JANE WELSH CARLYLE

AND HER VICTORIAN WORLD

The Carlyles in their ground-floor parlor, detail from "A Chelsea Interior" by Robert Scott Tait, 1857.

JANE WELSH CARLYLE

AND HER VICTORIAN WORLD

A Story of Love, Work, Friendship, and Marriage

KATHY CHAMBERLAIN

OVERLOOK • DUCKWORTH
NEW YORK • LONDON

This edition first published in hardcover in the United States and the United Kingdom in 2017 by Overlook Duckworth, Peter Mayer Publishers, Inc.

NEW YORK
141 Wooster Street
New York, NY 10012
www.overlookpress.com
For bulk and special sales, please contact sales@overlookny.com,
or write us at the above address

LONDON
30 Calvin Street
London E1 6NW
info@duckworth-publishers.co.uk
www.ducknet.co.uk

Cataloging-in-Publication Data is available from the Library of Congress

Book design and typeformatting by Bernard Schleifer
Manufactured in the United States of America
ISBN US: 978-1-4683-1420-5
ISBN UK: 978-0-7156-5165-0

FIRST EDITION
2 4 6 8 10 9 7 5 3 1

This book is lovingly dedicated to the following people without whom it would not have happened: Michael Zweig, Elizabeth Strout, Marcia and Marlin Brenner, and Aileen Christianson

CONTENTS

IMAGE SOURCES *8*

INTRODUCTION *11*

ONE: The Needle and the Pen *18*

TWO: The Servants: "A most important—a most fearful item in our female existence!" *37*

THREE: Friends and Conflicts *58*

FOUR: The Drama of 1844 *74*

FIVE: What Should a Woman Be and Do? *86*

SIX: Shaken All to Bits *101*

SEVEN: "My I-ity" *123*

EIGHT: Crisis in Nice *137*

NINE: A Fine Experiment *153*

TEN: Seaforth House *170*

ELEVEN: "What Is To Come Next?" *190*

TWELVE: "Threatening Shipwreck" *212*

THIRTEEN: Breaking Out *235*

FOURTEEN: "Such Shifting Scenes—Such Incongruities" *255*

FIFTEEN: A Green and Pleasant Idyll *274*

SIXTEEN: Sister Woman / Brother Husband *285*

SEVENTEEN: Changes *309*

EIGHTEEN: A Dash at the Wall *337*

EPILOGUE: A Last Word *362*

NOTE TO READERS *365*

NOTES *366*

ACKNOWLEDGMENTS *385*

INDEX *387*

IMAGE SOURCES

"A Chelsea Interior," by Robert Scott Tait, Carlyle's House, Chelsea (The National Trust), © National Trust Images / Matthew Hollow.

"Jane Welsh as a Girl," reproduced from *The Love Letters of Thomas Carlyle and Jane Welsh*, ed. Alexander Carlyle, vol. 1 (New York: John Lane, 1909).

Grace Welsh and Dr. John Welsh, from the Carlyles' albums, courtesy of the Rare Book and Manuscript Library, Columbia University in the City of New York.

"Margaret Aitken, Mrs. James Carlyle (1771-1853)," by Maxwell of Dumfries, © National Trust Images.

Jeannie Welsh (later Chrystal), by Spiridione Gambardella, reproduced from *Jane Welsh Carlyle: Letters to Her Family 1839-1863*, ed. Leonard Huxley (Garden City, New York: Doubleday, Page, 1924).

Geraldine Endsor Jewsbury, © National Trust / Geff Skippings.

"Chelsea, Carlyle's House, Cheyne Row," Look and Learn / Peter Jackson Collection / Bridgeman Images.

Charles Dickens, from the Carlyles' albums, courtesy of the Rare Book and Manuscript Library, Columbia University in the City of New York.

"The Governess," by Richard Redgrave, © Victoria and Albert Museum, London.

Mary Russell's maidservant Mary, from the Carlyles' albums, courtesy of the Rare Book and Manuscript Library, Columbia University in the City of New York.

"Sir Alexander Morison," by Richard Dadd, National Galleries Scotland / Purchased with assistance from the National Heritage Memorial Fund 1984.

Richard Plattnauer, from the Carlyles' albums, courtesy of the Rare Book and Manuscript Library, Columbia University in the City of New York.

Elizabeth Paulet, from the Carlyles' albums, courtesy of the Rare Book and Manuscript Library, Columbia University in the City of New York.

"Seaforth House, Lancashire," by J. P. Neale, private collection.

Thomas Carlyle, by Robert Scott Tait, © Charles Dickens Museum, London UK / Bridgeman Images.

Giuseppe Mazzini, © National Portrait Gallery, London.

Erasmus Alvey Darwin, by George Richmond, Historic England Photo Library.

Harriet Martineau, Alamy.

Jane Welsh Carlyle's copy of the forget-me-not poem, private collection.

"Charles Dickens Reading 'The Chimes,'" by Daniel Maclise, © Victoria and Albert Museum, London.

"Paul Pry at the Post Office," *Punch* Limited.

Lady Harriet Baring, by Francis Holl, Carlyle's House, Chelsea (The National Trust) © NTPL / John Hammond.

The Grange, Hampshire, Alamy.

Jane Welsh Carlyle, by Spiridione Gambardella, reproduced from *Jane Welsh Carlyle: Letters to Her Family 1839-1863*, ed. Leonard Huxley (Garden City, New York: Doubleday, Page, 1924).

Jane Welsh Carlyle, based on a sketch by Carl Hartmann, Edward Gooch / Getty Images.

Jane Welsh Carlyle and Geraldine Endsor Jewsbury, by Robert Scott Tait, Carlyles' albums, courtesy of the Rare Book and Manuscript Library, Columbia University in the City of New York.

JANE WELSH CARLYLE

AND HER VICTORIAN WORLD

INTRODUCTION

IS IT POSSIBLE TO PART THE CURTAINS, LOOK BACK THROUGH THE CENTURIES and discover the aliveness of a Victorian woman? Can she be glimpsed from fresh points of view, rather than through the sentimental scrims of her time?

Jane Welsh Carlyle (1801-1866) became, as Virginia Woolf put it, one of "the great letter-writers."[1] Her letters, always entertaining, can be funny enough to make a reader laugh out loud. Yet more than her epistolary brilliance has prompted *Jane Welsh Carlyle and Her Victorian World,* a story set in London during the 1840s, one of the most vibrant, turbulent decades of the nineteenth century, a time rife with controversy and change; in some uncanny ways, a time not unlike our own.

Born and raised in Scotland in the prosperous town of Haddington, near Edinburgh, Jane Baillie Welsh received a good education for a girl of her era, in schoolrooms and from private tutors. Her father was a doctor, and her mother—from a respectable well-to-do background—managed the household. Her parents counseled their only child as to her path in life, yet could never have predicted the surprising turns it would take.

Thomas Carlyle (1795-1881) was Scottish also, but born into a different social class: an extended family of stonemasons, peasant farmers, and domestic servants in the poorer, more out-of-the-way village of Ecclefechan. Unlike Jane, he had brothers and sisters with whom he was united in a network of kinship. Showing great intellectual gifts early on, Thomas studied at the University of Edinburgh where he befriended Edward Irving (later a notorious, controversial minister), who happened to be Jane's tutor. Edward was very fond of Jane, but he was engaged to another. He introduced her to Thomas, who eventually took Edward's place as Jane's mentor and began advising her on books to read and critiquing pieces she wrote, a relationship that evolved into a courtship.

In 1826, five years after they had met, Jane and Thomas married. After a brief residence in Edinburgh, they spent half a dozen years living on a hardscrabble farm of austere beauty, Craigenputtoch. Left to Jane by her father, the farm was (and is) located in an isolated section of southwest Scotland. With his brother Alexander helping to manage the farm, Thomas labored at turning himself into an author, and Jane learned to be a hardworking housewife. Although large families were then the norm, the Carlyles were not to have children. In 1834, to further Thomas's literary career, which was now showing promise and possibility, they rented out the farm and moved to the Chelsea section of London. There they would remain, and there Jane would write some of her most dazzling letters. Their well-preserved home on Cheyne Row is open to the public and can be visited today.

Known for her witty conversation and sense of fun, Jane Carlyle encouraged a romantic, humorous family legend that she was descended from John Knox, leader of the Scottish Reformation and founder of Presbyterianism, and, along a separate line, from a gypsy: "a cross betwixt John Knox and a Gipsey how that explained all." The combination underscored her Scottishness and could be used to account for her contradictions: her black hair; long-lashed dark, almost black eyes; and neat modest style of dress; her excitable interest in personalities and issues of her day—often with a forlorn *wae* or woeful strain woven through—and an underlying firmness to her character.

Though celebrity then was not the circus it has become in our era, Jane Carlyle's husband, after establishing himself as an author, came to be one of the most famous literary men in the British Isles, as well as in Europe and America. Known as the Sage of Chelsea, Thomas Carlyle authored books profoundly inspiring to his generation, especially his spiritual autobiography *Sartor Resartus* (1833-4) and his epic, poetic history *The French Revolution* (1837). In 1855, when many readers had grown weary of the increasingly reactionary opinions that Thomas favored as he aged, George Eliot testified to the enduring strength of his reputation: "[T]here is hardly a superior or active mind of this generation that has not been modified by Carlyle's writings; there has hardly been an English book written for the last ten or twelve years that would not have been different if Carlyle had not lived."[2]

For several sparkling years of the 1840s, Jane Carlyle was immersed in issues and controversies of her day, such as the British government's prying into the mail of private individuals; the treatment of the mentally ill; and the craze for mesmerism, or hypnotism, that swept through Victorian England. Because of her husband's fame and the fact of their dwelling in London, Jane met a range of outstanding Victorians, men and women whose lives and works matter to us today.

Among the fascinating friends and acquaintances who were part of the Carlyles' social circles, and who appear in these pages, were Charles Dickens, Ralph Waldo Emerson, Margaret Fuller, Frédéric Chopin, John Stuart Mill and Harriet Taylor, Erasmus Darwin (older brother of Charles), Alfred Tennyson, Elizabeth Gaskell, William Makepeace Thackeray, the prolific author Harriet Martineau, the feminist novelist Geraldine Jewsbury, and the translator / author of the *Rubáiyát of Omar Khayyám* Edward FitzGerald. The father of modern Italy, Giuseppe Mazzini, then living in exile in London, was an especially close friend of Jane's.

Yet halfway through this story, it is as if a line has been drawn through: what follows darkens, as Jane discovers that her husband has fallen romantically (though platonically) in love with a charismatic society hostess, the formidably intelligent Lady Harriet Baring, one of the tallest, widest women Jane had ever seen. Her secure and stimulating London life is suddenly thrown into jeopardy. Jane is severely tested as she attempts to cope with an opaque, perplexing, ever-changing situation—while being pulled out of her Cheyne Row existence into rounds of aristocratic country-house visits.

Even in her own lifetime, when nothing she wrote saw print, Jane Carlyle had a reputation as an extraordinary letter writer. Family and friends treasured the letters she wrote and passed them around, giving her a wider audience than a modern reader might imagine. Harriet Martineau left a record of the experience of reading a letter from Jane: "I have such a strong, singular feeling of welcome rise up at the sight of your envelopes as w*d* surprise you. . . . I generally put [your] letter apart, without breaking the seal, & leave it alone till the business letters & trifling & ordinary notes are disposed of. Then, when they are read & considered – & either burnt or put into the letter box, I stir the fire . . . draw the little table & lamp to my elbow,—rest my head on the cushion, & begin speech with you. My mind is still full of it, when I stare into the fire . . . before stepping into bed: & I wake in the morng with a sense of something very fresh & particular. They are wholly apart from all other letters."[3]

Jane's writing has a good deal in common with that other Jane, Jane Austen: both are sharply observant, humorous, ironic, and morally astute. Because of the gifts she displayed in letters and conversation, literary London sometimes suspected Jane Carlyle of being the author of the "the Jane Eyre books," before it became known that the Brontë sisters were behind the pseudonyms Currer, Ellis, and Acton Bell.

Jane Welsh Carlyle and Her Victorian World concentrates on a few years of Jane's life, which, as a whole, has often been greatly misunderstood. The 1840s are the years of her richest experience and development. Shining a light intensely on a portion of her life (1843 to 1849) reveals a truer, more complete picture than was possible before. By now, the first forty-four volumes of the magnificent Duke-Edinburgh edition of the *Collected Letters of Thomas and Jane Welsh Carlyle* (an ongoing project) include all of Jane's letters, journals, and other major writings. When she is seen close up during this decade, based on the great amount of information available from the Carlyles and their contemporaries, stereotypical images of this remarkable woman start to drop away.

Historically Jane Carlyle was too often portrayed narrowly by those who esteemed her as well as by those who did not, sentiments that served late nineteenth-century needs. The late Victorians who took Jane's side often saw her as the suffering wife placed upon a pedestal —or with one foot upon a pedestal—but sadly neglected by her overworked, self-absorbed husband, as she endured what her first biographer, in 1891, termed "her life of pain."[4] To those who took Thomas's part, Jane could be seen as a *barren* (later *menopausal*) shrew, who made her noble husband's life a misery. The old myths about Jane Carlyle as part of a couple who ought never to have married—which the Victorians and their descendants largely conjured up from their own urgent sex and gender anxieties—do not reflect the complicated lives of the Carlyles as presented in their collected letters, nor do they speak to us. Yet, most strangely, those stereotypes linger on. Even in the twenty-first century, the Carlyles have now and then been put squarely in the category of tragic literary spouses; or reduced to not much more than a self-sacrificing Jane Welsh who suffered from a tyrannical Thomas Carlyle.

Far better to search for the woman envisioned by Charlotte

Perkins Gilman, who in 1914 was herself trying to throw off Victorian shackles: "Here she comes, running, out of prison and off [the] pedestal: chains off, crown off, halo off, just a live woman."[5] When Jane Carlyle comes to life, the often-caricatured Thomas Carlyle changes also, becoming more dimensional.

The subject of this book is Jane Welsh Carlyle's unfolding, the story of her development as a woman and a writer. Writing was part of the way Jane spent nearly every day. Like many still in our time, she wrote within a private or limited sphere, yet she achieved what author Elizabeth Hardwick insightfully termed *a private writing career*.[6] Jane could even consider writing her business, as when she tells a cousin: "[N]ot that friendly correspondence is usually viewed as a 'business-matter'—but for us who have nothing to do with the 'cotton trade' or the 'Agricultural interest' or any other great world-business—letter-writing is as near an approximation to a *business-matter* as anything we take in hand."

With her work now published and available online, the fact that nothing Jane wrote appeared during her lifetime inevitably raises a question: could she or should she have written directly for publication, as several of her closest friends did? That Jane confined herself to the private sphere is something of a puzzle since she made several brave forays into the transitional spaces between private and public writing, trying her hand at memoir, fiction, parody, poetry, and translation, as well as more formal journal writing—all efforts that read as if intended for larger audiences. The life of Jane Carlyle offers insights into the mysterious writer-to-author transition, fascinating now as in her day—especially the assertion and the intricate arrangements of mind that the process can require.

For a woman who honored tradition and convention, Jane could not avoid the magnetic force of Victorian conduct books, which dictated appropriate wifely behavior. In the interest of facing up to social realities, such books advocated subjugation, sacrifice, and quietude. Jane made fun of them but did not escape their influence. She experienced pulls in opposing directions: toward subjection / toward aspiration. Toward love and romance / toward self-development and individuation. Toward service to others / toward the unfolding of her unique talents. As a Victorian wife, she was dominated by her marriage. Yet she was attracted to friendships with women and men who held progressive views. Drawn as if by an undertow to convention, she was tugged at by the thrilling new ideas of the 1840s, including, if obscurely, a sense of the value of liberation.

Rather defiantly a supporter, on the surface, of her husband's political ideas, including some of his most objectionable ones, Jane was, overall, more democratic-minded. And she never settled obediently into an anointed role. When she wanted to be, Jane Carlyle was a deft practitioner of the art of sedition through satire.

Although there was an increasing emphasis on education for women, during Jane's lifetime women were still not admitted to degree-granting programs in British universities. For a woman who observed, read books, thought seriously, and wished to live her life usefully and well, confusion reigned more often than clarity. More than most, Jane's near-contemporary Florence Nightingale understood the need to liberate oneself, yet retained a deep ambivalence about publically advocating the rights of women. Surprisingly, some of the most accomplished Victorian women opposed giving members of their sex the vote. It was the era of Coventry Patmore's narrative poem *The Angel in the House* (published in the 1850s), which glorified the impossible-to-emulate female giver and helper that Virginia Woolf, decades later, famously said that she had to kill in order to write.[7]

Jane Welsh Carlyle and Her Victorian World explores these tensions and the ways Jane handled them. She can voice the nearly inexpressible mysteries of a woman's inner life, as when after a spell of energetic charitable work to secure employment for young women, some of whom had thanked her for being their guardian angel, Jane confided to a cousin, "I do not know how it is; but I have somehow of late cut the cables of all my customary habitudes and got far out at sea—drifting before the wind of circumstance in a rather helpless manner . . . . To look at me *in action*, you would say that my whole heart and life was in it—and so it is; but then there is a something dominating my heart and life—some mysterious power which mocks my own volition and fore-thought." And she captured the elusive rainbow aspect of self when she wrote: "My views of myself are a sort of 'dissolving views,' never the same for many minutes together," taking her image from popular magic lantern shows where one scene melted into the next.

•

THIS PARTICULAR STORY of Jane Welsh Carlyle begins in their Chelsea home and neighborhood—not a fashionable or affluent area then and rather far from the city's center—on an unnaturally warm December morning in 1843. As the holidays approach, giving in to what she insists is an uncharacteristic impulse to be kind, and with several amusing tales to tell, Jane will pick up her pen to write a lonely governess in far off Devonshire. The governess will in time gain a friendship, and Jane will acquire a close observer of her life during these years.

CHAPTER ONE

THE NEEDLE AND THE PEN

"A word of encouragement and sympathy from a *fellow-sufferer* . . ."
– JANE WELSH CARLYLE

I

THE STORY BEGINS IN THE MID-NINETEENTH CENTURY, INSIDE A HOUSE in the Chelsea section of London. Built in the time of Queen Anne, it was part of an unfashionable yet still elegant row of attached homes along a street that sloped down to the River Thames. Near where it flowed beneath the old wooden Battersea Bridge, just before bending in a southerly direction, the Thames had muddy shores then and no embankment. It was a noisy working river bordered by shops and shipbuilding apparatus, crowded with steamers and barges, as well as smaller boats of varying sizes and shapes. The area reeked of tar and sewage and salt. There was a promenade to walk along, planted with trees, and the prevailing winds more often than not blew the noxious smells downriver and also kept the acrid smoke of the City of London away from the street, called Cheyne Row.

On the morning of December 18, 1843, the light of a warm temperate day filters in through the windows of the ground-floor parlor at No. 5 Cheyne Row, illuminating a pleasant but thriftily furnished room. A fire is burning in the grate, and on a sofa near the fireplace, a tallish, shapely woman sits darning stockings. She is wearing a well fitting black dress, its collar trimmed with a bit of blond lace, the skirt softly full. Her abundant black hair, parted down the middle, is looped about the ears and pulled neatly back in the fashion of her times. Her face has a prim expression, her mouth rather severe, as she plies her needle, taking back and forth stitches in the stocking cloth, mending hole after wearisome hole—the image of a patient Victorian Penelope. Only when she lifts her head from her work to gaze absently about can one see that her dark almost black eyes, what friends call her gypsy eyes, shine with a quick amused intelligence.

As always in a thrifty Victorian household, much sewing needs to be done (clothing, not yet available ready-to-wear, is far cheaper when made and repaired at home), and the woman, Jane Welsh Carlyle, has resigned herself to tackling her basket of work today. She would rather do the darning herself than hire a sewing girl to come in—such a nuisance to have a stranger girl around the house and underfoot. Besides, residing in close quarters with a single servant, and a most eccentric one, is problematical enough. Her maid-of-all-work is busy just now with the baking—a faint fragrance of gingerbread rises from the kitchen below.

On this December morning Jane is occupied with her sewing and her thoughts when there comes a heavy methodical tread down the stairs. Her husband descending. It does not bode well. At this hour he ought to be up in his study, locked in his struggle with the book he is attempting to write about the Puritan Oliver Cromwell—"his Cromwell in which he lives, moves and has his being at present," she had recently told her cousin, "as is always the way with him when he is writing a book."

As he strides into the parlor, Thomas Carlyle at once commands the scene. Wearing a long plaid dressing gown that flaps about his trouser legs, he is holding in his arms a large bundle, as gingerly as if he were carrying an infant. Jane lets her darning fall to her lap. Her husband, whose reputation as an author has been rising of late, is her principal subject to describe, one of the many characters who appear in the letters that she writes almost daily. Just now an Event seems poised to happen.

He crosses the carpet, his form long and lean, thick shaggy brown hair curved about his face, its expression grim, chin thrust forward, blue-violet eyes glowing fiercely. He shoves the bundle—a huge stack of papers!—onto the fire, giving it a definitive toss so it lands squarely on the nest of coals, throwing off showers of angry sparks.

Realizing it must be more than the contents of his wastebasket, Jane gasps in shock. He turns with an exclamation of satisfaction and nods—yes, just what she fears. He is making an official sacrifice of his Cromwell pages. Into the fire, the whole lot. "I discovered over night," he says, "that I must take up *the damnable thing* on quite a new tack! Oh a very *damnable thing* indeed."[1] The Carlyles both speak in their native Scottish accents. He says "a *verra* damnable thing."

Thomas seats himself on the nearest chair, an eighteenth-century mahogany and horsehair chair that had belonged to Jane's father, Dr. John Welsh. Ridding himself of the pages was a manly act. And good to have the deed witnessed by his wife (there were half a dozen fireplaces in the house where he might have made the gesture). "Dead Heroes, buried under two centuries of Atheism," he says now, of Cromwell and his allies, "seem to whimper pitifully, 'Deliver us, canst thou not deliver us!' . . . Confound it, I have lost four years of good labour in the business." He is talking half to himself, half to her, leaning against the hard chair back, legs thrust forward, feet braced upon the brass fender. "If the Past Time cannot become *melodious*, it must be forgotten, as good as annihilated; and we rove like aimless exiles that have not ancestors, —whose world began only yesterday!"

The discarded pages, having slid this way and that, flame and curl before them, emitting puffs of nasty smoke, most of which, fortunately, are drawn up the chimney flue. Jane has heard these complaints often enough. Oliver Cromwell, lord protector of England during that aberrant kingless mid-seventeenth-century era, has not yet received his historical due. Earlier accounts of England's Civil War, many dry and tedious, had not addressed fully enough the strength and sincerity of the Puritan hero's character and motivation.

Shock ebbing, she checks to make certain no sparks have landed on the carpet or her husband's trouser leg (Victorian fireplaces being fraught with dangers). "Providentially," she remarks crisply, picking her darning back up, "the chimney has been swept quite lately—saving us the awful visitation of *three* fire engines! besides a fine of *five pounds!*"—that the city levied for the kindling of a chimney.

Thomas laughs, a booming yet natural child-like sound, loud enough for their maid Helen to call from the kitchen to ask what has happened. Jane laughs too, raising her voice to tell Helen there is nothing to worry about; she should get on with the baking. Although there will be a fine mess of ash for the maid to clean up in the grate. With an air of "grim concentrated self-complacency" Thomas then confirms to his wife that he has indeed just burned "all his labour" since returning from his summertime travels.

A silence ensues, the room warms, and he begins to nod off to sleep, as Jane continues with her darning.

•

WHEN JANE CARLYLE wrote her marvelous letters, she sometimes included scenes, one of which she termed a "Drama in one Scene," a conversation between herself and her husband, written to amuse a friend.[2] Thomas Carlyle, historian, political writer, and biographer, also created scenes in his writing, using the word *visuality*, a term the *Oxford English Dictionary* credits him with coining, to mean seeing with the imagination in biography (as when, in his *Oliver Cromwell*, he imagines a summer afternoon two centuries before). Although this is a biographical narrative of Jane Carlyle's life in the 1840s, a nonfiction story of love, work, friendship, and marriage, it seems appropriate when the evidence is ample to include a "drama in one scene," such as Jane witnessing her husband's burning of his Cromwell pages. With so many letters, diaries, and memoirs available, it is not necessary to invent dialogue; what is "spoken" comes from accounts of the Carlyles or their friends. And since the Carlyles' sturdy commodious Chelsea house, with much of the original decoration and furniture, is, most fortunately, open to the public, it is possible to walk through their rooms today and picture what it would have been like to live and move about there.

Back in the late fall of 1843, Jane and Thomas Carlyle had been awakening to fogs, now yellowish, now dismally gray, which made their old house so dim and dark inside, the lamps had to be lit as early as noon. London had just been the scene of election excitement involving raucous anti-Corn-Law demonstrations. Protestors had taken to the streets to call for the repeal of the highly unpopular laws that regulated the sale of grains to favor the landed gentry, resulting in high prices of bread and much misery for the poor. The election noises had come from a great distance, but one evening in his study Thomas paused to tell a correspondent he could nevertheless hear "the faint *sough* of them." A few Anti-Corn-Law League candidates had managed to get elected, but now, as the holidays approached, the political commotion had died away.

Jane was spending hours alone in her parlor, reading, sewing, or just staring idly into the fire. As always, she was keeping up with her correspondence, also. She was then forty-two, her husband forty-eight, both of them lithe, spirited, and youthful looking, although after the unexpected death of her mother the previous year, Jane in deep mourning had suffered spells of ill health. Rather well now, she was nonetheless missing her mother and experiencing what she called *anniversary-feelings*, while Thomas agonized upstairs over his Cromwell book, and their maid, Helen Mitchell, struggled with pots and pans in the kitchen. Even with a fire kept burning all day in the range, the kitchen, which extended below the street level, was the darkest room of the old four-story house.

Jane had gone to considerable trouble to have a second floor dressing room converted into a study for Thomas, though she understood "his long projected life of Cromwell—is no joke—and no sort of *room* can make it easy." Scarcely big enough to hold his writing table and a shelf of supplies, the study protected against outside noise, which could rise to the level of cacophony.

Soon after the Carlyles moved to Chelsea in 1834, Jane had described their new neighborhood, which she had been happily exploring, in the exuberant pell-mell style she wrote in when excited. "Is it not strange," she reported to a friend back in Scotland, "that I should have an everlasting sound in my ears, of men, women, children, omnibuses, carriages glass coaches, streetcoaches, waggons, carts, dog-carts, steeple bells, doorbells, Gentlemen-raps, twopenny-post-raps, footmen-showers-of raps, of the whole devil to pay, as if plague pestilence, famine, battle, murder sudden death and wee Eppie Daidle [a mischief-making child] were broken loose to make me diversion." She added, referring to the six years she and her husband had spent on their remote Scottish farm, Craigenputtoch, "this stirring life is more to my mind" and joked that it had "besides a beneficial effect on my bowels."

Roosters still crowed at dawn in Chelsea—residents were allowed to keep hen coops behind their row houses. Dogs barked, pet parrots squawked, couples quarreled, organ grinders cranked out tunes, vendors hawked their wares, and the Old Chelsea Church clock chimed the hours. Most disturbing for Thomas, the girl in the adjacent house banged loudly on the keys of her pianoforte as she practiced diligently, right on the other side of the wall of the room it had been impossible to work in: the reason for the move to his dressing room study. But Chelsea still had a pastoral side. Scattered throughout the surrounding area were fields, orchards, and pastures, with grazing horses and cows.

Because Jane had arranged for the workmen to install a miniature fireplace, Thomas's study was pleasantly warm. When not complaining the space was too small to hold what he needed, he told people fondly that the wee cunning fireplace was like a saucepan, a porridge bowl, a snuffbox. A single window overlooked the walled garden in the back. From it he could see the neighbors' washing hanging up to dry, a stretch of red Chelsea rooftops and chimneys, and, just barely, through a haze of smoke in the distance, the top of Westminster Abbey and the dome of St. Paul's.

Above his writing table he had hung a cast of Oliver Cromwell's death mask, which lately had been gazing relentlessly, eyelessly down upon the author's unsatisfactory labors. When his day's work was over, Jane watched her husband pacing back and forth across the carpet of their parlor intoning such litanies as, "Peter of Russia built Petersburg, the imperial hightowered City, on a bottomless Bog of the Neva; 170,000 men had to die first in draining the Neva Bog, before the first stone of Petersburg could be laid. Courage!" The misery over not being able to write the life of Cromwell the way he wished was comprehensible enough. All those false starts. Paths leading nowhere.

Jane well understood his investment in the subject of England's lord protector, having heard him murmur of his subject "this belongs to thee, to thy own people." By that he meant that the old Puritans of England were "analogous to our Scotch Covenanters," or the religious tradition of his parents. Though as a university student he had broken from adherence to their theology, it remained the faith of his fathers. Though he had strayed far from the fold, he honored the fact of his parents' deep, sustaining belief, a pious faith and belief, which in this skeptical, self-scrutinizing, religious-crisis-prone nineteenth century continued to amaze.

•

THIS DECEMBER MORNING, as her needle takes its even stitches and her husband dozes in his chair, Jane wonders how she might tell the story of Oliver Cromwell landing in the fire. She owes a letter to her friend Harriet Martineau, living as an invalid in Tynemouth near Newcastle. Harriet is always eager to hear from "dearest Jenny," as she calls Jane. How to picture the conflagration for that prolix, energetic writer who (even in her sick room) believes "finding expression by words [is] as easy as breathing air"?[3]

After Harriet Martineau found a publisher and determined her method, she churned out her *Illustrations of Political Economy* (1832-34), the stories that made her a celebrity, almost like a writer-machine. Harriet's discovery that she might have a niche as a handmaiden to the intellectual men whose ideas she esteemed, interpreting their thinking for the many, had liberated her pen in that patriarchal era, which frowned on middle-class women's labor.[4] Construing her work as useful gave Harriet permission to become a hardworking author at a time when, it could almost be said, there was a culturally proscribed *ban* on work for women of her class.

The famous Miss Martineau would be sure to crow over the fireplace story. When she had visited the Carlyles one day, a glance at one of Thomas's proof sheets had suffused her with horror: "Almost every other word was altered; and revise followed upon revise."[5] Why would an author allow himself to suffer such torments? Recalling Harriet's astonishment and contemplating her fluent headlong style, Jane thinks wryly, "betwixt *writing* and *writing* there is a difference." (When Jane later does describe the burning of pages for her, Harriet will reply in character: "O dear! The suffering of writing with such effort, & then burning one's work must be unspeakably more painful than any thing that ever happens to me."[6])

Jane pauses now, gazing into the fire. Thomas had been holding his bundle of papers as if it were an infant. The project was a baby that could not get itself born. Somewhere she has heard an odd tale about that, what was it exactly? His irritation, grumbling, and insistence on needing "the utmost attainable solitude" for his work have come close to unbearable. *Would* be unbearable without laughter to break the tension.

She glances over. As he dozes, head now resting on the chair back, he looks almost pleased, the trace of a smile on his face, feet propped awkwardly on the fender, the shaggy, messy hair giving him a decidedly rustic look. A remarkably handsome man were it not for that air of rusticity. Does his craving for *solitude, solitude* imply he would just as soon have her remove herself to a different dwelling? "Cromwell *must* come to an end, or *he* and I will come to an end," she has more than once thought.

After all, Jane is darning *his* stockings. When Harriet Martineau was a girl and had her first essay published in the *Monthly Repository*, a Unitarian magazine her family subscribed to, her brother James, on discovering the author was his sister, had said to her, "Now, dear, leave it to other women to make shirts and darn stockings; and do you devote yourself to this"—the first time Harriet had received the balm of such words.[7] The general opinion in her family was that if a woman was forced to work for money, needlework was the only respectable means. Even after Harriet had become a professional writer, an aunt and a cousin pressed her to remove herself from the unseemly glare of public life and return to sewing and her daughterly duties—given her expertise with the needle, there was no excuse.

Although Jane matter-of-factly undertakes household chores, having a Scotswoman's brisk respect for housework, she views darning in its context and understands the dichotomy of the needle and the pen. Recently, after describing for a friend a vast quantity of needlework she had undertaken for "chaircovers sofa-covers all sorts of covers," she had declared in pride and irony that it "was enough to put Penelope for ever out of peoples heads as the model of industry and to set up M*rs* Thomas Carlyle in her place."

To women of Jane Carlyle's era who entertained hopes of becoming an author, it too often seemed like a choice: the needle *or* the pen.

•

IT WOULD SURELY have occurred to Jane that day that the burning of Cromwell pages was an uncanny repetition of a dire event that had occurred eight years before, something neither she nor her husband could ever forget. The tale is still told in our time. If people know only one story about the Carlyles, it is the burning of his *French Revolution* manuscript.

Thomas Carlyle had entrusted to his friend John Stuart Mill the only copy of the first volume of the book he was writing on the French Revolution. John Mill, too, was fascinated by that seminal event for their generation. He had considered writing about the subject himself but feared his known bias in favor of *liberté*, *égalité*, *fraternité* would prevent him from winning new converts. He therefore encouraged the endeavors of his less liberal friend, lending him countless books on the subject. When he asked if he might take away the manuscript to read, with a plan to make helpful notes in the margins, Thomas had acquiesced. Some days after, John Mill traveled to Cheyne Row to tell the Carlyles a confusing, astonishing, and terrible story.[8]

On Friday, March 6, 1835, as the Carlyles were drinking tea, a carriage rattled to a stop before their house, followed by a knock. A blanched, unsteady John Stuart Mill, looking "so like the ghost of Hamlet's father," stood swaying in the doorway. In anguish, he motioned for Jane to go down to the street to speak to his intellectual partner and platonic love, Mrs. John Taylor, who remained sitting in the carriage. With that, the usually dry, upright, self-contained man collapsed against Thomas's shoulder and had to be helped into the parlor.

Spurred by their friend's frightening demeanor, Jane hurried down the front steps in alarm. Her first thought: "Gracious Providence, he has gone off with Mrs. Taylor!" Despite the insistence that their love was platonic, she feared the pair had impulsively decided to elope, perhaps to the Continent, and had come round to bid the Carlyles a hasty farewell. Running off with a married woman would be the ruin, surely, of John Mill's reputation as thinker, writer, and editor.

Half hidden within the carriage, an elegantly gloved hand shading her face, Harriet Taylor began exuding in her iridescent manner an ever-changing array of tears and confusion, but saying nothing about elopement. Instead, she seemed to be throwing out a sheen of words concerning heartfelt sympathy, the impossibility of forgiveness, and manuscript pages.

For all her advanced views about women and reform, and her impressive erudition—she and John Mill were later to author major documents on the status of women—the petite Mrs. Taylor, with her pale heart shaped face, small chin, and large dark eyes, looked the part of an old-fashioned heroine of romance. As the horses restlessly lifted and lowered their hoofs and the cabman looked down at the two women with a quizzical expression, she uttered a few further moans, apologies, and expressions of sorrow through the carriage window to a very bewildered Mrs. Carlyle. Harriet Taylor then raised a gloved hand, signaled the driver to depart, and was borne away into the night, back to the home of her lawful husband.

John Mill, barely articulate, murmured and stuttered to the Carlyles in their parlor that night a confused version of unthinkable news. He had been careless, the borrowed manuscript had been left lying about. Someone, mistaking the thin pages for waste paper, had torn them into tatters for kindling. Though what he actually said then was not that specific, mostly despairing groans about *annihilated*, *destroyed*. The only thing certain: out of Thomas Carlyle's completed first volume, only "three or four fractions of leaves" remained.

Mysteries abounded. Thomas and Jane were unable to find out by whose hand, or where, the deed had been done. John Mill sat miserably in their parlor till midnight, too upset to be questioned. When they tried pressing for details, it pained him so terribly they had to cease asking. "[T]he poor man . . . seemed as if he would have shot himself" if forced to explain. Again they thought of Hamlet: "distraction (literally) in his aspect." And spoke of trivial matters to comfort *him*, despite their own acute pain. After, to protect his friend, Thomas Carlyle said little publically about what had occurred.

Though few lucid sentences were uttered that evening, the Carlyles came to believe that the manuscript, torn into tatters for kindling, had been burned. It was likely that John Mill and Harriet Taylor had been spending time in her Keston Heath cottage, as they often did, accompanied by Harriet's five-year-old daughter Lily[9] and a housemaid. Her oddly cooperative husband John Taylor had provided the pair with that convenient hideaway, near Bromley in Kent.

It is known that John Mill had been reading the manuscript aloud to Harriet Taylor so that they might evaluate it together. Perhaps, on impulse, tiring of Carlyle's complicated style with its annoying Germanisms, one of them had given the stack of pages a careless toss. Then the couple had gone out for a stroll on the heath, or along the bank of the Ravensbourne, and become caught up in a stimulating conversation about political reform, forgetting entirely *volume one*.

It would have been only human for Jane Carlyle to entertain suspicious thoughts. *Could it be* that Mrs. Taylor—Platonica as they called her—from some impulse of misguided loyalty, an urge to destroy what she perceived to be John Mill's competition—could it be that she had—or he had . . .? But no, *simply impossible*. Both were far too high-minded.

At the Keston cottage, then, the housemaid must have stumbled across a handy quantity of paper strewn about the floor, and noting its poor thin flimsy quality, good for starting a fire, had proceeded to tear it up, putting the pieces into a basket near the fireplace. Later John Mill realized, after a frantic search involving his family, that the manuscript was nowhere to be found. In desperation, he traveled back to Keston to consult Harriet Taylor, only to discover—.

If what the Carlyles came to suspect was true, he would not have been able to tell exactly what had transpired without exposing Mrs.

Taylor to dishonor. The world, already gossiping about them, would be sure to speak of the Keston Heath cottage as a love nest, or some equally false and loathsome phrase. Thomas Carlyle had once remarked sympathetically that the pair of them—who for their entire lives would insist that their love was "pure," not carnal, that is—had "the *innocence* of two sucking doves." Only a single calling would have been higher than telling the truth straight out: the need to protect the reputation of the woman John Mill so deeply and chastely loved, especially when he, too, had been careless. If he considered that his fiercest obligation, the lips of the gallant, unhappy man would have to remain forever sealed.

The night he was told the only copy of his manuscript had been destroyed, Thomas Carlyle had a dream that his father and sister Margaret had died a second time. When the horribly guilty John Mill insisted on supplying him with two hundred pounds to live on as he started his hard labor over, he accepted only half of what was offered and courageously set about rewriting, "a job more like breaking my heart than any other in my experience." He ordered reference books to make the task easier, installed new bookshelves to hold them, and acquired from his publisher a ream of tougher, higher quality paper.

Observing her husband sturdily going about these practical tasks, Jane had never tried harder to be a loyal supporting helpmate, and Thomas wrote in his journal one evening, "My dear wife has been very kind, and become dearer to me."

In Jane's estimation, her husband's rewritten volume was a phoenix arisen from the ashes; more magnificent, even, than the first draft. When published, the book proved a resounding success, helped along by a glowing review from the penitent John Stuart Mill, which opened with the words: "This is not so much a history, as an epic poem . . . . It is the history of the French Revolution, and the poetry of it, both in one; and on the whole no work of greater genius, either historical or poetical, has been produced in this country for many years."[10]

The seemingly ill-fated book turned out to be the making of Thomas Carlyle's literary reputation. It changed their lives. It was the start of his celebrity. And as his star began to rise, hers, as his wife, rose a little also.

As Jane Carlyle worked her way through her sewing basket that morning in December 1843, was her husband hoping for *fire* to work its phoenix-like magic again? Awake in his chair now, his expression was alert, as if new possibilities for his Cromwell book were coursing through. Busy with their separate thoughts, each had reason to feel lighter, Thomas from the relief of having made a bold decision, Jane from her plans to describe for friends his *voluntary* burning of manuscript pages. She knew a good story when she saw one.

II

DURING THIS SEASON Jane Carlyle had more on her mind concerning her husband of seventeen years than his tormented-author agonies. She was becoming more lucid in giving voice to darker strains between them, and connecting those to issues of the day. She wrote a letter of thanks to a novelist, Martha MacDonald Lamont, for having said a timely word to Thomas Carlyle "on the heterodox state of his opinions respecting us women. That he thinks us an inferior order of beings—that is, an order of beings born *to obey*; I am afraid there is not the shadow of a doubt!" She believed that her husband's views stemmed from a "self-complacency of full conviction" so automatic it hardly needed voicing. And added a sentiment expressed by many an articulate Victorian wife: "So these arrogant *men* may please themselves in their ideas of our *inferiority* to their hearts content; they cannot hinder us in *being* what we *will* and *can* be. Oh we can afford very well to laugh at their *ideas*, so long as we feel in ourselves the power to make slaves, and even fools of the wisest of them!"

Yet making slaves and fools of men amounted to Circe or seductress power, which at other times Jane Carlyle regarded with scorn. Potent though it could be, it was a disreputable, second-rate power. (Because an aristocratic Circe would eventually disrupt Jane's marriage and stimulating London life, she would become well placed, as we shall see, to observe such powers first hand.)

Shortly before they married, Jane and Thomas had anxiously negotiated where and with whom they would live. With his family? With her mother? In Dumfriesshire? In Edinburgh? As part of that discussion, in 1826 at the age of thirty, Thomas had written out for his future wife's benefit his views on the sexes: "*The Man should bear rule in the house and not the Woman*. This is an eternal axiom, the Law of Nature h[erself w]hich no mortal departs from unpunished. I have meditated on this ma[ny long] years, and every day it grows plainer to me: I must not and I cannot live in a house of which I am not head." He further stated, "[I]t is the nature of a woman . . . (for she is essentially *passive* not *active*) to cling to the man for support and direction, to comply with his humours, and feel pleasure in doing so, simply because they are his; to reverence while she loves him, to conquer him not by her force but her weakness, and perhaps (the cunning gypsy!) after all to command him by obeying him."

Though such sentiments were common at the time, Thomas infused them with a special energy. But he had an additional motive for laying down the law: his desire to avoid living in the same house as his mother-in-law to be. He feared that the widowed Grace Welsh (Dr. John Welsh had died some eight years before) might try to assume the role of queen of the household, usurping his place. He was quick to reassure Jane, however, that he did not intend to be "a harsh and tyrannical husband to thee. God forbid!"

Descended from peasants, stonemasons, and domestic workers, Thomas was uneasily aware of the discrepancy between his own family's relative poverty and the Welshes' middle class status and wealth. His first sight of Jane's gracious home in Haddington, near Edinburgh (he recalled in later years), had left him in awe: "The Drawing-room seemed to me the finest apartment I had ever sat or stood in:—in fact it was a room of large and fine proportions, looking out on a garden."[11]

For her part, Jane was glad enough to have a separate residence after her marriage. But *the Man should bear the rule*—who could forget such words?

•

ON DECEMBER 23, the temperature climbing to an unseasonable 60 degrees F,[12] Jane Carlyle realizes with a start she has not heard from a friend, a German woman working as a governess in Devonshire. Amely Bölte has become a protégée of hers—Jane helped her secure a job. Bright, impecunious, overqualified for her work as a glorified servant, the young woman is an exile from the land of Goethe and an advocate of the progressive ideas beginning to inspire many in Europe. Sitting down at her table, Jane picks up her pen to write Amely.

The resulting thirteen-page letter provides excellent examples of Jane Carlyle's epistolary art. She had recently described for a cousin her approach to letter-writing: "I have got so into the way of *splashing* off whatever is on my mind when I write to you, without forethought or back thought that I must go on so if at all, to the end of the chapter."

On this mild day, she will send a splash of her mind to Miss Bölte: "*Unmenschliche* [Inhuman One]! Are you become so inoculated with the commercial spirit of this England, that you will no longer write to me but on the debtor-and creditor-principle?" Jane demands to know, "What *are* you doing, and thinking, and wishing, and hoping—for in Devonshire I suppose people can still *hope*—even in December—*here* the thing is impossible—on the dark dismal fog, which we open our eyes upon every morning, there is written as over the gate of the *città dolente*, alias Hell: 'Lasciate ogni speranza voi che' entrate.[']" *All hope abandon, ye who enter here.*

To write an intimate letter at all to a woman she has been regarding as a project and toward whom irritation can flare ("Miss Bölte has been here but I absolutely refused to go down to her"), and will continue to flare, seems mysterious. More so when Jane confesses her motive for her "absurdly long letter!" is "that damned thing called the milk of human kindness," playfully alluding to Lady Macbeth.

Yet knowing Miss Bölte to be far from family and friends, Jane wishes to reach out. "I bethink me that on Christmas day you will be feeling *sad* . . . . I mean that you should read my letter on Christmas." Though Jane likes to declare she has conquered kindly impulses, her thoughts are spinning in this sentimental direction because—she cannot stop thinking about a book she has just finished reading.

•

THE BOOK WAS Charles Dickens' *A Christmas Carol*. This December Jane had been in a pensive state of mind, wishing at one moment to celebrate Christmas austerely and abstemiously, remaining quietly by her fireside with her nostalgic thoughts; and being drawn the next to cheerful glasses of Madeira wine and dancing parties with literary friends. Her changeable moods had not been eased by the peculiar weather. A letter in the *Times* attributed the abnormally warm temperatures to "some unusual planetary influence,"[13] and Thomas Carlyle had been speculating it would be "an open Yule"; they would not have to stay caged up indoors.

Customarily Jane did not make a fuss over any holiday, but the tale of Ebenezer Scrooge—Dickens had presented Thomas Carlyle with an early inscribed copy—had touched them both. They gave it as a gift to Jane's uncle, Thomas scribbling inside the cover, "Read with satisfaction; presented with satisfaction, and many Christmas wishes."[14] Jane spoke of the tale as the latest "literary novelty . . . really a kind-hearted *almost* poetical little thing, well-worth any Lady or gentleman's perusal."

Dickens' delirious descriptions of food, though, took them both aback. Jane found the story "too much imbued with the Cockney-admiration of *The Eatable*." The food emphasis prompted Thomas, as he strolled through the neighborhood, to realize, "All the world here is devouring geese turkies and other Christmas provender. It is really striking to see with what *admiration* the common people stand before the huge stacks of beef and mutton at Butchers' shops." And Jane became aware of the crowds of hungry people who were gazing at the handsome displays of food in local shop windows.

In Victorian England an unprecedented dialogue between readers and writers was underway. The liveliest interplay existed between the social realities that its educated citizens witnessed and wondered about, and what they were reading in contemporary novels and periodicals. Their reading intensified what they observed while walking or riding through London's most crowded, dirty neighborhoods, struggling to comprehend the immense changes being wrought by the Industrial Revolution. Unquestionably the condition of England—the wretched poverty (far worse than most of us can imagine today), the profit chasing, mechanization, industrialization, hard-heartedness, and alienation that surrounded them—made Charles Dickens' readers highly receptive to his novels. And certain readers, in turn, through private letters and conversation, could and did influence him.

Alert to condition-of-England questions, Jane Carlyle gave witness in her letters to what she termed social facts. Virginia Woolf praised her letters for "the hawk-like swoop and descent of her mind upon facts. Nothing escapes her. She sees through clear water down to the rocks at the bottom."[15] The famously fact-intoxicated Victorians turned out stalagmites of parliamentary blue books on every conceivable social subject, but Jane had a sharp eye for the *telling* fact, what, in "The Art of Biography," Woolf was to call "the creative fact; the fertile fact; the fact that suggests and engenders."[16]

Visiting a confectioner's in Piccadilly this December, Jane had observed a startling sight. While seated inside, enjoying a piece of sponge cake with hot jelly, she noticed the man next to her feeding his dog—

who also sat upon a chair—one hunk of cake after another. She winced, understanding how it must look to "the starved beggars who hang about the doors of such places to see a *dog* make away with as much *cake* in five minutes as would have kept *them* in *bread* for a week or weeks!" Earlier this season, she had depicted the gaunt, yearning faces of working people as they took the temperance pledge from a charismatic Catholic monk, Father Theobald Mathew, who had a dispensation to move freely among the poor. Jane had gone out of her way to witness Father Mathew work the crowds, deeply impressed by his efforts. Whisky on top of poverty only made a bad thing worse.

Jane also reported the effect that *A Carol* had on their immediate household: "the visions of *Scrooge*—had so worked on Carlyles nervous organization that he has been seized with a perfect *convulsion* of hospitality." At her husband's insistence, they did what they had hardly ever done, gave two dinner parties in a row. The menus included hare-soup, turkey with improvised stuffing (which turned out delicious), stewed mutton, bread pudding, and minced pies. It was with visions of Scrooge at work upon *her* nervous system that Jane Carlyle had resolved to write her letter to a lonely governess.

•

AFTER GIVING THE governess the first splash of her mind, Jane includes three vignettes, one tumbling after the other. She sprinkles in French, German, Italian, and Scottish dialect phrases, and refers to Dante, Shakespeare, Milton, and Burns. A natural-sounding cascade, the letter is structured, too; like *A Carol* it has three parts. The first vignette is the story of the Cromwell pages going up the chimney in a blaze. Recollecting the baby analogy that had teased at her memory, Jane conveys a bit of Continental gossip: "I begin to be seriously afraid that his *Life of Cromwell* is going to have the same strange fate as the child of a certain French marchioness that I once read of—which never could *get itself born*, tho' carried about in her for *twenty years* till she died!—a wit is said to have once asked this poor woman if 'Madame was not thinking of swallowing a tutor for her son'? So one might ask Carlyle if he is not thinking of swallowing a publisher for his book?"

Jane next tells Amely Bölte about a mystery letter that had arrived at her house anonymously. It opened by praising Jane's "*bright sweet* eyes! . . . there *is no escaping their bewitching influence.*" As a woman of forty-two, she tries not to feel flattered, working up "a due matronly rage," but "I read on however." Gradually it dawns on Jane that the bright sweet eyes are *not* hers at all, but belong to a thirty-year-old woman whom Amely knows, Miss Swanwick (Anna Swanwick, later an educator and suffragist).

The author of the mystery epistle turns out to be a journalist friend, John Robertson, who, furthermore, is writing to beg Mrs. Carlyle to convince Miss Swanwick of the beautiful eyes to undertake a job for him without pay. He wants the young woman to translate the "French laws on *pawnbroking.*" The spare time of young ladies is "so uselessly employed," he believes, that by setting her to work on his project he would be doing *Miss Swanwick* a favor.

Lastly for Amely's pleasure Jane describes a most peculiar gift brought to her from Germany by her friend Richard Plattnauer and handmade by his sister, a countess. After studying on the weird object and soliciting the opinion of friends—could it possibly be a *Devil's* tail?—Jane realizes, "The thing is the most splendid, most fantastical altogether inconceivable—bell-rope!" Did Richard Plattnauer imagine she might summon her tiny homely Scottish maidservant from the kitchen basement by pulling on "A countless number of little *chinese pagodas*, of scarlet net-work festooned with white bugles, [that] are threaded on a scarlet rope, ending in a '*voluptuous*' scarlet tassel, which again splits itself away into *six* little bugle-tassels"?!

Reflecting the somber side of Charles Dickens' tale, Jane's tone turns serious. "When one is far from one's own land and own friends; those *anniversaries*, however they may be cheered for one by *present* kindness, always bring the past and distant strangely and *cruelly* near . . . . A word of encouragement and sympathy from a *fellow-sufferer* . . . may be some little comfort to you[.] At all rates it is such comfort as I have to give—and if I had any better you should have it with a blessing—."

•

A FEW DAYS after sending her letter off to the governess, Jane Carlyle encountered Charles Dickens himself at a party. The excuse for the festive occasion: to raise the spirits of little Nina Macready on her birthday while her father, the Shakespearian actor William Charles Macready, was in America on a theatrical tour. Jane had not been feeling well, but having promised the actor's wife Catherine to help out, she forced herself to attend.

Charles Dickens, then in his early thirties, had an open mobile face with large round eyes of changeable color, quick to express good humor and fun. During what turned out to be a boisterous evening, he performed for the assembled throng a dazzling series of magic tricks.

Thrilled, after all, to be at a party, Jane wrote to a cousin—in another brilliant letter—that a "little knot of blackguardist literary people" had let down their hair in bacchanalian frenzy. The gypsy in her had been delighted to find herself on the fringes of respectability. "[I]t was the *very* most agreeable party that ever I was at in London," she said, describing the atmosphere as "joyous," illness all forgotten. "Dickens and Forster [the literary editor] above all exerted themselves till the perspiration was pouring down and they seemed *drunk* with their efforts! Only think of that excellent Dickens playing the *conjuror* for one whole hour—the *best* conjuror I ever saw—(and I have paid money to see several)—and Forster acting as his servant!—This part of the entertainment concluded with a plum pudding made out of raw flour raw eggs—all the raw usual ingredients—boiled in a gentleman's hat—and tumbled out reeking—all in one minute before the eyes of the astonished children, and astonished grown people! [T]hat trick—and his other of changing ladies pocket handkerchiefs into comfits [sweets]—and a box full of bran into a box full of—a live-guinea-pig! would enable him to make a handsome subsistence let the book-seller trade go as it please!"

The spirit of the evening swept Jane up. "Dickens did all but go down on his knees to make *me*—waltz with him!" She protested she could not but talked "the maddest nonsense" with him, Thackeray, and the others, until, against her will, she was compelled to dance a wild dance with John Forster. "[A] universal country dance was proposed—and Forster *seizing me round the waist*, whirled me into the thick of it—and MADE me dance!! like a person in the tread mill who must move forward or be crushed to death! Once I cried out 'oh for the love of Heaven let me go! you are going to dash my brains out against the folding doors'! to which he answered—(you can fancy the tone)—'your *brains*! who cares about their brains *here*? *let them go*!'"

Charles Dickens told a correspondent that pulling a pocket handkerchief out of a wine bottle during that wild whirling evening and cooking a plum pudding in a hat had made him "a tremendous hit," more popular "than I have ever been in my life."[17] After the party, he wrote Jane Carlyle, informing her that the guinea pig, so magically materialized out of the bran box, had sadly passed away. He added, "He left it in his will that he believed conjuring had done it; but that he forgave his enemies, and died (he was a very small Pig you know) believing in the whole Bench of Bishops."[18]

Although Jane Carlyle and Charles Dickens did not become intimate friends, they were part of overlapping circles of London literary people and held each other in esteem. Reading *A Carol* had influenced Jane to empathize with a foreign woman working as a governess in an alien land. She who had effectively used her pen to write down disturbing noises of barking dogs and squawking parrots that belonged to their Chelsea neighbors had in this case wielded it to console a friend. Her letter won Amely's heart on a lonesome holiday and was to carry the governess in years ahead through difficult moments with Jane.

She may have forgotten the letter that had danced out of her pen, but Amely never did. It formed her lasting opinion of Mrs. Carlyle. She told a friend, employing Victorian words of high praise, that she was a "rare woman . . . who combines the highest intellectual learning and strength of character with the most delicate femininity and the most profound and warmest emotionality. . . . [H]er wit and spirit are even greater sources of attraction than her husband's depth."[19]

The governess would weave in and out of Jane's life in the 1840s. In 1843, as Jane began to seek a more tangible purpose in life, assisting Amely to find employment was one of the first major challenges she took on. The following year the governess launched a correspondence with a man in Berlin that left a record of how Jane Carlyle, and her husband too, appeared to a European woman interested in progressive ideas. Amely's perspective as well as that of the Carlyles' literary friends whose work continues to matter to us today, like Charles Dickens, Alfred Tennyson, William Makepeace Thackeray, Edward FitzGerald, Ralph Waldo Emerson, and Margaret Fuller, help round out this story of Jane Carlyle.

CHAPTER TWO
THE SERVANTS: "A MOST IMPORTANT —A MOST FEARFUL ITEM IN OUR FEMALE EXISTENCE!"

"I was to sleep with Mary & our bed was in the kitchen & shut up in the daytime . . . . [I] slept soundly too for [all] it was only a straw bed—the straw cut up short."
—*The Diaries of Hannah Cullwick: Victorian Maidservant*[1]

FOR ALL HER PLAYFULNESS AND WIT, *WORK* WAS OF SERIOUS CONCERN TO Jane Carlyle, though she never expounded on the topic didactically, or even directly at any length. Rather she at times worried about how her life might be made more useful, as she searched during this decade for what her mission or purpose might be. The thread of her concern might take the form of a casual remark, hint, or glimmer, yet is always there. When she spoke of work she sometimes meant her writing.

However in the spring and summer of 1843 (several months *before* her holiday letter to the governess), Jane turned her efforts to a different kind of work: helping unemployed women find jobs. Might an enterprise of this sort become the fulfilling mission she was seeking? She had a model in her mother. In one of the few extant letters by Grace Welsh, she is attempting to find a position in a good home for an orphan lassie.[2]

Jane Carlyle was Scottish, Presbyterian, and practical-minded, as well as married to a man who not only advocated the work ethic but wrote inspiringly about it. All of which meant she was more interested in household matters than many a ladylike English counterpart.

Through his writings, Thomas Carlyle was helping to make work, a basic tenet of his philosophy, a foundation of the Victorian character. For instance in his *Past and Present*, published this year, he stated, "we do entirely agree" with the medieval motto *Laborare est Orare*, to work is to pray; or "true Work *is* Worship."[3]

Back in 1826 he had put forth his views on how he and Jane would work together as a couple after marriage. "Do you not think," he had told her, "that when you on one side of our household shall have faithfully gone thro your housewife duties, and I on the other shall have written my allotted pages, we shall meet over our frugal meal with far happier and prouder hearts than thousands that are not blessed with any duties, and whose agony is the bitterest of all, 'the agony of a too easy bed'? In labour lies health, of body and of mind." Enthusiastic at the heady prospect of setting up her first household in Edinburgh as a bride, Jane had concurred: "oh without doubt we shall be as happy as the day's long—happier in our little house at Comely Bank, than Kings and Queens amid the gilding of pallaces." Book writing and housework alike constituted sacred work.

•

YET, ASTONISHINGLY, OPERATING in opposition to this strong Victorian work ethic was the current social position of middle-class wives: work outside the home was essentially forbidden to them. Even work *inside* the home could be frowned upon if there was a staff to do the housework and educate the children. At the same time, working-class women were not so affected: those who needed to and could contributed to the support of themselves and their families, laboring away at a variety of jobs. They did not become cloistered like their middle-class sisters. By the mid-nineteenth century, nearly half the women of England were at work in "the factory, the workshop, and the field" or employed as domestics.[4] Tens of thousands of women worked as servants in people's homes.

Jane Carlyle enjoyed writing about the doings of cooks, washerwomen, governesses, housemaids, parlor maids, housekeepers, and sewing girls. She considered the servants a fascinating topic for her letters, asking a cousin, "[W]hy *do* you make bits of apologies to me for writing about the servants—as if '*the servants*' were not a most important—a most fearful item in our female existence!" And added, speaking of her friend Geraldine Jewsbury who lived in Manchester, planned to be a novelist, and was subject to frequent infatuations with both men and women, "I think, talk, and write about my own servant as much as Geraldine does about her lovers." Jane's own servant, the Scottish Helen Mitchell, a true character, was the Carlyles' maid of all work and only household help at Cheyne Row. She was "small, black haired—wiry—and very clever. She could do every thing. Cook sew wash iron—new-bake—all sufficiently well."[5] Despite being asthmatic, Helen managed to perform the roughest tasks.

Jane Carlyle's letters create an intimate picture of a Victorian home. She regularly helped out herself with the myriad jobs that needed doing, making her very cognizant of the details of a servant's life. Helen would have been grateful for any assistance her mistress could give her, for the daily grind involved in keeping up an old multi-level house required almost superhuman strength and stamina. A maid of all work had to cook, serve meals, pump water, wash dishes, feed the cat, make beds, open and close shutters, light the lamps, sweep the floors, and empty the slops. Going up and down steep flights of stairs several times a day would alone have been daunting. The half dozen fireplaces at Cheyne Row meant a constant cleaning of grates, as well as the building and tending of fires, and keeping up a steady supply of coals. Pictures, decorative objects, books, and furniture needed regular dusting, and the blinds a periodic cleaning. Shoes had to be polished and clothing brushed. Walls, carpets, stairs, the front steps and back flagstones had to be cleaned, also, as well as the privy out back. London households engaged in strenuous battles against soot, dirt, beetles, worms, bedbugs, moths, mice, and even rats. A maid had to hurry to the front door whenever a knock came from a tradesman or guest, and answer bells when her employer pulled on a bell rope. When a family member was taken ill, she was expected to assist with nursing tasks. Helen Mitchell often washed and ironed the clothes as well, though occasionally the laundry was sent out, or a washerwoman hired to come in.

Helen, as the third resident of 5 Cheyne Row, took a keen interest in her employers' lives, which could be a blessing and a curse. She looked upon them, for the most part, with an intense curiosity. Jane had to seal letters that she wrote in the evening so "that Helen might not edify herself with the contents in the morning—according to her usual fashion." And the maid was given to memorable utterances in her native Kirkaldy dialect that captivated Jane: she now and then jotted them down in a tiny notebook.

One day as they went about the housework, the two women, who were about the same age, fell to discussing the topic of remarriage after the death of a spouse. Helen made a comment that Jane relayed to a cousin with laughter. "[A]fter some interruption of dusting," said Jane, Helen had announced, "But I do think . . . M*r* Carlyle *will be* (admire the tense!) a very *desultory widow*! he is so *easily put about*—and seems to take no pleasure *in new females*."

Jane added, however, "there is one *new female* in whom he takes a vast [deal] of pleasure." She was speaking of Lady Harriet Baring, who was in the process of developing a close friendship with Thomas Carlyle. Though Lady Harriet did not yet appear to pose a danger, Jane was starting to keep a wary eye on the woman who would in time become a serious rival.

On another occasion when mistress and maid were re-shelving books, Helen put forth her view of Thomas Carlyle's difficult best-loved work *Sartor Resartus*. Pointing at the volumes, she said, "[T]ake care—that ane's the Maister's *sartor* RESART—and a capital thing it is—just *noble* in *my* opinion." As Thomas noted, "Helen was a great *reader*, when she c*d* snatch a bit of time." She had once delivered, in her inimitable dialect and from her indisputable vantage point, a critique of Harriet Martineau's officious *Guide to Service* pamphlet called "The Maid of all-Work."[6] Helen could write as well, and when Jane was traveling, they were able to stay in touch by letter.

Despite Helen's skills, her affection for the Carlyles, and attempts to please, she and Jane occasionally quarreled. Far worse, this pint-sized middle-aged woman was tempted by drink in an era when alcoholism was considered a defect of character. From time to time she went on a binge, wreaking havoc in the kitchen. It made Jane, as she coped with the damage, feel as if she "had adopted a child." One never-to-be-forgotten evening, Helen imbibed an entire bottle of whisky in the dark basement kitchen where she worked and also slept, in an improvised bed on a countertop slab.

Although Jane Carlyle advocated "recognition of *humanbeingism* in the Servants" as the mark of a civilized household, she did not, true to her time, believe in any fundamental equality. And did not think it necessary to provide Helen with a real bed or bedroom of her own. It was then far from unheard of for servants to sleep on improvised pallets in the kitchen, which would mean that they had to wait to go to sleep until their employers had no further use of the area.

Many wives in Jane's situation would have employed more than one servant, but the Carlyles were thrifty, having known very well what it meant to worry about money during their hardscrabble years on their Craigenputtoch farm in southwest Scotland, as Thomas was attempting to launch his literary career. Both Jane and Thomas paid attention to keeping the Cheney Row pantry and larder well stocked. It was often less expensive and more convenient to obtain supplies from Thomas's family in Scotland.

Thomas's family situation could not have been more different from Jane's. The tight-knit Carlyle family with their keen sense of kinship gave their "Tom," even at his most psychologically isolated moments, a strong connection to clan. In contrast Jane, though close to her uncle and his daughters in Liverpool, could experience the unique aloneness of an only child whose parents had passed away. Her Liverpool cousins Helen and Jeannie Welsh did not play a large part in the Carlyles' London life but were essential to her as correspondents. She treasured what they wrote her, and many of Jane's most fascinating letters were written to them. Her maternal uncle John Welsh, a widower and retired brass and copper manufacturer, presided over a household at 20 Maryland Street, Liverpool, that included his daughters Helen, Jeannie, Margaret, and Mary, and the family servants. (His several sons figured less prominently.)

Jane was the exciting older cousin residing in London with personal, political, and literary news to chronicle. When she sent a letter to the Welsh family, she was communicating with a circle of people on a range of topics. What she wrote, unless it contained very private matters, would be read aloud and passed around. Her cousins eagerly received and carefully saved her letters, which arrived at Maryland Street, it might be said, in installments—not unlike the novels of Charles Dickens and other authors whose work often appeared serially in Victorian periodicals. Jane was aware of the similarity of what she wrote to novel writing; and novelists in the 1840s often thought of *their* work as letters to the public. Yet in terms of family, despite this vital connection to her cousins, Jane was comparatively isolated.

Thomas, the eldest and most successful of his parents' children, behaved toward his brothers and sisters with a thrifty generosity, bestowing advice and aiding them with gifts and small timely sums of money. In turn his brothers and sisters sent the Carlyles products they had grown or made on their farms, or were able to purchase locally. Not all resided in Scotland. Thomas's father's son from an earlier marriage as well as his younger brother Alexander had immigrated to North America. The peripatetic Dr. John Carlyle, the sibling closest to Thomas and Jane, occasionally took on a job as personal physician to an aristocrat touring about Europe; he too aided other Carlyle family members financially.

The rest—James, Mary, Jean, and Janet—remained in Scotland near their mother, and it was they and their families who supplied the house on Cheyne Row with a great array of items: hams, cheeses, fowls, bacon, butter, eggs, peppers, honey, "sweeties," barrels of oatmeal for porridge, bottles of brandy, port, whisky, and sherry, as well as tobacco, pipes, brown soap, shirts, nightshirts, breeches, waistcoats, drawers, "wristikins," dressing gowns, and stockings that Thomas's mother knit from yarn she had spun. Even, at one point, dandelion pills, which may have acted as a diuretic.

Although Thomas wrote instructions to Scotland on stocking the pantry, Jane was in charge of running the house. Being house proud, she did not hesitate, when feeling well, to beat a mattress in the back yard to rid it of bugs or get down on her knees to scrub a floor. After a bout that she termed her *Cinderella* labors, she spoke of herself humorously as a maid of all-work who had the "improvisation and inventive-faculty of a woman of genius," admitting that she longed to balance out her exertions by lying for a fortnight on her sofa reading French novels.

When Thomas started earning more from his writing, however, doing housework could occasion outbursts of bitterness. After that particular Cinderella siege, which involved nailing down carpets for all the stairs and passageways, "a thing that Helen *can not* do," Jane's hands had become so "absolutely blackened and coarsefied" she had to wash them repeatedly and cover them with mittens. The carpet nailing prompted anger. "The fact is I have spoiled M*r* C," she told a cousin, "—I have accustomed him to have all wants supplied 'without visible means'—until he has forgotten how much head and hands it takes to supply the common resource of a good round outlay of money[.] When one had not any money—it was all well—I never grudged my work—but now that we have enough to live on it would be good sense in him to say 'get in a carpenter to nail your carpets.'"

If it seems strange that a spirited woman like Jane Carlyle refrained from telling her husband directly that she required extra help, one has to keep in mind that endless Victorian insistence on women being passive and obedient. Husbands legally controlled the family's financial resources, including the property their wives had brought to the marriage. Although Jane's father had left his Craigenputtoch farm to her, Thomas—who respected that reality—was nevertheless legal owner and official head of their household.

•

DURING THE SUMMER of 1843, Jane Carlyle—engaged in helping two sisters, Bessy and Juliet Mudie, to find employment—discovered she had somehow "'unconsciously' opened a bureau for destitute young women!" In jest, her journalist friend John Robertson drew up a mock document for her to send to correspondents whose letters she had failed to answer promptly. It explained that Mrs. Carlyle, "Sole Manager of the New Gratis Bureau for providing situations for Destitute Young Ladies," would like them to know she was in "absolute despair" that her preoccupation with those vital matters had prevented her from responding to their letters in a timely fashion.[7]

Joking aside, the situation of the Mudie sisters was grave. Their father Robert Mudie, a Scotsman from Dundee and an author living in London, had died. His family, a widow with several daughters and a son to support, suffered severely from the loss of his income. There were no saints here. The father may have been brutal toward his wife, the mother may have taken to drink. But the undertaker's bill had come to an unconscionable thirty pounds, and Mrs. Mudie and her children were forced to move to cramped quarters. Her only son, who was fourteen, died of typhus fever. Jane related their painful story: the women "starved on what they could earn," taking in any work they could find, such as "sewing what is called *slop-shirts* [made from second hand clothing] at a penny-farthing each—and stitching fine stays at eightpence a pair!" She asked friends anxiously, as she sought positions for the girls, "Do *you* want a needle woman?—or a nurse-maid?"

In spite of inevitable setbacks, this volunteer work—undertaken by loose networks of more well to do women—at first proved enriching to Jane and contributed meaning to her life. Her stories about helping such women entertained her husband and her correspondents. Though Thomas might step in and lend a hand, the work mostly occurred in a female realm involving conversations, letters, and exchanges of confidence he knew little about since men and women of their class occupied distinctly different spheres, no matter how frequently the public and private intersected and overlapped. The Carlyles, after all, lived and worked in the same house. But the female realm remained physically and psychologically separate, as the Carlyles had understood when they married: "you on one side of our household and I on the other."

In addition to ongoing efforts to help the Mudie girls, Jane was eager to find a situation for Amely, her principal project. (This was about four months before she wrote her December letter to the governess.) The Carlyles had apparently met Miss Bölte in 1841, after she had traveled to London with a letter of introduction from a German man of letters. By now they knew the governess rather well as an acquaintance, spelling her name "Emily" (it sounded like that), or more often "Amalie." Thomas described her as "a decisive, hardy, useful-looking, clear-sighted nimble little creature."

Amely Bölte extended Jane's horizons. The young woman had journeyed to England in the hope of earning enough money to return home and live independently. Her father, a jurist and mayor of Rehna, Mecklenburg, had died, leaving—like Robert Mudie—his family in need. Forced to support herself at the age of seventeen, Amely was equipped to teach German, French, and music. She would have been expected to know dancing, drawing, and arithmetic, as well as what was invariably added to such a list: *globes* (geography, presumably).

During this decade, she developed into an intriguing friend to Jane Carlyle. A foreigner and intellectual interested in progressive European thought, Amely also, because of working for a living, came to know intimately a cross section of British society: servants, genteel ladies, and the well-off individuals, including aristocrats, who were in the main her employers. The British caste system, with its confusing cues and myriad subtleties, greatly perplexed her, and she relied upon Jane to translate. Even Amely's own status confused her: a governess was a decided step up from an outright servant yet a step down from a lady, a distinction more pronounced in England than in Germany. At the same time, the position of a foreigner in London could be ambiguous; she was harder to place socially.

At this point, Jane had no idea how high and naively Amely had set her sights: the governess harbored a secret dream that she would one day work directly for Queen Victoria and Prince Albert. And considered herself entirely up to the task.

As Jane was sharply aware, Amely's dignified origins and range of talents were no guarantee against poverty. If Jane failed to help her, a dire pauper's fate might await her. For gentlewomen fallen on hard times, the workhouse loomed. A mid-century journal beseeched its audience to heed their plight: "Nor is this, O dear tender-hearted reader, an imagination. Go thou into our parish workhouses in dreary London, and investigate the past histories of some of those pale figures lying on the narrow couches of the female wards, and thou wilt find there drifted waifs and strays from the 'upper and middle classes' who pass long months and years in pauper clothing upon a pauper's fare."[8]

Women like Jane who sought to save others from that fate could labor creatively on their behalf. Yet their charitable work of course went unpaid, and outside small circles remained anonymous. They nevertheless performed a crucial function, for the institutions that existed were woefully inadequate. Jane knew of at least two formed at this time, "The Society for the Protection and Employment of the Distressed Needlewomen of London"; and a "Governesses' Benevolent Institution," launched, after faltering starts, "to raise the character of Governesses as a class, and thus improve the tone of Female Education."[9] An admirable if small-scale undertaking, the Benevolent Institution offered a free registry and placement services, as well as assistance in emergencies, and even made available a modest annuity program. Charles Dickens gave the institution his blessing at the inaugural dinner. It drew wide-ranging support and in some ways prospered. In time Queen Victoria herself lent her name to a school intended for the education of governesses, Queen's College. But in the earliest years the Governesses' Benevolent Institution could serve only the few.

Jane was often asked by London acquaintances why she bothered to concern herself with a German governess who exhibited some annoyingly odd behavior: Amely had the mysterious, unnerving habit when visiting Cheyne Row of sitting in the parlor and staring at Jane, following her with her eyes. Yet Jane discerned in this somewhat strange young woman special qualities of heart and mind.

She now wrote urgent letters, trying to secure a position for the governess, and in the process irritated the novelist William Makepeace Thackeray. He was responsible for the education of his two little daughters who had lived without their mother since the onset of her mental illness. Boarding schools had notoriously harsh, unhealthy conditions, as Charlotte Brontë would detail unforgettably in *Jane Eyre* (1847), as well as uncertain educational standards. If one had a family of daughters, hiring a governess to teach them at home was the safer choice. Yet when Thackeray received Jane Carlyle's request, he shot back, "For God's sake stop M*lle* Boelte—I have governidges calling at all hours with High Dutch accents and reams of testimonials. . . . [O]n going to dine at Punch by Heavens there was a letter from a German lady on my plate. And I don't want a Gerwoman; and all our plans are uncertain."[10] His martial handwriting, marching across the notepaper, underscored his indignation.

The context for Thackeray's refusal: at this time, when the British government did not put limits on who could enter the country, London was crowded with immigrants of various nationalities—Austrians, Italians, Frenchmen, Greeks, Hungarians, Poles. As commentators liked to note ironically, all were free to come and all were free to starve. Germans like Amely were among those arriving on England's shores, though in smaller numbers than later in the decade when political refugees would flood in (like Karl Marx, whom Amely, by then at home in the refugee colony, would briefly meet and entertain[11]). Ordinary workers seeking employment in all sorts of trades were coming too, "sugar-bakers, furriers, tanners, and tailors," according to one account; intellectuals and students who had suffered censorship under repressive European regimes; as well as "young middle-class women of no means," hoping to obtain higher wages in a somewhat wealthier country.[12] As Charles Dickens' novels memorably remind, London was the site of wretched poverty and misery. Yet it was also enthrallingly multicultural, a hive of those European new ideas, and home to stimulating foreign journals and newspapers, as well as organizations promoting the welfare of immigrants.

London in the 1840s teemed with people, both native born and foreign, searching for work. Something like fifteen thousand women hoped to become governesses, far more applicants than jobs available.[13] Tracking her social facts, Jane Carlyle once noted what she termed "Poor M*rs* Sterling's two hundred and eighty nursery-governesses," the number of women responding to a single advertisement in a newspaper. When an Italian artist friend had a similar experience after placing an ad for a housemaid, she exclaimed, "Does not this give one a horrible glance into life—as it is at present."

Jane veered between heroic efforts to find Amely a situation and annoyance at being pestered and importuned. "Miss Bölte has been here," she wrote one day, "but I absolutely refused to go down to her—She was here yesterday also while I was at Greenwich." Jane Carlyle had a temper. She would draw herself up to her full five feet five and three quarter inches, flash her dark hazel eyes, and stamp her foot at her Manchester friend Geraldine Jewsbury, a diminutive woman with strawberry blond hair who paid scant attention to her appearance, resembling at this time "a little boy in petticoats." Jane might call the petite young woman "a vile creature" whom she never wished to see again—only to reconcile soon after. (Geraldine could give as good as she got, and she endured: she became Jane's best friend for life.)

Female temper flare-ups were not an admired trait—far better to squelch unladylike bouts of anger before they erupted. In *The Wives of England: Relative duties, Domestic Influence, and Social Obligations* (1843), Sarah Stickney Ellis cautioned Victorian brides to be "unobtrusive, quiet, impartially polite to all, and willing to bend to circumstances." Mrs. Ellis took a clear-eyed view of the unequal relations between the sexes and taught the wives of England to face reality. She who marries, warned Mrs. Ellis, "has voluntarily placed herself in such a position that she must necessarily be [her husband's] inferior."[14] The ideal wife was subordinate and kept to her sphere, exerting when possible a gentle moral influence.

Jane not only had a temper, she liked to call attention to the gypsy blood said to be flowing in her veins, the proof being her very dark eyes and jet-black hair. Yet while making fun of etiquette book excess, which she and Geraldine ridiculed as the "Mrs. Ellis-code," Jane was also acutely aware of the proprieties. The strands of gentility braided into her personality often caused her to hide her temper for the sake of respectability and domestic peace. At best, anger made her satirical barbs bristle with energy. On more complicated occasions, it dove inward of its own accord, making her ill.

Among Jane's friends, her poor health was notorious. She suffered from chronic migraine headaches, biliousness, stiffness, and especially, a good portion of each year, from enervating colds and flu. As one of Thomas's sisters put it, Jane was "a bad winterer."[15] Although there was usually thought to be "nothing organic gone wrong," in a century replete with life-threatening influenzas, tuberculosis, cholera, and typhus, it would have been foolish to take illness lightly. The Carlyles, wisely, never did so, not even when it seemed possible that the cause might be other than physical.

Annoyances with Amely notwithstanding, Jane was slowly forming a more favorable opinion of her. In July 1843, with Thomas in Wales on a holiday, Jane was at home, holding what she termed her annual household earthquake. She liked to undertake cleaning and renovation projects at Cheyne Row when her husband was absent; it gave her a free hand for supervising. This month carpenters, paperhangers, and painters had been in the house pounding, banging, yelling, and singing.

In the midst of the unholy racket, the place reeking of paint smells and clouded with dust, Jane wrote a friend, "Sometimes I am seized with a passion for rural life—and then with *my own hands* I construct a gipsey-tent in the garden, out of clothes-lines—long poles—and an old brown crumb cloth!—within which I establish myself with the indispensabilities of life, a chair, a table, a bit of carpet—and the implements for writing and sewing—Woman wants but little here below!"

But as Jane sat in her back yard underneath her gipsy tent composing a letter one day, the entire structure collapsed upon her. "There!" she wrote, "—the tent has been down on the top of me again but it has only upset the ink—."

•

ONE WARM JULY day, Jane Carlyle and Amely Bölte are informally drinking tea, seated perhaps in the small back dining room at the table near the window overlooking the walled garden, where the improvised tent provides a spot of backyard shade. Jane's household renovations have subsided enough to allow her to entertain, at least in this casual manner. The dining room is the pleasantest place in the house to have a cup of tea, and the garden just now is lush with summer greenery.

Unexpectedly there comes a firm rap of the lion's head door-knocker, the sound echoing, as always, through the house. Helen Mitchell hurries to the entrance to see who is there, returning with a card and letter of introduction for Mr. Carlyle, still away on holiday. Picking up the letter from the tray, Jane at once recognizes the beautifully distinctive calligraphic handwriting: it belongs to the memoirist Karl August Varnhagen von Ense who resides in Berlin, someone the Carlyles esteem. For half a dozen years, he and Thomas have been exchanging letters and books, stemming from their mutual interest in the writer Goethe and German romanticism.

When Jane tells Helen she will speak with the man the letter introduces—a General Wilhelm von Willisen—the tiny maid, who has an eye for the grand guest, ushers the regal stranger in with a flourish. Gazing up astonished, Jane estimates the man's height to be "six feet two inches," his age to be about fifty.

Summoning her manners, she invites the officer to sit with them and have a cup of tea, tea being especially healthful on a warm summer's day. He readily agrees but, it is soon apparent, can barely speak English. When Amely offers to translate, they learn that the general, a professor of military history, has come to England to purchase horses for the Prussian army. To her pleasure, Amely discovers that he is acquainted with relatives of hers in the military. The two are soon chattering away in German, Amely animated and expressive.

Freed from the burden of hostessing, Jane sips her tea, now examining the foreign soldier towering over plain-faced "little Bölte"; now glancing into her garden where the fruit is ripening on the cherry and apple trees—perhaps wishing to be out there beneath her gypsy tent, in spite of the danger of its collapsing in a strong wind. Idly she ponders how to describe the man for her husband. She and Thomas, as always when separated, are writing each other nearly every day. "I was quite sorry you did not see [him]." "The very beau ideal of a Prussian Officer." "Plumb and more than plumb," knowing Thomas as the son of a stonemason will enjoy the builder's term. "[S]o highbred and intelligent and *brave* looking."

Amely pauses to tell Jane that her brave-looking guest has a mortifying problem. Varnhagen had lent General von Willisen his presentation copy of Mr. Carlyle's *Past and Present*, which contained a personal inscription; but in a fit of forgetfulness, the poor officer left it on the Derby Coach. ("Strange fate," Jane thinks, "for the book sent to Berlin!") He dares not return home without it. What is to be done?

As Amely sorts through this problem (it will be solved, a new copy inscribed, and the General will vanish from their lives), Jane listens, half comprehending the spoken German, and finds herself surprisingly impressed with the governess. Neatly attired and presentable, she is plain to the point of unfeminine drabness, but as Jane refills the teacups, her opinion continues to rise: Amely is turning out to be "a fine *manly* little creature with a deal of excellent sense—and not without plenty of german enthusiasm for all so humdrum as she looks."

•

THE MANLY YOUNG woman, however, had gotten herself into a true predicament. She was to experience quite a few predicaments during her time in England, but this one had a strange cause: Amely had been fired from her last job because of her views on the book of Genesis. The governess, that is, was a person who did not take the Bible literally. As a dreaded German Skeptic—the term referring to those German scholars who had begun applying critical analysis to Biblical stories—Miss Bölte was thought to pose a danger to the minds of the young.

Governesses who were not members of the Church of England—Dissenters, for instance, and Roman Catholics (French teachers were often Catholic)—could encounter problems with Anglican employers. But the accusation of skepticism was rare, suggesting that few governesses fell into such a nefarious category.

The charge intrigued Jane. Though her own religious beliefs are not entirely known, she had something of a reputation as a religious skeptic herself, and enjoyed shocking people by speaking of herself as a pagan. "I had got converted to Paganism in the course of learning Latin," as she humorously put it in a story about her childhood.[16] More seriously, she had developed religious doubts after the early death of her father in 1819. Though raised in a traditionally Presbyterian household, Jane as an adult did not live as an observant Christian, nor was she especially inclined toward the mystical-spiritual. Harriet Martineau, still a believer in this phase, complained to their mutual friend Fanny Wedgwood that Jane Carlyle's "scepticism is, with me, a bar to all confidence"; although Harriet, who now and then cast a jaundiced eye upon Thomas, was convinced there had to be "some sound faith at the bottom of her soul," for how else could she have "sustained herself and him all this time without it"?[17]

Sympathetic to Amely, Jane conjured up a plan. To circumvent the Genesis problem, she would find Miss Bölte a position with a guaranteed six months' employment. The arrangement would provide a new set of references and put her career back on track. She came close to negotiating a position for Amely as a companion to a rich lady on the Continent but the posts proved unreliable and the effort was dropped. A lady's companion might not have to work very hard, but Jane decided that the claustrophobic, symbiotic dependency involved in that job made it the very worst: "the soul is quite sufficiently taxed to overbalance the exemptions of the body." She concluded, "I would rather keep a school . . . and call my soul my own."

It was now August, and Amely was staying in Brentwood with "some stupid country parson," countering her irreligious reputation by attempting to play the role of a perfect saint, and as a result *perishing of ennui.* Letters flew back and forth. Without bothering to consult, Jane rejected an offer of a low-salaried schoolmistress job where Amely would have been "made into mince-meat" for "indiscriminate boardingschool misses."

Fortunately, old friends of the Carlyles came to the rescue. Charles and Isabella Buller, well-to-do members of the lower aristocracy, had years before hired Thomas Carlyle to tutor their boys. The Bullers now offered to take on Miss Bölte as governess to their goddaughter, Theresa Revis. (Theresa would become a three-volume novel of a little charge, but this was not yet obvious.) Miss Bölte would remain with them the full six months, "then *they* would be applied to for her character and would have no calumny to state about 'the first chaps of Genesis.'" When Jane related this scheme to Thomas, he offered rare words of praise: "The plan for Bölte is sagacity itself; really a neat plea for getting rid of that atrocious Genesis affair; truly glad am I that it is like to take effect."

But complications arose from crossed messages. The governess was glad to accept the Bullers' offer of sixty pounds a year, but meanwhile a better one got made: actor William Charles Macready, manager of the Drury Lane Theatre, and his wife Catherine told Jane that they would pay Miss Bölte one hundred pounds to work for them, the top salary for a governess. Only someone with excellent language skills could command it. The common wage for a governess then was about twenty-five to thirty-five pounds.[18] On the verge of his acting tour of the United States, Macready wished to sound out Miss Bölte before he left and assumed she would want to inspect his home and circumstances.

Jane wrote Amely to ask which position she preferred, but the governess temporized. Because actors were not thought respectable, the ambitious Amely feared that working for one would bring her career to an end. Finally, knowing her friend comprehended the unfathomable intricacies of England's social system, Amely begged Jane to make the decision for her.

The Carlyles liked and respected William Macready, an acclaimed tragedian. On the occasion of his upcoming tour, Thomas Carlyle wrote a letter of introduction to the American Ralph Waldo Emerson, assuring him that the actor's "dignified, generous, and every-way honorable deportment in private life is known fully." But wishing to protect Amely from unending chores, Jane worried that she would wear herself out caring for the Macreadys' large often ailing brood, "the *number* of little children—apt to fall sick—and every now and then needing to take medecine and have their stomachs rubbed with warm flannel." Though a nursemaid would normally be expected to minister to such ailments, a governess's job lacked demarcated boundaries; she was often forced to take over other servants' responsibilities.

After Jane told the Bullers that Miss Bölte would accept *their* offer, a letter arrived from Amely saying she had slept on the matter, dreamed of Jane all night, and awakened with the decision to take the position with the Macreadys. She needed to "make the money a compensation for all other little drawbacks." But she added, "You are a dear angel to trouble yourself with all the calamities of Eve about the poor German Sceptic."

Jane held firm, however. The governess should go to the Bullers' less-taxing household "and no more about it." Capable of taking her life in her hands and shaping its direction, as when she had adventurously set out to seek work in England, Amely complied without a murmur, revealing her dependence on her friend's advice. "A line from you will tell me if I have to come [to London] or not, or what to do," she wrote Jane submissively.[19] Without further ado, she settled in with the Bullers in Devonshire.

The nimble, enterprising young woman, who had spent time with an aunt, Fanny Tarnow, a writer back home in Germany, had also begun earning small sums by writing pieces for Cotta's *Morgenblatt*, a publication that brought news of English literature and politics to its German readership. When describing her qualifications for teaching jobs, the Carlyles and Geraldine Jewsbury all used the same phrase: as a governess, Miss Bölte was *first rate*.

Yet Jane Carlyle's long spell of "practical helpfulness" was beginning to take a toll. "To look at me *in action*," she wrote her cousin in September, "you would say that my whole heart and life was in it—and so it is; but then there is a something dominating my heart and life—some mysterious power which mocks my own volition and forethought." Speaking of her various employment bureau projects, she acknowledged, "The results are good so far—*useful*—contributory to 'the greatest happiness of the greatest number.'" She had been receiving letters from people she had assisted who, like Amely, touchingly addressed her as their guardian angel. Yet she found herself performing some of these tasks in a trance.

"I do not know how it is," she wrote; "but I have somehow of late cut the cables of all my customary habitudes and got far out at sea—drifting before the wind of circumstance in a rather helpless manner—not that I am become lazy or indifferent—I was never more full of energy and *emotion*." Beset by contradictory feelings—with an echo of Hamlet—she was attempting to give voice to the nearly inexpressible.

Something else had intruded on her time alone. With Thomas still away (in Scotland now), Jane had been hosting his brother, Dr. John Carlyle. For the most part she put up stoically with her brother-in-law's presence, but she now complained to Geraldine that John was becoming "an insupportable bore." To her cousin she wrote, "There is something so irritating at the very outset in having a man fix himself down in your house—palpably for *its* sake not yours—so that his material wants be all supplied . . . he will sit morning after morning munching away at his breakfast and gazing into vacancy without once addressing me as if I were the Chinese figure that one sees in some of the tea-shop windows!"

For his part, John Carlyle suspected that his sister-in-law malingered. He repeatedly tried to rouse Jane to get out and see the sights, believing, as a doctor, that touring about town would lift her spirits and improve her health. One day, in the manner of prescribing a medicinal dose, he insisted that she accompany him on an excursion to the Surrey Zoological Gardens.

Jane details the horrors of what became for her a long forced march. When she has at last returned home with a cruel headache, and is in her bedroom taking off her clothes, her brother-in-law knocks on her door, urging her to "come upstairs and look thro' his telescope at the four moons of Jupiter!!"

Her reaction: "'Oh' I thought 'if [only] *you* were in one of them!—or *quartered* into the four!"

It seems unfortunate if Jane missed an opportunity to encounter the moons of Jupiter when they were shining right upstairs. But her desire to escape to her own room for refuge, and also the many days of her life that she spent ill in bed, especially during London's winter season, brings to mind other Victorian writers. Charles Darwin, Florence Nightingale, Harriet Martineau, and Elizabeth Barrett Browning, to name a few, famously sought refuge from importuning relatives and friends in an invalidism that, however legitimate, bestowed considerable benefits. It liberated them from social and familial duties, and allowed them a chance to recoup their powers, and to pursue much more freely and prolifically their intense creative and intellectual interests. Jane Carlyle, too, may at times have benefited from a protective invalidism.

At the end of this letter to her cousin, which conveys a rare sense of her inner self, Jane uncovers a reason for her confusing low spirits. In a manner that feels modern, resembling as it does the talking cure, she has written her way to an insight: underneath her active bustling life, she has been deeply missing her mother. And her father, too, who had died so many years before. Busy with her employment bureau work, she is still in mourning: "[A]ll that remains for me in Scotland—two graves . . . . I am horribly sad always at the bottom of my heart—my external life is all smoothed over again, and flows on noiselessly enough—but underneath!— Happily the world troubles itself little [with] what we have *deep down*—and the thing to be chiefly guarded against in suffering is plaguing ones fellow creatures with ones individual griefs."

Jane's description anticipates the buried stream of our hidden selves the poet Matthew Arnold revealed in his moving, evocative poem "The Buried Life" (1852). We cannot know precisely what her individual griefs consisted of, beyond deeply missing her parents; but in his *Reminiscences* (1881) Thomas Carlyle suggested that Grace Welsh and Jane Carlyle, like many a mother and daughter who love and quarrel, had shared "the evidently boundless feeling of affection which knew not how to be kind enough."[20] Whatever its nature, a hidden river seemed always to flow beneath the surface of sociability.

•

DESPITE HER SOMETIMES-melancholic moods, Jane in this season successfully placed two of her lassies. Juliet and Bessy Mudie obtained work in Manchester with the help of Geraldine Jewsbury, who was keeping house there for her brother while she worked away at her first novel. Jane provided the Mudie girls with dresses, petticoats, and shawls. She briefly housed them in her own home to protect them from their beleaguered mother's uncertain morals, as they prepared for their respectable new positions. In late summer, she sent off the second one, Bessy, to Euston Square to begin her railway journey north. Jane pinned a note for Geraldine to the girl's stays, kissed her warmly, and gave her her blessing.

She did not know if the sisters would thank her or manage to keep their jobs, and Bessy, in fact, did not. In November Jane related the sequel to a friend. Bessy had become "lazy, heedless and *dirty* to a degree—and when her mistress tried to remonstrate with her she *lay down on the floor and kicked and screamed*!—So she was dismissed and when my kind Geraldine Jewsbury had found a home for her till she should get her one more trial in a[nother] place . . . the young lady informed her that her Mother wished her to return [to London]" where Bessy "expected to be companion to a Captains widow." Jane feared that "it was rather [companion] to a Captains self—for Juliet had told me of some officer that was in love with her Sister—The Mother I fear is quite lost to all right feelings if ever she had any—Juliet . . . is behaving herself excellently well—I had a letter from her mistress to tell me so the other day."

Bessy was not helpable, Jane concluded. A Captain in love with her? Many employers reflexively forbid their maids to have followers, what Jane called "The London Rule on Followers." What were the man's intentions? Could he support her? If he turned out to be a cad—only too likely—the next step might be the streets. *The workhouse or the streets* went the fearful refrain whenever a woman seemed in danger of falling, economically or morally. Not an unrealistic fear at a time when workhouses were degrading places, and, among the desperately poor, prostitution constituted a major female occupation.

Bessy Mudie's own point of view escapes from between the lines that Jane Carlyle wrote. What precipitated the firing: Bessy had sewn upon "a *black* apron with *white* thread." When her mistress reprimanded her for this lapse, Bessy lay down on the kitchen floor and kicked and screamed.

Housemaids all too easily lost their jobs for minor infractions. Geraldine Jewsbury, who lamented their lot in print, wrote of one who was fired simply for refusing to part "with a band of black velvet, which she had a fancy for wearing around her neck."[21] Worse, servants could be turned out on the street in a flash just for falling ill, if a heartless employer did not want the bother and expense of caring for them. Faced with a choice between being ordered to do incomprehensibly tedious tasks by a strange mistress in an alien city for ten pounds a year, or returning to her mother for whom she felt affection and an officer who loved her, as she believed, Bessy Mudie threw her tantrum.

Thomas Carlyle looked back much later on the Mudie episode, in memory lumping together the sisters who had "stalked fatefully . . . toward perdition." He wrote, "I remember these Mudies—flary, staring, and conceited, stolid-looking girls, thinking themselves handsome, being brought to live with us here, to get out of the maternal element, while 'places' were being prepared for them."[22]

Jane Carlyle devoutly hoped her plans for the girls would work out, that they would find and keep their respectable positions and escape the ravages of poverty. Juliet, a writer like both her parents (her mother attempted novel writing), possibly managed this. Geraldine told Jane some years later that Juliet Mudie had written a novel. Doubtful of its quality, Geraldine added sarcastically that it had been "'spoken of in the highest terms' by some unknown gentleman of the greatest judgment!"[23] No novel has been located, though "Poems on Various Subjects" by a Miss Mudie appeared later in the decade.[24]

To Jane, *flary* (gaudy or glaring) posed a challenge, not an obstacle. Helping the sisters was noble work. She had been moved by their stark destitution but could not guarantee results. When she heard about Bessy kicking and screaming in protest, even if her own grief stricken heart felt a quiver of sympathy, she could face reality.

Yet when Jane spoke of the mysterious power that mocked her "volition and forethought," her unconscious may have been sending a warning. Though she would continue, always, to help maidservants and governesses find employment, such work was not what she was best suited for. It could not, that is, constitute her special mission in life.

Down in Devonshire, meanwhile, the governess Amely Bölte began the onerous task of educating the scatterbrained eleven-year-old Theresa Revis, paying attention, as a good governess should, to the child's manners and moral training, as well as her intellectual development. The successful refinement of her charge was another miracle a governess was expected to perform. Overqualified though she was, Amely was grateful for the chance to work at a place where her employers, whose son Charles was a radical member of parliament, were unlikely to take offense at her philosophical and political views.

To Amely Jane wrote encouragingly and optimistically (for Theresa was to have surprises in store, including becoming a model for the most mischievous and amoral young woman in fiction): "A kiss to Theresa, who I hope is striding thro' all departments of human knowledge in *seven-leagued-boots* and carrying all the cardinal virtues along with her!"

CHAPTER THREE
FRIENDS AND CONFLICTS

"The cat is an angel in comparison!"
—JANE WELSH CARLYLE, 31 May 1844

ON NEW YEAR'S DAY, 1844, THE WEATHER HAVING TURNED COLD, JANE Carlyle, back from a snowy walk on Upper Cheyne Row, settles into a corner of her sofa, wraps a big shawl around her, and begins taking sips from a tumbler of brandy. As she is warming up, there comes a rap at the door. Helen Mitchell opens it to find a snow-covered Giuseppe Mazzini stamping his feet on the doorstep.[1] Nodding to Helen, he walks through the entranceway into the parlor, bringing the cold air with him.

A charming thirty-eight-year-old with dark hair and dark soulful eyes, the Italian revolutionary has a broad pale forehead and oval face made impressive by a full, neatly trimmed mustache. It is the countenance of a sensitive, grave, ascetic monk, though an urbane one—he enjoys a good Swiss cigar. Here in his London exile, he has been living a simple life, giving unstintingly to his political cause and to anyone he perceives to be in need, rarely using for himself the money that his mother has saved up to send him.

He is Jane Carlyle's *first foot*, or first guest this New Year's Day. According to the old Scottish superstition, if you like your first visitor, it means good luck in the year ahead. And like him she does. Very much. Tossing aside her shawl, she rises asking, "What on earth could tempt you to come out in a day like this?" Glad as Jane is to greet her slim elegant friend, clad in black clothing, worn in perpetual mourning for his fragmented Italy, she is disconcerted by the sight of "big drops of sleet hanging from the ends of his mustache." It might be funny were it not for the fact that he is recovering from serious dental surgery. She worries he might catch a cold, or worse.

As Giuseppe takes a seat near the fire, Jane offers him a glass of wine, tasty figs her uncle's family sent for the holidays, and a piece of fragrant, savory gingerbread that a sleepy Helen had managed to bake after attending a party with other servants in the neighborhood the night before. While the family dined in style above, Jane tells Giuseppe, the servants' own guests in the kitchen below, Helen included, "were kept all the time 'washing and *polishing* glasses for upstairs'!" It is clear as he listens that the neat, pleasant appearance of his hostess and her quicksilver interest in life's variety hold considerable charm for him. Thomas Carlyle is, at the moment, at work in his upstairs study, tied into knots over his Cromwell book.

Giuseppe and Jane relax into a confiding talk about politics. He trusts her, and freely—some would say incautiously—imparts information that few outside his movement have any knowledge of, including potentially dangerous secrets. He is confident that she will keep what he is saying to herself, telling no one but her husband, until matters become public.

Giuseppe Mazzini's commitment to his country goes deep. Unlike most, his personal and public lives form a pliant whole. Because of this unity, he strikes many who meet him as a rare pure spirit. Moved by his visit, Jane afterward writes her cousin that he "looked almost dazzlingly beautiful" as he sat in her parlor, a beauty that must be "the expression of some inward newfound joy!" She hopes against hope that it means things are going well for his cause.

•

GIUSEPPE MAZZINI, ONE of Jane Carlyle's most important friends, was another who widened her world. The Italian hero was born into a Genoa that had fallen under Napoleon's rule; and in 1831, in Marseilles, he organized Young Italy, the first Italian political party. Currently living in exile in London, he and his compatriots were working to unify their country's separate political entities. There was no common economy, and each section of Italy had a different court system, customs bureau, currency, and even, in several cases, a dialect unintelligible enough to other Italians to amount to a different language. Their goal was one Italy independent of the tyrants and foreigners ruling its various parts.

Mazzini had started a journal in London, *Apostolato Popolare*, as well as organizations to assist immigrants: a mutual aid society for artisans; a Union of Italian Working Men; schools for adult learners; and La Scuola Italiana, a school for impoverished children, such as the organ-grinder boys, hawkers of plaster casts, and trinket sellers who were common figures on London streets. Friends had warned Mazzini that these children, whom they generally regarded as overworked, apathetic street urchins, would not attend the school. But when it opened its doors in 1841, some two hundred had enrolled, including ten girls, to his delight, for he was a firm believer in female education. Among the supporters of his projects (some gave small sums while others helped out at the schools or with fundraising bazaars) were the Carlyles, Harriet Martineau, Geraldine Jewsbury, John Stuart Mill, Erasmus Darwin (brother of Charles), members of the Wedgwood clan (Darwin's cousins), Catherine Macready (wife of the actor), and in time Charles Dickens, the poet Robert Browning, and the American author Margaret Fuller.[2]

Concerned for lost children when they crossed her path, Jane Carlyle would have been bemused to know how an Italian organ-grinder boy had found his way to the streets of the great metropolis. Barrel organists were only too familiar to the Carlyles. On occasion they played right beneath the Cheyne Row windows, and if the noise—not considered music!—was driving Thomas mad as he tried to write, the maid's duties included rushing outdoors to shout "move on!"[3]

The Victorian historian Henry Mayhew, who conducted interviews with denizens of London's streets, recorded the story of one such organ grinder. As a boy of three or four, part of a large family living on a farm in the duchy of Parma, he had lost his father, leaving the family on the brink of starvation. Witnessing their destitution, an uncle determined to walk his little nephew to Paris and teach him to play a barrel organ. The mother had no choice but to relinquish her small son; it was a chance, at least, for a better life. "I was so poor," the man told Mayhew of his childhood, "I was afraid to die, for I get nothing to eat. . . . I went with my uncle to Paris, and we walk all the way. I had some white mice there, and he had a organ." ("Dancing" white mice could be part of an organ grinder's performance.) At nine or ten, the boy traveled on to London. He could now produce a variety of tunes: waltzes, Scottish country-dances, hornpipes, polkas—the polka being new and wildly popular—as well as pieces from Italian operas. As he played on a corner, a gentleman might step up, tap his foot to the tune, give a smile, toss a coin. If the gentleman took a liking to an opera selection, he might buy a piece of sheet music for a few shillings. In this manner, a London organ grinder might eke out a living.[4]

With heavy cares and concerns for others on his shoulders, Giuseppe Mazzini found a respite in his friendship with Jane Carlyle. They strolled together along Cheyne Walk, in sight of the Thames. She spoke with frankness to him of quarrels she had with her husband, and he told her of women who developed embarrassing passions for him. He mended Jane's pens. She gave him little gifts and helped in such practical matters as finding doctors when he was ill, housing when he needed to change his place of residence, and translators for his political essays. She helped out a bit with translation work herself, and now and then negotiated with his editors. She had in fact just commandeered Geraldine Jewsbury into translating an important essay Mazzini was writing on Dante. Signaling a rebirth of interest in Dante in the context of the burgeoning Italian nationalism, the essay would soon appear (April 1844) in the *Foreign Quarterly Review*.

This very year Giuseppe Mazzini said that Jane Carlyle was "the woman I value the most in England."[5] To stave off any alarm his Catholic mother, Maria Drago, might have about his friendship with a married woman (his mother had stayed in Genoa but remained vitally interested in all that concerned her son), he hastened to tell her that Mrs. Carlyle, four years his senior, was "neither beautiful nor plain—tall, thin, vivacious, but with very poor health." He also told his mother, contrary to what we know from Jane's accounts, "Some opinions about authors and insignificant matters have been the whole of our conversation." And he insisted that Jane (despite her declared skepticism) "firmly believes in God and in the immortality of the soul." Jane wished to assure Signora Mazzini that her son did not languish in his London exile, writing effusive notes to her in what was said to be garbled Italian, though in telling Maria Drago that "Giuseppe acknowledges me as a sister" (*Giuseppe ricognoscemi per sorella*), she was able to make her meaning clear.

With one note Jane enclosed a surprising gift, a golden brooch containing strands of her hair and his braided together. It meant that Mazzini then had to reassure his mother, "[R]ings and hair, which for us are precious tokens, and show the highest degree of love, are here mere tokens of friendship. I only love her like a sister." Signora Mazzini sent Mrs. Carlyle a ring inscribed with the admonishing words, "Love the martyr of Italy."[6]

Regarding each other as siblings would have helped Jane and Giuseppe handle any romantic feelings they might have had. For several years, theirs was a close and loving friendship. Elizabeth Fergus Pepoli, a Scotswoman married to an exiled Italian count, harbored dark suspicions about their degree of intimacy. Once when she made an unannounced visit to Cheyne Row, she caught sight of the two of them in "an unusual appearance of discomposure." But Jane explained the reason for their flurry of embarrassment: she and Giuseppe had been drinking wine together. When Elizabeth was announced, Jane had whispered to him anxiously to get rid of the evidence, whereupon he hastily stowed the wine glasses in the nearest receptacle, her writing desk.

Like many a brother and sister, they engaged in intense quarrels. A year before, Jane had related one of these, concerning a scheme she considered mad, to her husband, then in Ecclefechan with his family. You can almost hear Jane and Giuseppe shouting at each other across the drawing room as the pictures on the wall swing in their frames. Writing at a furious pace, Jane tells her husband: "[Mazzini] told me quite seriously that a week more would determine him whether to go singly and try to enter the country [Italy] in secret, or—to persuade a frigate [or warship] now here, which he deemed persuadable, [']*to revolt openly and take him there by force*.'" In her run-together words, we hear phrases of Giuseppe Mazzini's English as she heard him speak it:

> "[A]nd with one frigate said I you *mean* to overthrow the Austrian empire—amidst the general peace of Europe—'Why not? the *beginning* only is wanted'—I could not help telling him that 'a Harrow or Eton schoolboy who uttered such nonsense and proceeded to give it a practical shape would be *whipt* and expelled the community as a mischievous blockhead!' He was made very angry of course—but it was impossible to see anybody behaving so like '*a mad*' without telling him ones mind—HE a conspirator *chief*!—I should make an infinitely better one myself—What for instance can be mo[r]e out of the *role* of Conspirator than his telling *me* all his secret operations even to the

names of places when conspiracy is breaking out and *the names of people* who are organizing it?—*me* who do not even ever ask him a question on such matters—who on the contrary evade them as much as possible?—A man has a right to put *his own* life and safety at the mercy of whom he will—but no amount of confidence in his friend can justify him for making such dangerous disclosures concerning others—What would there have been very unnatural for example in my sending a few words to the Austrian government warning them of the projected outbreaks—merely for the purpose of having them *prevented*—so as to save Mazzini's head?"

Giuseppe had replied to her, "'What do you say of my head?—What are results?—is there not things more important than ones head?' And Jane responded, 'Certainly—but I should say that the man who has not *sense enough* to keep his head on his shoulders till *something* is *to be gained by parting with it* has not sense enough to manage or dream of managing any important matter whatever'—!" She concludes unnecessarily: "Our dialogues become 'warm'!"

•

As THE NEW Year unfurled, Thomas Carlyle wrote his friend Edward FitzGerald that he had by now thrown his Cromwell pages into the fireplace as many as six times but, at last, was discovering his form. The light began to dawn as he was making that first burnt-offering to the fireplace. Instead of attempting a full-scale history or biography, he would edit Oliver Cromwell's letters and speeches and include his own explanations. *Illuminations* he called these passages, later *elucidations*.

"Surely there was no such business," Thomas moaned to Edward, "as the writing a Life of Oliver Cromwell for the present race of Englishmen." The historical record was "a ghastly labyrinth, created for me by the stupidities of England accumulating for . . . two hundred years;—vacant Dulness glaring on one everywhere, with torpedo [benumbing] look, in this universal 'dusk of the gods,' saying with a sneer: 'Thou? Wilt thou save a Hero from the Abysses, where dark Death has quietly hidden him so long?'—It is frightful." He continued the metaphor that Jane had used, that they now all used, "[T]he Fates, I believe, have too clearly said that the child *Cromwell* cannot be born this year . . . he is a devil of a foetus to carry about with one!"

The recipient of these outcries, tall pudgy Edward FitzGerald, was then in his early thirties. Blue-eyed, round faced, with a receding hairline, Edward was not yet an author. His *Rubáiyát of Omar Khayyám* did not appear till 1859—when Thomas would be astonished to find that the book had been written by his old friend.

A sketch by William Makepeace Thackeray shows Edward FitzGerald wearing a pair of spectacles attached to a ribbon. He has the demeanor of the shy, fussy, intermittently kindly bachelor that he was. Edward's wealthy family had possession of much of Naseby Field, site of the decisive 1645 battle of the English Civil War, where Cromwell's parliamentarians had defeated King Charles I's royalists. Because of this connection, Edward was assisting Thomas with tasks that included identifying and sketching battlefield areas, and sending pieces of teeth, bone, and other Civil War relics discovered on the grounds.

Like Jane Carlyle, Edward FitzGerald had a rare talent for letter writing. He enjoyed recording impressions of Thomas Carlyle to entertain friends, viewing the older man with a loving yet critical eye. He worried that Carlyle would "spoil all by making a demigod of Cromwell, who was so far from wise that he brought about the very thing he fought to prevent—the restoration of an unrestricted monarchy."

In a letter, Edward pictured the study where the esteemed author worked, the dressing room that Jane had renovated for him. It shows the small separate world the study was, hanging as if suspended under the eaves: "I smoked a pipe with Carlyle yesterday. We ascended from his dining room carrying pipes and tobacco up through two stories of his house, and got into a little dressing room near the roof: there we sat down: the window was open and looked out on nursery gardens, their almond trees in blossom, and beyond, bare walls of houses, and over these, roofs and chimneys, and roofs and chimneys, and here and there a steeple, and whole London crowned with darkness gathering behind like the illimitable resources of a dream. I tried to persuade him to leave the accursed den, and he wished—but—but—perhaps he *didn't* wish on the whole."

A loather of city life, Edward FitzGerald believed that Mrs. Carlyle's attachment to London explained why he could not persuade her husband to live elsewhere, though he who greatly preferred the company of men had a habit of blaming his friends' wives. "London is very hateful to me," Edward said. "I long to spread wing and fly into the kind clean air of the country. . . . I tried to persuade Carlyle to leave his filthy Chelsea, but he says his wife likes London."[7]

This was true, although Jane Carlyle's relationship to her adopted city was complicated. Too often she was kept cooped up indoors because of illness or rough weather. Yet living in London was transforming her into a thoroughly urban woman—"so metropolitan," as Virginia Woolf later put it.[8] For the most part, Jane thrived on the mix of people, the bustling streets, the availability of books and periodicals, the gossip, the issues, the arguments—the variety a great city has to offer (though zoological gardens and tourist sights rarely tempted her).

Thomas, these days, continuing to suffer his creative paroxysms, had been provoking and irritating many of their friends, yet Jane was bearing with this behavior remarkably well. (The Carlyles' great quarrels were to come later.) She did not seem to mind unduly what others said of her husband, having an outlet for her own views in letter writing and conversation.

Anna Brownell Jameson, whose book *Characteristics of Women* (1832) had categorized and detailed Shakespeare's heroines, visited the Carlyles one day and afterwards told her friend Lady Byron, the poet's widow, that although she had found Carlyle "*great*!" as he thundered away about Cromwell, he had also, very disturbingly, "talked all breakfast time in defence of Slavery—and called the abolition movement 'Twaddle!'—in such grandiloquent phrases of Scorn mingled with grim laughter that I stood aghast." Somehow Anna located her courage and summoned her voice: "[W]ill you believe that I had the audacity to fight him—absolutely to contradict Carlyle?" She concluded that being married to the man must be "something next worse to being married to Satan himself." Yet she acknowledged that Jane that day had sat by "laughing and amused" to hear Anna take her husband on.[9]

Jane co-existed with volcanic conditions, the simmering sort as well as the occasional lava spill. Recently a few acquaintances, after witnessing Thomas ranting, had withdrawn from the Carlyles in distress. Harriet Martineau, not one to mince words, sent Jane a warning. She told her some people could not help pulling back because of Thomas's "hard mockery of all practical efforts to aid the suffering—particularly slaves. Some people who simply & honestly revere your husband's genius, & *read* him with delight, *cannot* bear to hear his talk of the abolitionists . . . less on account of the error & injustice of what he says, than of its 'withering' spirit." Harriet added, "There are some who wd keep young people out of his way, on this account."[10]

Miss Martineau, a slender, gray-eyed, plain and plainly dressed literary woman with a sober, pleasant appearance, had become impressed with the Abolitionists and their cause during a lengthy tour of America in the mid 1830s. She had visited the South as well as the North, spending much time gathering first-hand information about slavery. As she learned more, her mind grew clear regarding the horrors of the system, and the heroism of those who were fighting against it. Thomas Carlyle's contemptuous words on the subject of the Abolitionists, some of whom had become dear friends, pained and puzzled her.

Attempting to see the better side of Thomas Carlyle, who, after all, had influenced her whole generation with his inspirational *Sartor Resartus*, Harriet Martineau later said she believed that he felt deeper human sympathies than he could let on. A thin-skinned man, he did not know how to handle his seething outrage at human sufferings and human failings. "Till he got his coffee," said Harriet, searching rather more desperately for explanation, "he asked a list of questions, without waiting for answers, and looked as if he was on the rack."

Despite serious differences of opinion, Harriet Martineau had enjoyed teas and dinners at Cheyne Row when she stayed in London, and "the marvelous talk of both husband and wife." Famously deaf, she needed people to speak directly into her ear trumpet, and Jane and Thomas Carlyle had sometimes paid her the compliment of inviting her to visit them alone so that she would be able to hear better.

Like Edward FitzGerald, Harriet blamed Thomas's cantankerous outlook on the place where the Carlyles resided: much too close to the ceaseless babble of London. Of *course* Jane would be ill with colds and Thomas exhibit a disagreeable temper as long as they continued to dwell in a hundred-year-old house perched upon unhealthy Chelsea clay, down in the damp, foggy environs of the River Thames. Harriet who daydreamed of making a permanent home in the Lake Country (later settling happily in Ambleside) could not comprehend why the Carlyles would not heed her sound advice to remove themselves to "an airy quiet home in the country" built upon "a gravelly soil."[11]

The Carlyles' literary friendships, warm at first, sometimes growing cool to cold over genuine differences, could reach the breaking point. Yet, to a remarkable degree, members of their circles continued to quote, remember, and write about each other in letters, diaries, and memoirs. Their political conflicts and differences—serious ones, with mighty consequences for subsequent generations—appear in the 1840s as part of a single boisterous, contentious national conversation, rather than the disconnected discourse of alien camps. However often satire and stinging observation were brought to bear, they recognized each other as complicated individuals rather than merely as types.

In public Jane Carlyle rarely differed from her husband's political views. At social events she might echo an unpleasant sentiment or briefly defend his version of history. A few remarks only indicate that she might have liked to ameliorate the worst of his bigotry. In her 1845 journal, concerning his denigration of the Irish, she made the parenthetical comment: "pity but my Husband would pay some regard to the sensibilities of 'others' and exaggerate less!"[12] In 1850 after he had complained of a hideously uncomfortable journey by boat, telling her, "I suppose it must resemble that of the Slave-ships in the middle passage," Jane responded that she hoped having perceived such a connection would engender in him a degree of sympathy for "your black Brother." In her case, she told him, experiencing such misery first hand would create "a new sympathy . . . for another class of human sufferers."

But Jane Carlyle cannot be looked to for any systematic opposition to her husband's prejudiced opinions. The most that can be expected are a faint sympathy for those he opposed as the Other—as fellow victims—and occasional subversive jibes, or quick sharp punctures to his ego. There are two exceptions, however. Her views on Italy and on women, while uneven, tended to be considerably more liberal than his.

As for Thomas Carlyle, some unconscious connection involving projection seemed to exist between his reprehensible views on slavery and the Abolitionist movement, and his torment about his own writing-work. Unlike certain contemporaries, such as Charles Darwin, Thomas had no anti-slavery grandfathers and no experience of witnessing slavery. And he did not know personally any individual slaves, or former slaves.

His inner state—though this is necessarily speculative and certainly not an excuse—was more chaotic and unspeakable than many knew. The year before (1843), Jane had been shocked into awareness of his desperate agony over finding a viable genre for his Cromwell book. "Dear I will tell you a secret," she had written her cousin, "but see that you keep it to yourself—Carlyle is no more writing about *Oliver Cromwell* than you and I are!—I have known this for a good while." She had come across pages on "*The present fashion of mens coats*—about the rage for novelties—puffing every thing or any thing *except* '*Cromwell Oliver*'—I had no misgivings—I know he has such a way of tacking on extraneous discussions to his subject." But when she stumbled across a description of the late-twelfth / early thirteenth-century Abbot Samson, she inquired of her husband "and learned that Cromwell was not begun. . . . Nevertheless for I know not what Reason he lets everybody go on questioning him of his Cromwell and answers so as to leave them in the persuasion he is busy with that and nothing else."

That the extraneous pages turned into one of Thomas Carlyle's most fascinating, social-minded, and readable books, *Past and Present* (including a memorable discussion of Abbot Samson), does not diminish the pain of his protracted wrestle with the Cromwell material. It is no exaggeration to say that at the worst moments the dragon breath of madness blew down upon him. Enchained and enslaved to his work, believing himself in need of his own lash, forced by upbringing and beliefs to persevere, persevere, he viewed the doing of this work as an ironclad rule, a sacred duty, no matter how wretched it made him. Near-madness could alternate with stupefaction: the dark side of the work ethic. Abolition for himself—to abolish his project—was unthinkable, to say nothing of weak and unmanly.

The whole complex long-simmering gallimaufry was made no easier by deeply held beliefs, voiced much earlier in a stirring essay, "Characteristics" (1831): "Unconsciousness belongs to pure unmixed life; Consciousness to a diseased mixture and the conflict of life and death: Unconsciousness is the sign of creation; Consciousness, at best, that of manufacture."[13] The words have a romantic appeal, but as we know denigrating consciousness can doom a person to but slenderly know himself. In Thomas Carlyle's case there were hints throughout the 1840s that some kind of Vesuvius-sized eruption would one day occur, probably in print.

•

AMELY BÖLTE, MEANWHILE, was serving out her term with the Bullers and performing her job well. Jane Carlyle acknowledged the achievement, in which she could share: "She is an excellent Governess; the miraculous improvement she has wrought on Theresa proves *that* beyond all doubt." Mischievous, bratty, and hard to manage, little Theresa Revis appeared to be shaping up rather well.

Behind Theresa lay a story that had captivated Jane when Thomas first told it to her. On a visit to the Buller family some years before, he had observed the clever girl, then a slight, slim child of perhaps seven, watching her scamper in and out of the rooms making a great deal of noise. He conveyed her tale in an 1840 letter to his mother. Isabella Buller had confessed to Thomas "in all privacy that it [*it* is Theresa] was *an irregular production of her son Arthur's*!" Thomas reassured his mother, "[S]uspecting what it was, [I] never would take any notice of it, or so much as understand that it was running about and making a noise there." He reminded his mother how "kind and good," after all, the Bullers had been to him when he had tutored their sons, as if to excuse his presence in a house of ill repute.

Concerning the strange use of *it*, his audience must be kept in mind. He writes to his mother as if he has her image steadily before him, telling her, for instance, how the Quality are in town, distracting and disrupting him, causing him to eat dinner between the astonishingly late hours of "*six and nine o'clock at night*," hours she would have considered appalling, since dinner, especially among industrious peasants and workers, was traditionally served as early as noon to provide fuel for work. His mother's portrait, which still hangs today in the house on Cheyne Row, pictures a stiffer, more prim and primitive Whistler's Mother, with a starched ruffled cap fitted tightly about her face. (Aptly enough James McNeill Whistler in 1872-73 painted a portrait of his Chelsea neighbor Thomas Carlyle as a companion piece to the famous one of his mother. Whistler's *Father* it might be called.)

Margaret Aitkin Carlyle and her husband were faithful adherents of a strict protestant sect, the Burgher Seceder Church of Ecclefechan. Before marrying James Carlyle and giving birth to nine children, Margaret had worked as a domestic. In adulthood she labored to acquire the writing skills that would enable her to communicate with those of her offspring who lived far away. At the end of a letter her daughter Jean wrote to Thomas this January, his mother appended a note, "May God bliss you all and guid you by His holy spirit your Mother MAC."[14] Yet she had been the first to teach her son his letters.

With his mother's struggle to better herself in mind, Thomas Carlyle in this period when illiteracy was still widespread—in spite of becoming less progressive as he grew older—remained an advocate of universal education. In 1839 he had put forth in his *Chartism* pamphlet (an essay on the burgeoning Chartist working class movement) the proposition "That all English persons should be taught to read."[15] He wrote *persons* rather than *men*, a meaningful distinction.

When Thomas Carlyle had tutored the Bullers' sons Charles and Arthur in the 1820s, he had received two hundred pounds a year, university-educated male tutors being much better paid than governesses. Working for their family had been a turning point, widening his circle. Charles Sr. and Isabella had welcomed the unpolished tutor, and their boys could be cheering company. Son Charles loved boxing and Thomas found him "quite a bit of sunshine in my dreary Edinburgh element."[16] The friendships had lasted. Charles Jr., now large and imposing, well over six feet tall and making a name in radical politics, was still cheering Thomas and Jane with his company. Son Arthur, now the Queen's Advocate in Ceylon, was little Theresa's father. The child's mother was also named Theresa Revis, and her first husband, whose existence had at least rendered the little girl "legitimate," was said to be a scoundrel. Her current *caro sposo* was a Captain Bacon with whom she was residing in the South of France. Isabella Buller enjoyed flouting society's rules by remaining on friendly terms with her son Arthur's one-time paramour, the attractive, irresponsible Mrs. Bacon.

Picking up little Theresa's story, Jane made it her own. "She was the only *legitimate* child of a beautiful young 'improper female' who was for a number of years Arthur Bullers mistress . . . his Mother took the freak of patronizing this mistress, saw the child and behold it was very pretty and clever. Poor M*rs* Buller had tired of parties, of Politics, of most things in Heaven and earth: 'a sudden thought struck her,' she would *adopt* this child; give herself the excitement of *making a scandal* and *braving public opinion*, and of educating a flesh and blood girl into the Heroine of the three volume novel which she had for years been trying to *write*; but wanted perseverance to elaborate!—The child was made the idol of the whole house." For the present, with Theresa seemingly well in hand, the Bullers were pleased, a tractable idol being preferable to a naughty one.

When her temporary arrangement with the Bullers was over, Amely returned to London. Isabella Buller duly supplied the promised references and offered to help locate a new position for the governess. And Jane Carlyle found herself suddenly saddled with an unexpected guest.

•

SOMETIME IN EARLY May, 1844, Amely Bölte arrives without warning on the doorstep of 5 Cheyne Row, *trusting to Providence* that a new situation will soon materialize. As Jane Carlyle greets her—the young woman is burdened with boxes containing her belongings—she is not pleased.

Her maid Helen is about to go off on an extended vacation to Kirkaldy, Glasgow, and Dundee for a lark and to see relatives. Jane considers this proposed escapade a waste of the money that she has "with difficulty got [Helen] to lay up in the Savings Bank." She has agreed to let the maid go but is annoyed, and the house is in an uproar, the current cat running around underfoot, "the Devils own scrubbing and scowering going on." Helen wants to leave the place spic and span for her substitute, a serving maid named Maria, whom Jane will have to train. At the moment the industrious Helen is out back, washing down the flagstones.

Jane walks Amely up two flights of stairs to a large, airy, pretty three-windowed room with a charming fireplace,[17] the room that she had intended Thomas should work in until the loud piano music from next door had put a stop to the idea. Looking askance at the boxes, Jane tells Amely to stow them in a corner until Helen can come up to sweep and dust. Amely does as Jane requests, but, gazing about the room, can hardly concentrate on her friend's complaints about Helen's upcoming Kirkaldy trip.

Jane has placed her mother's best bed in here and arranged it with little things belonging to her mother to remind her of Templand, near Thornhill in Scotland, the gracious home of her maternal grandfather, her mother's last residence. Located atop its own hill, the well-loved house commands the rolling countryside. Jane once described the house as a "region of white sheets, and pretty chintzy curtains and soft carpets and green waving trees!" Her mother had made a garden at Templand, memorable for its yew trees and nesting mountain thrushes. Recently Jane had dreamed an idyllic dream that her mother was still alive and she was visiting her there.

When renovating this room, Jane had nailed to the floor patches of an old carpet, faded now to pleasing shades of blue. Her hand-coarsening labor had produced a happy result. Ample light filters in. Intriguing books line the shelves. Sometimes they call this the library.

The windows are open for airing today. Amely walks over to one, places her hands on the sill and leans her head out. The city air smells rather fresh, with only the slightest acrid tinge of salt, smoke, and tar. She catches a silvery glimpse of the Thames, and, on the far side of the river, the low green hills of Surrey. Turning vibrant green, as the spring deepens. The room will be a haven in which to daydream, write letters, and read—all those books on the bookshelves! *Heaven* after months spent attempting to mold the character of the bored, silly Theresa. A sense of good fortune washes over. "If you trust to Providence—"

With relief the governess takes off her dusty cloak and hat and gives Jane her heartfelt thanks. Jane can hear in Amely's voice how much it means that she has taken her in.

•

ROOM DESIGNATIONS CHANGED with some frequency at Cheyne Row, as the Carlyles nervously searched for the most conducive corners in which to eat, sleep, read, and write, so it is not always clear who was sleeping where. The Carlyles were famous insomniacs. "[A] sort of domestic wandering Jew," Jane once said of Thomas. She described one nocturnal house-traveling excursion of her husband's that, awake herself, she had tracked during the wee small hours: "There were wanderings about during the night—fires kindled with his own hands, bread and butter eaten in the china-closet!"

It is possible that Amely stayed in a small spare room at the back of the house, where one could look down upon the old walled garden with its newly leafy vines and lilac bushes, walnut, apple, and cherry trees. Wherever she was put, Amely was satisfied and her stay lengthened. Supposed to be a visit of two or three days, it turned into a fortnight.

Jane's annoyance surged. When visitors came, this uninvited guest, true to her habit, sat upon the parlor couch silent and owly, staring at host and guests alike. Jane expressed her vexation to her cousin: "When a person asks one to seek her a *lodging knowing* that one possesses a spare bed, nay having actually enjoyed the benefit of one's spare bed before, it is equivalent-to-saying 'will *you* take me in'?" Continuing to maintain that benevolence was not her style, Jane alluded to the book of Matthew and again to Lady Macbeth: *I was a stranger, and ye took me in*, and it was the fault of that damned thing called the *milk of human kindness*. The sight of the young foreign woman in the doorway weighted down by those pathetic boxes tied with string had made her capitulate.

Amely determinedly regarded Jane as a friend rather than a benefactress. When it was just the two of them, they enjoyed animated, stimulating conversation. But although Jane was gaining a sense of Amely's value, she could still experience her as a servant, on this occasion as a companion to herself falling short of the mark. Jane wrote her cousin that Amely *was* "a good creature, and 'not without sense' . . . [but] at no time an interesting companion for me." She would "sit hours together, especially when I am *doing* company, staring at me with her horn-eyes [*horn-eyes* having a film over them], and speaking never a word, till I feel somehow as if I were fallen under the power of a bad dream!" Jane had a knack for encapsulating a person in a phrase that others would find witty and repeat. Concerning Amely she landed on one: "But for a companion to *me*—! The cat is an angel in comparison!"

As for the staring, Amely was becoming ever more fascinated with Mrs. Carlyle. As for the silence, her English was excellent but perhaps it tired her to speak it all day. Or perhaps, even in the home of the cosmopolitan Carlyles, she was still afraid of uttering something improperly skeptical in front of their guests.

Days passed. Jane grew angrier, using words like *obtuse*, saying that Amely made her "blood run cold," seeming to forget the warm letter she had written to her five months before. It provoked Geraldine to inquire whether Jane was "finally delivered from your 'incubus.'"[18]

Once again, Isabella Buller came to the rescue—with news so good it was hard to take in. Miss Bölte was to be engaged at a hundred guineas a year to Lady Graham, wife of Sir James Graham, the Home Secretary in Sir Robert Peel's administration. Isabella told Jane that when she had informed Lady Graham that the governess was recommended by Mrs. Carlyle, the lady had exclaimed, "Oh certainly! M*rs* Carlyle's recommendation is to be received as *conclusive*."

With this grand situation before her, one that Amely firmly believed she merited—she who was worthy to work for the Queen—she at last departed the house on Cheyne Row. The salary was beyond expectations, "'the first chapters of Genesis' . . . silenced for ever!" As she firmly shut the door behind her guest, Jane Carlyle must have experienced all kinds of relief.

CHAPTER FOUR

THE DRAMA OF 1844

"There was not a single spark of life—a single feeling of honour—a single instinct of noble ideas or impulses throughout the House."

—GIUSEPPE MAZZINI TO JANE WELSH CARLYLE, 14? June 1844, *after Parliament put off his petition for redress.*

THE FIRST REPORTS ABOUT AMELY WERE ENCOURAGING, WITH LITTLE hint that she was soon to be a minor figure in a major political fracas. The governess had joined in the Victorian craze for autograph collecting, and her new employer, Home Secretary Sir James Graham, was providing her with some notable ones. As a courtesy, the Carlyles kept an eye out for contributions to the autograph collections of friends. For her cousin Helen Welsh, Jane rounded up the signatures of Goethe, Sir Walter Scott, Sir Robert Peel, the dandyish Count Alfred d'Orsay, Charles Buller, William Makepeace Thackeray, and Varnhagen von Ense, along with entire notes from Giuseppe Mazzini and Harriet Martineau. "Such distinguished names!" she teased her cousin. "To be sure, I said to myself, these will make her fortune."

The rage for autograph collecting represented a growing sense of the importance of the individual in this century, also seen in the establishment of national portrait galleries and the mass selling of photographic portraits of famous people. More particularly, it indicated the esteem felt for heroes or celebrated persons of genius and accomplishment, and a desire to touch something belonging to those special beings who were part of a wider sphere of life. Implied, also, was a yearning to connect to something beyond, the immortality of fame.

Amely had been working for the Grahams less than a month when

Jane heard bad news. Visiting Isabella Buller, Thomas discovered that "Lady Graham appears to be an entire goose." Amely, also present at the Bullers' residence that day, had told him a dismaying tale. When the Graham children inquired of their governess "What the Holy Ghost was like?" she had said in all honesty, "with all circumspection, she could not tell!" Thomas wondered if Jane could have conjured up an impromptu definition of the Holy Ghost. In the face of Amely's crime (apparently) her employers had dismissed her.

In other words, she had once again been fired for harboring skeptical or heretical opinions on religion, though the Grahams were allowing her to stay on till she made other arrangements. Always while in England Amely had to remain vigilant and watch her words. When accompanying employers on visits, she was forced to listen closely to ascertain "whether someone might have discovered a note of skepticism" in what she said. "I always felt as if I were standing on glass," she would remember, "and that feeling is awful. I had to appear as something I was not and yet all I ever wanted was to be truthful."[1] On this occasion, though, she was quite bewildered. The day before the Holy Ghost episode, the Grahams had voiced great satisfaction with her work.

Sir James Graham, a dedicated public servant and staunch adherent of the Church of England, and his wife Fanny would not have appreciated a Holy Ghost lapse. To Graham correct views on Biblical matters constituted the very glue that bound society together. Imbued with the belief that his was the class destined to rule England, he could be arrogant, sarcastic, and cold in manner. A contemporary account called him "always rough and unfair to his opponents," and charged him with having favored unconscionable legislation to rescue flagrantly indebted members of the landed aristocracy and gentry.[2] For England's *other* classes, the Home Secretary recommended frugality, and advocated cutting costs by lowering salaries and lengthening workdays.[3]

The stiff, fastidious man also believed that "The great characteristic of the present day, the prevailing national evil, is a constant thirst for change and love of innovation."[4] Alarmed by stirrings among the masses, he referred to the demonstrations and uprisings of the Chartists—that powerful, surging working class movement calling for the franchise and parliamentary reforms in their People's Charter—as "the mad insurrection of the working classes." On occasion he had ordered out the troops, fearing the Chartist movement might turn into England's French Revolution.[5]

•

THE YEAR 1844 SAW a profound moral and political scandal erupt in England. Since early March employees of Her Majesty's Post Office had been secretly opening the mail of Giuseppe Mazzini. On June 19, just as the controversy was coming to light, Thomas Carlyle published an influential letter about the matter in the *Times*.

Jane Carlyle was well positioned to observe what turned into "the major political event of 1844."[6] Amely's employer Sir James was at the center of the business. Though it was not at first clear what connection existed between this imbroglio and the precarious adventures of a German governess, they were intertwined. What happened illustrates the often-invisible yet powerful intersections of private and public lives, those intricately woven nets of society where a quiver in one corner sets the others to trembling in unexpected ways.

Giuseppe Mazzini was liked and admired from one end of the London social spectrum to the other, wherever room was made for exiles from illiberal European regimes. London had now become a haven for such refugees. But Jane Carlyle understood that her Italian friend was far from a wild-eyed ruffian. She humorously allayed the short-lived fears of Fanny Wedgwood on this point: "I can assure you, on the best authority, that you may send what invitation you like to Mazzini, without the slightest apprehension of his parading before your door with a stick—or sending you a challenge in the name of *La Jeune Italie* [Young Italy]." To the alarm of more conservative members of the extended Wedgwood family, Fanny had quickly become an ardent supporter.

Isabella Buller lost her head upon meeting Mazzini later this summer and hearing his "passionate pleadings for Italy." On the spot Mrs. Buller determined to carry a bust of him "*with his name on it in large letters*" to his mother Maria Drago in Italy, at the risk of being caught at the border and thrown into prison, or worse. At this time it was, as Jane put it, "*death* for any one in Italy to have a book of Mazzinis or a picture of him in their possession." Although Isabella Buller liked to live by her own rules and throw caution to the winds, Jane managed to persuade her that she need not literally lose her head over Mazzini.

Giuseppe Mazzini had also fascinated the wealthy society hostess Lady Harriet Baring. When Giuseppe had found himself seated next to Lady Harriet at a society soirée the previous year, he had teased her about what might happen to her as a member of the aristocracy come the revolution.[7] Not at all indignant, she had flirted with him. Taking Mazzini into her confidence in that crowded drawing room, confusingly for him (he could not figure out what she meant), she had signaled the existence of special secrets between them with her eyes. Jane used that encounter to call her husband's attention to his new lady friend's all-too-feminine wiles. In her letter, she adopted Mazzini's way of referring to Lady Harriet, "I am afraid my dear this Lady Baring of yours and his and John Mill's and everybody's is an arch coquette." Furthermore, Jane lost no time telling Thomas, Giuseppe had heard Lady Harriet commend the novels of George Sand, knowing her husband detested them beyond reason. *George Sandism* was a term of high opprobrium for Thomas, implying "phallus worship," the startling phrase that he used in private for what he considered modern forms of ancient, primitive fertility rites. While admitting the power of the French woman's novels (their power was the problem), he complained of her over-emphasis on romantic love—Sand seemed to suggest 'tis a *man's* whole existence—as well as their sentimentality and sexual explicitness. In this instance, however, he ignored his wife's warnings. Lady Harriet liked sending him "flights of charming little notes," which he liked receiving.

Recognizing seductress power in action, Jane pronounced the woman an Intellectual Circe. And was grateful to discover that the loyal Giuseppe, at least, would "not be caught by that syren." Yet because of her association with Giuseppe Mazzini, Lady Harriet's Tory father-in-law, Lord Ashburton, chastised her for "consorting with revolutionaries."[8] Jane had to acknowledge that "for a Tory woman of *her* distinction connected with the enemy as she is," it was a credit to Harriet Baring's open mindedness that she took an active interest in the revolutionary and his cause. Jane had no idea yet what a long, troublesome shadow this aristocratic woman was to cast across her life. Or how disruptive she would become to Jane's rich, fascinating London existence.

When Giuseppe had confided to Jane plans for secret uprisings in Italy early this year (1844), he was hoping that such incursions would prove to his compatriots they possessed the ability to gain their independence and would encourage them to persevere. But a foray into southern Italy had ended horribly, with the execution of two brothers who were captured in Calabria, Attilio and Emilio Bandiera. Caught in the tension of unfolding events, Jane wrote her cousin, "I am very sad about Mazzini the two young Bandieri are shot! God help their poor Mother." He was routinely blamed for such tragic incidents, even when, as seemed true in this case, he had tried to dissuade the participants because of the dangers.[9]

Believing her friend to be noble and dedicated, Jane was well aware of his role as an impassioned hero on history's stage. But regarding his political work, she who was not much drawn to politics for politics' sake wrote her cousin, "I never saw a mortal man who so completely made himself into 'minced meat for the universe! [']" Of all the women he had close friendships with in his lifetime, none saw him with Jane's sharpness and relative lack of sentimentality. In her letter writing, Jane often exhibits the clear-seeing eye of a socially observant English novelist who does not allow misty romanticism, susceptible though she may be to it, to blur her vision.

Sincerely concerned for Giuseppe and never battening on his fame, Jane cared more for his friendship, sympathy, and character than his—or anyone's—ideology. "I listen to his *programme* and miraculous hopes," she said, "with an *indifference* that drives him to despair." Yet it was not simple indifference—she feared that he might be risking imprisonment or death.

Neither a communist nor an atheist (he opposed both those *isms*), Giuseppe Mazzini held progressive views on many issues of the day, recognizing the urgent need in Europe for greater democracy. Thomas Carlyle disagreed about many of these matters, including, even, his plans for Italy. Despite considerable mutual respect, the two men were not enamored of each other. It was Giuseppe who said of Thomas that he "loves silence somewhat *platonically*." And in his *Reminiscences*, Thomas admitted he came to tire of Mazzini, who "fell mainly to *her* share; off and on, for a good many years, yielding her the charm of a sincere mutual esteem."[10]

Among the jealousies and jostlings rampant in London's literary and political circles, Jane Carlyle and Giuseppe Mazzini's friendship was remarkably warm and affectionate, although they were in many ways opposites. He disliked the ironic stance toward life, when irony was her métier. She distrusted airy theories and was suspicious of martyrdom, whereas he, with his whole heart, was a self-sacrificing idealist. Yet both were tolerant enough to befriend the tantalizing qualities in each other that they had disavowed for themselves.

The scandal of the opening of Giuseppe Mazzini's private letters by the post office began in the fall of 1843 when the Austrian ambassador in London, Baron Philipp von Neumann, requested that Sir James Graham, who as Home Secretary was responsible for police espionage, locate the Italian revolutionary's secret hiding place in London. Graham agreed, but to his immense irritation the London police could not (or would not) discover the address.[11] The police force had been in existence only fourteen years and the detective division a mere two, yet this was baffling. The Italian was living in Bloomsbury under his own name at 47 Devonshire Street, Queens Square, and openly visiting Jane and Thomas Carlyle and other friends.

In February 1844, when the police finally identified his residence, the Austrian ambassador requested that the British government spy on Mazzini. Concerned about Italian plots against the Austrian regime, Neumann wished to discover details of any political activities or travel plans. He persuaded Graham—though Mazzini had broken no English law—to gather information from the Italian's private mail, have it copied, and passed on to him. The Home Secretary had his reasons for complying with this request from a foreign country. Both he and the Austrian feared anti-establishment uprisings. And like the Austrian statesman Metternich, perhaps as a political ploy, they dismissed the romantic idea of a united *Italy* as "a mere 'geographical expression.'"[12]

A plan was devised in March 1844. Inside a secret room of the main post office, St. Martin's le Grand, the Devonshire-street mailbag was examined, letters identified, seals broken, pages unfolded, read, and copied. They were then refolded, new seals pressed down on top of old—often ineptly—and postmarks forged. The results pleased the Austrians. On 26 April Neumann wrote Sir James Graham, "Prince Metternich has desired me to express you his fervent thanks for the good important service you have rendered for the Cause of Peace."[13]

Based on the information secretly gathered, leaks to the press ensued. References in local as well as Italian papers aroused Giuseppe Mazzini's suspicions. When the writer of a *Times* article boasted of having seen *a mass of documents* containing details that only a few Italian exiles should have been aware of, he decided to test the system to learn if the mail sent to him had been tampered with. Jane Carlyle's playfully inventive friend had years of experience in France and Switzerland outsmarting spies and police, writing notes in codes and invisible ink, so it is unsurprising that he was able to come up with several clever tricks. He asked his correspondents to enclose nearly invisible "grains of sand, poppy seeds, or fine hairs" so he could tell, by their absence, if the letters that reached him had been opened. They also agreed to fold their letters in intricate ways hard to duplicate.[14]

When Jane discovered what was going on, Giuseppe asked her to say nothing until he had proof. But she grew concerned that the notes *she* was writing him were being opened and read.

When Chartist friends as well as a sympathetic clerk inside the Post Office uncovered ample proof, Mazzini with the help of the radical MP from Finsbury, and others, petitioned the House of Commons. The House, however, referred the matter: the silent majority, obedient as sheep, followed the lead of Home Secretary Graham. The moment he heard the dispiriting news, Giuseppe Mazzini rushed off an impassioned note to Jane Carlyle. "The *dumb* majority voted for Sir James Graham," he wrote her, "and all was over. There was not a single spark of life—a single feeling of honour—a single instinct of noble ideas or impulses throughout the House. Within two days, the Continental press will laugh upon *English liberty* and *loyalty*; but no body appeared to think of that."[15]

Punch published a cartoon on June 6 that Thomas called to Jane's attention, depicting Home Secretary Graham as "Paul Pry at the Post Office." It shows him wearing a country gentleman's top hat, high collar, frock coat, plaid pants, and knee-high boots, with an umbrella tucked under his arm, as he voyeuristically peers into the tube of a sealed letter.

A *Times* editorial on June 17 proclaimed the opening of letters "unconstitutional, un-English, and ungenerous." "Hitherto, it has been the peculiar boast of England that she is not as other countries, that her citizens are not liable to the same petty persecutions, the same rigorous police, the same insidious and incessant watching, the same dogging of their footsteps, opening of their letters, and prying into cabinets as harass the subjects of continental states." The *Times* also stated, "Mr. Mazzini's character and habits and society are nothing to the point."

In other words, the *Times* would speak out on the issue, but not on behalf of the man.

It was in response to this editorial that Thomas Carlyle wrote to the *Times* (a letter published June 19) testifying to Mazzini's character, which was under outrageous attack. He was variously accused of being a murderer, a gambler, and a maniac. Whatever their ideological differences, he never doubted the Italian's passion and sincerity. Mazzini was "a man of genius and virtue, a man of sterling veracity, humanity, and nobleness of mind, one of those rare men . . . who are worthy to be called martyr-souls; who, in silence, piously in their daily life, understand and practice what is meant by that." He further declared: "Whether the extraneous Austrian Emperor and miserable old chimera of a Pope shall maintain themselves in Italy, or be obliged to decamp from Italy, is not a question in the least vital to Englishmen. But it is a question vital to us that sealed letters in an English post-office be, as we all fancied they were, respected as things sacred; that opening of men's letters, a practice near of kin to picking men's pockets . . . be not resorted to in England, except in cases of the very last extremity. When some new Gunpowder Plot may be in the wind, some double-dyed high treason, or imminent national wreck not avoidable otherwise, then let us open letters: not till then."[16]

Jane Carlyle proclaimed the letter "glorious," and Mazzini sent a copy to his mother in Italy, who was "full of the most *fervid* gratitude." About these goings-on, Jane wrote her cousin: "I am 'very much excited'—more than ever needing to have my hair combed—if you have been casting your serious eyes on the Public Bruits you may have seen the affair of '*Mazzinis letters*.'" She confided, "[I]t is no news to *me* for I have been in the secret for months—but it is news for this FREE country of England—disgraceful news." And added that her friend Erasmus Darwin had advised her "'to apply for copies of all *my* letters to M. at the home office'—but my letters have a long while back been written more *for* the Austrian embassy than for the person they were addressed to—nay I lately said at the end of a note requiring dispatch that 'M*rs* Carlyle would be particularly obliged to the embassy to lose no time in forwarding it'!"

The letter-opening episode touched a mid-nineteenth-century British nerve. The social stratum Jane Carlyle was part of abounded in prolific letter-writers who indeed regarded their epistles *as things sacred*.

The writing and receiving of personal letters had become woven into the fabric of daily life, vital to human connectedness, intimacy, and entertainment. Increasingly in the Victorian era, letters were an expression of individuality, for men and women alike. The phenomenon was not unconnected to the awareness that Jane Carlyle called *I-ity*, an apparent female egotism that—from a modern perspective—indicates an emerging sense of personal agency.

The penny post, created in 1840, made the sending of letters cheaper and easier, and their importance only increased. Harriet Martineau waxed eloquent over the significance of the penny post for the many, extolling the "force and extent of its civilising and humanising influences, especially in regard to its spreading the spirit of Home over all the occupations and interests of life, in defiance of the separating powers of distance and poverty."[17] Private letters, to Harriet, were agents of civilization that could extend the feminine, moral sphere of the home into the rough and tumble masculine world of commerce.

In this instance, however, she wrote Jane: "I sh*d* not satisfy you quite ab*t* the letter-business." Although she believed no true gentleman would ever open another's mail, Harriet Martineau had not seen enough evidence to convince her that Graham, who had offered little explanation, was as culpable as he looked: "[T]he insults to Graham while he is silent, are cruel & dastardly,—& I for my part will wait."[18] Helen Mitchell, on the other hand, though she liked to peek inside other people's mail herself, weighed in firmly. In a pocket-sized notebook, Jane Carlyle carefully recorded the saying of her diminutive maid under the title "Helen on the Letter-opening question": "They're surely no sae particular now as they used to be; it is a most awfully *debauched* thing to open Letters."[19]

In the months to come, committees would be set up and hundreds of pages of parliamentary record devoted to the debate. The mail of Polish exiles, several Chartists, including, possibly, a Chartist MP, as well as that of various embassies had also been opened. It was hard to determine exactly what had been passed to the Austrians, but if names of men associated with the Bandiera brothers had been included, Italian independence fighters may, as a result, have lost their lives. No solid rationale was given for the opening of private mail, though tortuous explanations emerged. One had to do with the British Protectorate of Corfu, the Greek island from whence the Bandiera brothers' ship to

Calabria had sailed, and its connection to the peace and stability of "Europe." Translation: keep Italy safe for the Austrians.

As a result of the events of 1844, Giuseppe Mazzini and the Italian cause became wildly popular. As historian Thomas Babington Macaulay put it, tracking the debates as an MP, "the turning of the Post Office into an engine of the police was utterly abhorrent to the public feeling."[20] The mass production of photographs was now technically possible, and London shops sold pictures of Mazzini by the thousands. Thomas Carlyle's "a practice near of kin to picking men's pockets" became a household phrase. Newly won adherents stepped forward to volunteer assistance.

Many scribbled outside their letters "Not to be Grahamed!" Stickers expressing anti-Graham sentiments gave people a simple, doable form of political protest. *Punch* sold wafers, those small disks of dried paste used to seal letters, in the shape of hedgehogs that said "Keep Off." Others read "Deliver me from Sir James." Charles Dickens wrote merrily round the seal of a letter he sent June 28: "It is particularly requested that if Sir James Graham should open this, he will not trouble himself to seal it again."[21]

At one point Graham angrily declared the Italian hero to be a convicted assassin. [22] When he was forced to apologize for this, Mazzini refused to accept the apology. As the controversy wended its way, Jane Carlyle had harsh words for Graham, writing her cousin the following spring, "Have you been reading the 'debates' on the Mazzini question—good heavens what a *dirty* animal that Sir J Graham is! he does things which a street sweeper would not stoop to!—*The Murderer* [that is, Mazzini, the alleged assassin] takes it all *calmly calmly* . . . and we his friends can all afford to take it *calmly* knowing what a man he is!"

Reverberations spread far and wide. Frederick Douglass, who visited England soon after to lecture as an ex-slave on the subject of slavery in America, praised the English who came out to hear him speak. "They are the people," Douglass told his American readers, "who sympathize with . . . Mazzini, and with the oppressed and enslaved, of every color and nation, the world over."[23] Ironically, given Thomas Carlyle's opposition to the Abolitionist movement, on the issue of Mazzini and the post office, he and Frederick Douglass were on the same side.

The growing desire for individual liberties had joined an increasing revulsion against the machinations of the Austrian Empire. (The

European Spring of 1848 was approaching.) As a result of the post office affair, the secret inner room of St. Martin's le Grand was closed down. Warrants to open letters remained rare until the Irish Troubles of the 1880s. Private letters had been tampered with before, but the 1844 warrant had been issued at the request of an unpopular foreign government when no threat existed to what Jane Carlyle had termed, in her inimitable ironic-yet-ultimately-not-ironic style, "this FREE country of England."

In the midst of this drama, though few in the glare of public life had the least idea, a governess had lost her job. "Oh certainly!" Fanny Graham had said to Isabella Buller, "Mrs. Carlyle's recommendation is to be received as *conclusive*." But the day after Thomas Carlyle's letter appeared in the *Times*, the Grahams had turned against their governess, and not because of her Holy Ghost lapse. Amely had been deceived as to the cause of her dismissal. As Thomas explained to his brother, "[I]t is a fact, tho' one we keep strictly to ourselves, that Lady Graham, next day after the *Times* Letter, turned off poor Governess Bölte, who being a great favourite the day before could not in the least understand it;—Mrs Buller had given Bölte's character as originating here." That is, if *Mr*. Carlyle dared to write the papers in opposition to the Home Secretary, he and his wife would no longer employ a protégée of *Mrs*. Carlyle's.

Once again, Amely was jobless. As Jane described her, the governess was small and humdrum. As an unprepossessing and skeptical foreigner, how on earth was she to survive? Quick as a snap of the fingers, however, her wheel of fortune took another turn. When Isabella Buller learned what the Grahams had done, she invited Miss Bölte to accompany their family on a trip to the Continent, again as governess. Little Theresa was starting to exhibit an alarmingly precocious interest in the opposite sex. Mrs. Buller needed someone to chaperone as well as teach the child, and from her experience with Amely, she was confident the governess could handle both jobs.

When she heard of this offer, Jane, who was now out of town, visiting her uncle and his family in Liverpool, wrote her husband, "Oh I was *so* glad over Böltes new prospects," using her last name only, as all tended to do when thinking of her in her capacity as a servant. Amely sent Jane a brave note insisting that she actually preferred this. Her anticipation of a journey through France and Italy with the Buller family had made her, said Jane, "the happiest of creatures."

Curiously, until Sir James Graham's role became clear to the public, no one explained to Amely that the loss of her excellent position had to do with the Post Office affair. Perhaps what he considered calumnious newspaper and journal articles were kept hidden from servants and children in his household. At any rate, Amely spent about two weeks in the dark. Knowing that for Giuseppe Mazzini's own good it was incumbent upon her to keep his secrets, Jane had apparently said nothing. As late as June 26 Thomas wrote Jane that Isabella Buller "had strictly charged everybody not to whisper a word of Sir James Graham's proceedings to Bölte," but he added, "Of course all the world will know it."

A little later Thomas told Jane that he was coming to regard poor Sir James as having been "unluckier" than anything. Jane, however, remained impassioned on the subject, and her husband sympathized with her for having to keep a lid on her political views in her Tory uncle's Liverpool home. He understood that when the visit was over Jane would find it "a great relief . . . to get her mouth opened again, and that pent reservoir of Liberalism emitted!"

The post office drama had kept them on edge for weeks. They all, now, needed a respite.

CHAPTER FIVE
WHAT SHOULD A WOMAN BE AND DO?

"[T]oo much in advance of the Century"!
—JANE WELSH CARLYLE (1852)[1]

SOON AFTER HER HUSBAND'S LETTER TO THE *TIMES* APPEARED, JANE Carlyle set off on a visit to her uncle and cousins in Liverpool. Shortly before her departure, Helen Mitchell returned from Scotland with a strong smell of liquor on her breath but assured her dubious mistress it was only from a sociable glass of gin given her by "a most respectable pair of old people" with whom she had shared a cab from the steamboat. Jane was able to place Helen's substitute, the maid Maria, with a Cheyne Walk chemist, a swift successful piece of employment bureau work.

While Jane was away, Thomas remained at home working on his Cromwell. The Bullers were driving about London in their carriage, paying social calls and showing off Theresa—they would not be leaving for the Continent till September. Amely Bölte, as she waited to join them on their journey, would most likely have taken a room in a lodging house, what a governess typically did between jobs.

The words *depressing lodgings* were often spoken together, yet such rooms could be expensive. A governess required a good address in order to receive the visits of prospective employers. She needed to dress carefully, too, another expense, so that a lady inspecting her could see that she would not disgrace the household she was hoping to join. Yet even a modest room of her own would have provided Amely a space within which to collect herself, which she badly needed. Writing to Jane one evening, Thomas described the governess's ongoing agitation. He was only halfway through comfortably smoking a pipe, he told his wife, when "Bölte" had appeared at their door, perhaps hoping again for a place to stay. She agreed to take a cup of tea with him and to his great annoyance had "clattered in a wooden way, really very wearisome, about 'Sir James,' the 'Holy Ghost' and I know not what."

Knowing Jane would wish to hear about Helen Mitchell's doings, he tucked into another letter a glimpse of their maidservant in action, in the tone of voice he reflexively employed for little women: "Today a great smell of suds issues from the lower regions; I consider it is the bewildered little *dottle* of a body engaged in washing its bits of duds. She is forever busy, just as when you were here; and, tho' there . . . can be next to no cleaning of rooms [since he's having almost no company] . . . she never seems a whit nearer the end of her job. She cooks me my quarter of fowl in an unexceptional manner, and I do not interfere farther."

Around this time Amely was likely finishing a translation of Ludwig Tieck's historical novel *The Roman Matron; or, Vittoria Accorombona*. She must have had a knack for transforming a small dreary room into an island of freedom, since during her years as governess she accomplished a surprising amount of literary work. Thomas provides the evidence that the Tieck translation was hers (he too had translated some of the writer's early fiction), telling a correspondent who inquired, "The Translator of *Accorombona* is properly a Miss Bölte, a young Lady from Berlin . . . whom my Wife got placed with the Bullers." He adds, "some *English Lady*" may have helped out, "but this Fraulein Bölte, I am very sure was in it."

This novel meant a great deal to Jane. "Thank you *passionately* for giving me *Vittoria Accorombona*," she had written the Carlyles' good friend John Sterling, who had sent her the book in its original German the year before (1843), "—and thank you even more for knowing before hand that I should like her. Your presentiment that this was 'a woman exactly after my own heart' *so* pleases *my own heart*!—proves that I am not *universally* '*a woman misunderstood*'!" Or *une femme incomprise*. The French phrase had a special resonance for Jane, who later used it in two of her most formal writings. Like Tieck's heroine, Jane, too, had little bursts of feeling that no one on earth could understand her.

A romantic, quasi-historical, late Renaissance tragedy, *Vittoria Accorombona* opens in 1575 and is set in a strife-torn Italy, where murder, machinations, and mayhem reign. The heroine, in opposition to her times, is a free-minded creative woman, a philosopher and poet. The Vittoria of legend having captured Tieck's imagination, he set about rescuing her from earlier ambiguous or downright hostile accounts. As the author envisions her, Vittoria represents the most forward-looking spirit of a darkening age, and, indirectly, the novel addresses what a united, independent *Italy* might look like. Forced to adhere to the convention of marriage for the sake of her family, Vittoria holds on admirably to her self-confidence and sense of worth. Tensions exist in the novel between the external societal rules that govern a woman's life and the inner resources she might draw on to confront those restrictions—an appealing theme for mid-nineteenth-century readers like Jane.

More personally, Tieck's description of his heroine sounds like the young Jane Baillie Welsh, especially a charming miniature of her done in 1826 by Kenneth Macleary. Like Jane at the age of twenty-five, Tieck's Vittoria has a delicately formed ruby mouth; glossy, luxuriant dark curly hair; and "finely pencilled eyebrows of deep black [that] added to the animated expression of her sparkling eyes."[2] Playful in the way of any intelligent, spirited girl, Vittoria writes poetry, as Jane had also done. She surely would have taken note of the resemblance to her spirited younger self.

Beautiful noble Vittoria glories in contrarian opinions, especially on the subject of traditional arranged marriage. Under pressure from her mother to conform to custom and marry well, Vittoria proclaims, "I hate, I detest the thought of marriage; I would rather poison a man than submit myself to his legitimate control [referring to a legal system that gave sole authority to the husband]. [Marriage] seems to me the greatest crime, the most shameful prostitution." When it transpires that Vittoria *must* marry to save her family, the heroine declares, "As I am to be exposed in the market-place, it signifies little to whom I may be sold."[3]

The man she does wed at least seems innocuous. Although he turns out to be unpleasantly weak and idle, Vittoria makes the best of the bad situation, opening their home to friends and cultural events that stimulate and inspire her. In time she meets the scintillating older Paul

Giordano, Duke of Bracciano, who has had a career of military adventures to rival Othello's.

In a melodramatic turn of events, Bracciano strangles to death his corrupt and silly wife after discovering her infidelity. He thus avenges his honor and frees himself to marry the vastly superior Vittoria, who accepts the news of the Duke's dark deed with surprising equanimity, saying it is the *custom* of honor killing that is to be condemned. After her own spouse dies a mysterious death, she and Bracciano marry and for a time dwell happily together by the shores of Lake Garda. At length, however, he is undone by his enemies, as well as by his conscience, when reproachful ghosts of his first wife and Vittoria's husband appear before him in a magical woods.

After the Duke expires, Vittoria is murdered by men who had hated her husband. But she is murdered so sadistically it is as if the novelist felt compelled, in the end, to punish his heroine for having dared make herself into *a new genus*—to borrow feminist foremother Mary Wollstonecraft's phrase for a new category of woman. The murderer forces Vittoria to bare her bosom, then plunges in his dagger and turns it "slowly in the deep wound he had inflicted," while saying crudely "How do you like that?"[4] The symbolism is scarcely veiled: he rapes her as he kills her.

As the tale concludes, Tieck pens his moral: "That which is rare and noble is too often misunderstood and despised by men of little minds."[5] It is a dangerous moral, given the trail of dead bodies that paved the way for the union of the rare and noble pair.

After the English translation of "*The Roman Matron; or, Vittoria Accorombona*" had appeared as a three-volume set (1845), an anonymous review in *Fraser's Magazine* warned the reader away: "Nor let us imagine that it is possible to form a just estimate of any work from a translation." The review is notable for its omissions. Cautioning that one should not attempt judgments on the morals of a different era, the reviewer neglects to mention Vittoria's views on traditional marriage yet bemoans how cold and indifferent she is to her mother: "We are shocked at Vittoria's insensibility."[6] Ignoring the heroine's attitudes toward marriage while fussing over nuances of her filial transgressions stands in sharp opposition to the directness and force of the translated passages, and to the views of the heroine expressed by Jane Carlyle. The contrast makes Jane, to use her phrase, appear well "in advance of the Century."

Jane Carlyle's ironical eye did not desert her when she romantically immersed herself in novels of her era. Teasingly she had chastised her friend John Sterling for having said nothing to her, regarding Tieck's novel, "of *the* MAN AFTER *my own heart* so that Bracciano took me by surprise, and has nearly turned my head! My very *beau ideal* of manhood."

The Duke of Bracciano was a dangerous, satanic hero, like the Byron of Jane's girlhood. Many girls her age had been infatuated with the dashing poet, from what they had read and heard. Jane had written at least two poems about Byron. As she noted in her letter to John Sterling, the Duke of Bracciano had strangled his inferior, weak-minded wife "*with dignity*"; and she could "almost weep" that she "was not born two centuries earlier that I might have been—his mistress—*not* his *wife*!"

At Jane's urging, Thomas read the novel while on vacation in Wales. Engrossed, he found the Welsh countryside "a most solitary green region, very rainy too at present;—in which I feel hitherto very much like a man fallen out of the Moon. The people speak inarticulate Welsh . . . and they, and the whole world, except the rain-clouds, seems to be asleep or nearly so. I have Tieck's *Vittoria Accorombona*, and care for no weather today!" His verdict: he wrote Jane that the novel was by "far the pleasantest thing I have yet fallen in with . . . . A very gorgeous composition." But it contained too many showy "Bristol-diamonds" and was as untrue as an opera; though much *was* true and "genial-warm and very grand." Vittoria herself made "a right divine stage goddess," and he agreed she and Bracciano were well matched. However he concluded that he "could not but *abhor* that murder he did of the poor frivolous trembling creature [his wife]: it is detestable."

A disappointed Jane replied, "And you do not like my beautiful Vittoria!—Oh what want of taste!" Thomas nonetheless recommended the tale to his brother John, who also became absorbed in its dreamy, melodramatic, and bloody pages.

Jane Carlyle's passionate receptivity to literature involved the kind of relationship between writer and reader that both of them valued; though her husband saw himself more as the writer in the equation, whereas Jane identified as reader *and* writer. Through reading novels, middle-class Victorian wives, living within their narrowed sphere, could travel to exotic realms and vicariously experience forbidden, even *detestable* feelings and actions.

Jane Carlyle had a capacity to live in particular novels she read and take them to heart, allowing them to influence her own writing, although if she did not care for a work she could be sharp-tongued. When asked to recommend books for her uncle to read when he was convalescing from an illness and forced to eat gruel (a thin liquidy oatmeal), she produced a round-up of what she did *not* like: "'taking *a birds-eye view*' of all modern literature, I am arrived at the conclusion; that to find a book *exactly* suited to my Uncle's taste I must—*write it myself!* and alas, that cannot be done before tomorrow morning!" Dismissing several modern works in turn, Jane concluded, "Oh!—Ah!—Well! *Miss Austin*," adding, "Too washy—watergruel for mind and body at the same time were too bad."

Washy watergruel, Jane's opinion of Jane Austen's novels, was not then uncommon; both Thomas Carlyle and the Anglo-Irish novelist Maria Edgeworth said something similar. Yet, strangely, although Jane Carlyle rarely mentions Jane Austen, the two share uncanny similarities: novel-of-manners techniques; a concern with morality; a flair for humor, satire, wit; and an eye for the telling detail, including homely details of ordinary life. Was an anxiety of influence at work? Possibly, for when she talked of the other Jane in 1852, it was in a fanciful literary letter to Thomas that described an experience while traveling alone. It had made her feel as if she were inside one of Jane Austen's books, implying a closer identification with the novelist than she otherwise admitted to.

In that letter, Jane tells about a man she had observed at an inn, alluding to the scene in *Persuasion* where Anne Elliot and a strange gentleman (who turns out to be her cousin) notice each other in passing in a public place. And Jane Carlyle's gentleman, like Austen's character, will also reappear, although only to return a lost parasol. "He looked at me," Jane wrote, "but said nothing—and a minute or two after I saw *him* also drive past the window. Some twenty minutes after; I started myself, in a little gig, with a brisk little horse, and silent driver—Nothing could be more pleasant—than so *pirring* thro' quiet roads in the dusk—with the moon coming out—I felt as if I were *reading about myself in a Miss Austin novel!*"

Not only had Jane Carlyle been moved to action by Charles Dickens' *A Christmas Carol*, she would closely identify with contemporary novels such as Geraldine Jewsbury's *The Half-Sisters* (1848) based "almost word for word" on arguments the two friends had. About Charlotte Brontë's

Shirley (1849), Jane said that she and the author "must have been much together in some previous state of existence." When the pseudonymous Brontë sisters' books first appeared, rumors occasionally went around London that the author might be Mrs. Carlyle. At certain mid-nineteenth-century moments, life and literature seemed eerily in sync, as if Victorian writers and Victorian readers, who themselves took note of the coincidence, had been reading each other's minds.

Jane and Thomas Carlyle as writers, as a creative couple, shared a belief. She thought good letter writing involved the splash of the mind. When Thomas was dispensing advice to someone who asked him to explain how he went about preparing his historical works, he, too, stressed the importance of conveying the living mind.

Having to contend with congeries of bundled research notes for his interminable Cromwell project, to say nothing of reading through heaps of dryasdust tomes that he kept in irregular piles on the floor beneath his writing table, Thomas made several comments about this: "My Paper-bags (filled with little scraps all in pencil) have often enough come to little for me. . . . [K]eep the thing you are elaborating as much as possible actually *in* your own living mind; in order that this same mind, as much awake as possible, may have a chance to make something of it!"

And: "Only what you at last *have living* in your own memory and heart is worth putting down to be printed; this alone has much chance to get into the living heart and memory of other men. And here indeed, I believe, is the essence of all the rules I have ever been able to devise for myself."

A particular kind of reader is needed to receive the writer's words: another living mind, awake, supple, and receptive to impressions conveyed. Ideally, a highly desirable relationship is formed and a transmission from living mind to living mind takes place, romantically dissolving, for the moment, separations of body, space, and time.

•

ONCE JANE HAD returned to London from Liverpool, she was increasingly on Amely's mind. Like Giuseppe Mazzini, she admired Mrs. Carlyle more than any other woman in England. How might she secure a steadier attention from this friend who too often regarded her as an object of charity, as a servant, or a project? How could she force Jane to see and acknowledge more of her importance and worth?

Seated at a lodging-house desk one August day—we may imagine—Amely pauses in her translation work, settles back in her chair, and lets her thoughts drift. As happens rather often these days, they drift toward Jane as she wonders idly how she might strengthen her connection with the Carlyles. During her reverie, she recalls a countryman of hers whose memoir writings the Carlyles esteem, Karl August Varnhagen von Ense.

Amely had once met him in the company of her literary aunt, although since "unimportant events pass through one's memory like colorless images,"[7] she is certain he will not remember her. No matter. The question is whether she dares to write this Prussian soldier, diplomat, and man of letters. Dimly she foresees that by taking such a step, she, Varnhagen, and Jane and Thomas Carlyle might come to form a loose and unofficial quartet in the midst of their myriad other relationships and busy lives. As Varnhagen's correspondent, Amely might become the chief link, carrying messages, exchanging literary and psychological impressions, as well as revealing the as yet unsuspected extent of their political differences. Her curiosity about all of them is intense.

Varnhagan—he of the beautiful handwriting who had introduced the tall Prussian general to Cheyne Row—had studied medicine, literature, and philosophy in Paris and Berlin and served with the Russian and Austrian armies. In 1809 he had been wounded at the Battle of Wagram, where Napoleon had roundly defeated the Austrians. Not long after, he became a diplomat to Napoleon's court. Since 1837 he and Thomas Carlyle had been writing to each other and exchanging books. Amely was cognizant of their correspondence and mutual regard.

Admiration for Goethe and German literature formed the principal bond. Another was the Carlyles' respect for Varnhagen's memoirs depicting his adventures and wide acquaintance. Believing these volumes to be among the most entertaining he had read, Thomas wrote a complimentary essay about them for the *London and Westminster Review* (1838), singling out a significant scene Varnhagan had witnessed in 1810, featuring a very alive and fearsome Napoleon Bonaparte:

> "We had formed ourselves into a half-circle in the Audience Hall, and got placed in several crowded ranks, when the cry of '*L'Empereur*!' announced the appearance of Napoleon. . . . In simple blue uniform, his little hat under his arm, he walked heavily toward us. . . . The

> Emperor sought to appear sympathetic, he even used words of emotion; but this tone by no means succeeded with him, and accordingly he soon let it drop. . . . [I]n his farther progress some face or some thought must have stung him, for he got into violent anger; broke stormfully out on some one or other. . . [Napoleon] ra[n]ted and threatened, and held the poor man, for a good space, in tormenting annihilation. Those who stood nearer . . . not without anxieties of their own, declared afterwards that there was no cause at all for such fury; that the Emperor had merely been seeking an opportunity to vent his ill-humour, and had done so even intentionally . . . that all the rest might be thrown into due terror, and every opposition beforehand beaten down."[8]

Years later Varnhagen could still hear the frightening sound of Napoleon's "raspy, untamed voice" as he vented his fury on an underling. Thomas Carlyle highly valued passages like that, which brought the past to life. Such writing, which could overcome current-existence chauvinism, might jolt readers into a visceral experience: *they were once alive like you and me!*

He sent Varnhagen a personal letter of thanks and also praised his manner of describing the Congress of Vienna. What Thomas Carlyle wrote conveys his great love of the narrative form:

"That is what we call the *art* of writing,—the summary and outcome of many arts and gifts. The grand secret of it, I believe, is *insight*,—just estimation and understanding, by head, and especially by heart. Give a man a *Narrative* to make, you take in brief the measure of whatsoever worth is in the man. The Thing Done lies round him, with length, breadth, depth, a distracted chaos; he models it into order, sequence and visibility. . . . I rejoice much in such a style of delineation; I prefer it to almost all uses which a man can make of the spiritual faculty entrusted him here below. . . . [A] man had understanding given him, and a pen and ink, chiefly for that. In the name of the present and of future times, I bid you continue to write us *Memoirs*."

•

ON THAT LANGUID August day, the governess, contemplating what she knew of Varnhagen, took a deep breath and formed a resolve. She, Amely Charlotte Elise Mariana Bölte, would put her hand to the tiller and steer her life where she could. She would write to her illustrious compatriot, making use of some autographs she had gathered while working for the Grahams. She knew Varnhagen was accumulating an important collection; Thomas Carlyle had already sent him quite a few. "Dear Sir," she wrote on August 8, 1844, in her native German, "I hear from Mr. Carlyle that you are starting a collection of autographs. I recently received the enclosed signatures, including the coats of arms, from the Queen's Home Secretary, Sir James Graham."

Penning the note allowed Amely to salvage something from her time in the Graham household. Weary at the moment of England, she told her correspondent she could think of no better use for her autographs than to offer them "as a token of my gratitude to the man who has given every German a reason of even greater pride in Germany." She knew members of Young Germany regarded this legendary fifty-nine-year-old Berliner as a wise elder in sympathy with their liberal views. "[I]f my path should lead me back to Berlin one of these days," she added, ". . . I shall take the liberty of introducing myself to you and bring you regards from our mutual friend, your fan and admirer, Mr. Carlyle, and I shall be certain of a friendly reception from you."[9]

Amely intuited rightly that he would be fascinated by anything she might have to say about Jane and Thomas Carlyle. A month later he replied briefly, acknowledging the note and autographs that Fraulein Bölte had sent him. A correspondence that would contain many observations of the Carlyles had been launched.

•

THE HIGHLIGHT OF Varnhagen's colorful life had been meeting and marrying a woman fourteen years older than himself, Rahel Levin, a Jewish *salonière* living in Berlin. Jane Carlyle admired Rahel Levin Varnhagen, as did Amely, who would one day dedicate a novel to her memory. Rahel's aura was part of Varnhagen's allure. Her contemporaries had described the small, vivacious woman as not wealthy, beautiful, or especially well connected, but recognized that through her salon soirées, which began in the 1790s, Rahel had brought together talented people from many walks of life.[10] They said she possessed intellect, wit, and a rare gift for friendship. Despite the legal constraints and prejudices she was subjected to as a Jew—and her troubled sense of identity that developed as a result—her salons were mind-expanding occasions, carrying on the spirit of the Enlightenment.

In England during the second half of the eighteenth century certain literary and intellectual women, or bluestockings, had experienced moments of liberation and respect unknown to most women by Jane Carlyle's time. They wrote, their works often saw print, they mingled and conversed, knew everybody, and flourished.[11] Rather quickly, however, as conservative reactions to the French Revolution set in, enthusiasm for all radical causes, including the rights of women, diminished. As the nineteenth century wound on, according to George Eliot, Mary Wollstonecraft's *A Vindication of the Rights of Woman* (1792) languished almost unread. Copies became scarce to the point where it was difficult to find one to read.[12]

Bluestockings were never many in number, but their rise and fall needs to be kept in mind when contemplating the changed circumstances that promising middle-class Victorian women had to endure. Harriet Martineau, born a year after Jane and like her well educated for the times, left a record of what it was like for a girl who loved learning in the early nineteenth century, another case of needle versus pen:

> "When I was young, it was not thought proper for young ladies to study very conspicuously; and especially with pen in hand. Young ladies (at least in provincial towns) were expected to sit down in the parlour to sew,—during which reading aloud was permitted,—or to practice their music; but so as to be fit to receive callers, without any signs of blue-stockingism which could be reported abroad."[13]

The prejudice against bluestockings subtly influenced Jane despite a Scottish education that had included schoolroom time and private sessions with outstanding tutors, such as the future controversial and charismatic London preacher Edward Irving, and her husband-to-be, Thomas Carlyle.

The changes from one century to the next were complex, but they shaped the narrowed, restricted conditions that formed the context in which Jane Carlyle lived her life. During the generations that preceded the Victorians, as the new industrial classes developed apace, they engaged in institutionalizing and codifying emerging bourgeois manners and mores. Evangelical Christianity was an influence on those values, strengthened in opposition to flagrant Regency immorality.

One way to signal a rising status was to imitate aristocratic modes, such as the feudalistic protection of the lady. To have a wife of leisure like an aristocrat implied an elevation in class. Anxious for respectability at a time of rapid social change, codes of decorum were fostered that confined middle-class women, whose labor could increasingly be dispensed with, to their families and homes. Conduct books telling them how to behave—women, ironically, authored some of the most popular ones—found a wide audience.

An unofficial ban on useful labor for middle class wives was in place by the 1830s.[14] Some early-Victorian women had been quick to call this unwritten prohibition archaic and silly: "The onset that refinement has made against useful exertion, is but a worn-out relic of feudalism." They remembered nostalgically how different things had been in the days of their hard-working eighteenth-century grandmothers: "[M]any were the gentlewomen, in our great-grandmothers' days, who lived in honoured independence, though they kept small shops."[15]

With the influx of the rural poor into cities, as industrialization and enclosure legislation drove them off farms, domestic servants had become available in abundance and were inexpensive to hire. Middle class women who might once have worked hard at housekeeping and taking care of and teaching their children no longer had to. Exceptions existed. Jane, as we know, was willing to plunge into housework when health allowed and kept only a single servant. Yet the trend was toward wives of leisure, who came to seem like ornaments for display, enhancing the status of their husbands.

Jane picked up and played with the ornament image. When the Carlyles' beloved friend John Sterling sent her an article and several poems of his to critique, a task she wished to avoid, she disavowed *playing at Editors* and wrote him that she could not respond adequately to his request since she "was clearly born for the *ornamental* rather than the *useful*."

The Carlyles did not believe that John Sterling, a man of many talents, had a gift for poetry. They had once sat trapped in their parlor while he recited to them a poem of his called "The Sexton's Daughter." In his overall warm and generous *Life of John Sterling* (1851), Thomas Carlyle rendered the verdict he and Jane had arrived at: "We found the piece monotonous, cast in the mould of Wordsworth, deficient in real human fervour or depth of melody, dallying on the borders of the infantile and 'goody-good.'" Worst was the unnatural, mechanical, overly rhythmic way that Sterling read his poem, "that flattest moaning hoo-

hoo of predetermined pathos, with a kind of rocking canter introduced by way of intonation, each stanza the exact fellow of the other, and the dull swing of the rocking-horse duly in each."[16] Stiff in their chairs, attempting to keep straight faces, Jane and Thomas had been forced to listen to verse after hoo-hooing verse.

When Jane Carlyle told John Sterling "I was clearly born for the *ornamental* rather than the *useful*," she was trying to evade harsh words about his poetry so as not to hurt his feelings. But her statement is a good example of her hall-of-mirrors style of ironic reflection. In the space of that single sentence, for those who know her mind through her writing as a whole, one sparkly dimension after another exists. Not only does she tactfully avoid giving offense. She signals that she understands society's meaning of the ornamental wife, and fears she might have become one. Ironically, at moments she longs to be one. Yet she has stated her desire to lead a *useful* life, wondering what will become of her if she does not find work she can do. At the same time she suspects the motives of do-gooders who stride about loudly proclaiming themselves useful. And with her sense of *dissolving views* of the self, taken from magic lantern slides where one image fades into the next, she cannot be sure *what* one was born for. When Jane is funny and serious simultaneously (as so often), it becomes difficult to discern just where her irony lands. Keeping several dimensions in play may be the point.

For all that there was a woman on the British throne, archetypally potent despite her nominal rule, a queen who in addition to her roles as wife and mother was known to busy herself with her dispatch boxes and to assume (when well) numerous other monarchal duties, the external world, in terms of power, remained a man's world.

Rahel Levin's ephemeral salons, begun in the late eighteenth century, provide a glimpse of an alternate universe. Men and women; gentiles and Jews; aristocrats, military men, diplomats, artists, writers, actors, and sculptors mingled freely in her rooms. She was the kind of woman, unique and innovative, who, through the very life that she lived, opened new spaces, new ideas, about what a woman might be and do. Jane Carlyle breathlessly described Varnhagen to her cousin as "*husband of Rahel.*" Thomas Carlyle, awed by the quality of her presence in her husband's memoirs, wrote to Varnhagen of "the high, tranquil-mournful, almost magical spirit of your Rahel shining over them with a light as of stars!"

When Ludwig Tieck fashioned his Renaissance heroine, he had in mind female contemporaries like Rahel Levin Varnhagen and the French-Swiss author Germaine de Staël, another salonière. When his fictional heroine Vittoria appears before a Vatican court after her first husband has been mysteriously murdered, Tieck takes the opportunity to dramatize the patriarchy's condemnation of salons.

Although it is clear in the novel that Vittoria is innocent of any crime, one of the judges, flailing about for reasons to accuse her, lands on the creation of a salon in her home as proof of iniquity. Implying that the salon made her no better than a courtesan, the judge excoriates Vittoria for having converted "her house into a poetical academy, a rendezvous for foreigners and authors, a stage for the exhibition of public performances, poetical compositions, music and song, and all sorts of offensive and unfeminine discussions, to which she gave the name of philosophy."[17] A clear list of *don'ts*. But dressed like a princess, behaving with both dignity and high spirits, Vittoria successfully defends herself before the Cardinals.

Such heroines became models for Victorian women. They enabled those who admired them, like Jane Carlyle, to set their sights higher, although dire warnings existed simultaneously, exemplified by Vittoria's cruel, untimely demise. Models like the fictional Vittoria and the real Rahel, stars and heroines of their own lives, complicated the understanding of what a nineteenth-century woman was supposed to be and do.

Varnhagen had published letters by and to his wife Rahel (who had died in 1833). In his review of Varnhagen's memoirs, however, Thomas Carlyle said that he found her letters too "vaporous, vague," as well as uncertain in grammar (a complaint he voiced about Jane's writing when annoyed with her). Rahel effused too emotionally. It was wasteful "to *feel about Feeling*! One is wearied of that." Yet from certain passages, Thomas also found Rahel to be "a woman of genius, of true depth and worth," in fact "a woman equal to the highest thoughts of her century."

In his review Thomas struggles with what seems to him a very disturbing fact. Despite genius, talent, and greatness, "Rahel did not write."[18] Though a handful of her letters had been published anonymously in her lifetime, he meant that she did not write for publication.

Like Jane Carlyle, like most gifted female letter writers of that era, Rahel expected that much of what she wrote would be read aloud, passed around, commented on by friends and family, quoted to others, and—it was to be hoped—carefully kept. But unless they were published as books, like Mary Wollstonecraft's reports from Scandinavia (*A Short Residence in Sweden, Norway and Denmark*, 1796), even brilliant prolific letter writers had to settle for what amounted to private writing careers.[19]

"She sat imprisoned," Thomas Carlyle says of Rahel as he tries to imagine what it would have been like not to have the outlet of authorship; "or it might be sheltered and fosteringly embowered, in those circumstances of hers." He goes on to wonder, "Is a thing nothing because the Morning Papers have not mentioned it?"

The question regarding Rahel—and Jane—haunted. How to evaluate talent that had not seen the light of the public arena? Thomas said finally of Rahel, as if not quite able to work the conundrum through, "Silence too is great: there should be great silent ones too."[20]

As for Jane, she had returned home from her visit to her Liverpool cousins filled with fresh inspiration and resolve. Where her own private writing might take her—whether it might be considered her work, her mission—such thoughts were glinting at the back of her mind.

CHAPTER SIX

SHAKEN ALL TO BITS

"Ourself behind ourself, concealed— /
Should startle most—"!
—EMILY DICKINSON

LONDON FELT EMPTY IN THE LATE SUMMER OF 1844, MANY OF THE CARLYLES' friends and acquaintances having fled to the countryside to escape the heat. Jane wrote the cousin she had just been visiting, "The soul gets leisure to listen to itself in this silence—and to form 'good intentions'—if it could but keep to them!" Her travels had resulted in a degree of health and well-being, and finding herself with a rare moment of solitude, she fell to devising a program of self-improvement.

For two or three hours each morning in the quiet house Jane sat on the sofa in her upstairs drawing room engaged in a "critical reading" of Voss's German translation of *Homers Werke*, "the only translation which gives a person ignorant of Greek any adequate idea of the real Homer," though her German was proving rusty. Not to be deterred, she embarked on a translation project, a poem she had begun in the past (by Goethe or Schiller). Possibly Amely's work on Tieck's novel had motivated her to try her hand? "I am translating—or to speak accurately *I have bought foolscap for translating*," she told her cousin, hoping to see the work bear fruit "before I die."

Jane was also writing a letter a day, hemming tea towels, reading articles "in Jeffrey's miscellanies," forming plans to purchase a new piano, and "making extensive and enlightened repairs of the household linen!" "And," she added insouciantly, "I *think* a great deal!"

She who thrived on response said "Carlyle looked very pleased to have me back at first but he is already relapsed into his usual indifference." After Jane's return, he had quickly disappeared back into his study. This summer Thomas had taken to calling Jane his *dearest little Necessary Evil*, using a phrase from Goethe's *Wilhelm Meister's Apprenticeship* that they both found funny.

Their close friend Erasmus Darwin, a lanky, reticent man and perennial bachelor, had postponed a short trip expressly to welcome Jane back. Although Erasmus had earned a medical degree, he did not, in profound contrast to his industrious younger brother Charles, apply his fine mind to practicing medicine or to any long-term project. Erasmus, it seems, had forsaken his profession from a lingering sense of invalidism. Wedgwood and Darwin relatives who accepted and respected him as he was made vague mentions of rheumatism, low spirits, and lung trouble, as if his bony physique and the shadow he had grown up under of being apt to die young were explanation enough. Sustained by a generous allowance from his father, Erasmus lived a calm life, dedicating himself to favorite friends, among them Jane and Thomas Carlyle, Harriet Martineau, and his beloved (married) cousin Fanny Wedgwood. He was famous for performing small commissions for others: sending, for instance, matches, shoes, and books to his brother Charles when on his Beagle voyage (he and Charles were very fond of each other); and oysters, champagne, and sums of money to Harriet Martineau during her convalescence in Tynemouth.

Erasmus Darwin valued the ways in which Jane Carlyle was unlike him: talkative, hospitable, playful, brisk in her movements. When Erasmus first met Jane he had called her "a divine little woman,"[1] though women he liked, whatever their height, were invariably *little*, that so-common patriarchal diminutive. And he enjoyed Jane's sense of fun. One of his sisters told Jane after a dinner party that they had "just been remarking to one-another that everybody that has sat next *you* thro the evening has been one after another in incessant fits of laughter!" Although Erasmus was mostly a good listener, he himself had a ready sardonic wit. He could deliver a sting and was once said to have frightened Jane's mother.

Jane had called Erasmus "the likest thing to a brother I ever had in the world." But on this occasion, she complained that after not having set eyes on her for weeks he ambled into her parlor with such a nonchalant air "one would have said he could have dispensed with a sight of me till the end of the world." Since Jane depended on response and approval, his appearance of indifference caused real dismay.

In early August 1844, a publisher arrived at Cheyne Row, likely Edward Chapman of Chapman and Hall, to confer with Jane about alterations to *Zoe*, Geraldine Jewsbury's first novel, scheduled to appear in February. Still residing in Manchester with her brother, Geraldine was grateful to have the well-connected Mrs. Carlyle act on her behalf. Jane found the discussions tedious yet complained rather proudly, "I had better have written the book all over myself than have had so much intermediation to transact!"

For months she had been involved with the manuscript of *Zoe*, counseling Geraldine, whose prose could be vague and prolix, on how to revise, and attempting to tone down the melodrama. Their friend Elizabeth Paulet had helped out, too. The three women, writers all, had discussed the daring views Geraldine was putting forth on sex and religion, and debated the fate of her novel's hero, a Catholic priest, whom she had naughtily named Everhard Burrows.

Father Everhard, who has lost his beliefs in a spiritual crisis, passionately loves the eponymous heroine, a married woman. In the throes of passion, he awkwardly, impassionedly clasps Zoe in a chapel as he is rescuing her from a fire, although in the interests of novelistic decency they part forever immediately after. (It was permissible in Victorian novels for a man to embrace a woman fervidly while saving her from fire or flood—Tieck's Vittoria is saved from drowning in an astonishingly fervid manner.) To complicate her tale, Geraldine has Zoe fall in love with the French revolutionary Mirabeau, adding a historical flavor.

Geraldine's letters reveal echoes of the friends' laughter as they talked over the project, an ambitious undertaking that went beyond mere melodrama. *Zoe* explores what a woman's genius (or talent and energy) can do in a society that provides her with "no ready-made channels to run in."[2] That urgent, subversive question was in the air, and novels like Geraldine's, modeled on works by European women like Germaine de Staël and George Sand, became seditious bearers of new tidings. Even as the walls closed in for the majority of educated middle-class Victorian women, protests like Geraldine's were underway.

But the news, which, if widely heeded, might have stood tradition on its head early on, was to travel oddly over the next century and more. As far as the majority were concerned, it could dive underground for a generation at a time, so that there would be many a place where a smart, alert girl could grow up hearing scarcely a word about how a woman might be ambitious and productive in the wider realms of life; and without any warning about the degree of suffering she might experience if her dreams were thwarted.

At one point in the novel-writing process, Geraldine and Betsey Paulet had written Jane asking her to comb through a draft of *Zoe* for improprieties, gaily claiming they had tried themselves but had no knack for discerning the indecent. Jane undertook the task with seriousness and flair, finding a good deal to disapprove of. Geraldine wrote back, "Your criticism made me laugh till I was half-dead, for you little know all our strivings after decency. If you had seen the work as it was first schemed, you would have had something to complain of; indeed, it struck us that people might get scandalised."[3]

A free spirit, Geraldine could dwell happily in what she referred to as the *debatable* land of imagination. Jane whose talent lay in nonfiction prose admired her friend's imaginative gift, if not her syntax or sense of propriety. In fact, reading through Geraldine's manuscript, Jane grew amazed by the energy of the novel, the mix of bouncy action and inspired contemplation. The February before, Jane had finally cast her reservations to the winds, exclaiming: "[B]y the powers it is a wonderful book!—Decidedly the CLEVEREST english-womans-book I ever remember to have read." Though Thomas had not read it, she persuaded him to pen a note of recommendation, and went out of her way to find a publisher who might take *Zoe*.

She wanted to make sure that Geraldine, currently dependent upon her brother Frank's generosity, could earn her own money. As she had done for others on the margin, like Amely Bölte and the Mudie sisters, she fretted over Geraldine's economic future: "[W]hat is to come of her when she is old—without ties, without purposes, unless she apply herself to this *trade*?—and how is she even to have a subsistence . . . should her Brother take it into his head to marry? all these considerations have made me very anxious to find a Publisher for her *first book*."

Against the odds, Jane succeeded. In March when she journeyed to the Strand to hear the verdict of Chapman and Hall, she discovered that after a favorable reader's report they had decided to publish Miss Jewsbury's book on generous first-novel terms. "[T]he MS is accepted on the principle of half-profits!" she reported back to Geraldine. "The very most Heaven-high success that could befall a young Ladies *first* book in 'the existing state of the book trade'!" Excited at having her judgment confirmed, Jane "rushed into a silk mercers—and bought myself a new gown!!"

As she pointedly told Geraldine, rarely had a path to publication been so smooth. That had not been the case for either John Mill's *Logic* or Carlyle's *Sartor*, both of which had required prolonged efforts before seeing print. Geraldine responded graciously, quoting a local Manchester merchant: "The more nonsense there is in a book the better it sells; people can't stand sense, they want something racy."[4]

Racier than Father Everhard's rescue of Zoe from the burning chapel is Geraldine's description of Zoe's spotless stepdaughter Clotilde who unknowingly entices a man whose children she is teaching to dance: "[H]er back was to the door, so she did not perceive his entrance, but went on with her lesson; she stood with her dress raised above her instep, and her little flexible foot pointed before her; she was laughing with gentle merriment at some blunders of the children's . . . when the little ones bounding away, calling 'papa! papa!' caused her to turn round in too much confusion to hear his well-turned compliment on the graceful sight he had so unexpectedly witnessed."[5] Since only scoundrels were capable of facile well-turned compliments, the reader of *Zoe* is not surprised to discover that the man, after shamelessly leading the girl on, fails to propose. Clotilde of the small sexy foot enters a convent.

•

A COMPELLING *REAL-LIFE* drama came along that caused Jane Carlyle's self improvement schemes to get *dadded a' abreed*, Scottish for shaken all to bits. We might note the speed with which she abandoned a solitary, uncertain literary task to concern herself with a project that could bring the immediate comfort of performing a womanly duty: helping a human being in need of her care.

The human being in this case was her friend Richard Plattnauer, a young German about thirty years old, now residing in London. Attractive, witty, and personable, Richard had come to England for adventure, but once his money ran out, he had no choice but to try supporting himself as a private tutor. Recently this essentially sane and rational man had begun to exhibit signs of distress.

When she returned to London, Jane had found a letter from Richard lying on her mantelpiece. Immediately opening it, hastily perusing it, she grew very concerned. Although Richard was "a man not given to foolish enthusiasms," he had suddenly been seized by the latest "new ideas," which caused him, he told her, to go from being "the most wretched [to] the happiest of human beings." This confession elided into a statement that his only wish, now, was to dedicate himself to the service of the Carlyles. That was silly enough, but Jane felt a superstitious shudder at his claim of happiness, believing that (in her underscored phrase) "*Happiness if there was such a thing at all seeming to me of the nature of those delicate Spirits which vanish when one pronounces their name.*"

What to make of Richard's oddness? "It *did* cross my mind," she told her cousin, "that he might be falling into insanity—but I struggled against the idea as too horrible." She replied to his letter but heard nothing back. If it weren't "for the english ideas of propriety," she said, she would have grabbed bonnet, gloves, and shawl and headed out the door to discover what could be the matter.

One gray drizzly August afternoon the Bullers came by Cheyne Row with their goddaughter. As they gathered in her parlor, Jane gave voice to her anguish about Richard, admitting she had been yearning to jump into a street cab and go in search of the lodging house where he had taken a room. She felt not only a warm affection for the pale young man but a disturbing sense of kinship she could not explain. She acknowledged to the Bullers, though, that in this staid country, a respectable married woman could not very well dash off to visit an attractive unmarried man. Or could she, under the circumstances?

Theresa Revis, now close to twelve years old, still small and slight, gazed up at the tallish, agitated Mrs. Carlyle and burst out, "[Y]ou shall take Godpapa's carriage—and Godpapa himself [old Mr. Buller] and the Servants and [']*then there will be no Impropriety*'!"—quick as a whippet, in her precocious way, to get around the tiresome adult fuss over decorum. "And off she ran," Jane reported approvingly, "and came back in two minutes, and told me all this precautionary equipage would be at my orders in half an hour—clever Child! Off then I went." It was still raining as the crowded carriage made its way, the metal-bound wheels rattling and clattering over the cobblestone streets. With difficulty, they located the lodging house where Jane had a word with Richard's landlady—who had not seen him for days.

Amely Bölte later recalled that the young man's life at this time "was most sad." He had been attempting to earn a living writing for German newspapers, but, as she noted sourly from her own experience, "writing did not help a German survive in London." She had hoped that Jane might use her name to do more for him, find him teaching positions as she had done for Amely, yet despite her urgings, nothing transpired. Amely thought "his pride and her tact did not allow this."[6] Jane did not want to seem the patron, nor he the object of charity. Before his disappearance, Richard, who had not been eating enough, had become wan, thin, and peaked. Was he possibly *starving*? His clothing was worn, his mood dark—until he had happened upon those stimulating new ideas.

His landlady did produce a strangely worded forwarding address, the Accordium, Ham Common, Surrey. Always impatient with airy idealism, Jane wrote her cousin that "the name—and situation taken together suggested to me at once one of those dreadful *vegetable, fraternal, universal-religion* establishments which Alcott and the like of him have originated on this long suffering earth!" Jane would have had Fruitlands in mind, the short-lived co-operative vegetarian community that Bronson Alcott had founded near Harvard, Massachusetts; and also Alcott House, a school in Ham Common established on similar principles and named for him. Annoyed that the idealistic Alcott when in England had proselytized tediously about adhering to a diet of vegetables, Thomas Carlyle had called him "a good man, but a bore," and liked to use his London nickname, Potato Quixote.

The vegetarian community Richard moved to in Surrey was apparently associated with the Alcott House establishment. Ham Common, land that had survived an ancient enclosure, was possibly symbolic to the Accordium's founders of communal property and happier days, and redolent for Richard of the utopian ideas that had seized and excited him.

But news arrived from a mutual friend that confirmed the worst. Richard Plattnauer was indeed said to be insane, "the horrid word." It turned out that at the Accordium he had at first worked happily enough in their garden but grew angry that "they *did not carry out their own principles*." Jane paused in a hastily written account for her cousin to remark that this showed a "noble detestation of humbug surviving even in the wreck of reason!" When Richard suggested certain innovations to the Pater (the way members of the community addressed their leader), he, in irritation, had shunned the young man's ideas for improvement—and the situation grew dangerous.

In protest against the lack of adherence to principle, Richard descended from his room "stark naked." Or else, as another report put it, "He was found in the garden digging '*mit nodings on.*'"[7] And there was more. In his fury that the community did not live up to its ideals, and his frustrated inability to influence them, Richard "burst into frightful violence and proceeded to strike at them all and break everything within his reach," including (said Erasmus) "all the windows."

As Thomas Carlyle explained it (seeming to refer to the Accordium), the place offered the water cure or hydropathy, that popular Victorian remedy for every sort of ailment, which involved drinking of plenty of fluids and being wrapped in ice cold body packs. Richard "plashed, and dabbled; and did I know not what, till his wits suddenly quitted him! A kind of thing like a brain-fever." They all, Amely said, felt it an agony to watch "a fine mind perish so miserably!"[8]

The Pater speedily obtained a magistrate's warrant and had the violent now-clothed Richard "conveyed to the nearest gaol where he passed the night in a dark cell and was found in the morning raging mad." The jailers bound him with ropes and chained him to the floor. In frustration and despair, Richard tore at his clothing and linen till his garments were shredded. The chains lacerated his body and left raw wounds that would linger long. A friend managed to get him out of the jail and into a private house in Richmond, Jane reported; but when he proved too much to handle, he "was conveyed to the Wandsworth Lunatic Asylum" and deposited there as if he were "a person belonging to nobody!"

The night she heard that Richard Plattnauer had been taken to the asylum, Jane Carlyle tossed and turned in her red-curtained bed, greatly disturbed, unable to sleep. Through her wry, ironic comments comes the sure sense that she cared greatly for this brilliant, endearing young man in need of her assistance. "What I felt in hearing all these particulars," she told her cousin, "you may *partly* conceive—I wished it were morning—to *do* something—tho what I knew not—all night I thought and thought—To go to the Asylum and *see* the locality and his doctor—to get him proper medical assistance . . . *to see himself* if the Dr would suffer it—All these things . . . were clearly enough to be done—and I got up with an agitated mind to do them."

•

BY THE FIRST light of dawn, Jane Carlyle is out of bed and making arrangements. She has received a response to a note dashed off the evening before to Erasmus Darwin. Yes, he will happily drive dear Jenny to Wandsworth in his carriage. As soon as she has dressed herself in her most respectable dark-colored gown, her face pale, hands shaking a little, she pens an answer about when and where to meet Erasmus. In times of distress, this scion of the Darwin family, described by Harriet Martineau as "so thoroughbred too in impartiality of calm catholicity,"[9] becomes a bastion of steadiness. The famous nonchalance seems soothing.

Jane wishes to travel in this statelier manner, rather than taking an omnibus, to give "an appearance of *respectability*." The point is not adherence to conventional codes of gentility, or to save money, but to impress the medical establishment with her status so as to make sure of acquiring respectful answers to the questions she needs to ask. The Surrey County lunatic asylum, an institution for paupers, is six or so miles south of the Thames, not far from the leafy lanes and knolls where her husband likes to go walking and horseback riding.

The journey passes in a blur of anxiety and tears, with Jane anticipating that she will find Richard, as she tells Erasmus, "chained in a dungeon."[10] The asylum turns out to be located in a park of nearly a hundred acres. As the carriage approaches, a redbrick edifice looms in the distance, a forbidding pile, and Jane pulls her shawl more tightly about her shoulders. The place is a high, impossibly wide castle-like structure from a gothic tale, with peaked gables and crenellated towers that look as though they might be guarded by hidden shooters, their weapons poised to aim through the evenly spaced openings at the intruders below.

The vehicle rolls to the front entrance, and Erasmus Darwin helps Jane Carlyle to descend, holding her firmly by the arm till her slippered feet are safely pressed upon the gravel. He will wait outside with horse and carriage, for this is her business to transact. She walks bravely through a strangely high narrow portal, looking fragile and vulnerable in bonnet and shawl. Once inside, a vast chamber and a maze of soaring galleries ringed with corridors confront her. In the first dizzying moments they appear to be turning about her. To whom should she speak? Where is Richard being held? Was it folly to come? Can she do any good at all?

A trim upright gentleman is striding toward her. He introduces himself, explaining that he is the inspecting physician of lunatic asylums in Surrey.[11] Ordering herself to be calm, Jane tells Sir Alexander Morison—she has heard of him—that she has been severely alarmed by reports of her friend Mr. Plattnauer's condition, whose care is of the greatest concern.

Sir Alexander, in his mid-sixties, has a high domed forehead, curly light-colored hair, and features at once stern and pleasant looking. To put Mrs. Carlyle at ease, he escorts her to a nearby office where they can sit and speak privately. He tells her immediately what she needs to know. Mr. Plattnauer is already being treated with the most enlightened methods. It is the institution's policy to frown on the overuse of restraints like shackles and strait-waistcoats. Further, with his extensive background in physiognomy and phrenology, he has, during his interview with the patient, carefully scrutinized Mr. Plattnauer's features, facial expressions, and general demeanor, and has formed the opinion that the young man will soon be cured.

Jane expresses astonishment, not having expected anything so hopeful. Yes, the doctor repeats, having seen similar cases, he firmly believes Mr. Plattnauer, with his strong intelligence and sympathetic nature, will improve rapidly under their care. But it would be best if she did not see the patient today. Let their regimen have its chance to work.

Having heard the Scottish lilt in her voice, the doctor lets her know that he was born at Anchorfield, near Edinburgh. She is fortunate that he was inspecting the Wandsworth asylum today, could examine the patient, and be present to receive her. He has often witnessed the phase the patient is now experiencing, just after melancholia has given way to maniacal excitement. He has lectured widely and written on mental diseases such as these. When Jane, who likes to read medical books, inquires, he tells her that among his works are *Cases of Mental Disease, with Practical Observations on the Medical Treatment* and *The Physiognomy of Mental Diseases*.

She discovers that the fearsome fortress of Wandsworth is actually the most contemporary of institutions, having opened its doors only three years before. Such modern devices as a steam heat system have been installed. For the paupers residing here, healthful practices are followed. It was Richard Plattnauer's great good luck to have been brought to an asylum based on benevolent Moral Treatment principles, developed by Quakers well versed in Enlightenment thinking. The patients, when possible, contribute to the community through their labor. The entire staff is dedicated to the reformed treatment of the insane. (It was to be a halcyon moment, however, maintained only as long as the number of patients remained relatively small.)

During cold weather—Sir Alexander explains the procedures to Mrs. Carlyle with the reassuring manner of a benign patriarch—they provide fires in the fireplaces for the patients of the female wards, and take care to guard these fires. In warm weather, such as they are now experiencing, the sunk fences around the "airing courts" allow patients to enjoy in safety the vista of the surrounding Surrey countryside.[12] As part of a supervised regime of daily living, the male inmates, like Mr. Plattnauer, if up to the task, have the opportunity to work outdoors in the garden and farm, growing fresh vegetables for the kitchen.

Communal gardening seemed to have become a theme in Richard's travails.

•

NOT ONLY DID Jane Carlyle cry on her way *to* the asylum, fearing the worst, but according to Erasmus Darwin she cried in his carriage on the way back to Chelsea, from, as he put it, "the pleasure of finding it such a nice place & such a nice set of people who assured her he would soon be well."[13]

Meeting a doctor who was a wise and sensible Scotsman had been an incredible relief. To Jane who enjoyed myths and fairy tales as a child, including the *Arabian Nights*, it might have seemed as if a genie in dark elegant clothing had arisen from a lamp at the most fortuitous moment, offering with a bow to be at her service. At the end of a long letter to her cousin detailing what had happened—and in spite of her relief that Richard seemed in the best of hands—she agitatedly wrote, "But I must stop—for I am writing myself into *delirium tremens*—"

Ten days later Jane told her cousin that because "I have had so much *writing* to do about that poor man, and . . . so much mortal anxiety about him," her conscience did not reproach her for having neglected her correspondence. She was using the phrase *that poor man* to avoid Richard's name, so her cousin could be discreet when reading Jane's letter to others. The Carlyles understood the importance of preserving Richard's reputation if he were to have any hope of future employment. They notified close friends and did their best to protect his privacy otherwise.

Already Richard had become well enough to write Mrs. Carlyle "a long excellent noble letter!" For his doctor, she continued to have only praise: "the Blessing of Heaven be on the head of that good old Sir Alexander Morison, who has treated him so skillfully and so humanely—in other hands I have not a doubt but that he would have been driven into permanent insanity—for this man is the only *real physician* I have seen since I lost my own Father!"

Essential to Jane Carlyle's identity was the fact that she was the daughter of Dr. John Welsh of Haddington. She had lost her father when she was only eighteen. An intelligent, considerate surgeon, he had died of typhus, caught from a patient he had been treating. Dr. Welsh had allowed his daughter to accompany him on country drives to visit patients in the district he covered. During companionable rides in his chaise, he—an often-silent man—would sometimes speak eloquently to his child, lauding high ideals of genius and talent, and discussing her future and his hopes for her.

Jane's mother had not especially wanted her daughter to be educated. According to a late nineteenth-century biographer, Grace Welsh "kept to the old traditions" and "considered Latin and mathematics sadly out of place in the little girl's education."[14] But when Jane as a child had jumped out from beneath a table and surprised her parents by reciting "*Penna*, a Pen; Pennae, of a pen . . . I want to learn latin—please let me be a boy," her father had overridden his wife's reservations and supported his little daughter's ambitions.[15] In addition to her schooling, he provided Jane with private tutors, keeping a careful record of the sums he paid them in tiny account books (that still exist).

On one of these trips, near the end of his life, in the course of a slow jog down a country lane in his open vehicle, the taciturn Dr. John Welsh had offered rare words of praise for Jane, telling her "she was a good girl, capable of being useful and precious to him and to the circle she would live in; that she must summon her utmost judgment and seriousness to choose her path, and *be* what he expected of her." Yes, her

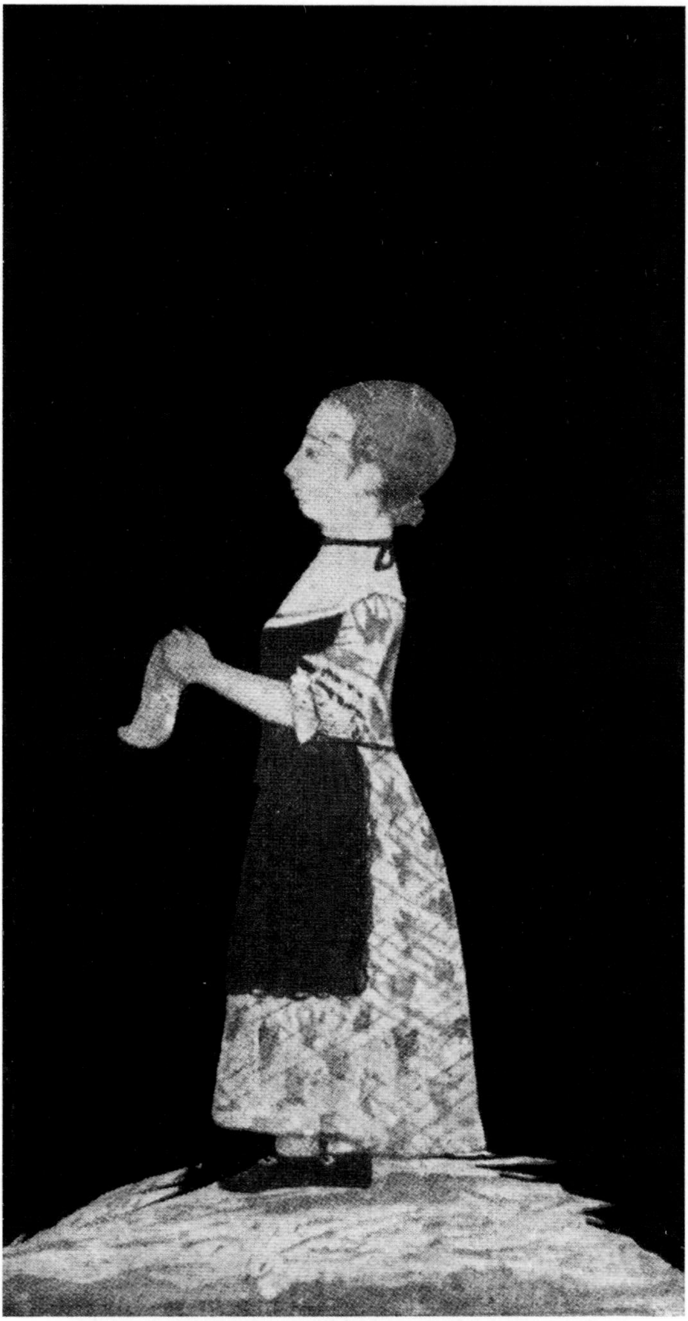

"Jane Welsh as a Girl." This charming though rather stiff portrait (artist unknown) does not convey the lively sense of herself as a child that JWC retained into adulthood. To her nurse Betty Braid, she was "fleein', dancin', lightheartit" and fearless.

JWC's mother and father: Grace Welsh, in a white lace mantilla; and Dr. John Welsh. They resided in Haddington, near Edinburgh, where Jane grew up as an only child.

TC's mother: Margaret Aitken Carlyle by Maxwell of Dumfries, 1842.

Above left: Jeannie "Babbie" Welsh of Liverpool was JWC's cousin and favorite correspondent. Her portrait is by Spiridione Gambardella (1843). Above right: This image of JWC's novelist friend Geraldine Endsor Jewsbury hints at her petite boyishness and strawberry blond hair.

On the far left below: the Carlyles' house at no. 5 Cheyne Row (later no. 24), TC's image in relief on the façade. It is part of the Cheyne Row terrace, built in 1708, and the River Thames can be glimpsed at the end of the street. Virginia Woolf's father Leslie Stephen and other late Victorians organized the purchase of the house, which has been open to the public since 1895.

Charles Dickens

Opposite page: Novelist Charles Dickens, from the Carlyles' albums. His name at the bottom is in an unknown hand.

"The Governess" by Richard Redgrave, 1844. The artist portrays the governess in the shadows, while two of her charges enjoy bright sunlight. The girl in the middle, a book on her lap, might be the child most influenced by her teacher.

"Mary" was a maidservant of JWC's trusted family friend Mary Russell of Thornhill, Scotland. The image of the poised young woman is from the Carlyles' albums.

This evocative oil painting, "Sir Alexander Morison" by Richard Dadd, 1852, is a portrait of the physician JWC consulted about the care of her mentally ill friend Richard Plattnauer.

Richard Plattnauer, a Prussian exile friend. The photograph was taken perhaps ten years after his brief stay, while ill, at the Carlyles' home. From the Carlyles' albums.

Artistic, cultured Elizabeth "Betsey" Paulet was chatelaine of Seaforth House near the River Mersey, wife of the Swiss merchant Étienne Paulet, and one of JWC's best friends in the 1840s. From the Carlyles' albums.

"Seaforth House, Lancashire," from an 1819 engraving in J. P. Neale's Views of the Seats of Noblemen and Gentlemen in England, Wales, Scotland, and Ireland. *For JWC Seaforth House, not far from Liverpool, was a place of renewal.*

father acknowledged, she had often been told she was "good-looking and good." That was fine but insufficient. He wished his daughter, his only child, "to be wise, as well."[16]

Their closeness and mutual respect shaped her interest in many aspects of mental and physical health. The frequency of her illnesses and how she handled them, often remaining imprisoned for long periods in her room, suggest that in addition to what adequate treatment required, she might have gained psychological comfort from doctoring herself.[17] It was perhaps a way of staying close to the father she revered and still acutely missed. Her sense of herself as a doctor's daughter also made her keenly observant of symptoms and the effects of remedies, and she followed with special interest medical issues of the day.

Such a relief, then, to discover that Sir Alexander Morison, like Dr. John Welsh, held enlightened beliefs. He had told her that if "any judicious D*r* or friend [had] been beside [Richard Plattnauer] at the commencement[,] nothing of all that"—referring to the chains and the ropes the jailers had used to bind him—"need ever have been!"

"And what is more," Jane wrote her cousin, "I have *seen* him!" She had again gone to Wandsworth in the carriage of the co-operative Erasmus Darwin. (Thomas liked to joke about how much Erasmus Darwin enjoyed driving friends around, dubbing his vehicle "*Darwingium Cabbum.*"[18])

The resident doctor—not Sir Alexander this time—who greeted Mrs. Carlyle suggested that she view Richard Plattnauer's improvement for herself. He urged her to go out to the asylum garden, "where my poor friend was sitting on a bench apart from the other patients—." As Jane described it: "He recognized me a great way off—further off than *I* could possibly have recognized *him* except by his starting up, *passing his fingers thro his hair* (the only little movement of human weakness he betrayed)—and then with a free erect air hastening towards me—no awkwardness—hardly any surprise—but such joy!—He was dreadfully pale and in the uncouth dress of the Establishment [in later photographs, patients wore rumpled romper uniforms with round child's collars] so that the first look was sad enough—but in a minute we were walking arm in arm thro the garden as if we had met after our long separation under the most natural circumstances in the world. During all the half hour that I staid with him he was perfectly rational and composed." She added, "[N]othing could be more manly and dignified than his whole way of taking the thing—even to his last action—insisting *dressed as he was*—in attending me to the carriage in which he *knew* Darwin was waiting for me, and apologizing to him in the most courteous manner for having detained me so long. You may fancy Darwins astonishment!"

Dignified was the word they all used when describing Richard's princely posture.

An unexpected event followed the scene in the garden. As her pen hastened over this series of letters to the Welsh family in Liverpool, Jane Carlyle—well versed in eighteenth-century epistolary novels like Samuel Richardson's *Sir Charles Grandison*—was fashioning not polished set pieces but rather an epistolary tale of her life on the wing, replete with dialogue and drama. Richard Plattnauer was her character of the moment, though his tale is woven through letters that address a wide variety of matters.

As he passes his fingers through his hair in the asylum garden, Jane brings him to life with the phrase, "the only little movement of human weakness he betrayed." And segues easily into her next scene, "You will wonder if I have not become insane myself when I tell you *the sequel.*"

Little more than a week after her second visit, as Jane and Thomas were about to leave for a "Cockney-Sunday-excursion to the Regent's Park to be helped out with tea at M*rs* Macready's," there came a rap of the lion's head doorknocker. As Helen answered, "a gentleman's voice at the door [was] inquiring for *me*— I had heard that voice only once before in my life but I recognized it instantly as Sir Alexander Morison's— What on earth had brought so busy a man to my own house?"

Fearful that Richard Plattnauer might have escaped, or might even have committed suicide, Jane felt the blood leave her face. In her rush up the stairs "white as milk" to the drawing room to greet the physician and hear his news, she caught her light muslin summer dress on something and it tore—a telling detail selected to show anxiety and haste. Ignoring the ripped dress she waited, Thomas at her side, to discover what had brought the doctor to Cheyne Row. Nervous as Jane was, she was touched by the courtesy he showed by paying a personal visit.

He indeed had an important announcement. Mr. Plattnauer had "appeared before the Committee on the previous day [and] been pronounced *cured*.'" As Jane wondered how the transformation could have come about in so short a time, the physician gave an additional urgent reason for this visit. The young man had proved ready for release, "but," he demanded abruptly, "where will he go?"

A pause ensued. "I looked imploringly at Carlyle," Jane said, "who, good as he always is on *great* occasions, said directly 'Oh he must come *here* for a while till he sees what is to be done next'—"

In handling arrangements for Richard's transfer to their home, Jane spent another, nearly full day at the asylum, telling her cousin, "A *happier* day I hardly ever past in life—At seven at night I landed him here in *a fly* and here he has been ever since and will be for some time yet—." To be greatly needed, to deploy her skills in the care of a troubled person for whom she felt sympathy—that was satisfaction indeed. Once she got Richard home, she was surprised to find that "Carlyle seems to take to him most *lovingly* and shows him the uttermost kindness!! Still I have much to keep me anxious," she added, admitting the grave difficulties, "for not only does his future lie most perplexedly before us but—whatever the D*rs* and Committee have judged—*I* do not consider him by any means *sane*."

Jane and Thomas Carlyle spoke about Richard Plattnauer's excitability, wild whims, exalted moods, and, at times, sheer rambling incoherence, trembling on the verge of violence; this phase having followed an earlier one of low wretchedness, sadness, and despair. Their descriptions indicate he suffered a form of what we would call bipolar illness, *melancholia followed by maniacal excitement* to use Dr. Morison's phrase. In between episodes, Richard was for the most part thoughtful and sane. He stayed perhaps three weeks at Cheyne Row, and even though Thomas regarded him lovingly, he considered the young man his wife's responsibility.

Isabella Buller, Jane reported, was "worrying herself to death with the fear of [Richard's] killing me." In fact these were dangerous "days of *insane* murdering." Recently Jane had heard of the brutal murder of the mother of a servant girl in her uncle's household, a horror difficult to absorb. Madness seemed to linger in the air like a contagion, haphazardly striking now an acquaintance, now a friend.

Believing Jane to be in danger, Isabella showered her with caresses when they met, as the Bullers were preparing for their autumn journey to France and Italy. The whimsical, tactless Isabella mothered Jane and made a pet of her only intermittently. Needing her maternal attention now, Jane believed Isabella to be sincere, though Thomas, observing more neutrally (and probably more accurately, given later events), thought the woman essentially heartless. Isabella was warmly affectionate when the mood struck her.

Caring for Richard was a "heavy charge," yet Jane did not agree that he posed a danger. She had come to the rueful conclusion: "No madman will ever hurt a hair of *my* head—I have too much *affinity* with them—" Identifying and empathizing with Richard, she seemed to know what he was thinking before he said it. But watching anxiously now, making sure that he ate, something stirred darkly and uneasily in her own mind. The feeling ran deep, she was unsure why. Her most disturbing moment, she confided to Amely, had occurred during one of those visits to Wandsworth when Richard, who seemed to have found at the asylum the harmonious utopian life he had been fruitlessly searching for, told Jane he believed that the place was "some kind of institution for kindred spirits, with no difference of rank, everything all peace, love, and unity. And she deserved to be a part." What Jane felt upon hearing that the lunatic asylum was where she belonged, Amely reported, "cannot be described!"[19]

In the midst of this drama, Thomas Carlyle abruptly left the house. He had decided to pay a visit to the Grange, a country estate in Hampshire belonging to Lady Harriet Baring's father-in-law, Lord Ashburton. It was to be the first of many jaunts to this mansion, located on some seven hundred acres. The Barings were then in residence at the colossal edifice that had a stunning high columned Greek-style portico. Its over-the-top splendor provoked extreme reactions, either thrilling or shocking the insignificant mortal who chanced to gaze up at its Olympian grandeur.

Jane—who had not yet seen the place—wrote her cousin, "[A]s the Lady Harriet like the Queen must have her Court about her wherever she goes or stays she has summoned Carlyle down to the Grange for a week at the least—and *he—never* by any chance refuses a wish of *hers*—the clever woman that she is!" Thomas left Jane at home not only to care for Richard, but to oversee her annual re-papering, painting, and carpeting projects.

Close friends visited Jane, among them Erasmus Darwin, Giuseppe Mazzini, the Bullers with Theresa Revis, and Amely Bölte. During one social event, Richard was "in a state of violent talkativeness," creating "Bedlam." On a different occasion, when he came across a chattering guest in her parlor to whom he took a dislike, Jane reported that he told her later "he had been 'strongly tempted to seize a poker and dash [the man's] brains out (!) and so put an end to his eternal clack in that way since nothing else could stop it.'" She chided Richard, saying "it did not become one visitor in a house to dash out the brains of another—a statement which he at once perceived and admitted the justice of—"

Jane found that if she evoked the name of the absent Mr. Carlyle, she could persuade her patient to do as she wished, yet she knew "his madness is far deeper in him and more complicated than we at first suspected." Although she could handle him, he was worse than "the most impatient of spoiled children." When she could catch a moment of leisure, Jane would collapse into her easy chair, rest her tired feet upon the ottoman, and work at the nearly hopeless task of sewing up his shredded clothing from the chaotic night he had spent in jail.

Thomas had escaped his fraught household for a majestic change of scene. His friend Edward FitzGerald caught wind of his going about "in a grand nobleman's carriage to see [the nearby] Winchester Cathedral."[20] He had dodged a responsibility (Jane makes this clear in a letter), leaving his wife alone to cope. Yet she does not complain. She depicts his behavior humorously and as a salute to her own skills: "Every body else was terrified for my being left alone in the house with him—But C. has no idle apprehensions [;] he payed me the compliment of supposing that I had presence of mind and cleverness enough to manage perfectly well without any protection—and I am quite of his opinion—." She underscores her take-charge behavior: "*In this instance at least* while others talk I act."

Writing in this manner to her cousin, in fact her letter writing in general, gave Jane Carlyle opportunities to do more than exercise a literary gift that has aptly been called the "joyous, playful deployment of her great comic complaint."[21] It allowed her to control the narrative of her life, to shape the way her actions were interpreted, to indicate to her audience how she wished to be seen. She could attempt, at least, to edit her life through her letters, and make of living something like art.

Although Jane Carlyle and the youthful, attractive Richard Plattnauer had been left in the house together, no one questioned the propriety of that—even though *gardening naked at the Accordium* evokes an image of an appealing, muscular Adam surrounded by greenery and tanned by the late summer sun. Perhaps the lack of gossip was due to Richard's illness, or to Helen Mitchell's presence. Or perhaps Mrs. Carlyle was regarded as beyond reproach.

An additional reason may exist as to why Jane did not object to Thomas's departure for the Grange—something that was *not* said. In 1817 when his mother Margaret Aitken Carlyle was about forty-seven, after he had left home for the university, she had suffered a mental breakdown. Her symptoms were not unlike Richard's (though less violent). Her family reported that this pious woman had become sleepless and awakened others while they were sleeping. She sang, got angry, offered unsolicited advice, ran away, was brought back, and once or twice dashed about a farm field astride a horse, riding bareback.[22]

They compared Margaret Carlyle to a cousin of hers, Jean of Haregills, who smoked a great deal of tobacco and rode a pony far and wide to pursue "thinking persons" in order to converse with them "on all subjects," once getting as far as Edinburgh. According to Thomas Carlyle's colorful description of Jean of Haregills—his language itself captures her eccentricity—she had dressed "like no one else;—veils, multiplex wrappages and appendages, all as if thrown on by a pitchfork; spoke like no one else, in wild low chaunt or *lilt* (cadences not unmelodious) in words largely borrowed out of book, high-flowing, sure to be at least *mispronounced*; . . . [with] a malicious little sting of sarcasm now and then."[23]

From a distance of two hundred years, it is not possible to disentangle those eccentric symptoms from nineteenth-century views of how women were supposed to behave. The neighbors, apparently, did not perceive much amiss in Margaret Carlyle's behavior. When informed she had lost her reason, they wondered if it might not be due to her son Tom's atheism, a reference to the university student's radically changed beliefs, the profound break with his past, which deeply upset his parents; and which older villagers who shared his parents' religious outlook could not fathom. Thomas Carlyle would have likely experienced some guilt about his mother's illness.

A modern reader might see in Margaret Aitken Carlyle a much-put-upon woman who had given birth to nine children and found herself, on the brink of menopause, about to be free of an endless round of pregnancies and angry at how confined her life had been. The record is sparse. More cannot be known, but one can at least sense her exhilaration, temper, and sudden burst of abandon.

Thomas's mother recovered after a stay with her brother-in-law's family who nursed her back to health, later claiming that whisky secretly administered against the doctor's "No, no, no!" had calmed her down and brought about a cure.[24] Her son John reported that their mother was again reading her religious books and, finally, "behaving always decently."[25]

Whatever the truth of the episode, Margaret Carlyle had suffered an excited agitated state that greatly upset her family. It was the single time that Thomas had seen his doughty father cry. At the extinction of his mother's reason, he recounts in his *Reminiscences*, his father burst "into quite a torrent of grief; cried piteously and threw himself on the floor, and lay moaning," which caused his son to feel awe at the "unknown seas of feeling [that] lie in man."[26]

In relinquishing Thomas to the Grange without much to-do, Jane may have understood that Richard evoked disturbing memories in her husband. This strange, moving episode with a mad man no doubt stirred vague fears for them both about their own mental states. Jane was a father's daughter and Thomas a mother's son. Like most people, they held idealized yet complex feelings about the parent of the opposite sex who had favored them. Jane revered a father who had nevertheless deserted her by dying. Thomas idealized his mother, yet his life so greatly surpassed hers that the wide arc of their difference is difficult even to grasp. As well as retaining extensive memories of the real people, each had, of course, internalized these figures, who had simultaneously boosted their offspring's self-regard and created doubts. Parental imagoes lurked in the shadows of the Carlyles' marriage, unwitting ghosts that on occasion flew out and pushed the two of them into confrontation, or pulled them apart into baffled isolation.

In a poem she wrote after her father died, "Lines to Lord Byron: From his daughter, Ada" (1822), Jane Carlyle implied how the loss had affected her. Like many girls who enjoyed an adolescent infatuation for Byron, she had been deeply moved by thoughts of his daughter, deserted by her father when the poet and his wife separated and he went into exile. Jane's poem begins: "Father! what love that word reveals!" It concludes:

> Deceitful hopes! my years roll on
> And each new day is like the past;
> Still, still I live unloved, alone,
> Ah! this fond heart will break at last![27]

Thomas Carlyle's knowledge of what his mother had gone through in 1817 may have caused him to behave in that especially kindly way toward Richard. He employed a euphemism to describe what had happened to both: they had fallen prey to a brain fever. About his escape to the Grange and Lady Harriet, he would look back with remorse, scribbling on a letter from this time the words "alas, alas, how tragic-looking now!" But from the perspective of time, he complimented his wife on her "heroic and successful charity."[28]

Jane Carlyle had handled Richard as a competent asylum physician might have done. For a moment, she had become, like her father, a doctor. When she and Thomas had lived on the Craigenputtoch farm, she had been "considered a skillful Dr," nursing extended family members and hired help. Just this month, August 1844, she diagnosed from afar a Liverpool cousin's complaint—biliousness, for which she recommended the blue pill—saying, "I know both by observation and experience more about this sort of illness than most D*rs* do." She criticized the theoretical approach of the Liverpool doctor who attended only to a person's ears and throat, "as if a humanbeing were made up of entirely detached members—that is stupid—All these ailments are but *symptoms* of some central-ailment—to find which and cure it would be the business of a right Doctor[.]" Good medicine involved considering and treating a human being as a whole.

Seven times this summer Thomas Carlyle had addressed his wife in letters with the phrase *dear little Necessary Evil*. He now ceased making that derogatory joke. After Jane sent to the Grange some pills he had forgotten, he thanked her and called her, instead, "dear little Doctor!"

Jane kept Richard stable until arrangements could be made to send him to his family in Silesia. Amely assisted by writing letters in German to his brother-in-law, Count Oskar von Reichenbach, begging for assistance, especially needed travel money. The Count replied, money was found, tentative plans laid. If not cured, Richard was able to embark on his European journey. Back from the Grange some ten days later, Thomas wrote his brother that their patient had lately been very quiet with Jane but was "mad and ever madder in his notions."

Richard left them September 20, 1844, taking the Rotterdam steamer, planning to head up the Rhine toward "Switzerland and lighter air." "So much for Plattnauer," Thomas growled. For more than a month they had worried over him. But Thomas had a final task, to write the Prussian ambassador, pronouncing the young man close to being cured, and providing a string of accolades. He assured the ambassador that although Plattnauer had suffered "a kind of brain-fever," he "had never been, in the least disaffected against his native Government." The argumentative Richard, free to come and go once he got to Chelsea, had on occasion "kick[ed] up rows at the Embassy!" In an era of severe political tensions, Thomas could by no means take it for granted that Richard's government would distinguish between madness and sedition.

When Richard departed, Jane Carlyle, too, experienced relief. But a last-minute mad scheme she had persuaded him to put off reveals the regard he had for this woman, who for several weeks had ruled ably and respectfully over the complicated kingdom he turned out to be. The scheme, Jane told her cousin, involved his joining the English army, "rising to be a Commander in two years," and giving her "a large territory to rule over . . . at the head of things." (He seems to have relinquished the new idea of no difference in rank.) Whether he meant by his grateful tribute that she should reign as queen or prime minister, he felt certain it was a position in life that Jane Carlyle "ought to fill."

•

YEARS LATER (1857) Geraldine Jewsbury published "Agnes Lee," a story that resonates uncannily with this episode.[29] In Geraldine's fictional version, Agnes Lee, an orphan who becomes a lady's companion, finds that the man she loves, on the eve of their wedding, has turned into "an uncaged wild beast," "a furious maniac." His "dress disordered and torn, and covered with mud," he is taken to a lunatic asylum. A fever, we learn, precipitated the illness, which at first involves his being "irritable, nervous, and full of strange fancies."

Accompanied by a respectable friend, Agnes Lee visits the asylum and eventually persuades the head physician to allow her to bring the man into her home to care for him, and then marries him (Geraldine having grown rather more concerned about decency). He is so "dangerous and ungovernable," friends are amazed that Agnes does not fear for her life. Like Richard who came close to seizing a poker and dashing out the brains of one of Jane's guests, the man says of Agnes's guests, "If they had stayed a moment longer I would have killed them!" She exerts a "wonderful power" over her patient, who in turn tells people,

"I will make her great—I will!" The physician, wondering if Agnes is "accustomed to mad persons," praises her skill in handling him.

In time Agnes Lee effects a cure but at a price. Her tragedy is that her grateful patient, now husband, no longer loves her as she loves him. He respects and honors Agnes as his caretaker. But once she exhibited such manly attributes as strength, self- reliance, and self-control, however much he benefited, he cannot feel for her the way he had before. Speaking of the virtues he admires but now cannot love, Geraldine Jewsbury ruefully concludes that "people must brave the defects of their qualities." An ironic, sobering moral to the tale.

But *love*? It would have been fascinating to overhear Jane and Geraldine's private conversations about Richard Plattnauer, to know the extent of Richard's feelings for Jane and hers for him. The story provokes further questions. If a woman takes charge, exercises power, remains intelligent, rational, and calm in the face of chaos and crisis, is her femininity called into question? Does she risk losing love? Is there always a price to pay?

CHAPTER SEVEN

"MY I-ITY"

> "'I am half sick of shadows,' said /
> The Lady of Shalott."
> —ALFRED TENNYSON

SOON AFTER RICHARD'S DEPARTURE, JANE RECEIVED TWO LETTERS FROM him, "the first highly satisfactory, the second more flighty." Amely traveled to the Continent with the Bullers, staying with the family at the Hôtel de Mirabeau in Paris, then at Chalon-sur-Saône, en route to Nice. Thomas's friend Lady Harriet Baring and her husband were also headed for Nice, on their way to Italy.

Keeping at his Cromwell work, Thomas wrote determinedly in his journal October 1, 1844, "I must persist, persist till I succeed."[1] His close friend John Sterling (who had given Jane *Vittoria Acccorombona*) had died after a long illness—the Carlyles had received the sad news the day Richard left. Feeling the pressure of *time's winged chariot hurrying near*, Thomas sorely missed John Sterling and his warm praiseful friendship. Sterling had believed that even Carlyle's maddest flights of prose would tingle the ears of angels.[2]

Jane completed the purchase of a secondhand piano, using money of her own. The Carlyles had turned over to Jane's mother the money that the rents from Craigenputtoch provided, but since Grace Welsh's death they had been receiving the extra income. In addition to the allowance her husband gave her for household expenses, Jane had an account in a savings bank, and she now took out enough to cover the twenty pounds or so that the piano cost.

After the labors of the day were over, with the evenings growing darker, she would enter their "long, dim-lighted, perfectly neat and quiet room,"[3] light an additional lamp, open her piano, spread out her sheet music, and sit down to play a little Beethoven or Camille Pleyel. Her talent was modest but she played and sang expressively. What she mostly played for her husband were lively Scottish rondos and airs such as "Duncan Gray," "Will Ye Go to the Indies, My Mary," "Life Is Darkened O'er with Woe," "Flowers of the Forest," "The Blue Bells of Scotland," "Come Be Gay and Banish Sorrow." A favorite was Robert Burns' "Ye Banks and Braes":

> How can ye bloom sae fresh and fair?
> How can ye chant, ye little birds,
> And I sae weary, fu' o' care!
> Thou'll break my heart, thou warbling bird.

If Thomas wished to hear a little music, he traditionally said, "Jane, will ye play me a few of those Scotch tunes."[4] *If* the Carlyles were getting along, the wae Scottish tunes could solace them both.

•

ON A MID-OCTOBER day, Jane is lying on her chaise longue, shifting her position in a vain attempt to avoid its prickliest horsehair sections, which she is trying to keep covered with a shawl. Her head is aching badly but she has a matter on her conscience, an epistle to answer from her cousin Helen Welsh concerning another governess in need. When Jane can no longer ignore the call of duty, she rouses herself to go to her table. A friend of her cousin's has had to quit her position (for reasons unknown) and is looking for work.

Head still throbbing, Jane begins, "[I]f I hear of any thing likely to suit her, you may depend on my putting all my energies into action on her behalf—for I think her a very true and thoroughgoing person—besides that she is *your* friend." But she must be frank. Prospects appear dismal. Mrs. Macready might still be interested in hiring a governess, but since she requires a knowledge of languages, "it were idle to propose to her an Englishwoman who had never lived in foreign parts[.] As she gives a hundred a year of salary she has a right to first rate accomplishment."

Jane's thoughts turn naturally to Amely who "is performing the functions of *Courier* and *Interpreter*" for the Bullers in France, "rather than those she bargained for—of *Governess*." Although Jane had kept Amely from being made into mincemeat by boarding school girls and protected her from nursery tasks, not every indignity could be avoided. Besides, what choice would a governess have when asked to take on, at an employer's whim, the duties of tour guide?

More ominous are signs that Theresa Revis is turning recalcitrant. Jane sighs to her cousin, "The Child Theresa will probably run off with some mustachioed count before long . . . [her] premature Genius for *flirtation* . . . being from all accounts something *tremendous!*" The changeling child's gift for coquetry seemed to the baffled Bullers to have sprung up out of nowhere.

Before sealing her letter, Jane indulges in a description of how ill she feels, with "a violent rheumatism in the back of my head and neck—whereby I have been as if *nailed* to a sofa on the flat of my back for five days—today 'thank*s* God' I can sit up by snatches—but I am still as stiff as a crutch and my head aches." Time to close the curtains against the glare, return to her couch, and call for a cool cloth for her forehead.

•

JANE'S RENDERINGS OF illness, which can approach the articulation of the unsayable, bring to mind Virginia Woolf's comment that "English, which can express the thoughts of Hamlet and the tragedy of Lear, has no words for the shiver and the headache." She believed a new language was needed for this, one more "primitive, subtle, sensual, obscene."[5] Jane Carlyle at times seemed to have found it.

As for Amely, a governess was a gentlewoman fallen on hard times. She was a friend of the family she worked for. She was no better than a servant. She was servant *and* friend, yet not quite either. When mentioning Amely's literary work, Thomas Carlyle referred to her as Miss Bölte or Fraulein Bölte, the translator, "a young Lady from Berlin." When considering her primarily as an employee, they all slipped into *Bölte*.

Alas, poor Bölte. Before she left for Europe, Amely had brought around to Cheyne Row a Madame Lyser from Dresden. Erasmus Darwin was present in the Carlyles' parlor also. Writing of the visit to his brother, Thomas called the woman a "singular little German Improvisatress," and described a strange performance: "She is a little black-eyed, angular-visaged, wise, curious little Sibyl of a body, this Lyser; totally unacquainted with English . . . . Neither Darwin nor I could make any hand of speaking [German]; but she is quick as a little witch. We gave her 14 end-rhymes, and in an inconceivably brief time . . . she had a most respectable little Sonnet crystallized upon them! I have seen nothing come near it in the improvising line,—a curious, but alas a barren one."

A poignant, indelible image, a foreign woman of undeniable talent performing in the manner of a trained animal what Thomas considered a clever, witchy, barren art (the Victorians were reliably intrigued by such curiosities). The art was mechanical, the artist to be dismissed with a patronizing "ess." "Improvisatress" as in "poetess." Madame Lyser was to perform the next day at the Hanover Square concert rooms, but Thomas predicted she would make hardly any money there. Erasmus Darwin had a softer impression, calling her "an enchanting little woman" who "made really quite beautiful poetry in an instant." Of Thomas he said, "I think his stony heart was rather touched."[6]

Madame Lyser, about whom no more was heard, existed, like so many, on the edge of the economic precipice. Thomas Carlyle's British Museum research assistant on his Cromwell project, Dr. John Christie, was paid a pound a week. Thomas pointed out to his brother the stark fact that Christie was not quite so expensive to keep as a horse. London was filled with literary workers with odd careers, laboring arduously to scrape a living together. Women with creative aspirations and the need to earn their bread might, very understandably, twist and torque themselves into whatever niche society allowed, a state of affairs that could encourage a cramped if brave and admirable eccentricity.

Madame Lyser dancing like a nimble marionette to the random tune of others formed a peculiar image, but Amely herself was to provide a stranger one—as she lay stretched out cold and stiff in Isabella Buller's drawing room.

A craze for hypnotism, called mesmerism or animal magnetism, had begun sweeping through Britain. The phenomenon was not entirely new to Jane. Charles Buller Jr. had offered to magnetize her a couple of years before, "provided I will give him an *hour* and not laugh." After the event, she told her cousin Jeannie, "Well—I have undergone the process of Animal magnetism and with the impracticability of the Bass-Rock," which proved to Charles "not that his animal magnetism is a piece of downright nonsense but that I 'have an ill-regulated mind.'" In May this year Geraldine wrote Jane that she had just witnessed the hypnotizing of a young dressmaker who during her trance, to the astonishment of her audience, had "delivered a most furious anathema against the Catholics, devoting them all to perdition very eloquently."[7]

Sometime this fall, Isabella Buller invited a practitioner to perform his feats in her parlor for assembled guests. Jane later wrote an account of the evening for her uncle. Astonishingly, the hypnotist mesmerized Amely Bölte in the space of fifteen minutes by "gazing with his dark animal-eyes into hers, and simply holding one of her hands, while the other rested on her head."

•

THE WEATHER THIS December 1844 was as icy as the last had been unseasonably warm. Having spent a great deal of time sick in bed, Jane Carlyle had grown lonely and bored. Thomas's custom, when she was ill was to take the briefest breaks from his writing table, pop his head between her red bed curtains three times a day, and say, "How are you now, Jane? Have you had anything to eat? You are not thinking of getting up yet?"[8]

On December 10 Thomas paused in his work to describe for Edward FitzGerald the severe frost they were enduring in London. In Suffolk Edward had also been experiencing "a most desperate East wind, all razors," worrying what "all the poor folks [are] to do during the winter?"[9] But he was at least near enough to the shore to be "sung to sleep by the voice of the Sea." In depicting for Edward the grim cityscape, Thomas alluded to Dante's *Inferno*, a work his brother John had just begun to translate:

> "London is frightful; full of dust, storm and frost; jingling with tenfold noise . . . nothing but bluenosed cabmen in dreadful "comforters" [woolen scarves wrapped around their throats]—a bluenosed ugly population generally, all the women and their carriages being imprisoned by the cold. We have almost forgotten that there ever was any Sun; any sky except a hideous Coverlid woven out of coal-soot . . . . Per me si va nella Città Dolente! [Through me you pass into the city of woe!] Today there has been no daylight at all; the Heavens have fairly surrendered. I have sat with candles all day."

As her husband was depicting the hideous Coverlid of coal-soot, Jane was lying imprisoned in the city of woe: inside a house, inside a room, inside a bed hung with protective vermilion curtains, attempting to keep warm. Her cold and cough, bronchitis perhaps, had been brought on by the weather. Following her husband's advice, she told friends, she had "*walked*, walked" outdoors and stayed away from fires, as if "by *force of volition*" she could tough it out and prevent herself from falling ill. She now knew better, but the question of what *volition* might accomplish or not remained on her mind. What might one's will power control?

On December 13 Jane felt well enough—just—to rise from her red bed, migrate to her tub chair pulled close to the bedroom fireplace, and write to her Uncle John Welsh. Fortunately for Jane, too sick to do housework, the forever busy, bustling Helen Mitchell had been trudging up and down the stairs several times a day. Up with the weighty coal scuttle, down with the sloshy bedpan. On this dark, freezing evening Helen had managed to keep a fire burning in the bedroom grate—so essential to have a bedroom fire when one was ill.

"Oh uncle of my affection," Jane begins her letter, "such a season! did you ever feel the like of it? *Already* solid ice in ones water jug!"[10] But she must be improving, she tells him, for she feels "'a wholesome desire'—to smoke." (Jane was beginning to enjoy smoking some cigarittos that Geraldine had sent in thanks for helping with her novel.)

The excitement of getting out of bed had made her long to speak to someone, but since Thomas was out dining with Erasmus Darwin "the only possible talking for me [is] on paper."[11] She tells her uncle, "The next best thing I can think of is to write to *thee*;—beside one's bedroom-fire, in a tub-chair, the family-affections bloom up so strong in one!" Jane is writing in the flickering glow of firelight and candlelight, "a little live bundle of flannel shawls and dressing-gowns."

Her uncle had solicited Jane's opinion of what everyone was then talking about: Harriet Martineau's accounts of mesmerism appearing in the *Athenaeum*. They were called "Letters from Tynemouth," where she still resided, and the series had opened with a catchy directness: "It is important to society to know whether Mesmerism is true."[12]

Propped against her bank of pillows, desultorily turning the pages of the *Athenaeum*, Jane would have seen seasonal advertisements for cough, cold, and influenza remedies, and endless varieties of candles. The pages contained advertisements for magic lanterns, dissolving views, phantasmagoric lanterns, photographic cameras, and microscopes. In 1844 mysterious other dimensions seemed to hover in the very air. The door of speculation was wide open partly because electricity and magnetism were not yet well understood. James Clerk Maxwell, who developed a scientific understanding in the 1860s, was not to publish his *Treatise on Electricity and Magnetism*, containing "Maxwell's equations," until 1873.

Christmas and New Year's gift-books were also advertized in the *Athenaeum*. Charles Dickens' *A Christmas Carol* was in its tenth edition, his new holiday story *The Chimes* soon to see print. In fact on December 2 Thomas had gone to John Forster's apartments in Lincoln's Inn Fields to attend Dickens' reading of his latest story, which the novelist hoped would strike "a great blow for the poor." Dickens had asked for Mrs. Carlyle to be present, a special honor since such gatherings were usually for men only. As he put it to Forster, "Carlyle, indispensable, and I should like his wife of all things: *her* judgment would be invaluable."[13] But weather or ill health had kept Jane away.

In the event, the artist Daniel Maclise had sketched a picture of the assembled group. Charles Dickens glows as he reads his work, sunbeams radiating from his head. Fond as an author could be of his new creation, he especially liked having Carlyle in the audience; but in the sketch, listening to that long worthy tale of goblin chimes, head resting on his hand, Thomas seems to be shielding a bored, pained, "*please* let me go home!" expression.

In her *Athenaeum* articles, Harriet Martineau narrates her own experiences as well as those of a nineteen-year-old girl she calls J., for her Tynemouth maid Jane Arrowsmith, her landlady's niece, who had been waiting on her for nearly five years. Harriet claims that mesmerism has miraculously allowed her to recover from years of illness (apparently caused by uterine tumors), referring to her time as an invalid as "a life passed between my bed and my sofa." Mesmerism, Harriet testifies, has also enabled her to recover from a dependence on opium, that all-too-common Victorian remedy, taken to relieve her pain.

As her own health improved, she and her mesmerist of the moment, Mrs. Montagu Wynyard, a genteel widow fallen on hard times (mesmerism seemed to be opening up new careers[14]), practiced upon the maid. In her dramatization of the conversations that transpired between J. and her examiners, during what she terms a séance, Harriet provides snappy dialogue: Mesmerist: "Will our minds become one?"

Subject: "I think not." "What are your chief powers?" "I like to look up and see spiritual things. I can see diseases: and I like to see visions."

In an exasperated aside, Harriet complains of the maid, "I have often longed that she had a more copious vocabulary."

In her letter, Jane—as stimulated by reading Martineau this December as she had been by Dickens the last—first surveys the ways in which humans are made to blush, tremble, feel tickled or cowed by mere looks or comments, without being actually touched. "I perfectly believe then in the power of magnetism to throw people into all sorts of unnatural states of *body*," Jane declares, "could have believed so far *without* the evidence of my senses, [but] *have* the evidence of my senses for it also—I saw Miss Bölte magnetized one evening at M*rs* Buller's by a distinguished Magnetiser who could not sound his *hs*."

In a drama in one scene, Jane then relates to her uncle what had happened to Amely and herself that night. With her swift sharp portrayal of several characters, what she writes reads like a page from a novel of manners:

> "[H]e had made her [Amely] into the image of death—no *marble* was ever colder, paler, or more motionless, and her face had that peculiarly beautiful expression which Miss Martineau speaks of—never seen but in a dead face or a mesmerized one—Then he played cantrups [tricks] with her arm and leg and left them stretched out for an hour in an attitude which no awake person could have preserved for three minutes. I touched them and they felt horrid—stiff as iron—I could not bend them down with all my force—they pricked her hand with the point of a penknife she felt nothing—and now comes the strangest part of my story—
>
> The man who regard[ed] Carlyle and me as Philistines said, "*Now* are you convinced?"
>
> "Yes," said Carlyle, "there is no possibility of doubting but that you have stiffened all poor little Miss Bölte there into something very awful."
>
> "Yes," said I pertly, "but then she *wished* to be magnetized. What I doubt is whether anyone could be reduced to that state without *the consent of their own volition*. I should like for instance to see anyone magnetize ME!"
>
> "You think I could not?" said the man with a look of ineffable disdain. "Yes," said I, "—I defy you!"

"Will you give me your hand MISS?"

"Oh by all means," and I gave him my hand with the most perfect confidence in my force of volition and a smile of contempt.

He held it in one of his and with the other made what H. Martineau calls some "*passes*" over it—as if he were darting something from his finger ends—I looked him defiantly in the face as much as to say, "You must learn to sound your HS Sir, before you can produce any effect on a woman like *me*!" and whilst this or some similar thought was passing thro' my head—flash—there went over me from head to foot something precisely like what I once experienced from taking hold of a galvanic ball—only *not nearly* so violent—I had presence of mind to keep looking him in the face as if I had felt nothing and presently he flung away my hand with a provoked look, saying "I believe you would be a very difficult subject, but nevertheless if I had *time* given me I am sure I could mesmerize you At least I never failed with anyone yet."

Now if this destroyed for me my theory of *the need* of *a consenting will*—it as signally destroyed *his* of *moral and intellectual superiority*—for *that* man was superior to *me* in nothing but animal strength as I am a living woman! I could even hinder him from *perceiving* that he had mesmerized me by *my* moral and intellectual superiority!

In this passage Jane uses dialogue somewhat as Harriet did, but, as if competing for the fun of it, greatly outdoes her.

Harriet Martineau had by now gained a firm reputation as a popularizer of contemporary issues. Her *Life in the Sick-Room*, based on her years spent indoors, had made invalidism interesting and respectable. (When Jane received a presentation copy, she had read the book at once.) Harriet dignified the subject by showing how invalidism provided an opportunity to gain a deeper spiritual perspective and an improved character. She revealed that one little room could become an everywhere, especially, in her case, with the aid of a telescope from which to view Tynemouth Harbor from her window. She claimed to have been able to see on the decks of far off ships the "sailors' lips mov[ing] in the utterance of a foreign tongue."[15] The Carlyles had visited Harriet in Tynemouth three years before, so Jane would have been able to picture the scenes for herself.

A very personal testament is hard to dispute. "A few days after the arrival of my kind Mesmerist [Mrs. Wynyard]," Harriet writes, "I had my foot on the grass for the first time for four years and a half."

The shock of the change is so great she feels haunted "by the stalks of the grass, which I had not seen growing for so long." She also claims to have seen, during those years, only one tree.[16] But now, in no time, she is ambling about outdoors "as self-possessed as any walker in the place," and seeing lovely visions besides. Her nearly irresistible account would tempt many an invalid to experience a wild surge of hope.

Standing up to the charismatic male mesmerist and opposing Harriet Martineau's contagious advocacy of magnetism in the *Athenaeum*—reflecting as it did the current social craze—would have required from Jane considerable strength of mind. Harriet's "Letters from Tynemouth" are so passionate, convinced, and sure, they tumble forth like a force of nature—and after all, the *New Testament* abounded in miracles.

Yet even though she read these claims while lying in bed in a weakened condition, Jane was able to think her position through. From the galvanic jolt she herself had experienced and from witnessing what happened to Amely, she realized something extraordinary transpired during mesmeric séances. She respected the potency and mystery. But she was alert to what common sense told her, and wary of hysteria and humbug. For one thing, Harriet Martineau claimed that the maidservant had demonstrated clairvoyance, saying that J. had foreseen details of a shipwreck that occurred later on near Tynemouth.

On that dark evening as she sat in her chair before the fire, Jane registered her disbelief, telling her uncle, "Of the *clairvoyance* I have *witnessed* nothing—but one knows that people with a diseased or violently excited state of nerves *can* see more than their neighbours. When my insane friend [Richard Plattnauer] was in this house he said many things *on the strength of his insanity*—which in a mesmerized person would have been quoted as miracles of clairvoyance—Of course a vast deal of what one hears is humbug—this girl of Harriets seems half diseased—half make-believing—I think it a horrible blasphemy they [Harriet and the mesmerist] are there . . . *exploiting* that poor girl for their idle purposes of curiosity!"

The strong could exploit the weak: Jane had put her finger on a true danger of mesmerism. Harriet Martineau and Mrs. Wynyard showered J. with the closest, most flattering attention to get her to cooperate, and, cleverly, encouraged the maidservant to take her own turn at playing the role of hypnotizer.

Exhausted at last from the excitement of writing about such an engaging subject, Jane concludes her letter to her uncle by saying that she regards "Animal magnetism" as "a damnable sort of tempting of Providence which I 'as one solitary individual['] will henceforth stand entirely aloof from—And now having given you my views at great length I will return to my bed and compose my mind."

The fire is dying down. She will have to ring for Helen to bring up more coals. Her mind still racing, she will no doubt have a hard time falling asleep this dark chilly night.

•

JANE CARLYLE WITHHELD from her uncle a story that she had related to Charles Buller Jr. Visiting Cheyne Row *before* the *Athenaeum* articles had started to appear, Charles (as he told Lady Harriet) had found Mrs. C. huddled "by a blazing fire" and full of a letter she had just received from Harriet Martineau. Jane related to Charles "wondrous tales about Miss Martineau's recovery. She has walked five miles, she sees visions, two of which she is going to publish an account of: but the two first are of so *awful* a nature that she cannot communicate them to any human being. She did once begin to try to tell them to the lady, who has magnetized her [Mrs. Wynyard]! but in two minutes the lady started up begging her not to talk in such a terrible style, & telling her that if she did she must call the servants. From which . . . I conclude that the far-famed Harriet was talking improperly." The image of Miss Martineau talking improperly suggests the outlet, and even fun, that mesmerism could provide for pent-up people.

According to Charles Buller, it was Jane's opinion that a "long course of *Iodine*" Harriet had taken earlier, not mesmerism, had been responsible for her so-called miraculous cure.[17] As Jane's skepticism about mesmerism increased, her feelings of friendship toward Harriet Martineau were undergoing a change. Although Harriet continued to write her as Dearest Jenny and express sisterly affection, a patronizing note had begun creeping in. At the same time, while continuing to admire Thomas Carlyle's deft pen portraits, Harriet was growing weary of his political opinions. For his part, Thomas had been finding Miss Martineau ever more tedious and didactic. Among all of them, that is, annoyance was mounting. Yet a degree of affection mixed with a tinge of respect lingered on.

By the end of the month, Jane had become even more exasperated with the subject, writing a Scottish friend that in London they were now sick of hearing about Animal Magnetism. By then the *Athenaeum* had printed more of Harriet Martineau's articles, along with an editorial rebuttal attacking her claims of clairvoyance, which Harriet understandably viewed as a betrayal. The rebuttal showed how the maidservant could have independently gathered facts about the shipwreck, since rumors had been flying all over Tynemouth.

"Harriet Martineau expects that the whole system of medecine is going to be flung to the dogs presently," Jane told a Scottish correspondent, "and that henceforth instead of Physicians we are to have *Magnetizers*! May be so! but 'I as one solitary individual' (my husbands favourite phrase) will in that case prefer my sickness to the cure—one knows that sickness at all events comes from God—and is not at all sure that *such* cure does not come from the Devil—The wonder is that sensible people who have heard tell since ever they were born of witchcraft and *demonaical possession and all that sort of thing* should all at once fall to singing *te deums* over magnetism as if it were a new revealation! Nay anybody that had ever seen *a child* tickled might have recognized the principle of Animal Magnetism without going further!"

Skeptical Jane, ironically, seemed half to believe the Devil was still afoot, and she was not alone. Harriet Martineau, soon after moving from Tynemouth to her beloved Lake Country, where she began practicing mesmerism upon naive neighbors, reported gleefully, "The people round [here] say they fear 'the lady does the cures through the Old 'un.'"[18]

When Jane Carlyle told her uncle of experiencing moral and intellectual superiority over the mesmerist, she was striking a note of hard-won confidence. She had stood up to a man of lower class stature by drawing on a strong sense of who she was, and by utilizing the force of her *volition*, despite the galvanic charge she had secretly felt. She drew on her class status to resist the man, rather than any rights of women. And portrayed herself in sharp contrast to Amely, who for some strange reason had wished to be magnetized, entering willingly into that death-in-life state.

Knowing Amely's story, though, we might wonder if in that drawing-room among the distinguished guests she had felt the prod of Isabella Buller's finger in her back and heard a whispered command like, We need another volunteer, Bölte. Quick quick, get up there and amuse them! Too often, according to a recent article in *Fraser's Magazine* (which the Carlyles had likely seen), governesses were relegated to hearing "the echoes from the drawing-room" for "in a house full of people, they dwell alone," their predicament being compared to prisoners in solitary confinement.[19] To be among the guests, then, had been a privilege, and a governess might feel obligated to repay an employer for such magnanimous inclusion.

Or was Amely, a naturally curious person, anxious to experience for herself what all society was talking about? Or eager to be, for once, the center of attention? Mesmerism could be a great equalizer, making potent figures of formerly marginalized governesses, clergymen's widows, and dark-eyed men who could not pronounce their *h*s.

Jane's sense of superiority seems partly real. Jane Baillie Welsh, a doctor's daughter and much-valued only child, had grown up to be a witty educated woman and notable letter writer, married to a well-known author, and more—sister-friend, for instance, to an Italian hero. Yet her stance seems half defensive, too.

Jane Carlyle once used the word "I-ity" (*I-ety* in the *Oxford English Dictionary*, where she is cited): "[I]n spite of the honestest efforts to annihilate my *I-ity*, or merge it in what the world doubtless considers my better half; I still find my self a self-subsisting and alas! selfseeking *Me*." In that same letter (to John Sterling) she quoted from a Goethe novel, "*I too am here*!" Believing, early on in their marriage, that Thomas was receiving the lion's share of attention from friends had provoked both comments.

A push and pull existed in Jane, sometimes unconscious, sometimes not, between the allure of the shadows—passivity, privacy, invalidism—and the desire to stand up for herself and assume a role on the social stage. The dialectic between public and private—passive dependence and assertive independence—could be as confusing to Victorian women as it remains today for women in many parts of our world. It was a central conundrum of Jane Carlyle's life.

She had a need to assert self-worth and had been exhorted by her sympathizing friend Geraldine to "patronise the pronoun 'I' as much as I do myself!"[20] A similar impulse would lead Charlotte Brontë to make "*I*" the governess Jane Eyre's favorite word. It was as if a group of Victorian women had just stumbled across the underused pronoun and seized it as their own with the enthusiasm of a fresh discovery—

I-ity as the necessary starting point, a formerly hidden source of the Nile. Jane's account of resisting the powerful dark-eyed man portrays both the difficulty of asserting her ego as a Victorian wife all too aware of the Mrs. Ellis-code rules of compliant behavior, and the true triumph of a small success.

Her husband's opinion of mesmerism was blunt, as when he complained of several boring Edinburgh duds who had arrived unannounced on the Cheyne Row doorstep wishing to discourse with him about *au courant* social trends. "Miserable snaffles [weaklings] too," Thomas had called them, "full of animal magnetism, free kirk and other mere rubbish;—I had some doubts whether not to rise with red hot oaths, and pack them all instantly into the street." In the event, he served the duds tea and walked them out the door on the pretext of having an errand to perform in Kensington. So much for mesmerism!

Jane and Thomas essentially agreed about the sort of mesmerism suited for parlor display. In an 1845 notebook entry, Jane tells a funny story about a maidservant who "could not *wash heavy clothes* without mesmeric help"—she had to be hypnotized by her clergyman before she could manage to do the laundry. But Jane remained open to what she later referred to as *spiritual magnetism*. In 1861, writing to the American actress Charlotte Cushman, who had asked if she believed in that concept, Jane responded, "Most assuredly! I believe in it absolutely and entirely! It is the Great Central Fact of the Universe for me!—The concentrated Essence of Life!" By spiritual magnetism Jane appeared to mean a kind of mental telepathy practiced by kindred spirits, "one human will having power over another even thro' some miles of other human beings." The magnetism practiced by Harriet Martineau, the dark-eyed man, Mrs. Wynyard, and later practitioners of table-turning séances, Jane dismissed in the same letter as "knaves and idiots" with "all their brutal nonsenses."

On *that* aspect of the question, she had firmly made up her mind.

CHAPTER EIGHT
CRISIS IN NICE

"As if mere 'Chaos' had broken loose there and
the Night-Empire were threatening to break in,
presided over by Unwisdom!"
—THOMAS CARLYLE, 22 December 1844

AMELY LYING STIFF AND DEATH-LIKE. JANE REACHING OUT TO TOUCH her friend's extended arm, the feel of her fingertips against the too-still flesh: *No marble was ever colder, paler.*

What Jane wrote reads like a prevision, for within days of sending the mesmerism letter to her uncle, Jane heard alarming news. Isabella Buller wrote from Nice to say that Miss Bölte had "lost her senses in a fever." To compound the trouble, it looked to Jane like the Bullers were "very anxious to be rid of her."

In bed again with a cold or flu, Jane had for a while been receiving worrisome tidings from France, where the Bullers, Barings, and other friends were still traveling. Reading through their letters, she had become aware of additional hardships Amely was enduring, yet was not at first very disturbed. As the recent *Fraser's* essay on the plight of the governess had put it, given her tangential position in a family as an extra, an add-on, she might as well be called "Madame de Trop."[1] But sometimes one just had to accept reality.

The situation in Nice, however, had all at once turned alarming. Not only was Theresa acting up, and worse, but Amely lay dangerously ill. The journey to storied cities in temperate climes, which Amely had so much anticipated, seemed about to founder on the rocks.

The facts were not easy to discern in the muddle of messages flying back and forth, but it appeared that, first of all, the socially precocious Theresa had lost interest in her studies and rebelled against her governess. Had she made fun of Miss Bölte's French accent? For Theresa spoke French like a native. Did she refuse to sit still for drawing? Did she balk at learning globes? It seems clear that to get out from under the protective wing of her governess-chaperone, Theresa told lies about her. One friend, reporting from the scene, wrote Jane that Theresa, or Tizzy, as she was nicknamed, had been acting "the most artful little Devil." As Jane put it, she "has got provoked with Miss Bolte for too much repressing her premature tendencies to *unfortunate femalisings* and tells M*rs* Buller all sorts of lies to get her turned off which M*rs* Buller is silly enough to believe." They could handle their goddaughter as they liked, Jane added, but predicted that ridding herself "of the only person who has succeeded in having the upper hand of her" would be Tizzy's "first decided step towards '*the streets*.'"

It transpired that Amely Bölte had been stricken with typhus, the reason she was so ill with such a high fever that she had become delirious. Theresa had caught some illness too and the Bullers who "had no sympathy or cares to bestow on anyone else" had taken their entourage up the hill to a villa, abandoning the governess to a hotel. Their excuse: Miss Bölte was too sick to be moved. Dr. John Carlyle told Jane this was nonsense, as long as the job was done with care. To complicate matters, the glamorous elder Theresa Revis, Tizzy's mother (former mistress of the Bullers' son Arthur) who resided in the south of France now entered the scene with her Captain Bacon in tow, the man who "for the time being she calls *her husband*!" as Jane acerbically put it, adding "Really, all this is a little too strong for even *my* morality!"

With the Theresa Revis-Bacon party crowding in, there was no room at the villa for a sick governess, especially one who was not a good patient. Lady Harriet wrote Thomas Carlyle, relaying the Bullers' point of view: "the Bölte" had "a deranged head—and a positive will of her own—and energy to carry the said (will) out [, which] no one seemed to have energy to resist—so she ate when she ought not, and got up when she ought not and has been very seriously ill—"[2]

Jane rushed off information to Nice about Amely's family in Germany—could they send her home to her mother? She supplied the address. But Amely's condition worsened. On December 17, 1844, the Carlyles received word that she was unlikely to live.

With Jane terribly anxious and Thomas understanding very well how such tragedies could end in death, they had been discussing her condition daily. They still did not know the governess intimately and allude in their letters, without sentimentality, to several Biblical injunctions about the stranger: I was a stranger, and ye took me in. [T]hy stranger who is within thy gates . . . may rest as well as thou. Be not forgetful to entertain strangers: for thereby some have entertained angels unawares. Amely, the German skeptic, however much she might annoy, provoked such thoughts in the Carlyles, themselves Scottish strangers-of-a-sort in London.

Richard Plattnauer, perhaps fearing political repression or family conflicts, had not ended up in Silesia with his sister, as planned, but had taken himself off to Nice. Mad though everyone claimed he still was, he did not now seem violent and had undertaken a program of writing at least once a week to Mrs. Carlyle, whom he continued to view as his manager. He now sent Jane word that Lady Harriet might come to Amely's rescue, though tension and uncertainty prevailed. She will. She won't, it's unnecessary. No, she will after all.

When in England, the formidable Lady Harriet presided ably over the Baring-Ashburton town and country residences, each grand and impressive. She held what amounted to a salon, reigning over a circle of political and literary luminaries with her daughter-of-an-earl confidence. Whatever self-doubts she may have possessed, she had developed an imposing social presence. Though somewhat in the older bluestocking tradition, her salon had an essentially Victorian character, meaning that the queenly Lady Harriet might reign as a bluestocking if she so chose; but when the whim struck her, she could with impunity relegate women like Jane Carlyle to the conventional wifely sphere (once, in the future, even to the housekeeper sphere).

Thomas Carlyle, despite early grave misgivings concerning the aristocracy as a class, had been drawn to the imposing Lady Harriet as a moth to a lamp, iron filings to a magnet, or, more aptly, a medieval knight to his lady. Clichés come to mind perhaps because of something mythical / archetypal in their growing attraction. Jane, who hardly knew her at this point, described Lady Harriet as "immensely *large*," one of the tallest, widest women she had seen. It was because of the woman's charismatic allure for men that Jane had called her a Circe and Siren. That Jane was about four years older is hard to keep in mind because of Lady Harriet's regal air and stately bovine elegance. Just by looking as she did and being who she was, she elicited projections from men and women alike. Thomas certainly idealized her. And their friendship had begun to bother Jane.

William Bingham Baring, a rather shy man with a placid temperament, liked and admired Thomas Carlyle and did not seem to mind his wife's more-than-friendship for a literary man. When he returned to London, he brought additional letters from Nice for the Carlyles. On December 21 he sent word to them that Lady Harriet, still in Nice, was on the verge of taking Amely Bölte under her protection. With that news, as Thomas put it, "a clear door of deliverance opened."

•

IT IS A DARK December evening when Thomas Carlyle, seizing the opportunity to do a possible good, places himself at the desk in his small, warm dressing-room study, with its fireplace the size of a saucepan, to write Lady Harriet.[3] In the last month or so they have been exchanging friendly, intimate letters. The lady's notes have made no mention of Jane.

The little study under the eaves is quiet. Is it approaching midnight? Will the old Chelsea clock soon strike the hour? As his pen scratches across the paper, Thomas writes in close communion with his friend, giving her the weight of his encouragement and approval of her plan to rescue the governess, so long as it does not endanger her own health. Although Lady Harriet has declared her intention to assist Miss Bölte, he is well aware that the deed has yet to be done. Plans may yet go awry.

"You have done a beneficent, humane and right thing," he tells Lady Harriet encouragingly; "for which we are all very grateful to you here, of which I for one am very proud! . . . your act, so far as I understand it, is a real subject of satisfaction to me." What he has learned, he states explicitly, is "that Bölte is to go to you, so soon as she is fit to be removed; that you take charge of the poor Bölte, and give her shelter."

To shore up the cause at the moment that Amely lies dying in her lonely hotel room, Thomas Carlyle—providing, incidentally, a fascinating picture of what has been transpiring in Nice—turns Lady Harriet into the heroine and star of a medieval morality play:

> "In fact there have come nothing but disastrous, bad, confused news from the Buller side of Nice, ever since you wrote. As if mere 'Chaos'

had broken loose there; and the Night-Empire were threatening to break in, presided over by Unwisdom! Sickness, disaster, distraction,—'houses too small,'—dark nameless Figures occupying place there, with whom the Daughters of Light could have no communing,—and poor Bölte lying sick, insane, among strangers in a hôtel; apparently sick to death,—and no use for her recovering if she could! . . . it did seem a real bit of Chaos come again, and that it was like to end as Tragedies do with the loss of life."

He continues: "Very pleasant it has been to me, Ma Dame, to figure you all along as a Beam of Light in that miserable element of Darkness; spreading round you what of order, settlement, humanity, good sense and nobleness was possible there. My blessings on you;—mine, and those of the afflicted and the stranger that was forsaken within your Gates!"

Though he does not say so here, Thomas believes Isabella Buller to be essentially heartless and is attempting to summon a counter spirit. Lady Harriet has an opportunity to play the part of an interposing goddess, a *dea ex machina*. Who could turn down the role of Bringer of Light to the Night-Empire?

Appealing first to the lady, then to the prospective employer, Thomas switches tone and provides next a judicious character reference for Amely. The governess has always seemed "a decisive, hardy, useful-looking, clear-sighted nimble little creature;—in whom there were utilities of many kinds . . . and general wholesomeness of mind." But he has a caveat: "there might be some hysterical flaw in her constitution." On the whole, she is "calm and practical." Yet he had personally witnessed, astonished and disturbed, that preposterous scene where she had allowed herself to be mesmerized. What did such nonsense imply about her character? He also recalls the mad notion of Amely's that she might become a "Governess in the Queen's House itself." And furthermore, he has observed a lack of tact.

He concludes, however, on a positive note. Miss Bölte "has first-rate talents for teaching, and is a thoroughly honest creature." He will leave the handling of the situation to Lady Harriet's judgment, and urges her to take the opportunity to turn the governess into her own private German tutor: "One good result I anticipate from this good deed: that you will now actually learn German. . . . There is no reading elsewhere in the least comparable to German for one like you."

As he puts down his pen and leans back in his chair, he might justifiably feel he has accomplished a very creditable job of persuasion.

•

REGARDING AMELY BÖLTE'S character, Thomas Carlyle years later recalled her as "a bustling, shifty little German Governess," which some took to be disparaging. But by *shifty* he meant resourceful, or able to shift for oneself, having used the word previously to describe efficient, practical women, including his wife back in 1835 when she had hired a young girl to help out in the house: "Shifty Jane has already found a *little* g[irl] of suitable promise." His observation of Amely's lack of tact or reticence is more complicated. A phrase that later stuck to her was Household Spy, a sobriquet given her by a friend of Varnhagen's after his letters to Amely were published; his responses to her revealed how closely she had observed the Carlyles. She had in fact been taking careful notes at 5 Cheyne Row. With hindsight, it seems that Amely was developing an almost scientific interest in the Carlyles, exhibiting what we might call today a psychological-anthropological curiosity—or a *biographical* curiosity—Boswellian, that is, rather than gratuitously inquisitive.

In his letter to Lady Harriet, Thomas Carlyle went on to talk of other things, a frank, ranging conversation indicating the excellent terms they were on. This season the lady had been writing him fulsome descriptive notes, and while they contained nothing that could directly give Jane ammunition for complaint, Lady Harriet was enough at ease with "dear M*r.* Carlyle" to confide her feelings: "you must . . . write to me again, for I am alone and sometimes feel It very much."[4]

Jane Carlyle was right to be disturbed. The following summer she would become deeply alarmed. But on this occasion, Thomas's principal motive for writing the lady was Jane herself: "My Wife has been in great trouble about poor Bölte; almost daily talking of her." He wanted to be able to assure Jane that Lady Harriet would step in and do the right thing.

Little by little, against predictions, Amely began to revive. That willfulness about eating and exerting herself, indicating an active spirit, possibly aided her recovery. Some three months later, Lady Harriet would keep her promise and bring the governess back to England.

Meanwhile Lady Harriet was quick to set the record straight concerning her alleged good deeds. She replied frankly to Mr. Carlyle's letter, "I have done nothing at all—of any kind—to deserve any praise of any body *in re* Bölte." Moved and touched by his praise for her, she nevertheless told him it was "because I do not think little or lightly of what you say that I want you to keep to that noblest quality of real friendship—Truth." Do not exaggerate, she meant, speaking of his high-flown courtly language and his praise. Yet she would "take a little of it as reward where *my wisdom* puts it, and keep the rest as strength when my heart is sick—as it sometimes is sorely."

Overcome by being alluded to as a Daughter of Light, Lady Harriet had perhaps missed the force of his rhetoric. If he so strongly emphasized the nobility of the deed, would she have any choice but to execute it? In her response she dutifully details for him just how she went about fulfilling the role he had created for her: "I took my landlord, who is also the Buller's, in hand and succeeded [in] making a much better arrangement for all parties—getting [Amely] a bedroom and sitting-room and fireplace, a thing many rooms do not boast of here, in a small house adjoining, but communicating, with the Bullers. And there she is going on quite well—tho' still weak and looking poor thing, what she has suffered, but in good spirits." Because of "*folly on all sides*," Lady Harriet continued, "it seems she is not to continue educating the child."[5] In a manner of speaking, Amely had again been fired.

Amely Bölte later claimed it was actually *Richard Plattnauer* who had saved her. After his "roamings had led him incidentally to Nice," it was he, who desired to serve others and enjoyed concocting schemes, who had dreamed up a rescue plan. Speaking of good deeds, Amely was to claim that while Thomas Carlyle liked to hear of and encourage them, he usually did "not want the responsibility" of getting embroiled himself.[6]

Lady Harriet also related to Mr. Carlyle a startling piece of news. While in Nice, Theresa's mother, Mrs. Bacon, had caught a fever and died. Lady Harriet frankly considered this "one obstacle the less in the way of good to her child—but only one—& the others are fearfully many to that young life."[7] In the space of a month, little Theresa had lost both her governess and her mother.

•

JANE NOW TOLD her cousin definitively that "Miss Bolte thank god [is] in the way of recovery at last—," though many details of that episode remain unknown. Letters that might have provided more information, like those Richard Plattnauer wrote Jane, are non-existent.

Letters are the fragile genre, too often misplaced, torn up, thrown away, put to the flame. In a fit of pique this holiday season, hoping for a letter from Jeannie Welsh that did not arrive, Jane crumpled up one of Geraldine's and tossed it into the fire, watching the pages curl and burn. She was petulant that her cousin had not written her, whereas letters from Geraldine were frequent and could be counted on.

Letters that Jane had written to her mother were burned, and later most of those she wrote Geraldine. Jane had requested that they be destroyed. Missing therefore are what might have been her most revealing communications. Letters she wrote to Thomas immediately after her mother's death also disappeared. Charles Dickens was to burn his letters from the Carlyles. Only a few of the notes that they and Erasmus Darwin sent each other have survived, which means a sparse record exists of the lifelong relationship between the Carlyles and their perhaps closest friend. One letter that Erasmus Darwin wrote got preserved only because Thomas had used the other side of it to write a page of *Past and Present.*[8]

Harriet Martineau forthrightly advocated the burning of personal letters. "Our correspondence," she believed, "has all the flow and lightness of the most sacred talk."[9] Self-consciousness about writing for posterity or saving letters for posthumous publication would ruin that precious intimacy and freedom. Much better consign them to the fire—easy enough to do with all those fireplaces so near at hand.

Jane Carlyle and Harriet Martineau argued about this. Jane reported their debate to her cousin at a time when Harriet was "demanding thro'out the whole circle of her correspon[d]ence which is almost as wide as the world—that there should be a general thorough conflagration of her letters." According to Jane, Harriet's problem was "fear of their publication at her death—and this she calls—not what it really is, a diseased anxiety about her future *biography* but '*her protest against the laxity of society in the matter of letters.*'" Jane continued, "I felt it *my* duty (without varnish) to tell her that I considered the whole uproar '*unworthy* of her'"; but Harriet "goes on exciting this letter-conflagration as if it were 'the burning-up of all the sins of the world'—I have *done* the *practical* in the matter—keeping only an autograph for Helen [Welsh]—but for the rest, have told her that I must be allowed to retain my own *opinion.*"

Harriet Martineau believed she stood on principle. "We all know how the present action of our new civilization works to the impairing of Privacy," she had written formally in *Life in the Sick-Room.* "I would keep our written confidence from being made biographical material, as anxiously as I would keep our spoken conversation from being noted down for the good of society. I would keep the power of free speech under all the influences of life and fate,—and leave Biography to exist or perish."[10]

But reading an especially garrulous plea for letter burning that Harriet sent to Fanny Wedgwood—it is tinged with anxiety, repeating the phrase "*My* letters are all written speech"[11]—one wonders if she perhaps also feared that certain of her dashed-off letters were not so much prose as a wearisome onrush of words. If some resembled the murmur of intimate, indiscreet speech, would not Miss Martineau, as a far-famed author, wish them to escape the judgmental eye of posterity? Did she envy the more articulate, amusing letters of Jane Welsh Carlyle?

She in fact told Jane that hers were "wholly apart from all other letters," generously praising them as witty, entertaining, and kind.[12] But she did not save them. Although Jane claimed that she had gotten rid of Harriet's letters, she actually preserved quite a few. Though to protect her friend, she likely burned any that could be considered indecorous, such as the one where Harriet suggested that she had communicated mesmeric visions to Mrs. Wynyard in improper language.

A twenty-first-century chronicler who longs to look back and learn how things were feels grateful for every scrap saved from conflagration. Yet Thomas Carlyle wisely implied, after wending his way through endless piles of dryasdust tomes, that *oblivion* could also be the historian's friend.[13]

•

JANE SAYS LITTLE more about Nice. The crisis has passed. She focuses instead on a gift Thomas surprised her with on Christmas day: he slipped a woman's cloak over the chair at the foot of her bed as she slept.

Recovering from her illness, Jane discovers the cloak while getting dressed and feeling sorrowful about her mother, the holiday / anniversary feelings she is subject to. Thomas had worried she would not like the garment, for he had, as she put it, gone into a shop and "bought it 'by *gass light* . . . quite desperate about it when he saw it in the morning.'" The cloak was "warm, and not *very* ugly—and a good shape—only entirely unsuitable to the rest of my habiliments! being a *brownish colour* with *orange spots* and a brown-velvet collar!!" But she decides she will wear it. In writing her cousin, she underscores her husband's kindness and consideration in making the gesture.

Could he have kept his courtly love language for Lady Harriet (my Queen, ma Dame, my Lady) a complete secret? Jane, at the moment, perhaps badly needed to cling to the thought of his special gift for her.

In the coming months as Jane witnessed her husband's growing interest in another woman—in Lady Harriet Baring—there was a secret knowledge that would have contributed to her sense of vulnerability and insecurity: the apparent absence of physical affection in their marriage.

In the late Victorian era and beyond, the Carlyles' sex life, or supposed lack of one, became the subject of a vast amount of prurient speculation, most of it based on posthumous hearsay that cannot be verified. Younger members of the extended Carlyle family supplied counter evidence, most of that based on hearsay as well. The debate concerned urgent, complicated late Victorian anxieties about Heroes, Great Men, and Manliness. It involved a destruction of the High Victorian Sage-Father, which Carlyle had come to represent, by his Sons of subsequent generations. What if the great manful author who commanded British literature had been *impotent*?! That highly detailed, convoluted, time-specific argument, wherein many gallons of ink were spilled, began decades after the events detailed in this chapter. Because the controversy did not affect the Carlyles in their lifetimes, those endless attacks and counter attacks cannot concern us here.

Based on the evidence from Jane and Thomas's extant letters, where the subject of their sexual intimacy is never directly addressed, they appear to have had some kind of warmly affectionate physical relationship during the first years of their marriage. They sound excited about being married to each other, writing at times like ardent lovers. There are mentions of embracing and kissing, a deep desire for each other's presence, and fulsome expressions of endearment. We do not know and have no way to find out to what extent they engaged in sexual intercourse.

Jane and Thomas lived for six years on their farm at Craigenputtoch and unquestionably knew the facts of life. There is a hint, at one point, that they believed Jane might be pregnant. A letter Thomas wrote her from London, September 14, 1831—they had not yet moved there but she was about to join him for an extended visit—concludes, "Good bye, my Dearest! Heaven send thee safe to me and soon. Take every care of thyself, Wifekin: there is more than thy own that thou carriest with thee. A thousand kisses; and farewells, which will soon be welcomes!"

No other references in their sometimes-wordy letters of this time hint at a pregnancy, which casts doubt on that interpretation. Yet by *more than thy own* he could hardly have meant clothing or manuscripts. Jane's letter of about September 7 or 8, which prompted his, is missing. Did she later suffer a miscarriage? Had she been mistaken, after all, in thinking herself pregnant?

A little later, in the spring of 1834, shortly before they moved to London for good, Thomas wrote a poem that appears meant for the free-spirited Jane and her housewifely accommodation to life in their Craigenputtoch desert. He composed "To a Swallow Building under Our Eaves" after an Edinburgh friend, Francis Jeffrey, had criticized Jane for mismanaging her life, accusing her of reading too much German literature and being insufficiently sociable. Thomas concludes what he says of the swallow approvingly: "God speed thee, pretty Bird! May thy small nest / With little ones all in good time be blest! / I love thee much! / For well thou managest that life of thine."[14]

Perhaps it is a stretch to connect this little poem about a swallow with their personal lives, but it might suggest that the Carlyles were still hoping to have children one day, *all in good time*. Jane made a copy of the poem and kept it all her life.

Years later the Carlyle family recollected stories about Jane's expressions of "maternal hopes" during that period and relayed memories of her packing up baby clothes. There is a reference to an alleged drawer of saved baby clothes that she took with her when they moved to London.

Despite the closeness Jane and Thomas enjoyed while living at Craigenputtoch, whatever specific forms it did or did not take, a withdrawal of physical affection apparently set in rather soon after their move to London. Thomas at first told his brother, "We sleep aloft, in our old Bed, which is all rehabilitated." But both suffered bouts of insomnia, and they soon took advantage of their spacious new home to have separate bedrooms. Living side by side with someone without being able to express one's sexuality would have been a very great source of frustration. So far as is known, neither Jane nor Thomas had the outlet of a physical heterosexual or homosexual affair.

All that probable abstinence and celibacy has to be taken into consideration. It might help explain her edge of hysteria and hypochondriacal nervousness. It might shed light on his savage agonies of feeling lashed to a rock, or being a volcano that could not or ought not to explode. But in that pre-Freudian era, few advocated sexual happiness in marriage as being of essential importance to the lives of an urbane literary couple. Intellectual soul mates John Stuart Mill and Harriet Taylor, for instance, were said to have a celibate marriage. Then, too, many of the Carlyles' friends commented on their companionableness, mutual laughter, and array of interests in common, indicating a degree of marital equality unusual for the time.

The Carlyles were sophisticated, if easily shocked, and passed on sexual gossip to each other. One example: while discussing in 1847 the French Duke of Praslin's scandalous murder of his wife, the mother of his ten children, so that he might pursue unobstructed a liaison with the family governess, Jane conveyed to Thomas in delicate language a startling piece of information. It was said that the Duke had engaged in sexual intercourse with his wife right before killing her as a ploy to cover his tracks. (Lady Harriet, who had been acquainted with the Duchess, had repeated the gossip to Jane.) In her letter, Jane refers to "Something that took place immediately before the murder—either because on going into her room he had found her awake—and needed to make some pretence for coming there—or—that the *examination* afterwards might prove the good terms he was living on with her." She assumes Thomas will know what she means—and he does: "Good Heavens, my imagination refuses to conceive the unspeakability you intimate; I am forced to believe it a conversational exaggeration!"

Throughout their lives, Jane and Thomas were often preoccupied with each other's physical well being, expressing their concern, nearly always sympathetically, through endless questions about ailments and illnesses, real and imagined. They also worried over each other's physical discomforts caused by lack of sleep, indigestion, and inconveniences experienced while traveling. Countless letters express such intimate anxieties. A displacement, perhaps, but it may have been a way of continuing to care for each other's bodies.

A well-intentioned effort; a hopeless clash of colors. The brown cloak with orange spots that Thomas gave Jane reminds her ironically—she mentions it in the same letter—of a time she had shaken his faith in her housewifely know-how. She had purchased for her soberly dressed curmudgeonly Victorian husband a garment that "made him 'an ornament to society in every direction.'" Was she thinking to complement the surreal blue-violet of his eyes? Did she have a yearning to costume him as the hero of a Regency romance? Whatever the motive, she had presented him with a sky blue coat bedecked with yellow buttons.

And what of the hopeless clash between the lively Theresa Revis and her intelligent, cultivated governess? More interested in men than in learning lessons, Theresa had turned against Miss Bölte. Was Tizzy, perhaps, "small and slight in person" with eyes that "were very large, odd, and attractive"? Had she "never blushed in her life—at least not since she was eight years old . . . when she was caught stealing jam out of a cupboard by her godmother"? Did she say of her schoolroom "I wish it were at the bottom of the Thames, I do"; and of Miss Bölte, that if she had fallen in, "I wouldn't pick her out, that I wouldn't. O how I should like to see her floating in that water yonder, turban and all, with her train streaming after her, and her nose like the beak of a wherry"? Did she humiliate the woman in charge of her education by speaking French more easily and colloquially? Did her acts of defiance include the flinging of an abridged version of Doctor Johnson's dictionary out a stagecoach window? For these things happen in the first chapters of *Vanity Fair.* Theresa Revis was—Becky Sharp.

William Makepeace Thackeray's famous novel would begin appearing in 1847. Several possible models from real life exist for his protagonist, and his characters were often composites. Canny author that he was, he did not divulge his real-life sources. But his daughter Annie Thackeray Ritchie, among others, testified "Miss Tizzy Revis . . . was supposed to be Becky."[15]

We can sympathize with Amely Bölte in this latest turn of fortune's wheel. Not only had she been brought to the brink of death in Nice, she had been given, in a manner of speaking, the thankless task of attempting to educate, civilize, and enlighten Miss Becky Sharp.

Jane later claimed that Theresa's education, which involved having first-rate governesses like Amely, had been too *showy*, placing her in a false position. And she blamed the Bullers for plucking the child from obscurity, then teaching the fetching, cosseted urchin to live in a high style—for when her grandparents died, Tizzy would claim they had hardly left her enough to live on.

Jane Carlyle, who could say to herself at bitter moments "too much of schooling hadst thou poor Ophelia," is not always trustworthy on the subject of women's education. It would have been hard not to internalize something of her mother's views when Grace Welsh, we recall, had believed that *Latin and mathematics were sadly out of place in the little girl's education.* Jane who had possessed dolls enough, and at the age of nine had begged her father to allow her to learn Latin like a boy, later took a strange satisfaction in announcing to relative strangers that in childhood she had been "made a scholar," as if forced, but "would rather have had a doll."[16]

Regarding Theresa, it was a sentiment of the era to feel that girls of so-called questionable origins or lower orders should be taught to know their place in a more practical sphere of life. Complaints were made in the press about the perils of teaching them too many refinements, which would only lead to false expectations and subsequent unhappiness. Literacy and the acquiring of basic skills might be suitable, but even among progressive reformers the full sense of education for women was not necessarily intended to encompass *them.* In an analytical era with an earnest, energetic interest in social remedies, this class-bound sentiment, sometimes expressed non-ironically as "the mania for rising in life," could go unexamined.[17]

Theresa Revis had not been able to take advantage of what an intellectual like Amely Bölte had to offer, but the Bullers certainly bore their share of the blame. Despite Isabella Buller's generous, timely assistance to Miss Bölte earlier on, she was ready to jettison her, the only person who could handle Theresa, at the first hint that the governess might become an inconvenience—that is, sick enough to die.

From this day forward, Amely was indignant regarding Isabella Buller. But Isabella, who perhaps scarcely understood why there should be any reason for animosity, was said to remember the governess kindly. Lady Harriet Baring delivers the most scathing criticism of Isabella. In a letter to Thomas Carlyle written some weeks after Theresa's mother had died, she says, "As for M*rs.* Buller I cannot get on with her at all . . . the most foolish woman I ever met." Lady Harriet, whose own childhood had been lonely, pitied Theresa. "As for the fate of that child—& what can come to her but misery with such a childhood? Mrs. Buller says she has given up the idea of making her an accomplished woman in acquirements or cultivation, that she intends to devote the next two years to developing & taking care of her beauty, for which she has begun by cutting off her eyelashes that they may grow longer and darker." Lady Harriet asked in disgust, "What can one do with such a woman? What can one say to her?"[18]

Despite the lies her little charge had told about her, Amely Bölte attempted to stay in touch with Theresa, to exert influence if she could. But the precocious girl continued adept at outfoxing her former governess, cleverly attempting to turn *her* into a devilish villain by hinting to others of Amely's alleged attempts at *unnatural*, or sexual, influence, probably having discerned in her governess a preference for women.

Several years later (1849) Jane referred to Theresa as "that little viper," telling Amely that staying involved and trying to help the girl could lead her into serious moral difficulties. Jane left that comment unexplained, other than warning the governess that she was "the most indiscreet little woman in the world." Jane advised her, "All you say to Tizzy—out of mistaken compassion is repeated . . .—and you are made to look a sort of Demon lying in wait for her *soul*—so pray be *quiet* if you can."

Many in London society wondered aloud what the fate of Theresa Revis would be. If she did not end up in the streets, as Jane Carlyle had feared, she was to have a wild time in India (after being sent there to live with her father and his wife) where she "produced the most extraordinary *furor* at Calcutta." High-ranking judges, years older than she, proposed to her, whereupon she "refused them point blank." According to another account, Theresa, about whom devil imagery clung, "appeared one night at a fancy-dress ball attired as his Satanic Majesty with a long tail. All the old gentlemen present went wild about her." To jump very far ahead, Theresa was discovered in the 1880s to be living by herself in London, a countess of sorts and a cat lady, in trouble with local police for not properly feeding or controlling her numerous feline familiars that had the run of her house and neighborhood.[19]

Nevertheless, this wild, out-of-control, flirtatious, exciting, sometimes malicious but also much put-upon child and teen inspired more than one literary work. She had a starring role in at least four "novels." In addition to *Vanity Fair*, where Thackeray in a burst of poetic justice, perhaps, consigns Becky to the position of governess, there was his *Pendennis* (1850). When that book appeared, Jane Carlyle said that Theresa was also the inspiration for the character Blanche Amory, though not "*quite* such a little devil as Thackeray who has detested her from a child has here represented—but the looks, the manners, the wiles, the *Larmes* [tears] 'and all that sort of thing['] are a perfect likeness." As we have seen, Theresa was the heroine of Isabella Buller's never-written three-volume novel that she had "wanted perseverance to elaborate" in print. And Theresa is a compelling figure in what amounts to a novella about her, woven like a ribbon through the letters of Jane Welsh Carlyle.

CHAPTER NINE
A FINE EXPERIMENT

"And so these two Women *Green* by name and
Green by nature sat down and talked
like *Mountain-brooks* for a good hour—"
—JANE WELSH CARLYLE, 24 April 1845

IN LETTERS THIS WINTER AND SPRING, JANE CARLYLE DEPICTED THE shifting, changing lives of her friends, who continued to intrigue, amuse, and absorb her. Beneath these social concerns, ambition stirred. Her view of herself as a writer was subtly altering. Might writing become her mission in life? But she glances off that subject, for the most part. As creative development occurs in a shadowy twilight between the conscious and unconscious, her unfolding as a writer can be hard to discern.

The spotlight was on Thomas Carlyle as he worked at editing Cromwell's letters and speeches. Jane told her cousin the "(moral) atmosphere" inside their home was becoming "*sulphury* and *brimstoneish*," portraying her author-husband as a humorous character with a satanic tinge. Thomas himself contributed to the picture, groaning about his Cromwell project in a letter to Ralph Waldo Emerson, and in the course of it blaming his audience: "Such a scandalous accumulation of Human Stupidity in any form never lay before on such a subject. No history of it *can* be written to this wretched fleering, sneering, canting, twaddling godforgetting generation. . . . I am sunk in the bowels of Chaos."

Edward FitzGerald, too, offers a glimpse of the character Thomas

Carlyle, now worthy of being reported on, no matter how unremarkable the encounter. "I spent one evening with Carlyle," Edward told a friend in January 1845, "but was very dull somehow, and delighted to get out into the street." As the door to 5 Cheyne Row creaks open, we can imagine Edward, a bit pudgy, jauntily descending the steps. A rectangle of yellow light shines out into the darkness as Thomas stands framed in the doorway, tall, slender, dark-clothed.

"An organ was playing a polka even so late in the street," Edward continued, "and Carlyle was rather amazed to see me polka down the pavement. He shut his street door—to which he always accompanies you—with a kind of groan. He was looking well—but he says he gets no sleep of nights. This comes of having a great idea, which, germinating once in the mind, grows like a tape worm, and consumes the vitals."[1] The polka was the latest thing, a current craze; and Edward, according to his sisters, was an excellent dancer. Happy to escape the dull, brimstoneish atmosphere of the tormented author, something Jane had not the freedom to do when cooped up indoors in the winter, Edward in the spirit of a jailbreak danced his way down Cheyne Row to an organ grinder's tune.

Edward FitzGerald, who liked sketching portraits of literary friends in his letters, lamented that both Carlyle and Tennyson were currently engaged in writing (very different) elegies of Oliver Cromwell and of Arthur Henry Hallam, which became the poet's *In Memoriam*. "Don't you think the world wants other notes than the elegiac now?" he wondered wistfully. Not as earnest, adulatory, or worshipful as many of his contemporaries, Edward was partly out of sync with his Victorian world. Those for whom mourning was a sincere, almost holy ritual, however, yearned for the elegiac, and both books would meet with a welcome reception. Edward also reported that Alfred Tennyson had just taken the water cure, was unfortunately "drinking a bottle of wine daily," and had just come up to town.[2]

Jane Carlyle learned of the poet's presence in London for herself. When her husband was dining out one night, Alfred Tennyson paid a visit to Cheyne Row. Jane's account of that January evening (written to her cousin Helen) exhibits her own flair for pen portraits. In the course of her sketch, she offers a revealing glimpse of relations between the sexes in the 1840s. What characteristics *womanness* might encompass was under discussion in her circles, and Jane had been turning the term over in her mind.

> "I . . . had made up my mind for a nice long quiet evening of *looking into the fire*," she begins, "when I heard a carriage drive up, and mens voices asking questions, and then the carriage was *sent away*! And the men proved to be Alfred Tennyson of all people and his friend Mr Moxon [Edward Moxon, his publisher] – Alfred lives in the country and only comes to London rarely and for a few days so that I was overwhelmed with the sense of Carlyles misfortune in having missed the man he likes best . . . . Alfred is dreadfully embarrassed with women alone—for he entertains at one and the same moment a feeling of almost adoration for them and an ineffable contempt! Adoration I suppose for that they *might be*—contempt for what they *are*! The only chance of my getting any right good of him was to make him forget my *womanness*—so I did just as Carlyle would have done had he been there; got out *pipes* and TOBACCO—and *brandy and water*—with a deluge of *tea* over and above."

Jane winds up taking flight in one of her dazzlingly flexible sentences:

> "The effect of these accessories was miraculous—he *professed* to be *ashamed* of polluting my room 'felt' he said 'as if he were stealing cups and sacred vessels in the Temple' but he smoked on all the same—for *three* mortal hours!—talking like an angel—only exactly as if he were talking with a clever *man*—which—being a thing I am not used to—men always *adapting* their conversation to what they *take to be* a woman's taste—strained me to a terrible pitch of intellectuality—When Carlyle came home at Twelve and found me all *alone* in an atmosphere of tobacco so thick that you might have cut it with a knife his astonishment was considerable!"

•

NEWS CAME OF other friends. Fully recovered, Amely was preparing to leave Nice and return to England as part of Lady Harriet's entourage. Hopes were high for new employment and the translation of Tieck's *Vittoria Accorombona* was about to appear, yet Amely harbored many complaints. Lady Harriet wrote that when she got back to England Mrs. Carlyle should visit to "hear 'the sorrows of Bölte'—as I don't mean *her* to flood my carriage with them on my way home. She must be happy during our journey & her grief shall begin when she falls on Mrs. Carlyle's neck."[3]

Richard Plattnauer had shown up in London and was visiting Cheyne Row more often than Jane liked, but she did not want to turn him away, fearing it might trigger another episode of madness. All who saw him were concerned by what Jane described as "an everlasting *chase* of strange *expressions* over his face." One day, growing more and more irritated with a visitor of hers, a man with a reputation for being talkative and effeminate (which possibly threatened him), Richard "started from his chair at last, seized the *Cat*—danced her in the air a while like a Baby—then pitched her on the floor—and asked if he might go up stairs for some of his books still here." He "went off—*not* up stairs but down to the kitchen where he marched to and fro smoking and talking very loud to Helen." Jane speculated that Richard might have taken this action to prevent himself from doing mischief to her guest.

Distractions of an amorous sort were swirling about, also. Jane found herself caught up in Geraldine Jewsbury's affairs. On the eve of the publication of her novel *Zoe*, Geraldine had befriended "a learned Egyptian," the way all referred to Charles Lambert, who, after moving to Egypt a dozen years before, had converted to Islam.[4] Originally from France, this mining engineer with one glass eye liked to dress in Egyptian costume and did not dissuade acquaintances from believing rumors he had gone native, even to the extent of keeping a harem.

Charles Lambert had been captivated early on by Saint-Simonianism, a proto-socialist movement that advocated a scientific reorganization of the means of production for social harmony; enlightened new views of Christianity; and the gradual emancipation of women. (One wonders if members of the rumored harem would have been encouraged in that direction.) In the practical sphere, he had been involved in very preliminary work for the building of a Suez canal. A rugged, imposing figure, he was known as a dynamic, philosophical conversationalist. With her lifelong penchant for exotic, knowledgeable men, Geraldine regarded him as a mentor, a wise man from the East; and her emotionally intense and dependent connection with him—it is not clear how reciprocal it was—had caused talk.

Yet when *Zoe* was launched this February, Jane observed that at the same time Geraldine was coming more into her own as an independent person. "In the fuss and flurry of finding herself just emerged into publicity, and busy too as busy can be," Geraldine was writing a long letter to her every Sunday and also translating a new pamphlet Giuseppe Mazzini had written, *Italy, Austria, and the Pope*, which he had sardonically dedicated to Sir James Graham for having authorized the opening of his mail. When Jane waved one of Geraldine's admirably thick Sunday epistles under Giuseppe's eyes, he exclaimed, "[B]ut, my Dear . . . that is *more clever* than Zoe! for upon *my* honour I have sent her last week work enough to leave her not time to eat—and it is all done."

Jane had worried whether *Zoe* would sell: "I wait to see the fate of this book with a considerable curiosity, and with some anxiety when I think how much Geraldine's own fate is likely to be decided by its [publication]." As a favor, to spread the word, Giuseppe sent a copy to the French novelist George Sand, a friend of his. Geraldine had attempted to emulate Sand by writing daringly, smoking cigarettes, and affecting a boyish tatterdemalion style; although lately, as she emerged as an author in her own right, she had taken to arranging her strawberry blond hair more attractively, as well as dressing with greater care.

Once *Zoe* was published, a reviewer commented that it had been "written with masculine energy."[5] Giuseppe, who admired the novel's boldness and cleverness, told Jane he disliked "its want of *womanness* —'it is the book of what shall I say—a *man* upon *my* honour!'" Yet Geraldine was not proposing to turn women into men, but exploring the currently much-talked-about concept of *womanness* and attempting, through her protagonist, to widen its meaning.

With its outspoken treatment of sexuality and religion, *Zoe* inevitably caused commotion, some complaining it was "a most dangerous book *shaking the foundations* of all sound doctrine!" As tension mounted over how it would be received, Jane reported, "Geraldine's Publisher [Edward Chapman] has just been here and said he would apply to *me* to *bail* him if he were taken up for bringing out Zoe!" She did not think the book was all *that* subversive, however, and was amused to find the hullabaloo had assured its sales. As it turned out, the most moral people Jane knew voiced the fewest objections; the least moral professed to be the most horrified.

The biggest surprise: Geraldine appeared to be "in the fair way of getting a Husband by it!!!" Commented Jane, "THERE is encouragement to young ladies to write *improper* books." The man in question was not Charles Lambert, who already had at least one wife, but a different lover (as the Victorians used the word, not necessarily implying a sexual relationship). He was Jane's friend, the free-lance journalist John Robertson, who had been acting editor of John Stuart Mill's *London and Westminster Review* (a position thought necessary to protect Mill's job at India House). Thomas Carlyle had described Robertson as "a burly Aberdeen Scotchman . . . full of laughter, vanity, pepticity [good digestion] and hope."

After reading *Zoe*, John Robertson launched into an avid correspondence with Geraldine. The two, in their early thirties, speedily became infatuated, as a chorus of friends protested their *Midsummer Night's Dream* style madness. Jane had fun relating news of their drama. Caught in the middle as everybody's confidant—including Frank Jewsbury, on the brink of losing his sister-housekeeper—she described Geraldine as "fast taking 'a *fit*.'" As for the burly Robertson, Jane thought he was "*doing* the Mirabeau," that is, imagining himself to be the dashing, rather fierce historical hero Geraldine had put into her novel to give Zoe a worthy admirer. Harriet Martineau, now settled in the Lake Country, also got drawn in, writing to Jane, "I wonder what ill star brought the man down to make love to Geraldine & then out here to beg me to assist them to elope!"[6]

A marriage was on the verge of taking place. Then all went dark, with Geraldine suddenly crying out to Jane, "Oh write to me *can* I break off; for I am *frightened* out of all *love*." Although breach of promise, or ending an engagement, was a potentially serious moral and even legal matter, Jane provided her friend with an enlightened reply: "[O]nly fools marry for the sheer sake of keeping their promise."

It is not clear what had frightened Geraldine. Harriet Martineau, who thought Robertson egotistical and believed he held "doctrines of 'oriental strictness to women,'" claimed that he also had a dangerous *enticing* side. She asked Jane, "Poor Robertson! . . . Can't he be somehow labelled, so as to guard young ladies from him. There was a man in Nott[ingha]*m*, the other day, with a large 'DEAF' printed & put on his hat behind,—w*h* we thought was a sensible & courageous way of preventing him being run over. C*d* not one do something like this to prevent R's riding roughshod over young ladies' hearts as he does?"[7]

Why did they all object so strenuously? John Robertson not only had an eye for the ladies—other flirtations may have been going on—he seems not to have had sufficient means to support a wife. Or perhaps Geraldine, who adored being infatuated and loved both women and men, wished deep down to avoid the fate of becoming a Victorian wife. Unlike Harriet, Jane considered Geraldine to be the culprit; Robertson was a fool suffering a brain fever for allowing himself to be twisted around the novelist's little finger.

A later observer thought the man's primary motive had been opportunism, that he was not so much infatuated with Geraldine as interested in furthering his journalistic career by hitching himself to a rising literary star.[8] Or based upon Geraldine's willing labor for Giuseppe Mazzini, he perhaps believed he could cajole her into becoming his unpaid amanuensis, something he had already tried with Anna Swanwick. The situation is murky, but when Geraldine became frightened and the engagement ended, even though she had wanted it to, she was—briefly—shattered. The Egyptian and her brother Frank, anxious to get his housekeeper-sister back to manage his Manchester home, arranged to take Geraldine to France to divert her and prevent any lingering influence that might issue from the man's enticing side.

Oddly, a lovers-and-jealousies carousel with a larger cast of characters had begun to swirl around Jane Carlyle, with strains of madness in its music. The wives of both Anthony Sterling (brother of John) and Arthur Helps (a literary man) believed that their husbands were in love with Mrs. Carlyle. Charlotte Sterling behaved and was treated as a true Victorian madwoman in the attic, "madder than twenty March hares," although her bouts of insanity came and went. Jane reported that Anthony "had to lock up his wife in two rooms, she having been running about like a wild cat flinging the poker at people and things." Charlotte's rooms were "*boarded* off from the rest [of the house] with improvised planks—lined with *flock* to prevent her noise being heard." A doctor and three trained attendants waited on her in her flocked wallpaper cell, sometimes restraining her in a strait-waistcoat, in stark contrast to the enlightened Moral Treatment methods followed at the Wandsworth asylum where Richard Plattnauer had been.

"[A]ll the madness," Jane noted, occurred "in my sphere—*the idea* of her *Monomania* is, that her husband is *my Lover*!!" Anthony Sterling reported that his wife thought Jane "a dreadful person" and believed he was plying her with gifts, referring in particular to the frugal Mrs. Carlyle's own carefully budgeted new piano and carpet for her dining room. The basis upon which the accusation rested: Anthony had once presented Jane with a crockery jug. Though in truth all the Sterling men, beginning with the father Edward (who had been a leader writer, then co-proprietor of the *Times*), adored Jane Carlyle and made a fuss over her.

"[I]t is slightly annoying," said she who had never warmed to Charlotte Sterling, whom she called a poor creature and unhappy woman, "to have ones name uttered *in shrieks*, before assembled Drs and servants—and coupled with the most ignominious epithets." Jane attributed the madness to the plight of the ornamental wife. Mrs. Sterling had "done nothing—absolutely nothing—these many years but read *novels*."[9]

Bessy Helps, though not mad, had also become jealous of Mrs. Carlyle. Thomas, Jane told her cousin, found her role in these dramas quite funny: "Carlyle is making himself very merry at what he calls '*the judgement* come upon me' and calls me oftener than 'Jane' or 'my Dear' '*Destroyer of the peace of families*!'"

The carousel starts spinning ever more dizzily, motored by large doses of jealousy, unrequited love (real or imagined), and possessiveness. Bessy Helps and Charlotte Sterling love their husbands. Their husbands love Jane. Arthur Helps and also Richard Plattnauer are jealous of Erasmus Darwin because of Jane's "sunshiny cordial looks of welcome, and hearty shake of the hand for *him*." Jane loves Thomas (in her fashion). Lady Harriet loves Thomas. Thomas is becoming increasingly smitten with Lady Harriet. (In fact, the mad Charlotte / Anthony / Jane triangle eerily shadows and mocks the Jane / Thomas / Lady Harriet one—soon to crescendo into seriousness.) Geraldine loves Charles Lambert and John Robertson, who may not love her as extravagantly. Geraldine also loves Jane. And John Robertson—it comes almost as a relief—loves himself.

Jealousy, which can of course afflict anyone in any era, flourishes in a dearth of attention and opportunity. Their leisured ornamental status would not have been mitigating for Victorian wives—Jane had a point about Charlotte Sterling's having done absolutely nothing but read novels. Geraldine, single and a writer, was yet to be fully launched in her career. The only two who appeared to float above the jealousy fray were the ones who could be said to have had the most: the wealthy, aristocratic salon hostess Harriet Baring and the increasingly well-established Thomas Carlyle.

•

LIFE FOR JANE simmered along this spring with a series of memorable visitors to Cheyne Row; further turns of the mad-lovers carousel; and spells of the debilitating colds and headaches that she suffered, even more than her friends, during London's harsher months. Being sick meant long days spent in bed, her nightcap on for warmth, staring at the yellow tassels of her red bed curtains and listening to her heartbeat.

April 1845 opened with the weather "windy, cold, and *clashy*," as heavy spurts of rain struck at the windowpanes of the house on Cheyne Row. Still experiencing a little physical depression from illness, Jane reported that she was getting better and becoming more active about the house: "All this week I have *done* nothing else but drive my needle." She had invented a method for making slipcovers look like upholstery, tighter and neater. Plying her needle to recover the furniture was labor that preserved the household budget; the cloth cost only seven and a half cents a yard. Sewing assiduously also took her mind off her friends' shenanigans.

On April 13, though, having done her housewifely duty, Jane put down her needle and picked up her pen: she began to keep a journal notebook. It was to be an experiment, unprecedented for her, in a more public form of writing.

In her letters of this month, something can be seen of the state of mind that led to this new kind of writing. Psychologically, she had begun experiencing excitable surges of confidence, speculating that she might do "such wonderful things." She tells her cousin about a dinner party she had given, describing the scintillating talk of each person present. Of herself she says (always with a touch of irony), "every opening of my lips was sensibly felt—and Miss Jessy [Fergus, a Kirkcaldy guest] must have gone away with the feeling that she had seen for the first time in her life a woman of superhuman intelligence!"

Jane had been experiencing her familiar push and pull between conduct book behavior and a freer nonconformity. The dramatic tension of her inner life can be traced through allusions and images in her April 1845 letters. In one to John Forster, who had been ill and in need of company, she says that as a woman she dares not go alone to pay an innocent visit to him in his chambers—she must adhere to convention. Yet a stronger-than-usual pull toward a freer state of mind can be seen in a dream-like image from the same letter. She tells him she has just purchased a new "gold pen with a *platina point!* Upon my honour the thing writes of itself! And *spells* too better or worse. And then the Maker assures me that it will 'last for ever.'" She has found herself in possession of a magic pen.

A second free flowing image, this time of mountain brooks, appears in a letter about the visit of a young lady and her mother, Henrietta Greene, to Cheyne Row. Young Miss Greene was "*Lancashire-witchish*" and her speech "had a naturalness and *gumtion* in it which gave the idea of a girl shaped after her own notions rather than the London notions" (*London* representing conventional views). The two women sat in Jane's parlor, talking "like *Mountain-brooks* for a good hour," and she found the mother's gossipy indiscretions a treat. Their uninhibited, uncensored, natural flow of speech—"*Green* by name and *Green* by nature"—captivated her.

They exemplified the witchy gumption it could take for a woman to launch a new writing project. Also, Jane related sympathetically the story of a naïve lady who had been seduced. In other words, at this moment, she found herself intrigued by marginal, unconventional females: a witch, a gossip, and a seduced lady, with the proviso that each was essentially innocent, or behaving naturally. It was *society* that misunderstood. When faced with a new, uncomfortable project, Jane had to let go of a certain inhibition. The links seemed to be: loose women, loose tongues, loose pen.

The journal she wrote in was small—6½ by 7¾ inches—with "a hard mottled cover and marbled paper edges."[10] At the time she began it, Thomas was "busier than ever," as he told his mother, "with the Printers jingling away at my heels [Chapman and Hall had now agreed to publish *Cromwell*], and a whirl of paper-clippings and confusions of every sort about my ears!" His being well occupied was doubtless beneficial to the other writer in the house.

Jane likely kept what she was doing a secret from him. During most of her adult life, she was shy about her occasional forays into non-epistolary genres: memoir, fiction, parody, poetry, and translation, as well as commonplace book and diary entries. With few exceptions, she hesitated to show this other writing or to speak of it. As her husband recalled in his *Reminiscences*, "She wrote at various times in Note-books; refusing all sight of them even to me." When a visitor once had the audacity to open a notebook she had left lying unlocked and read an autobiographical passage—which he found charming—she cut out the pages and burned them. Thomas believed that Jane had "destroyed nearly every vestige" of what she had written in her notebooks,[11] which lends importance to the pages that she did save from the fire.

In her current notebook, Jane quickly introduced her topic: "all the people who come about our house" and the tales they told her. She had been growing more conscious of the parade of singular guests who graced her parlor. Eccentric individuals. Figures in society. Men and women of talent. With her pen portrait of Tennyson as he sat smoking, she had captured a famous poet in prose.

Future biographers were on her mind. After mentioning a wife who had neglected to alter an annoying tic of her husband's (the man would give a "weary '*chick*' with one corner of his mouth, in every pause of his sentences!"), Jane comments, "I have driven more than one such tendency out of *my* Husband, of which his future Biographers will never know to thank me."

The first formal entries in her notebook mark a distinct departure from her letter writing. Though recognizably in her style, the tales and vignettes sound more controlled than her letters. The pace, even when playful, is statelier. The entries read as if she is consciously attempting to write for a public beyond her usual circles of family and friends.

A number of entries are dated April 13th. She might have had a few pieces on hand to copy in. Some entries "are clearly written, with some words or phrases crossed out firmly and alternatives written in, indicating a second reading." (Although the notebook has been published in its entirety, the original remains in private hands.)

Jane narrates in the persona of Mrs. Carlyle, wife of the author, and invokes *Sartor Resartus*, her husband at his inspiring best. She first describes a visit of Alfred, Count d'Orsay, a well-known man of fashion and notorious dandy, noting details of his clothing and the changes that growing older have wrought in him. "Today, oddly enough, while I was engaged in re-reading Carlyle's *Philosophy of Clothes*, Count d'Orsay walked in! I had not seen him for four or five years. Last time he was as gay in his colours as a Humming Bird—blue satin cravat, blue velvet waistcoat, cream-coloured coat lined with velvet of the same hue, trousers also of a light colour—I forget what—white french gloves—*two* glorious breast-pins attached by a chain—and length enough of gold watchguard to have hanged himself in. Today, in compliment to his five more years, he was all in black and brown."

In uncharacteristically balanced cadences, she compares the Count to Francis Jeffrey, the Carlyles' old friend and editor of the *Edinburgh Review*: "Lord Jeffrey came, unexpected, while the Count was here; what a difference! '*The Prince of Critics*' and *the Prince of Dandies*. How *washed out* the beautiful dandaical [sic] face looked beside that little clever *Old* Man's! The large blue dandiacal eyes, you would have said, had never contemplated anything more interesting than the reflection of the handsome personage they pertained to in a looking glass; while the dark penetrating ones of the other had been taking note of most things in God's universe—even seeing a good way into millstones!"

Jane attempted parallelism, tried and true openings, some of them strained, and the insertions of morals, as if testing out phrasing from books she had read to see how it would sound. She had freed herself to *begin* her journal notebook, but was finding her way through descriptions rather stiff and formal for her. One section opens self-dramatizingly: "Mazzini Plattnauer and I were talking of Count Krasinski's immortal activity of Body." (The elderly Polish count was preternaturally active for his age.) Occasionally she inserts a strained-sounding moral: "Pity that Benevolence would not oftener *look before it leapt!*"

The next section, different in tone, shows the influence of Charles Dickens. Jane delves into the subject of those who dwell in poverty in London's slums. How might middle class people who feel the prick of conscience render assistance? What are the motives of charitable givers? The work she has done to find employment for women in need has given her insight into the matter.

She tells the story—another tale told in her parlor—of a Chelsea neighbor, a shopkeeper and intrepid temperance missionary, himself a reformed alcoholic, who ventures into the Seven Dials district to seek out individuals willing to sign the temperance pledge. A taboo area, with its labyrinth of narrow lanes and closes, its jumble of steep-staired houses, Seven Dials was dark, crowded, and dangerous. Two decades earlier, Thomas Carlyle, then a visitor to London, had written, appalled: "I saw St Giles's Seven Dials, and Dyott street: it is a city of *Cuddy-*

lanes [just large enough to ride a donkey through]. There dwell 100 thousand Irishmen, in the lowest state of filth and poverty. Their children were puddling in the gutters, ragged, wild and careless: it made me sad to think that most of them were breeding for the hulks and the gallows!" The Seven Dials had remained distressingly impoverished.

The temperance missionary, as Jane Carlyle relates his story (writing rapidly and sometimes careless of spelling), climbs several flights of stairs to "a wretched garret" where he comes upon "a middle-aged man, horrid-looking with sickness and want—his clothes in rags, and his shoes *tied on his feet in seperate pieces*." The man turns out to have been a well-to-do physician in Glasgow, a Dr. Wood. When both he and his beleaguered wife, a woman of about forty and a drinker also, sign the pledge to keep away from alcohol, the missionary finds them better lodgings, raises a little money on their behalf, and obtains for the man a bit of writing work. After relating his good deeds, Jane wonders: "Can *I* do nothing?"

She calls the burly John Robertson to Cheyne Row to find out if he might secure additional literary work for Dr. Wood. Robertson visits the man, who is out; speaks to the wife; and returns to report.

"Is there any thing *interesting* about her?" Jane finds herself asking, with what she calls "true femenine silliness."

"No," replies Robertson, "—she is a decent-looking very scotch-faced woman with—if the truth must be told—a *red nose*."

Jane analyzes her reactions: "Alas for poor human Benevolence especially of the female gender! how fantastical, illogical, irrational it is apt to be! the mercury of mine sunk many degrees under these two monisyllables 'red nose'! What could be more natural than that the habit of drunkenness in this woman should have produced such 'outward visible sign'? . . . While figuring her with something of the 'interesting female' saved from her degradation . . . I had entertained devout Imaginations of going to encourage her well-doing by my personal attentions." But Jane now wants "further proofs of her reformation."

"The mercury of my Benevolence," she notices, "rose again a little, when he told me she had 'no gown; only an old thin shawl over some sort of wrapper'; and fell again when he went on to say that like all poor people entertaining angels *awares* she 'seemed to feel it incumbent on her to evince *a good deal of piety*.'" But when he reports the wife as saying her husband's daily prayers were for repentance, "*again* it rose—and this was the last variation—on hearing of 'a sort of choking in her throat' when she spoke of . . . those who had been kind to them. Indeed I rather believe the *no-gown* and the *choking in the throat* raised it to the same boiling point at which it had stood before the chill from the red nose."

John Robertson did ask for samples of the man's writing to be sent to him and said he would try to help—but the outcome of his efforts is unknown.

The temperance missionary had another tale about common thieves and prostitutes in Drury Lane who had kindly helped care for a young man dying of consumption. When the missionary cautioned them about their wicked lives, "they told him 'they knew all that as well as he did, but *what could they do*? their characters were gone—nobody would give them honest work.'"

When Jane repeats this story to Thomas, he exclaims, "They could do *this* at least—*die*—rather than go on in such a coil of infamy."

"But dear Carlyle," she points out, taking care to differentiate her position from her husband's, "is not life sweet even to 'the scum of Creation'? Is it not very very hard to make up ones mind to *die* rather than *crib* a gentlemans silk handkerchief?"

—Astonishingly, all the above, and more, Jane dated with a single date, April 13th.

In her last major notebook entry, dated April 27, her magic pen is at work. The passage concerns the unexpected visit to Cheyne Row of a group of Irish nationalists who were law students: Charles Gavan Duffy, John O'Hagan, and John Edward Pigot, accompanied by fellow nationalist Frederick Lucas. They wished to see the Act of Union of 1800 between England and Ireland repealed, and were fervent activists on several fronts.

Thomas Carlyle, who had written derogatorily of the Irish, was perplexed by their desire to see him, telling his mother shortly after, "They are all sworn disciples of *mine*, they say; which astonished me beyond measure. They came to complain of my unfairness to Ireland; I had called them 'all liars and thieves,' which was hard talking! . . . They are all ready for 'insurrection,' for 'death' &c &c I strongly advised them to make a general insurrection *against the Devil* first of all, and see what came of that!"

Jane's account of the visit starts out: "Last night we had a novelty in the way of Society—a sort of Irish *rigg*— Mr Lucas came in before tea with a *tail*, consisting of *three* stranger-Irishmen – real hot and hot live Irishmen—such as I had never before sat at meat with; or met in 'flow of soul'—newly imported Irishmen with the brogue 'rather exquisite' and '*repale*' [repeal] more exquisite still! They came to ADORE Carlyle and also remonstrate with him, almost with tears in their eyes, on his opinion as stated in his *Chartism* that 'a finer People (than the Irish) never lived only they have two faults; they do generally lie and steal'! The poor fellows got into a quite epic strain over this most calumnious exaggeration (pity but my Husband would pay some regard to the sensibilities of 'others' and exaggerate less!)."—With this last comment, Jane is again taking care to differentiate her opinion from her husband's.

Her eyewitness report is written as if dashed off in excitement. As she stretches her sentences to capture life in the moment of occurrence, she is writing like *Mountain-brooks*, in the style of her Green guests, words tumbling energetically with no sign of stiffness: "The Youngest one Mr Pigot [about 23]—a handsome youth of the romantic cast—pale-faced with dark eyes and hair—and an Emancipator-of-the-Species-melancholy spread over him, told my Husband after having looked at and listened . . . with *How to Observe* written in every lineament" that "my Husband was not *in his heart* so unjust toward Irland [sic] as his Writings led one to suppose." The young man therefore decided to retract "the strong feeling of *repulsion* with which he had *come* to him that night."

"Why in the name of goodness then *did* you come?" Jane had to ask.

She continued: "They were speaking of the scotch intolerance towards Catholics—and Carlyle as usual took up the cudgels for *Intolerance*."

"Why," said he, "how *could* they do otherwise—if one sees one's fellow creature following a damnable error, by continuing in which the Devil is sure to get him at last and *roast him in eternal fire and brimstone* are you to let him go on towards such consummation or are you not rather to use all means to save him?"

"A nice prospect for *you*! to be roasted in fire and brimstone," Jane turned to exclaim to Mr. Lucas, "the redhottest of Catholics."

"For all of us," Lucas answered, laughing good-naturedly, "for we are *all* Catholics!"

"Nevertheless," Jane wound up, "the evening was got over without bloodshed."

Actually, though, some blood *was* shed "involuntarily whilst they were all three at the loudest in their defence of Irland against the foul aspersions Carlyle had cast on it and 'scornfully' cast on it; one of their noses burst out bleeding!" It was John O'Hagan's nose, and he let it "bleed into his pocket handkerchief privately till nature was relieved."

"The third—(Mr Duffy) quite took my Husbands fancy and mine also. . . . With the coarsest of human faces—decidedly as like a horse's as a man's he is one of the people that *I* should get to think *beautiful*—there is so much of the *power* both of Intellect and Passion in his physiognomy."

As for the young Pigot, with his "handsome but *fatal* looking countenance," Jane worried: "if there be in *his* time an Insurrection in Irland as these gentlemen confidently anticipate; Mr Pigot will rise to be a Robespierre of some sort—will cause many heads to be removed from the shoulders they belong to—and will '*eventually*' have his own head removed from his own shoulders."

The Irishmen went out the door with heads intact but "*without their hats*; and had to return into the room to seek them; two of them found theirs after a moderate search—the third, the one whose nose bled had *hid* his under the sofa where *I* discovered it by the help of my aforementioned *second sight*. I have now seen what Sir James Graham would call '*fine foamy patriotism*' dans sa plus simple expression [expressed most simply]."

Despite the fierce disagreements, the Irish disciple-antagonists left Cheyne Row fond of Thomas and fonder of Jane. According to Charles Gavan Duffy, from a letter written at the time, O'Hagan and Pigot "declare they would rather cultivate her acquaintance than the philosopher's. She is no longer handsome, but full of intellect and kindness blended gracefully and lovingly together."[12]

The Irishmen escaped the worst of Jane's fears for them. Though tried for treason, Duffy was acquitted on appeal and eventually immigrated to Australia. In 1892 he wrote a book about Thomas Carlyle that opens with excerpts from Jane Carlyle's notebook account of this visit (which had by then been published).[13]

Writing about the hot live Irishmen whose presence she had witnessed first hand allowed Jane Carlyle to locate a richer vein than in the earlier notebook entries. It is as though she had been working through a creative problem she had set for herself. After experimenting with what seemed a more public form of writing, beginning somewhat stiffly and unnaturally, she ended up with a voice that turned out to be very close to the voice of her best letters.

She set the notebook aside and would not take it up again till 1847, but the later entries were cursory. This particular experiment was over. Importantly, she did not destroy these pages. Stretching herself this way had prompted further thoughts about what her mission might be, a concern she would explore in the following months.

CHAPTER TEN

SEAFORTH HOUSE

"Fate . . .
Bade through the deep recesses of our breast
The unregarded river of our life
Pursue with indiscernible flow its way;
And that we should not see
The buried stream, and seem to be
Eddying at large in blind uncertainty,
Though driving on with it eternally."

—MATTHEW ARNOLD, "The Buried Life" (1852)

IN EARLY SUMMER JANE CARLYLE EXPERIENCED A SUDDEN "FRIGHTFUL depression of spirits—giving me occasional apprehension that I was going out of my sane mind." Confused and ashamed, she tried to suppress the terrible mood that unexpectedly waved over her, at first keeping it a secret from her husband and friends. Eventually she revealed her fears to Geraldine Jewsbury in a letter that does not survive.

From Geraldine's response we can guess at the depth and severity of what Jane was going through. Free of melancholia for a long spell, Geraldine remembered her own pain. "I know from horrible experience all you are suffering," she wrote Jane from Manchester in July 1845. "That depression which falls upon one in a moment, enveloping one, body and soul, for hours or days, as it may be, and the horrid lucid interval which we spend in dread of its return, knowing full well that it will come. . . . For two years I lived only in short respites from the blackness of darkness. . . . If the most intense fellow-feeling can be any comfort, you may have plenty from me."[1] Franker than many of her contemporaries when describing feelings, Jane also held back a great deal, which could provoke the more outspoken Geraldine to render advice like, "It is far better to work off your irritation in the due course of nature, and let it evaporate, than to suppress it. . . . Better to scold, scold, scold."[2]

Jane who knew so many *mads* was horrified to think such a shadow might be falling over her. Experiencing sleeplessness and loss of appetite, she believed her condition to be physical—intensely in the body, versus all in the mind—but "*that* consciousness did not make it the less painful and alarming." It only made her more fearful.

Although an aura of mystery surrounds her depression, Jane's letters offer some definite clues. The first sign of trouble appeared mid June: "My house in ineffable disorder and my soul—what with one devilry and another, I have not had an hours peace these three weeks." The Carlyles had just endured a series of houseguests. Her Uncle Robert's oldest son from Edinburgh, a callow youth, had lingered on and on. Geraldine, back from Paris, spent some two weeks at Cheyne Row, yet, calmed down now, she looked attractive and well. But when Amely Bölte, too, came to stay, Jane found her irritating, since as usual the governess's eyes kept following her hostess. And Amely's unrealistic employment expectations exasperated Jane: "She is now gone to a very good situation where she has a hundred a year. . . . I have determined if she cannot stick there; to wash *my* hands of her future."

Another source of upset was her birthday. On July 14, Bastille Day, Jane would turn forty-four. The question of what she might accomplish in life weighed on her: "how fast they come these birthdays of mine! and how little are they marked by any good done—"

It would not have been surprising if she had expressed regret at the absence of children. The late Victorians who wrote about Jane Carlyle and tended to be worshipful of maternity thought her childlessness significant. But in her extant letters she rarely comments on that. When she does allude to the subject, as when she recorded in her April notebook a charming tale of a two-year-old boy she had found toddling about by himself in King's Road, her touch is so light it is hard to discern any anguish. After informing the police, Jane took the toddler home until his family could be located. When Thomas wondered whether its mother might not have *purposefully* left the child on King's Road so that some naïve woman would stumble across it and adopt it, Jane commented, "This was giving me *a new idea* 'rather exquisite[.]'

I began to look at the child with a mixed feeling—of terror—and interest—to look at it *critically* as a possible possession, while little ideas of an educational sort flitted thro my brain."[3] This intriguing train of thought was brought to a close by a knock at the door: the infant's sister arriving to claim him. Jane relinquished the child without further ado, realizing the fascinating creature who had sat on a tablecloth spread over her carpet, while consuming large quantities of bread and butter, had provided her with a good story to tell.

Jane's principal problem appeared to be of a very different nature. Toward the end of June she wrote her uncle, "I was taken to the Opera the night before with Lady Harriet Baring—my *debut* in fashionable life." The party saw Donizetti's *Robert Devereux* and also *La Sylphide*, in which the Italian ballerina Marie Taglioni performed. Though Jane had never seen a ballet dancer before, her perturbed response may indicate distress at more than this particular performance. She was astonished to see "some thousands of the grandest and most cultivated people in England all gazing in ecstasy, and applauding to death, over a woman, not even pretty, balancing herself on the extreme point of one great toe, and stretching the other foot high into the air." After the dancer had flouted Victorian mores in that blatant manner, the grand personages in the audience began tossing floral bouquets at her—twenty-five of them. Jane counted.

Another social event involving the Barings occurred in early July. "I had to dry my eyes and go off with the Lady Harriet to Addiscombe for four mortal days!" Their country place, ten miles south of London near Croydon, was full of impressive guests. The pressure to be amusing, what Amely called "making incessant wits," and the strain of dressing for dinner each evening increased Jane's headaches, sleeplessness, and fatigue. "[H]ow gladly would I have exchanged my Throne-like bed—with cambric sheets bordered with lace (!)," she wrote her cousin, as if the class extremes of the French Revolution were on her mind, "to have had the deep sleep of a Peasant on the top of a dung cart!"

It was here at Addiscombe that Jane made a jolting discovery. Thomas had taken to spending Sundays with the Barings. She knew that, of course, and that they made over certain rooms to him, as they did for special guests. She had not been unduly alarmed. But on this visit she learned a new fact. With seeming casualness, the explosive detail hidden in parentheses, she informed her cousin: "(he has established a small permanent wardrobe there!)."

The definitiveness of *permanent*! Jane now began to dread what her husband's friendship with Lady Harriet might portend, though she did not see the business with any satisfying clarity. It would long remain a fraught, murky, complex matter.

Two years before, in spring 1843, Jane Carlyle had met Lady Harriet. When Isabella Buller introduced the two women at a social event, she had insisted that Jane should "see a little into the thing" with her own eyes. It was already a thing. On that occasion Jane had stood back and coolly analyzed: "I liked her on the whole—she is immensely *large*—might easily have been one of the *ugliest* women living—but *is* almost beautiful—simply thro the intelligence and cordiality of her expression." Jane did not experience the lady as haughty, contrary to her reputation. She thought her clever, witty, and a bit brusque, "with many aristocratic prejudices."

Lady Harriet, in turn, had given Jane appraising stares, and wrote Thomas soon after (a letter Jane saw): "I meditate paying my respects to M*rs.* Carlyle as soon as I am able to pay visits. She is a *reality* you have hitherto *quite suppressed!*—"[4]

Why suppress the reality? It would likely have interfered with the sizzle of a courtly love romance, a knight swearing allegiance to his idealized lady, a motif that had been there from the first. When one reads Thomas Carlyle's letters to Lady Harriet, different pairings come to mind. Not only Knight and Lady, but Vassal and Queen. Son and Mother. Mentor and Student. Sometimes, Best Friends. The two had much to offer each other. He opened up worlds of literature for her. She opened up social worlds for him. The exact nature of their friendship cannot be determined, nor can the degree of Thomas Carlyle's conscious awareness of what it all meant, but it seems certain that potent psychological energies were involved.

Right after that first encounter, Jane had employed the power of her pen to tell her cousin that Lady Harriet was an "Intellectual Circe" and "a very loveable spoilt Child of Fortune—that a little *whipping*, judiciously administered would have made into a first rate woman." Although that image of violence immediately arose, Jane insisted, "I am singularly inaccessable [sic] to jealousy," attributing the emotion to Geraldine on her behalf, saying instead that she was "pleased rather that he has found *one* agreeable house to which he likes to go and goes regularly." While Jane was apprehensive, there was no sign then that Lady Harriet's friendship with Thomas terrified her.

During her upsetting visit to Addiscombe Farm these two years later, Jane's only respite came one evening when she took an hour's walk in the dark with Lord Ashburton, Lady Harriet's father-in-law. The old Tory had a casual, self-assured manner and no need to compete, perform, or fill the silence with inane chatter. It may have been July 4, the night of the ebony moon, when the darkness would have felt sheltering compared to the sunshiny glare and din of society. During that nighttime stroll, Jane said, "I felt myself human again—able to talk." As if she flourished in darkness, whereas Lady Harriet, a lover of sunshine, craved the glare.

It is likely that this June and July of 1845 mark the point where a dark vertical line might be drawn through Jane's life to indicate when the richness of her sparkling London existence was put into jeopardy. In her pilgrimage through life, if the first part—to use Jane Austen's words about *Pride and Prejudice*—"wanted shade," the second part would be characterized by deepening shadows. In years to come, Jane would at times be afflicted by confusing troubles of the heart that surfaced, died away, and returned; even as she resiliently coped and rose to the occasion, and more.

What was not yet clear: with this debut into fashionable society, Jane was to be partly pulled out of her own existence and into someone else's orbit. Despite the Victorian curtailment of women's opportunities in the 1840s, Jane's London life had become unusually varied. After all, she knew poets, novelists, journalists, politicians, preachers, actors, and revolutionaries from several countries. She had relatives she liked in Liverpool and intimate friendships (involving literary matters, too) with Geraldine Jewsbury and Giuseppe Mazzini. She had her employment bureau work; a steady involvement in the running of her own home; an interest in her friend Richard Plattnauer's mental condition, and other medical matters; and an engagement with trends of the day like mesmerism. Most recently, she had ventured on a new writing experiment.

But now—what exactly did the *small permanent wardrobe* imply? Back home in Chelsea after the visit to Addiscombe, unable to hide her low spirits from her husband any longer, she fell into a fit of crying. No evidence exists that she directly confronted him with her fears. But Thomas was shocked by her visible misery. His network of loyal brothers and sisters providing a firm structure of connectedness, he appeared to think that Jane's "feeble, and often dispirited" condition stemmed from the fact that she was "very solitary in the world now." He was convinced of the need for action, and with his encouragement and Geraldine's support, Jane formed a plan to try a change of scene. She would visit her uncle and his family, then travel a little farther on to Seaforth, a mansion on the seashore she had visited previously, for some country air.

Toward the end of July, Jane left her husband in Chelsea correcting his Cromwell proofs and journeyed to Liverpool for a brief stay. In her uncle's familiar, bustling, hectic household, perpetually smelling of roast beef, she became more herself. At the beginning of August she left for Seaforth House, and there found the change of scene that she needed.

About four and a half miles northwest of Liverpool, it was the home of Mark Étienne Paulet (probably pronounced like *ballet*), a Swiss merchant with a business in the city, his cultured English wife Elizabeth, or Betsey, and their three children. (Jane already knew Betsey rather well. Back in 1842, she, Geraldine, and Betsey had decided to collaborate on a work of fiction. At one point, Geraldine and Betsey had sent Jane pages to read, but finding their plot overly turbulent, she had withdrawn from the project, as Betsey eventually did also, with Geraldine going on to write *Zoe* alone.)

The Paulets were renting Seaforth House, which visitors commented on as curiously bare, from John Gladstone (father of the future prime minister), who had built it during the second decade of the century.[5] Mr. Gladstone had renovated so many times—opening up the rooms, one imagines—that his daughter had nicknamed it "Guttling Hall."[6] Large and airy with spacious verandas, it was located in the township of Litherland, adjacent to an estuary of the River Mersey, near where it flows into the Irish Sea, and was surrounded by a hundred acres of tidal flats, meadows, and farmland. Wild roses and sand hills abounded. The winds and tides could be dramatic, even dangerous, but when dryer conditions prevailed, the broad beaches were firm enough to gallop a horse across. Colorful merchant vessels carrying goods to and from Liverpool plied the waters. According to an account written just before the steamship era, if countervailing winds detaining sailing ships in Liverpool suddenly changed course, it could happen that "one hundred and fifty, or two hundred sail of ships, bound to foreign and coasting Ports, go to sea in one tide."[7] Visitors continued to see moving sights: the mountains of Wales might be glimpsed in the distance, also a Cheshire lighthouse. Secluded as it was, Seaforth opened out to the world.

Soon after arriving, Jane relayed to Thomas an instant sense of renewal: "If I am not content with my environment *now*, I need never expect to be so—away from home. I have found Seaforth all that it was last year and somewhat more." The suddenness of her changed outlook suggests that circumstances, rather than physical problems, had been the impetus for what Geraldine called "the blackness of darkness."

Guests at Seaforth were free to write letters, read, chat, argue politics, and philosophize. The term they employed for engaging in a free flow of ideas—controversial ones welcome—was *speculating*. They undertook excursions and bathed in the sea from bathing machines, those little Victorian caravans pulled into the waters where a swimmer could change clothes privately before plunging in. The location on a lonely bank of the Mersey and the relative bareness gave one the feeling of dwelling in an improvised camp. Here Jane Carlyle discovered what it was that she liked: an "unformal speculative, civilized-gipsey manner of life." For one summer month, Seaforth became her ideal place.

In various homes she had visited, Jane had been constrained by the more rigid sort of Victorian decorum: overstuffed parlors and tiresome social regimens, including mealtime rituals involving a constant changing of clothes. In contrast, she lists for her husband Seaforth's civilized-gypsy freedoms:[8]

"One puts on ones clothes in the morning—and has nonthing [*sic*] more to think about *dressing* till one takes them off at night." Seaforth was known for its gardens, orchards, and wandering peacocks. Guests had "the run of the paddock"; all could "walk on the turf instead of the gravel walks . . . *pull* flowers as well as look at them, and *eat* the fruit . . . one may lie about on all the different sofas in all the different rooms—every where there is *freedom* and a great big *fire*." Jane is also constructing an argument: the Paulets' home has an entirely different and better atmosphere than Lady Harriet's Addiscombe. The two country houses stand at opposite poles.

The food at Seaforth, though by no means as elaborate or well prepared as at Addiscombe, was informally served. On a typical day, the Paulet family dined at 1:30 or 2, had tea at five, and supper at 9:30. Jane hoped to put on a little weight and return home "fatter." She had grown thin while suffering her low spirits and was a person for whom two or three pounds meant an altered appearance, a rounder, smoother face, suggesting the bloom of health.

When giving no evening party, the Paulets went to bed early, and a guest might sit in her upstairs chamber writing letters by candlelight until the flame sputtered out, and could sleep as late as she liked in the morning.

This civilized life, it goes without saying, was a class privilege, requiring a staff of servants, seven according to the 1841 census, and a plentiful supply of money.[9] But one of the best features for Jane was a "recognition of *humanbeingism* in the Servants." The servants appeared to reciprocate, finding a degree of *humanbeingism* in those they worked for. "[T]he housemaid," Jane told Thomas, "'recollected M*rs* Carlyle did not sleep with the *quilt*'—'liked a bit of the shutter left open'—recollected every thing—and looked so *friendly* and glad to see me again." Jane's budget for this Lancashire excursion was a little over ten pounds, which included, as was usual, tips for the servants.

Jane Carlyle is setting forth her idea of a utopia, and good relations with the servants form a part. In fact, *the servants* was a topic currently under discussion, and the following year Geraldine Jewsbury wrote an essay, influenced by conversations she had had with Jane and Betsey, advocating humane treatment. According to her, the present system, with both classes behaving badly, was unchristian, vicious, and selfish. But it might be changed from above if the servants were treated as fellow beings instead of as inferiors. (For all of them, it should be noted, humane treatment did not imply social equality.) "This may sound Utopian," Geraldine acknowledged, "but there is no other secret whereby good and faithful servants are to be made."[10]

Important for Jane personally, Étienne and Betsey Paulet were demonstrably glad to see her; and their children Julia, Charles, and eight-year-old Frank, whom they called Pup, were fun to be around. Étienne played chess with Jane in the evenings. When she tried on a bonnet of Betsey's one day, her generous hostess, seeing how attractive it made her, promptly asked her seamstress to prepare another for Jane.

The Paulets kept their guests busy with concerts, horseback riding jaunts, parties, picnics, and carriage rides along moonlit roads. Jane's only real complaint: Betsey kept an *untidy* house.

Jane illustrates the spontaneity possible with a startling account of rearranging her hosts' wall decorations. "[W]hile at breakfast 'a sudden thought struck me' to '*put down*' a Crucifixion which M*rs* Paulet had hung-up in the Diningroom," she tells Thomas, with a frisson of Puritan revulsion at the idea of the crucifixion looming over them as they ate. "[I]t has been shocking my religious feelings ever since . . . [and] might have hung there till the day of judgement had I not set M*r* Paulet on it this morning in her absence—We got a beautiful landscape hung up in its stead."

One day Jane got lost. After wandering over the grounds to the post office to mail a letter to Thomas, she "strolled on solitary, in a spirit of adventure, to try whether I could not *get up a sentiment*, more or less towards *Nature*." Meandering through the pleasant countryside, she came upon "a little boy—seven years old—herding cows—and—smoking a pipe!" When she inquired, the boy could not say how he came to be smoking a pipe and gave her rambling, confused directions about returning to the house. She ended up at a little village named Crosby, and had to walk several miles to get back.

After Geraldine Jewsbury arrived, she and Jane sometimes escaped upstairs to smoke cigarittos and gossip. Jane described for Thomas a day when she had been ideally pampered: "M*rs* Ames came to dinner and staid till this morning—She sung me delightful songs from Don Giovanni while M*rs* Paulet and Geraldine *rubbed my feet!!*—My dear I wish YOU would *take a notion* to rub my feet! it is so soothing to the feelings."

•

GERALDINE REMAINED GERALDINE, though, and human passions, as they invariably do, broke in upon utopia. To convey what transpired, Jane put it in the form of a little drama for Thomas:[11]

It is Tuesday, August 19, 1845, around 2 p. m. Jane Carlyle and Geraldine Jewsbury are seated side by side at the Paulet family's dinner table. Dinner being a blessedly casual affair, they are eating picnic style with the children and have been chatting, joking, and "speculating." Talk and laughter go echoing through the large bare rooms as the light shines in through the tall French windows, and late summer breezes, scented with the fragrance of salt spray roses, toss the curtains about.

The footman Robert knocks and enters, bringing the day's post. He hands Mrs. Carlyle a packet from Chelsea—her husband has forwarded her letters—and goes round the table making other deliveries. Looking through her stack, Jane finds a note from someone who has neglected to put a signature; three brief notes from Amely Bölte; and a thick letter written "in the palest ink." Putting these aside, she fingers one from her husband, which she plans to read first.

Étienne Paulet startles them all by loudly exclaiming from his end of the table, "Miss Jewsbury, what have you in the name of God?"

Jane swivels in alarm to look at her small friend beside her, who is "pale as milk and then all over crimson" by turns. Has Geraldine received bad news from her brother? But Geraldine's eyes are fixed not on her own pile of mail but on Jane's pale ink epistle, as if she could see straight through to the inside.

Jane asks who the writer might be, for she has not recognized the handwriting.

"I—*I* can can tell you," gasps Geraldine. "It is from the *Egyptian* —and why he should have written to *you* instead of *me* is a mystery I cannot pretend to fathom—" Charles Lambert, as John Robertson had been in the spring, is (once again) Geraldine's "*declared lover* for the moment."

Has Geraldine become clairvoyant? Does she see through envelopes? Handing over a different one, Jane teases, "And can you tell me who *that* is from?"

Another gasp. "Yes, it is from Robertson!" And the whole table laughs, even the Paulets' youngest, Pup, whether at the display of Geraldine's occult powers or from the fun of her having all these lovers.

As the afternoon winds on, Jane realizes that Geraldine, an angel so far on this visit, has a devil in her today. Petite but potent, her red-blond hair all mussed, she has been crying, sulking in corners, looking "*daggers*." Later, when they are sitting in the drawing room with Betsey, Geraldine goes a step further and is openly impertinent to Jane, speaking "at" her, Jane feels, with "the most inconceivable rudeness."

Jane has finally had enough. She rises from her chair "in a good hearty rage" saying, "Geraldine, until you can behave like a gentlewoman—if not like a woman of commonsense, I cannot possibly remain in the same room with you." Drawing herself to her full height, Jane stalks off to the library. Betsey, in solidarity, having also had enough of the pettishness, marches away in another direction.

In a scant half hour Geraldine appears at the library door telling Jane, who is collapsed into a chair—perhaps desultorily cutting the pages of a new French novel—that she had "*hurt her feelings*" at dinner. But Geraldine will not specify how. If she tried to explain, she says, Jane would not understand, nor would Betsey. It was something in Jane's *manner* of speaking to her that "that grated on her soul." Geraldine makes apologies, but Jane, who dislikes having her manner mysteriously criticized, is not appeased.

After a bad night of upset and sleeplessness, Jane's anger evaporates the next morning after Geraldine apologizes again, cries some more, and showers her with kisses. She herself has—just—received a letter from the Egyptian, but only a brief one "because," as he (rather sadistically) informed her, "he had spent all his time in writing to M*rs* Carlyle."

That is, Jane had received letters from *two* of Geraldine's lovers, without thinking how this would make Geraldine feel. She ought to have known better. Jealousy was *of course* "at the bottom of the phrenzy of yesterday."

When the party gathers in the drawing room for evening tea, Étienne Paulet, having watched the little drama unfold in his home, makes the final pointed though perplexed pronouncement on the business in his accented English: "I could understand that if *I* made much courtships to a particular Lady my wife might be jealous—but to be jealous of a little *old* decrepit glass eyed Egyptian with one wife already—*that* I can *not* understand."

•

AN EXPLOSION OF what Geraldine herself called *Tiger-Jealousy* had occurred at Seaforth the year before, which had somewhat prepared Jane for the current incident. But the jealousy then had a different cause. Geraldine had accused Jane of giving her "such a *stab* to her feelings as she had never suffered the like of from man or woman," all because Jane had changed her mind about spending a few days with her in Manchester. Scenes and hysterics had ensued. "[H]er vageries exceeded my reminiscences of M*rs* Jordan in *The Jealous Wife!*" Jane had written Thomas at the time. "It was a *revealation* to me not only of Geraldine but of human nature!—such mad *lover-like* jealousy on the part of one woman towards another it had never entered into my heart to conceive—. . . . In fact I am not at all sure that she is not *going mad!*"

It is interesting to note Jane's surprise at the revelation that one woman could excite such passion in another. Yet confronted by the phenomenon, Jane was quick to adjust her understanding of "human nature," promising to go to Manchester after all. Recovering at once, Geraldine could laugh at herself. "[W]ith her hair all dishevelled," Jane reported, "and her face all bewept she thereupon sat down at my feet and—smoked a cigaritto!! with all the placidity in life!"

Geraldine's intense crushes on both women and men could produce tantrums of jealousy like a child's—gushing forth, running their course, finding resolution with the ministration of a few calming words. On this current visit, the two friends were soon back on good terms, and Geraldine laughingly confided to Jane a dark secret about John Robertson. Tantalizingly, Jane wrote Thomas that it was "the most *ludicrous* piece of unmentionability it ever entered into the heart to conceive—I have not laughed so much over anything for the last dozen years—If I accumulate a great many atoms here, as I intend to—and consequently increase in *moral courage* I shall tell you this wonderful history—*from under the table*, or in *some* modest position—when I come [home]."

Whatever the unmentionable secret, it made Jane change her mind about who was to blame for the termination of their engagement: "No wonder poor Geraldine *bolted*!"

•

WHILE AT SEAFORTH, Jane encountered a fascinating variety of people. She described for Thomas a talky, contentious party at the home of the singer, Mrs. Ames. Present was the forthright Martha MacDonald Lamont, who had earlier challenged Thomas Carlyle's old-fashioned views on the subject of women, winning Jane's appreciation. At another point, Jane found herself defending Oliver Cromwell in an argument with a Mr. Yates. Echoing her husband, she defended Cromwell's bloody atrocities against the Irish people—claiming the massacres had been necessary to prevent further bloodshed.

That evening James Martineau, Harriet's brother and a Unitarian minister, sat down on an empty chair between Jane and Geraldine and launched into the subject of "*animated mud*," based on a pre-Darwinian book everyone was then reading (later discovered to be by Robert Chambers), *Vestiges of the Natural History of Creation*. Jane includes this scene in a letter as well.[12] "Geraldine and M*rs* Paulet were wanting to engage him in a *doctrinal discussion* which *they* are extremely fond of—" Jane wrote, when—

> "Look at Jane" suddenly exclaimed Geraldine—"she is quizzing us in her own mind—You must know (to Martineau) we cannot get Jane to care a bit about *doctrines*."
>
> "I should think not," said Martineau, "M*rs* Carlyle is the most *concrete*—woman that I have seen for a long while."
>
> "Oh," said Geraldine, "*she* puts all *her* wisdom into what she calls *practice*—and so never gets into *scrapes*."
>
> "Yes," said Martineau, "—to keep out of *doctrines* is the only way to keep out of *scrapes*."

Commented Jane, "Was that not a creditable speech in a Unitarian?"

Habituated to doctrinal scrapes, James Martineau later invited a popularizer of Emerson and Carlyle's teachings to preach at his chapel, understanding that some saw the inspiring ideas of these men as amounting to a kind of religion. In these last two years, a leap forward had occurred in Thomas Carlyle's long-growing reputation. New editions of *Past and Present*, *Critical and Miscellaneous Essays*, and the *Life of Schiller* were published. Ralph Waldo Emerson reported on "the great literary & fashionable army which no man can count, who now read your books" in America.[13] The poet Elizabeth Barrett (not yet Browning) had written anonymously, and lyrically, for an American publication that Mr. Carlyle had "knocked out his window from the blind wall of his century," illuminating all, and had spoken to her generation in a "soul-language."[14] Disciples, like the Irishmen who had visited the Carlyles in April, were making themselves known in greater numbers.

In a letter written after Jane's Seaforth visit, Betsey Paulet referred to Thomas Carlyle as "the great man of Europe" married to "dear Democratic Jane."[15] The great man designation was surprising enough for both Carlyles to comment on, although Thomas had not lost perspective, saying he felt himself (when in Scotland) "the Smallest man in Annandale almost!" Yet the accolades intrigued him; and as her husband's social position continued to rise, Jane Carlyle's did also. With adolescent hyperbole, Betsey's daughter Julia expressed adoration of them as a couple. To her family, she said, Mrs. Carlyle was "some kind of angel married to some kind of god!"[16]

•

IN SEAFORTH'S ENHANCING, nurturing environment, Jane had perhaps never been so confidently witty, teasing, and playful. The idleness of Seaforth, she discovered, was a "preparation for future exertion, a gathering of new strength from touching the bosom of Mother Earth." The security and restoration experienced there seem to have provided her with the strength to allow certain subaqueous disturbances to arise and find expression. A sense of burgeoning powers, surely intensified by her notebook experiment in April, had both excited her and caused anxiety. Hidden from her friends, an inner life drama concerning what her purpose or mission might be had begun to unfold. Since Jane Carlyle does not expound directly on such matters, to discover what she was turning over in her mind it is necessary to heed the words she repeats and note the resonating memories that arise.

Jane and Thomas Carlyle were, as always when separated, writing each other nearly every day, but Thomas's current comments on his wife's letter writing take on a troublesome tone. At first what he says seems not to upset her. July 26, when she is still in Liverpool, he writes: "Thanks, dear little Wifie, for your delightful little Letter. . . . And tell *me* about all things. No danger of boring me,—my little Vehemence; not me!" July 27: "Thy clever bits of Letters are a great cordial to me; equal to sparkling champagne in a forenoon, and much wholesomer!" August 1: "[T]hy bright little Missives are a real consolation to me in my solitude here."

Jane's letters to Thomas at this time include lively passages of dialogue with her Tory uncle—when he voiced support for Sir James Graham over Giuseppe Mazzini, she complained of his "detestable politics." Yet uncle and niece also enjoyed a rapport. Her uncle was playing cards at a small parlor table with his son one day, as the women in the family silently read or sewed around them. "[S]uddenly the little table flew into the air on the point of my Uncle's foot! and a shower of cards fell all over the floor!—'*Damn* these eternal cards' said he fiercely, as we all stared up at him in astonishment—'*Hang* them! *Curse* them! *Blast* them!—Blast them to Hell!'" Whereupon the assembled group, uncle included, burst into laughter.

Her letters this summer show her talent for capturing character, stance, and voice in swift strokes, and her ability to cover several topics at a great speed. References, allusions, quotations, metaphors come tumbling, as if from several dimensions. Jane Austen's praise of her character Emma's "wonderful velocity of thought" comes to mind. The effect is of a writer sensing her own brilliance and giving it play.

The conclusion of a letter to Thomas provides an example. It involves a reference to Betsey's mother, Elizabeth Nodes Newton, who lived near Seaforth with her husband, the Reverend Robert Newton, an acclaimed Wesleyan Methodist preacher. In breathless style, Jane details the different religious paths that seven of their adult children had taken:

> "What an amazing feeling it must have been for that mother to see all her children so soon as they came to the years of reflection dash off into *new religions*—M*rs* Paulet a freethinker—Julia a roman Catholic —Emma an *emancipated Evangelical*—writing books to show the evils of Sectarianism and how [']all christians' should meet together 'on the broad basis' of *Crayst* [Christ]—Rebecca a strong Church of England Woman—Caroline adhering alone to Wesleyan [Methodism] Noedes an Epicuraean Philosopher and Frank a Unitarian minister!!! A hen beholding her brood of ducklings take the water were a feeble comparison for such a case as poor M*rs* Newton's—Suppose a hen to see one day her brood all take wing one to water another to air another to fire! what a cruel surprise! worse than Basil Montague's damp gunpowder refusing to go off at the critical moment! What '*babbles*' I am writing God bless you dearest / Your own Jane[.]"

When Thomas responds to this high-velocity passage with—again—"Thanks for your charming bits of Letters," Jane explodes. *She* might say "what babbles" but did not want *him* continually talking of *bits*. Not any longer. "'*Monsieur le President!* I begin to be weary of the treatments I experience here'!—Always my 'bits of letters' and 'bits of letters' as if I were some nice little Child writing in half-text on ruled paper to its Godpapa!—Since Jeffrey was pleased to compliment me on my 'bits of convictions'; I have not had my '*rights of WOMAN*' so trifled with! *He* payed the penalty of . . . losing from that time forward my valuable correspondence; with *you* I cannot so easily cease to *correspond* . . . . So let us hear no more of my *bits of letters*."

A memory had returned. Back in December 1833, Francis Jeffrey, editor of the *Edinburgh Review* (the old man of her April journal, who had also become a judge and politician), had written a letter to Jane that caused her to become so furious she broke off correspondence and ordered him to return a miniature of her, even though he had been an important friend to the Carlyles when they were living on their isolated Craigenputtoch farm.

Jane Carlyle and Francis Jeffrey had engaged in arguments over approaches to life. He had accused her of "moping and pining" at Craigenputtoch, reading too much romantic German literature, and not managing her life well.[17] He had a habit of repeating truisms she thought fatuous like "to be happy, and to make happy, is the chief end of man."[18] He wanted her to become more positive and social, less quarrelsome and satirical. The letter that angered Jane the most was the culmination of a series of hectoring notes he had written in the tone of an infatuated, meddlesome parent.

She was a woman of thirty two and he a man of sixty when he wrote her, "My Very Dear Infant—I thank you a thousand times for your letter . . . God bless you, my large hearted, high minded child—for you are but a child you know—after all—with your pretty bits of lessons and exercises—and your magnanimous purposes of *fighting* for your pet fancies—or convictions as you call them—Fighting is about the worst kind of child's play."[19]

In this patriarchal society with its emphasis on the ornamental wife, men often used fond diminutives when addressing women; it was a rhetorical mode. But Francis Jeffrey and Thomas Carlyle had a knack for deploying patronizing, infantilizing words, which they would have justified as endearments. It had been a dozen years since Francis Jeffrey's demeaning letter, but Thomas's *bits* had brought the old hurt and fury right back.

Thomas replied to Jane's *Monsieur le President* letter by saying, oddly, "do not *bore* yourself writing to me." Angry himself he added, "And pray, my Goody, let me call your Letters by any name I like. . . . [I]f I call them 'bits of Letters,' it is perhaps all the better for them, from a soul so sulky, dispirited, dead and buried, as mine now is, in this horrid business of mine [reading his Cromwell proofs]!"

After the Carlyles argued and apologized by turns over his dilly dallying about when he would join her at Seaforth, Jane ended her next letter saying: "[T]he marriage-state" may not quite yet have come "precisely to immortal smash" (referring to German ideas about the institution); but "the matrimonial-question may lie over till I write my book on 'the rights of women'—and make one *Egyptian* happy!"

In his letter Charles Lambert had just told Jane that she ought to write a book about women. As he put it (in French): "Woman; as free from all masculine influence as she can be."[20]

Although Jane did not take that particular idea seriously, the thought of a book started something churning. The Egyptian's remark had given her the courage to bring up the possibility that she might author a book of her own. Thomas responded (in what we might today call Carlylese): "I know not if you mean to take Egypt's Advice, and write some Book? I have often said you might with successful effect: but the impulse, the necessity has mainly to come from within. . . . So we will be content with Goody whether she ever come to a Book or not. One way or other all the Light and Order and Energy, and genuine *Thatkraft* [energy] or Available-Virtue we had does come out of us, and goes very infallibly into the God's-treasury living and working thro' Eternities there;—very infallibly, whether the Morning-Papers say much about it, or say nothing. . . . Greater, I often think, is he that can hold his peace."

However well intentioned, it was the kind of discouraging encouragement that Thomas had doled out to Jane on the subject of authorship from the time of their courtship; he would often counter a positive statement with a negative, as if there were always a degree of sabotage involved. In this instance, you could do it; I have said so. But after all, it is best not to try.

In 1822 Thomas, as an older learned suitor, had acted the part of Jane's mentor. He had pressed her, with her already apparent gifts for writing social comedy, to pen a historical tragedy. He claimed to have found the perfect subject: Britain's doomed warrior queen, Boadicea (or Boudicca). After the Romans had crushed Boadicea's native army, the tall, valiant, bright haired, grim-faced, righteously revengeful national heroine downed a goblet of poison—and expired. Jane, in the process of searching for a literary project, had reacted to that idea in dismay: "I am not capable of designing a tragedy at present—Indeed I do not see how one can make the story of Boadicea sufficiently interesting." It was, surely, corrosive advice to have given a twenty-year-old girl with a playful sense of humor.

•

AFTER THEIR SERIES of irritated letters, Thomas Carlyle did briefly join his wife at Seaforth House. He, too, appreciated the place, especially the "solitary sea-beach of many miles of which I had the run; nothing but a few rabbits in the neighbourhood; Liverpool with 'the smoke of its torment' hanging all in the safe distance."

The second week of September, the Carlyles again parted ways, Jane traveling home to Chelsea to oversee household renovations; Thomas heading north to visit his family in Scotsbrig for a post-Cromwell rest. When separated, each wrote a revealing note to another person. From Scotsbrig Thomas effused to Lady Harriet Baring, "[Y]ou seem beautifuller to me here from Hades then you ever did before." She was a streak "of Heaven's own brightness," a Figure of a realized Ideal. The opposite, that is, of his wife, the Reality.

Jane wrote a note to their Irish revolutionary friend Charles Duffy, which mentions her concern about finding a mission in life. He had just sent Jane a beautiful book he had edited, *The Ballad Poetry of Ireland*. She thanked him and asked, "When *are* you purposing . . . to break into open Rebellion? I have sometimes thought that in a Civil War I should possibly find my 'mission'—*moi*! But in these merely *talking* times, a poor woman knows not how to turn herself; especially if, like myself, she 'have a Devil'—always calling to her 'March! March,' and bursting into infernal laughter when requested to be so good as specify; *whither*!" This summer dear democratic Jane, born on Bastille Day, had on her mind civil wars, rebellions, and the class extremes that provoke revolutions.

She had used the word *mission* soon after her arrival at Seaforth in a letter to her husband: "If *I* were going . . . to take up a '*mission*' . . . instead of boiling up *individuals* into *the species*—I would draw a chalk circle round every individuality and preach to it to keep within *that*, and preserve and cultivate its identity at the expense of ever so much lost giltlacker[lacquer] of other people's *isms*."

Woman's mission, a much-used Victorian phrase, had diverse meanings. Nineteenth-century women from Hannah More to Baroness

Angela Georgina Burdett-Coutts, Charles Dickens' friend, employed the term to confer dignity upon women's philanthropic work. To others, it meant a woman's proper duties in the sphere of the home, and Jane could use the word satirically in that conduct-book sense. But she was well aware of Giuseppe Mazzini's belief. As one of his adherents phrased it: "He saw life as a Mission—not as a search after happiness."[21] To find some purpose greater than one's own daily existence is what inspired Jane.

But what might her work in this greater sense, be? Jane spoke now, dispiritedly, of her housework: "if I do not get on with my work—such as it is—what am I here for?" Thomas responded with a tenet of his philosophy: "all work; if it be nobly done, is about alike." Her criticism of *bits* having finally begun to sink in, he was quick to assure Jane that her letters were far more entertaining than Betsey Paulet's.

But that word *entertaining* provoked another memory. Jane replied, "[*M*]*y mission*—mine—is to—amuse! As M*rs* Basil Montague [Anna Dorothea Montagu, an early London friend] told me years ago 'every body in the world, it seems to me, has *some* mission and yours Jane is to *write little notes*[']! One might question whether it were worth while to 'have given oneself the trouble of being born' for such a mission—but happily I had no choice—I mean as to being born."

Francis Jeffrey's bits of convictions, Thomas's bits of letters, Mrs. Montagu's opinion that Jane's *mission* was to write little notes; dear little wifie, "My Very Dear Infant . . . you are but a child you know": their authoritative voices must have seemed to converge in a chorus.

Jane had proved that she could make her pen fly across the page. In April she had tried out that new type of writing in her notebook, experimenting with a more public voice. Her letters during this period include set pieces on a variety of topics and a surprising number of dialogue passages, as if she were practicing—all indicating flares of ambition, as well as that yearning, upon entering midlife, for a greater purpose.

But just as Jane Carlyle was gaining a sense of her powers, it was as if she heard ancestral voices prophesying fear. It can be very hard to discover the right forms for one's exciting, disturbing creative energies; and Jane was trying to do so in a daunting context: the restricted opportunities for middle-class Victorian women. The promotion of compliant, obedient wives. The culturally-prescribed ban on work, except for the handful of occupations open mainly to widows and spinsters. The lack of university and professional degree programs, and the self-esteem and confidence the achievement of such credentials could provide.

Perhaps most pernicious: the deep, pervasive belief that assertion or egotistical display in a woman was unnatural, like the ballerina balancing upon her great toe. It was not ladylike, decent, or respectable. *Or was it?* A breath of hopeful change was in the air, but we have seen that Jane was also angered and discouraged by the belittlement and denigration that previous acts of assertion had brought in their wake.

During her late summer days back in London, having recovered her spirits during her overall happy Seaforth visit, Jane Carlyle was leading a full and busy existence. Her drop into depression had been quick and frightening, with portents of troubles to come. But most of what she wrote at this time details her London life, rather than interior matters concerning what her mission or soul's work might be. Yet mysterious, slippery, and difficult to fathom, those concerns were part of the half-hidden river flowing beneath the surface of daily life. They would remain on her mind for a long time to come.

CHAPTER ELEVEN

"WHAT IS TO COME NEXT?"

"I wish I might know what is to become of me!—
that is *all* I pretend to—a modest request!"
—JANE WELSH CARLYLE, 19 January 1846

THE YEAR AND A HALF AHEAD WOULD BE A TIME OF CONFUSION, EVEN bafflement, heartbreak alternating with hope. From one month to the next Jane Carlyle could not be certain what was happening or where events would take her—as if a gale force wind had blown up and whirled her into a different dimension where the dreamlike terrain looked at once familiar and alien, and it was nearly impossible to find a footing.

Yet for the moment, restored by her Seaforth visit, Jane had her full London life back. Re-engaged in her metropolitan existence, she was seeing friends, attending cultural events, and supervising housework. Moths had gotten into the mattresses, which had to be taken apart, the wool boiled and dried. She was decorating the lower halves of the library windows, pasting on cut outs of half moons and stars, a better covering than ugly shutters, and undertaking other household improvements.

The Carlyles were enjoying their current separation, Jane's urban, Thomas's pastoral. Still ensconced with his family at their Scotsbrig farm near Ecclefechan, Thomas was recovering from his hard slog of Cromwell work amidst green pastures; while Jane, the sounds of the city humming about her, was poised to take in a special production of Ben Jonson's *Every Man in His Humour*.

Charles Dickens and John Forster (Fuz) had invited Mrs. Carlyle to their amateur theatrical event, which they and their troupe had been enthusiastically preparing during the month of September 1845. John Forster had reserved a seat for her in the dress circle, and her husband begged Jane to report to him on the "Fuz-Dickens dramaturgy. . . . I long to hear the history of it."

On a rainy, sloshy Saturday night, attired in evening dress and accompanied by her brother-in-law, Jane Carlyle hired a fly for eight and sixpence and was driven to Miss Fanny Kelly's gaslit theatre, 73 Dean Street. Though the London season was not yet underway, some five hundred excited, dressed-up theatre goers—Dickens had requested that they wear their best—stepped around the mud puddles and made their way indoors, several having arranged special trips in from the countryside. "The Duke of Devonshire travelled a couple of hundred miles, in one direction, to be present," Charles Dickens told a correspondent, "and Alfred Tennyson (our friend) travelled a couple of hundred miles in another. . . . We newly painted all the scenery; newly-carpentered all the Machinery; and had the dresses (they were bright colors you may be sure, to please my Managerial eye) made expressly, from old pictures; and worked away at it, rehearsing and rehearsing, night after night, and day after day, as if it were the whole business of our lives." He confessed that he had always "had a misgiving, in my inmost heart, that I was born to be the Manager of a Theatre. And now, I am quite sure of it."[1]

On stage that evening, Dickens played Captain Bobadill, the cowardly, boastful soldier, and Forster played Kitely, the jealous merchant. Interestingly for Jane and her friends and their recent rounds of lover-madness, the play explored the theme of excessive jealousy, one of the eponymous humors.

From Forster's account, we know that Charles Dickens rehearsed his part in the manner of a modern method actor. Dickens, he said, "took upon him the redoubtable Captain long before he stood in his dress [costume] at the footlights . . . talking and writing Bobadil, till the dullest of our party were touched and stirred to something of his own heartiness of enjoyment."[2] Jane confirmed that he disappeared into his role: "Forster preserved his identity even thro his loftiest flights of *Macreadyism*, while poor little Dickens all painted in black and red, and affecting the voice of a man of six feet, would have been unrecognisable for the Mother that bore him!"

If Charles Dickens was thrilled by the success of *Every Man in His Humour* and the splash their troupe of amateurs indubitably made—"I have known nothing short of a Murder, to make such a noise before"[3]—Jane Carlyle was less than impressed. She told her husband, "[T]he acting was 'most insipid,' not one performer among them that could be called *good*, and none that could be called absolutely *bad*." Furthermore, the money spent on the production stunned her: "scenes painted by Stanfield—costumes according to the strictly historical style of Macready—*cost* 'no object'—. . . and all this for *one* night." She exclaimed to her cousin, "'To think of the *loaves*' . . . that their frolic might have supplied to 'the poor people'!"

At some point in the evening, Jane joined Catherine and William Charles Macready in the special box Dickens had reserved for them. The noted actor kept to the shadows, since many in the theatre were observing—and smiling at—John Forster's blatant imitation of Macready's tragedian's style, striding about, hand over heart, orating in heavy, woeful tones. (Macready, who had advised Forster on his part, went home that night, after wading through pools of standing water, to nurse a very bad cold, his wife later complaining that the newspapers had been more generous in their praise of Dickens and his amateurs than they had ever been to him, the consummate professional.[4])

During an intermission Jane spotted Alfred Tennyson. She was uncharacteristically dressed in evening clothes, and the poet at first did not recognize her: "Passing thro a long dim passage I came on a tall man leant to the wall with his head touching the ceiling like a *Caryatide*—to all appearance *asleep*, or resolutely *trying* it under most unfavourable circumstances! '*Alfred* Tennyson' I exclaimed in joyful surprise—*Well*!' said he taking the hand I held out to him and *forgetting* to let it go again. 'I did not know you were in town' said I—'I should like to know—who you are'! said he—'I *know* that I *know* you but cannot tell your name'!—and I had actually to name myself to him—Then he *woke up* in good earnest, and said he had been meaning and was still meaning to come to Chelsea[.] 'But Carlyle is in Scotland' I told him with due humility."

•

THE EVENING AFTER the play, Jane Carlyle, reclining on her parlor sofa, is suffering a bad headache brought on by the mélange of gaslight glare, sloppy streets (horse manure mixed with mud), gaudy costume colors, dirty theatre floors—and all the crash of noise and crush of people a theatrical production could engender.

Downstairs in the kitchen, Dr. John Carlyle, present again as a guest, is having a smoke. He has been spending considerable time in the kitchen lately, having made Helen Mitchell his principal confidante (according to Jane), though this evening the maid is off visiting servant friends at a neighboring house. John has been favoring the kitchen because he and Jane are not getting along. She has been complaining about him as—at worst—"babbling and boring." (He would soon take rooms at a nearby lodging house, wishing to escape the bother of Cheyne Row repairs and needing to concentrate on his prose translation of Dante's *Inferno*.)

There comes an unexpected knock at the door, and Alfred Tennyson is standing before Jane, tall, languid, caryatid-like, head threatening to attach itself to the lintel. With Helen absent, Jane busies herself preparing tea. Candles and lamps cast a warm glow, throwing moving shadows of the hostess against the walls as she lays out her very best pink-and-gold teacups and saucers with their delicate, classic design—china her mother left her—and slices of cake.

Her brother in law, having hurried up the stairs to greet the poet, soon monopolizes him, as does another guest who drops in later. Jane does not get much chance, on this occasion, to converse with Alfred Tennyson herself. But despite the several men talking and smoking in her presence, she finds that her headache has vanished.

•

AFTERWARDS JANE WROTE her husband about Tennyson's visit: "[B]y a superhuman effort of volition he had *put himself* into a cab—nay *brought himself* away from a dinnerparty, and was there to smoke and talk with me! by myself *me*!" And gave as her explanation for the disappearing headache, "perhaps a little feminine vanity at having inspired SUCH a man with the *energy* to take a cab on his own responsibility, and to throw himself on Providence for getting away again! He staid till eleven." Thomas, captivated by his idealized Lady, was being sent a message. His wife the Reality had inspired a sought-after man to honor her with a special visit, difficult as managing life's practical tasks was for the absent-minded poet.

Thomas sent back a disappointingly laconic response: "Thanks for the Narrative of the Fuz-Dickens dramaturgy; of Alfred Tennyson . . . and all the rest." Yet his request for the history and thanks for the narrative provided a framed space for Jane to pen a description of the play. To perform her epistolary writing, Jane, like any letter writer, had to rely on relationships with her correspondents. Any violation of their pact might cause, in addition to the more obvious personal upset, a writerly distress; an interruption of her epistolary autobiography, her life's story in progress. A request for a history, on the other hand, was an inspiration to shape a tale.

Soon after the play, Jane dreamed an odd dream, which she also conveyed to her husband. It alluded to a theologian and professor the Carlyles knew, F. D. Maurice. Thomas had once caricatured the man's thought as "moonshine and *spitzfindigkeit*" [subtleness]; and Jane had said, "I am never in his company without being attacked with a sort of paroxysm of mental cramp!" In their offhand, breezy opinion, Maurice was known for rigid, rather loony mental intricacies.

Sadly, some months before, his wife Anna had died after a lingering illness.

Like all dreams, Jane's has the nature of a riddle and a gloss. "I went to bed as wearied as a little woman could be," she writes, "and dreamt that I was plunging thro a quagmire seeking some herbs which were to save the life of—M*rs* Maurice! and that Maurice was waiting at home for them in an agony of impatience while I could not get out of the mud-water!"

A sickly wife; an anxious, difficult husband with a labyrinthine mind; losing her footing in boggy waters (inspired by the muddy trip to the theatre); seeking healing herbs: the dream seemed to hold subterranean concerns about her own marriage.

•

IN KEEPING WITH the rhythms of the Scottish moorlands, meanwhile, Thomas Carlyle's pace had slowed. Although his *Cromwell* index had been sent and required scrutiny, he was busy restoring body and soul. Four local tailors arrived at the farm to make the author of *Sartor Resartus* a new set of clothes: "trowsers, waistcoats, flannel- shirts, drawers," as well as a black coat and a dressing gown. After visiting a sister who had five little ones running about her crowded cottage, he told a correspondent, "I feel least annoyed when left entirely alone, to saunter about the moors here, and converse with the ghosts of the Past after my own fashion."

On his solitary walks he found himself viewing the natural round of country events—market days and preparations for the annual Dumfries Rood Fair, or cattle show—from the psychological distance created by his years away. Yet he examined the surrounding fields like a true son of farming people. The potato blight, soon to wreak havoc in Ireland, was making its first appearances in the British Isles, having spread north from the Isle of Wight and Sussex. "Crop good," Thomas observed, "except Potatoes, which, like everybody's, have taken to rot."

Margaret Aitken Carlyle, now noticeably weak and elderly, continued her affectionate, religious ways. Thomas marked her "interest in all that is divine and noble according to her own version of that." A very different sort of person than his wife, his Calvinist mother was given to dire utterances on the heinous nature of the times, which tended toward the doom-eager and rambling; but when well she also exhibited a strong faith in the protective benevolence of God toward His believers. From her nook of Scotland, his mother took a wide view. Infinity, eternity, and judgment hovered as living presences, a perspective she had passed to her son.

Thomas wrote Jane that late one day, "I drove my Mother along thro' the still Country with the wind on our backs, handsomely enough. Sun was setting over the steeple-tops, Galloway hills, and windmill 'Observatory' of this old Town [Dumfries] as we approached it: one of the beautifullest bright-stern melancholy scenes for me I ever saw." However alienated, now, from his former existence, he was back in home territory.

•

WITH HIS GROWING fame and their increasing closeness to the Barings, the Carlyles were both taking a sharp fresh look at social disparities. Jane wrote her husband about an unexpected visit Lady Harriet had just paid to Cheyne Row in her famous brougham—her lightweight enclosed carriage pulled by a single horse and driven by her coachman. She had come by with a letter to deliver. Helen Mitchell accepted the letter but with her wits about her had lied and declared her mistress was not at home. Jane explained, picturing herself as a Cinderella: "I was in the act of nailing down the dining-room carpet with black hands—a not over clean face—my dressing gown on—and my stays only partially laced to meet the exigency of the occasion." In this hurried note she also said, "I am 'a *middle-aged* woman in difficult circumstances!'"

Thomas wrote Jane about his newfound view of the lives of his sisters. "My Sisters both *wept* when I came away; there sit they, fighting along in their obscure department, amid clouds of children and confused elements of destiny; I have to go else-whither and fight otherwise."

In this series of letters, the Carlyles also go back and forth over who can best describe ambient noise. They don't make anything of this—they just do it—but it reveals how each needed to secure the other's attention, how attuned they could be to each other's words. Jane writes an energetic mock epic piece on the silencing of a dog's annoying barking: "'Bow-wow-wow,' roared the Dog," she concludes, "till the whole Universe seemed turned into one great Dog-kennel!" Stirred to compete, Thomas describes for her the sounds of the Scotsbrig farm: "clogs of women's feet, creaking of door-hinges, masons breaking whinstone." With their marriage on the brink of its most severe test, it is necessary to keep in mind their very great need when separated to receive letters from each other.

To say that the cause of the approaching turmoil was Lady Harriet and the romantic triangle that she, Thomas, and Jane found themselves in, while true, flattens the complexity of what was to transpire. This phase of their story—several chapters long—is not simple, involving in addition to love, the question of work and fundamental issues of friendship, self-esteem, and the position of women, particularly of wives, in the nineteenth century.

Nevertheless, Lady Harriet Baring dominates. Sheer largeness is a theme: her physical height and breadth, the forcefulness of her personality, her queen-like social status, and the impressive multiple residences at her disposal.

There was the wealth of William Bingham Baring's father, Lord Ashburton, perhaps "80,000 pounds a year" as the catch phrase went, suggesting some unimaginably vast sum. Wittingly or not, the charismatic lady could evoke archetypal energies in others, and perhaps experienced them herself. She had a persistent opaque quality, an imperviousness that made her hard to comprehend. And she possessed, too, "a festive nature," according to one of her contemporaries who devoted a chapter of his memoirs to her and experienced her as "so complex a character."[5] She could seem to embody for others their own wishes and fears.

Lady Harriet, as we have seen, had been looming at the edges of Jane's life ever since Isabella Buller, two and a half years before, had given Jane that sharp tap of her fan, warning her to take a good look at her husband's new friend. When Isabella had introduced the women at the soirée, Jane had been struck by the lady's stately presence and bulk; and she had given Mrs. Carlyle those *prodigious* looks, taking surprised notice of her as a reality her husband had suppressed.[6]

Apart from Lady Harriet, though, Jane Carlyle's own life was currently keeping her well occupied. And it seemed natural enough that a rising author like Thomas Carlyle should attract members of the aristocracy. That is what happened with writers of stature, as if invitations constituted part of their wages. But the changes Jane had lately become aware of had greatly increased her apprehension—that permanent wardrobe, as well as the expectation that she would now become part of their entourage.

Thomas once remarked that Jane was "a spirited woman, of very democratic tendencies." Why then was it so necessary for her to become part of an aristocratic circle? How would she fit in? How could she and Lady Harriet manage to get along on an intimate, long-term basis? The exceptionally hard-to-figure-out lady was, as Geraldine put it after reading through one of Jane's accounts, "a moral mystery."[7]

Both Jane Welsh Carlyle and Lady Harriet Baring were witty, intelligent women with a strong dose of what Jane had called *I-ity* in an era that encouraged types. Both were childless (Lady Harriet had lost a baby). Neither fit Victorian female stereotypes, such as the submissive saint that later came to be called "the angel in the house" (after Coventry Patmore's poem, inspired by his wife). Yet each had been raised to respect social conventions.

Jane did feel dazzled by the Arabian nights / magic carpet quality of the Barings' lavish dwelling places. Entering their portals was to find oneself in a fairy tale. She was highly conscious of the honor bestowed. But a nagging worry persisted: "I have an unconquerable persuasion that she does not and never can like me!" In a letter to Thomas about a forthcoming visit to Bath House, the London home of the Ashburtons, she expressed her concern: "I dare say in spite of M*rs* Bullers predictions we shall get on very well together—altho I can see that the Lady has a genius for *ruling*—whilst I have a genius for—not being ruled!"

Thomas responded, "There is nothing to hinder you, in spite of Mrs Buller's prediction, to get on very well there . . . . Persons of sense, with no talebearer or other piece of concrete Insanity between them, can get on very well. The Lady Harriet has a genius for ruling? Well, I don't know but she may. And on the whole did you ever see any Lady that had *not* some slight touch of a genius that way, my Goodykin! I know a Lady—But I will say nothing, lest I bring mischief about my ears. Nay, she is very obedient too, that little Lady I allude to, and *has* a genius for being ruled withal, Heaven bless her always!" He unwisely concluded with a Scottish widower's unflattering sum up of his wife: "She and I did ay very weel together; and 'tweel it was not every one that could have done with her!"

Soon after, he admitted to one of his sisters that Lady Harriet was "a very great, noble and imperious person, capable of being *either* all sunshine of the brightest, or all lightning at the hottest." Complaints of the lady's witty lightning strikes made the rounds. "I do not mind being knocked down," one such story went, "but I can't stand being danced upon afterward."[8]

Yet Jane had other concerns. In this time of worrying over her purpose in life, she was thinking of herself more consciously as a writer. She said in a letter to her husband, "[W]hen I sit down to write, I have so many things to tell always that I am puzzled where to begin! Decid-edly, I was meant to have been a subaltern of the Daily Press . . . a Penny-a-liner—for it is not only a faculty with me but a necessity of my nature to make a great deal out of nothing!" Able to conjure easily out of airy nothing, she could fleetingly picture herself as a productive hack journalist.

To gather thoughts for letter writing required solitude. After Thomas returned to London, Jane showed how his presence could interrupt her concentration: "I have no facilities for writing such as I used to have—Carlyle sits always in the same room with me since he returned, with no work on-hand—and you know I cannot write in the presence of a fellow creature—especially one who is apt to say when I have finished a letter: 'now read it to me'!"

On November 27, 1845, Thomas Carlyle's *Letters and Speeches of Oliver Cromwell* finally saw print. Jane indicates her favorable opinion in a note she wrote John Forster about his *Examiner* review, which she found "quite as meritorious as the book itself—only there is not so much bulk of it!" She concludes, referring to an acquaintance, "As M*rs* [Caroline] Norton would say 'I *love* you for writing it.'" Surprised and pleased by the book's popularity, and the money he received, Thomas discovered in less than a month to his great dismay that he was not yet done. New letters had come to light, necessitating a second edition (which would appear the following June).

On the day of *Cromwell's* publication, the Carlyles were at Bay House, Alverstoke, embarked on a six-week visit to a different establishment of the Barings. Lady Harriet had lured them there with a promise of her beloved sunshine: "One day's sun shines brighter than another on the glistening sea all round our windows. I walk before breakfast & with a Parasol."[9] For six long weeks Jane was to give up what she cared most about, her life in Chelsea—and that was a compromise. Lady Harriet had at first insisted they be her guests for three months, until Parliament met in February.

Having been pulled into rounds of aristocratic country house visits—a different world—Jane did not yet realize all she was sacrificing. But she would now have to leave her Chelsea home for weeks at a time, the way house-visiting tended to be done, and to bear a heavy emotional burden.

She took note of her Bay House surroundings: "a large fantastical looking *New* Building on the shore of the Sea & belonging to Lord Ashburton but made over for this winter to Lady Harriet." Across the Solent, some four or five miles away, lay the Isle of Wight. Jane viewed the area differently than her hostess: "all that body of cold water which immense ranges of windows look out on." But "Inside, it is warm enough and magnificent as money and taste can make it."

The insomniac Carlyles had a small suite of rooms, and Jane was guardedly hopeful, attempting to comply with her husband's admonitions to be sensible. She told her cousin, "I feel as if I should get on here in an even, middlingly pleasant sort of a way. I am not in the horribly excitable state I was in when I went to Addiscombe [last July]—I take things now very calmly—almost coolly—Lady Harriet seems a woman of *good sense* and perfect good breeding—and with a person of that sort one need not, unless one be a fool oneself have any *collisions*—at the same time she seems to me so *systematic* and *superior* to her *natural feelings* that however long and pleasantly I may live beside her I am sure I shall never feel *warm affection* for her nor inspire her with warm affection—her intercourse will remain *an honour for me* never be a heartfelt delight—"

In letters to others, the Carlyles complain of idleness and *donothingism*, owing to the extravagant amount of time the English aristocracy managed to waste at house parties. Although relieved to be away from dirty London fogs and at a place where late-season geraniums and dahlias were still in bloom, they experienced a surfeit of leisure: battledore and shuttlecock, games of chess, horseback riding, music in the evening, a fair amount of staring out of windows, walks on the pebble beach dotted with small gorse bushes. Always, a corps of servants hovered nearby to cater to their needs.

In the midst of the leisure and lassitude, conversations about the Corn Laws took place. Pressured by the failure of the potato crop and famine looming in Ireland, Sir Robert Peel, despite powerful forces arrayed against him—agricultural landowners who had once been his allies—was contemplating abolishing the laws. William Bingham Baring, an MP, began as a Whig but had grown more conservative. He served in the Peel administration, first as secretary to the Board of Control, currently as paymaster-general. Politicians like the younger Charles Buller joined family members and literary men at these gatherings as they discussed, in a deceptively idle manner, the issues of the day, strengthening their connections with each other.

More often, though, houseguests sat around talking nonsense and indulging in spurts of "making wits." They wrote letters and read—the Barings subscribed to half a dozen newspapers. Democratic Jane made herself useful by teaching the head cook how to make oatcakes from meal sent from Scotsbrig (the price of oatmeal had been rising). At Lady Harriet's request, Thomas had enrolled her in the London Library, and he now read Goethe to her in the evening, as he had once done with Jane. Oatmeal from Scotland, German books, the procurement of a library card: they were but tiny ways to repay such elaborate hospitality.

Interested, scared, out of her element, Jane observed and analyzed as best she could. She wrote Amely Bölte (employed again and looking *fat*, or healthy, these days) that she admired Lady Harriet, who was behaving in a kindly manner. But used to intimate, confiding friendships, Jane added, "I fear she is too *grand* for ever letting herself be *loved*—at least by an Insignificancy like me,—I *could* love her immensely if she looked to care for it—" Revising her Circe accusation, she told her cousin, "In fact she is a *grand* woman every inch of her—and *not* 'a coquette' the least in the world—if all the men go out of their sober senses beside her how can she help *that*?"

Closeted in a room reserved for her use one afternoon, seated at a table writing to her cousin, Jane had scarcely scribbled the words "how can she help *that*?" when Lady Harriet opened the door. The great personage darkening the entryway said something like, Now then, come to me and I shall tell you of a thrilling development (one of her famous commands). Did Jane in haste, her heart beating fast, cover what she had just written with the palm of her hand?

As she described the scene, "Lady Harriet opened my bedroom door and asked me to come into her dressingroom to hear great news—*not* the repeal of the cornlaws—but that *snow* had fallen to day near Winchester—whilst here we have had almost summer sunshine."

When Jane finally, gratefully, returned home to Chelsea on December 26, life became at once busier and more peaceful. She tried to evaluate. To her cousin Jeannie she gave voice to the misery she had experienced during the holidays at Bay House, intensified as always by anniversary feelings: "Your letter and the beautiful purse were a great Godsend to me on the Christmas morning—it was my only letter—and away there—amongst entirely new people and new things I felt dreary to death on that day, so unlike any Christmas day that I had ever lived before." She wrote Mary Russell of Thornhill, who had known her mother, "This Lady Harriet Baring whom we have just been staying with is the very cleverest woman—out of sight—that I ever saw in my life—(and I have seen all our 'distinguished Authoresses') moreover she is full of energy and sincerity—and has I am quite sure an excellent heart—yet so perverted has she been by the training and life long humouring incident to her high position that I question if in her *whole life* she have done as much for her fellow creatures as *my mother* in *one year* . . . . The sight of such a woman should make one very content with one's own trials even when they feel to be rather hard!"

Jane goes back and forth, her perceptions of Lady Harriet unstable. How can you know another person, really? Especially one encompassing so many aspects? She can only be sure of one thing: beneath it all she is upset and uneasy.

•

DURING THE FIRST months of 1846, her friends were preoccupied with their own concerns, leaving her without the cushion of support she customarily had. Jane needed her friends to confide in and talk through her perplexities, although concerning her husband's friend she would have had to be discreet.

Harriet Martineau was still writing Jane letters that she found *very nice* while acknowledging that Thomas would consider them twaddle. In fact, Harriet wrote to him, also, pressing her case for mesmerism in a manner sure to annoy. But occupied with building her dream house, The Knoll, in Ambleside, Harriet Martineau was slowly fading from the Carlyles' lives. Betsey and Étienne Paulet were in London so that he could have eye surgery. Jane was seeing them and their doctor appointments were going fairly well; but the city, not Betsey's natural milieu, made her nervous and edgy. She and Jane were not at ease with each other here, as they had been at Seaforth. The Macreadys, too, were absorbed by their family and his work, though the actor took time to send theatre tickets to the Carlyles.

Richard Plattnauer came and went. He would appear very well, then deeply troubled. Jane now understood this would be a pattern all his life. After she tried talking stern sense to him, Richard, in an especially pale, unkempt phase, began avoiding her.

In March a most startling event occurred. With Queen Victoria soon to give birth to another baby, Richard Plattnauer forced his way into Buckingham Palace! He had conjured up the notion that the queen had summoned him there, requiring his assistance during her confinement, apparently as midwife. He "knocked down one of the ushers" at the palace and was soon apprehended and hauled off to the Marlborough police office. The police must have realized the man was mentally disturbed, and possibly influential friends intervened, because although Jane searched for it, she did not find his name in the newspapers. Richard then went to France determined to carry out grandiose political work. He was going to "settle Poland." The "very man for *actually* shooting Louis Philip[p]e" Jane commented sarcastically, referring to a recent attempt on the life of the unpopular French king. At least,

Richard had told a friend he met on a London street that he was going to Paris—had he only imagined his travels?

Jane knew that if worse came to worst, he would be sent back to Wandsworth and receive adequate care. If he seemed friendless and homeless, it would be easier for him to gain admittance to the asylum, intended for paupers. With Thomas twisted in agony over his second edition of Cromwell and needing quiet, Jane dared not invite Richard to stay in their house again.

When Giuseppe Mazzini visited or they strolled together in Chelsea, she worried about him also because of the slow, torturous, dangerous path toward the liberation and unification of Italy. "Mazzini does not go mad—but I do not know whether it would not be better for him if he could,—these long many years of failed hopes and destroyed illusions seem to be taking effect on him—not on his health—or sanity—but on his *temper*—he is grown so *captious* and *silently irritable* that one knows not what to make of him—every word one says provokes a contradiction or a reproach."

As for Geraldine, she had developed a sudden, highly annoying (to Jane) crush on the American actress Charlotte Cushman, who had gone on tour in England, playing the part of Romeo to her sister's Juliet. Geraldine had met the actress in Manchester. In response to what Jane considered a ridiculously infatuated letter ("Geraldine . . . is all in a blaze of enthusiasm about Miss Cushman"), she gave her friend "such a screed of my mind as she never got before." Jane sounds jealous herself. She apparently accused Geraldine of the *habit* of spouting meaningless, gushy, fickle sentiments in the course of her rotating affections for various women and men. And perhaps of hypocrisy: falling for Charlotte Cushman at the very moment she had been professing to be jealous of Jane's friendship with Betsey Paulet. (Since Geraldine destroyed most of Jane's letters, it is necessary to guess at Jane's words from her friend's replies, or from what Jane told others.) "It is no good your getting up a theory about me," Geraldine responded. "I was born to drive theories and rules to distraction, and I want to beat yours to powder and then stamp upon it."[10]

More calmly, the two women discussed Geraldine's journalism. She had begun to write more often for periodicals, a necessity if she was to earn her living, and discovered that she enjoyed balancing novel writing with this different sort of work. Hesitantly at first, she sent her drafts to Jane. When Jane responded, including critical comments solicited from journalist friends, Geraldine expressed her gratitude. "I am so glad you like that little essay," she wrote, "—more glad than I can tell you . . . because I was afraid you did not care for that sort of subject." The piece may have been "Hiring Servants," which Geraldine wrote for *Douglas Jerrold's Shilling Magazine*. She now came to a decision: "I shall send you everything without misgiving."[11] Jane had become her official first reader, even for minor pieces.

As Thomas Carlyle labored over his second Cromwell edition, Amely Bölte reported that he was not "in the rosiest of moods,"[12] and a young visitor, Caroline Fox, scribbled in her journal that Mr. Carlyle looked thin and was "grumbling at all Institutions."[13] At one point he proclaimed a desire to go live in the countryside; and Lady Harriet issued an imperious invitation to Jane to join her in Rome the following winter. In this context with her future uncertain—were they to move? would she be traveling to the Continent?—Jane exclaimed to her cousin, "I wish I might know what is to become of me!"

In the next moment, though, her tone alters. She announced she was on improved terms with Lady Harriet, who had been sending her carriage for Jane. First impressions were changing. Although the lady never said outright that she liked someone, Jane believed her behavior told a different story: "she proves by all her behavior that she is rather fond of me—the mere fact of her having *kissed* me at parting and meeting again proves more affection for me than twenty reams of protestations from a Geraldine would do—for her Ladyship is *sincere* to death—and would think much less of boxing the ears of a person indifferent to her than of kissing her! for my part I *love* her now as much [as] I *admired* her in the beginning— She is the only woman of *Genius* I have found amongst all our pretenders to it."

Jane's saying *I love her now* made Geraldine (in Manchester) and Betsey (still in London) jealously fear that they might be in danger of losing their favorite friend. Jane Carlyle and Lady Harriet Baring appeared to be on the verge of an extraordinary female friendship that might overpower all others. In this era of separate spheres and constricted opportunities, women depended upon close friendships with each other for the very breath of life—love, intellectual stimulation, self-expression, entertainment. With other women, a rich private world of warmth and shared confidences could be created. That might be true in any age, but there was an aspect of the harem to this Victorian sisterhood, essential bonds of survival formed in enclosed spaces. Any new addition might threaten disruption.

Geraldine begged Jane for details of Lady Harriet, bursting out with "I would give anything to see her." She promised *not* to throw a tantrum this time: "I do really feel pleased that you have someone near at hand to love, and who desires to be loved by you. What you tell me interests me very much . . . . [D]on't fear [my] making an explosion of jealousy."

Lady Harriet had a mother, the dowager Lady Sandwich. But as an upper-class child brought up in echoing nursery quarters by governesses and servants, some unpleasant, even cruel, she had *felt* motherless. Attempting to analyze, Geraldine said, "Some fine day [Lady Harriet] will let you inside that moral mystery. . . . She was not brought up by a mother, you once told me, and that's the secret of her! She was not treated kindly, and was driven within herself, and then she had no one to trust. . . . There is something hard, not natural, in all women who have had no mother!"[14] Because her own mother had died young, Geraldine had pondered the subject.

She now repeated what Betsey Paulet had finally concluded: "though she thought you had begun to care for Lady [Harriet], she felt sure you could care for us all the same."[15] When she next wrote, Geraldine declared that Jane's new friendship might even strengthen her self-esteem: "I am very thankful you have got her . . . . [S]he has had long practice in standing on her own basis—and it's like learning to stand on ship-board, one's 'life-legs' are as apt to come to one as one's 'sea-legs.'" The lady, Geraldine imagined, "cares a great deal more for you than you suspect . . . . Go on telling me about her, because I feel as if anybody who belongs to you concerns me too."[16] More than anything, she wanted Jane's letters to keep coming.

Thomas Carlyle was now writing to Lady Harriet ever more effusively. "Sunday, yes my Beneficent, it shall be then:—the dark man shall again see the daughter of the Sun, for a little while; and be illuminated, as if he were not dark! . . . My wife will follow, on Monday or on Tuesday, according to your will." In closing he said, "Adieu my sovereign Lady. Take care of these ugly foggy evenings; we cannot quite afford to have you unwell! Also be patient with the dark man, who is forever loyal to you. / Yours to command / T. C."

His discourse with the lady, falling into courtly love cadences, reveals his need to worship a woman he can imagine, or play at viewing, as a goddess with powers over him. With Margaret Aitken Carlyle now frail and declining in health—having become, that is, another Reality—it may have been difficult to maintain his early, necessary idealization of her. He told himself that his mother's love for him had been unqualified. He actually wrote his mother this spring saying, "[You] would have loved me ever truly, had I been reduced to beg my bread, nay I suppose to die on the gallows! It is not every one that has such a Mother." He had perhaps transferred early feelings for his mother, who had loved and managed (and punished) him, to the Lady.

For a friendship involving that degree of adoration, he might have felt an urgent, helpless need. Erasmus and Charles Darwin both spoke, half seriously, of the lover in subjugation to the beloved as being a Negro slave.[17] Thomas describes himself to Lady Harriet as the dark man, implying a romantic, wild, Byronic (satanic), rough, disturbed figure. There are implications in this of a different race—such intoxicating images in a time of Empire being always at hand. The dark man is not a pale, etiolated Anglo-Saxon. A large, strong, beautiful, merciful (at least to him) woman, capable of unqualified love, might force the dark man into a sunnier orbit.

The sun imagery had originated with her. Lady Harriet comes to life in the light, yearns for trips to southerly regions (*going to meet the sun* as she puts it), and describes sunny scenes from the South of France. "[T]oday was the most glorious day that ever shone in the heavens," she had written Mr. Carlyle the previous year. "Such a sun & sea that but for the food of mellow light on the horizon would have looked like a teaboard so deep and bright a blue—I started on a kind of long, lank, tumble-about Sun beam I have got here, for a long ride, up rocky paths and thro' olive grounds & vineyards."[18]

All who described Lady Harriet attested to what her portraits, too, reveal: she was far from conventionally beautiful. Thomas agreed, yet flatters her, "Blessings on your bonny face . . . . Surely you are the best of women . . . . wise and kind now and always."

It seems highly unlikely that Jane knew specific details of these notes. As he was writing them, Jane was portraying Lady Harriet as: "The *wittiest* and most high-bred woman of her time—a woman who is a sort of queen in London society—and *deservedly*." Soon after, Thomas wrote to his brother, "Jane is gone up to Lady Harriet's tonight; the Lady sends her carriage of an evening for Jane, and they spend a couple of hours, talking, reading a thought of German (this I believe is rather *rare*), more frequently playing *chess*." (There is no record of who won the chess games.)

All appeared well. Then on March 10 Jane wrote her cousin that "in a world where one meets [the Devil] at every turn, one may as well take a little arsnic at once and spare oneself the sin and sorrow of being nothing but a Spooney [fool] in Gods universe." She had been experiencing terrible insomnia. "The consequence was such a state of nervous excitation as nobody ever saw in me before—Carlyle declares me to have been 'quite mad' for half an hour—and I can well believe him—I have for a long while back been dreadful haunted with the apprehension of going *mad* some day."

It was a recapitulation of her depressed state the summer before. Jane continued to hear about instances of madness: Charlotte Sterling had suffered another episode. She had, it was said, gone mad in Rome and "*exposed her person* before the male servants." Her husband Anthony had to bring her home by force, at great expense. Furthermore, Edward FitzGerald would soon worry aloud that Thomas Carlyle, whom he and Alfred Tennyson one day heard railing savagely against bishops, might be going mad. Although in declaring bishops to be (according to Edward) "ever so many rows of stupid, fetid, animals in cauliflower wigs—and clean lawn sleeves—" (etc. etc.),[19] Thomas may have believed himself in good Miltonic argumentative tradition, braced by Scottish exaggerative humor. But even when *mad* was used loosely or glibly, behind it lay genuine fears that a slim wavering line, only, separated the sane from the insane. Jane's words "I have for a long while back been dreadful haunted with the apprehension of going *mad* some day" have a ring of childlike fearfulness.

In the arsenic letter she announces, calmly, another country house visit. "On the 20th [of March] I am going with Lady Harriet to Addiscombe for a month. [A]nd that will be good for me I suppose. . . . We two *women* go alone. . . . I profess never to this hour to have arrived at a complete understanding of her—but *that* I fancy is just a part of her fascination—the insoluble phsycological [sic] puzzle which she is and bids fair to remain for me!"

Addiscombe Farm being only half an hour from London by railway, the city remained accessible. With amazement, Thomas remarked on what he was witnessing in his lifetime: "One is now free to go almost anywhither; railways are ready for one everywhere." Wednesdays Lady Harriet could travel to London for her drawing lessons, and Jane could stop by Cheyne Row to keep her household account books up to date. The lady's efficient brougham would also be traveling back and forth: if Jane wanted the latest issue of *Douglas Jerrold's Shilling Magazine* in order to read Geraldine's articles, or any journal, the coachman could deliver it to Addiscombe Farm. Thomas Carlyle, Bingham Baring, and Charles Buller were to join the women on weekends.

On the eve of her Addiscombe visit, Jane Carlyle quarreled again with Amely Bölte, but in a mean-spirited manner. Tired to death of letters complaining of the governess's employers—the latest had spoken of some "devilish slight and malice"[20]—Jane thought her too quick to blame Cruel Destiny when she might instead try exercising patience and common sense. Amely, she told a correspondent, was "much esteemed in every family she has lived in—but too *exacting* ever to be content with the best treatment that one can get *in a conditional* World." In saying this, Jane overlooked the Bullers' cruel and negligent treatment of Amely in Nice, when she had been on the verge of death.

When the governess wanted to come by for a visit, Jane, busy packing, wrote in irritation, "I cannot ask you to come this evening for we are to dine at the Ashburtons' and the day is not looking as if it would permit me to call for you. . . . I would have answered your last note, if I had seen any probability of doing the least good by repeating the same thing over and over again . . . when I have once had my say I feel an absolute need of having done with it." Did Jane's new friendship with a member of the aristocracy mean she had no time for a governess? Amely, who had just expressed extravagant admiration for Mrs. Carlyle in a letter to Varnhagen, was hurt, and Jane knew that she was.

At Addiscombe, Jane Carlyle included in a letter one of the violent images that seemed to accrue to Lady Harriet: ear boxing, whippings, hot lightning strikes. "I have been here for a week with Lady Harriet Baring," she wrote Thomas's mother, "whom you have doubtless heard Carlyle speak of with enthusiasm. A very clever woman, and very lovable besides—whom it is very pleasant to live with—if she likes you—and if she does not like you, she would blow you up with gunpowder rather than be bored with your company."

Though claiming things had gone well, by the end of this stay Jane said she had "a mind all churned into froth." When she returned to Chelsea, Lady Harriet sent her a scarf from India. "She rails at *sentiment*," Jane wrote her cousin, "and never puts any into her *words* but it peeps out often enough in her *actions*. She would not put an *affectionate* sentence in her letters for the world but she will put *violets*—leaves of *the flowers one likes*—sometimes sends me envelopes by post containing nothing else!!"

Kisses, India scarves, violet petals in envelopes, and, on Jane's part, some extravagant praise: these two women who had not chosen to be friends, but had been forced together because of their connection to Thomas Carlyle, were making impressive efforts to get along.

Or was some subtle, dangerous game being played? Undertones and subtexts ripple beneath the surface. "So my aristocratic *connexion* goes on extending itself," Jane concluded. "*Ach Gott*! If I had not such an eternal hund[red]weight of leaden thoughts on my heart I might live *pleasantly* as other people do but once for all life is *not* pleasant for me and the best I see in it is that it does not last very long[.]" Her visit with the psychological puzzle has gone well yet she is grateful life is short? Jane could not or would not explain further. She seemed, still, to hold out a hope that Lady Harriet might be brought to genuinely care for her.

Writing her cousin Helen after her return to London, Jane penned a critique of the aristocratic way of life. She must have been thinking the subject through during her visit. In a light self-deprecating manner, she identified the genre, with its penetrating observations of social class: it is *a moral essay*.

"The more I see of aristocratic life," this excellent essay-letter begins, "the more I wonder how people with the same system of nerves as oneself, and with the same human needs, can keep themselves alive in it—and *sane!* Lady Harriet especially, who is the woman of largest intellect I have ever seen—how *she* can reconcile herself to a life which is after all a mere dramatic representation, however successful, fills me with astonishment and *a certain* sorrow. . . . [A]nd nobody, I fancy knows till he try how difficult it is to tear himself loose from the network of Lilliput[i]an packthreads in which our nobility grow up from their earliest days. [A] *poor* woman has enough of serious occupation cut out for her by the nature of things—sometimes *more* than is good for her—and therein lies *her* grievance—[.] [W]e in *our* sphere have also something given us to *do*—how far it may suit our taste is another question and a secondary one—we see at least how our activity may be turned to account better or worse. [B]ut a great Lady—should *she* take a notion to wrap herself in a blanket and go to sleep like *Beauty* for a hundred years; what would stand still that needs to go forward?—only herself!—and should she take the better notion to put away Great-Lady-things and lead a rational useful life how is she to set about it? how extricate herself from the imposed *do-nothingism* of her *position?*— As Lady Harriet herself once said to me 'one would have to begin by quarrelling with all one's husband's relations and one's own' . . . No! it is not *easy* for a Great Lady in these days to be anything but 'an ornament to Society in every direction,' and *that* her Ladyship succeeds in being—to perfection!"

Jane concludes, "Now, what has tempted me into this moral-essay style, I have not the slightest conception!—when I sat down to write I did not feel at all *preachingly*-disposed[.] But I am in the habit of letting my pen go its own way, and this is the way it has gone." She must have been pleased with what she had written. An epistolary essay like this renders ridiculous patronizing phrases about charming bits of letters.

Jane could now see that even Lady Harriet, caught in intricate aristocratic nets, was affected by the ban on work and the necessity of being an ornament to Society. It is fascinating that Lady Harriet had confided to Jane Carlyle that in order to discover *her* purpose in life, "one would have to begin by quarrelling with all one's husband's relations and one's own." The unconventional opinions the women shared illustrate the potential for a friendship that others saw.

As if Jane had not difficulties enough, her husband again spoke of taking a house in the country. Worse, when feeling unwell he hinted darkly at returning to Scotland to live. "I feel myself no longer in a *home* but in a *tent*," Jane complained, "to be struck any day that the commanding officer is sufficiently bilious." Like many a Victorian wife, she was a private in her husband's army; if he issued marching orders she would be forced to obey. She might put her foot down about minor matters, but what could she do if her husband, the breadwinner and property owner, should resolutely announce it was mandatory to leave London for the sake of his work? "What is to come next," she said, "Heaven knows—"

She was bemused when others failed to discern her mood. When she called at the Macreadys one day in May and told stories about

Thomas's horse, she made all of them laugh. (Because his horse Bobus was proving restive and expensive to stable, he was planning to sell it; the growing number of railway crossings—because trains scared horses—had been making horseback riding much less enjoyable.)

Jane wrote her cousin: "By and by M*rs* Macready, who is in the family-way began to talk of the dreadful 'depression of spirits' she occasionally laboured under—'Ah said I, everyone I suppose has their own fits of depression to bear up against if the truth were told' – 'Do you say so' said Miss Macready [the actor's sister]— 'Oh no surely!—some people are never out of spirits—*yourself* for example I really believe you do not know what it is to be ever sad for a minute!!! one never sees you that you do not keep one in fits of laughter!' I made no answer—but congratulated myself on having played my part so well."

As a writer and conversationalist, Jane Carlyle was in essence a comedian, not a tragedian. Humor, wit, satire, parody, the mock epic form, and irony—especially irony—were her modes. She often entertained people and made them laugh, a gift her friends enjoyed and appreciated. It defined her. But the difference is the fundamental stance one takes toward life's trials. Comedian and tragedian may see the world from sharply different angles but they see the same sort of world—as Samuel Johnson put it, a world that is too often "bursting with sin and sorrow."

Jane ends her Macready story with a cry of the heart concerning not Lady Harriet but her own purpose in life, showing how much that question remained on her mind. "I wish I could find some hard work I *could* do—and saw any sense in doing— If I do not soon it will be the worse for me—"

She intuited, correctly, that one way or another serious trouble was approaching. One thinks of *Macbeth*: "Something wicked this way comes."

CHAPTER TWELVE
"THREATENING SHIPWRECK"

"Ah, sad and strange as in dark summer dawns
The earliest pipe of half-awakened birds
To dying ears, when unto dying eyes
The casement slowly grows a glimmering square;
So sad, so strange, the days that are no more."
—ALFRED TENNYSON, "Tears, Idle Tears"

TOWARD THE END OF JUNE 1846, OR THE BEGINNING OF JULY, THE Carlyles had a bitter, angry quarrel. The threat of *shipwreck*, or separation, hovered in the air. Since their letters do not provide a full explanation, a variety of circumstances—the context for their quarrel, that is—has to be considered.

On Jane's part—some who wrote about the Carlyles put the blame on her—her forty-fifth birthday was fast approaching. No evidence exists that at this time she was taking opium. Menopause was probably not a cause, since the onset likely occurred later. Although she twice expressed fears for her sanity, she was never entirely specific as to why. Love complications most definitely played the major part in the accelerating tensions between husband and wife.

But Jane herself had spoken of *work* when she lamented in her letter of May 19, "One escapes so much suffering by dying young!—all the good one *could possibly* have enjoyed in longer life is not it seems to me to be put in the balance against the evil which one *must necessarily* have suffered. Surviving one after another of all one loved—one after another of all one's beautiful illusions and even most reasonable hopes, surv[iv]ing in short one's original self!" In a sort of limbo,

Jane was looking forward and backward in apprehension, fearing she had lost touch with her original self, the playful, promising girl she had been, and worrying what the future might hold.

She was keenly conscious of mortality and her place on the timeline. Though Jane Carlyle may seem rather young to us, life expectancy was then around forty-five, the very age she was approaching. "[T]he latter part of ones life," she continued, "may be cruelly *embittered* by the reflection, that ones best years, which might perhaps have produced something good have been suffered to run to waste, fertile only of tares [weeds] and nettles!" After relating that the Macready women had laughed at her amusing stories without glimpsing her underlying depression, Jane had written those telling words: "I wish I could find some hard work I *could* do—and saw any sense in doing— If I do not soon it will be the worse for me—"

By hard work Jane Carlyle might have meant a memoir-writing project like that in her journal notebook, describing intriguing visitors to Cheyne Row and the curious stories they told her. She might have been thinking of moral or autobiographical essays, or collaboration on a novel with Geraldine Jewsbury—a door that was always open. In the next paragraph she added, "Meanwhile all *around* me goes on as usual—C is just getting done with *his* work—"

Did the advance of his work make hers seem suddenly all the more tenuous and elusive? Although difficult to factor into Jane's state of mind, her husband's work was part of the picture.

He reached another milestone with the second edition of *Oliver Cromwell's Letters and Speeches*, finished at last. It saw print June 16 and marked a change in the Carlyles' financial situation. Busy with various editions of his work for publishers in England and America, Thomas Carlyle no longer had to fear poverty: "It is really a blessing and deliverance not to be haunted by the base Terror of Beggary any more."

This same month, the long-hoped-for repeal of the Corn Laws took place; and with the passing of the legislation, Thomas's respect for the conservative prime minister grew. The disaster of hunger in Ireland, as well as fears of social unrest and pressures to increase free trade, had made it imperative for Sir Robert Peel to act. Weakened, however, by the break the legislation caused with his former Tory allies of the land-owning class, he soon resigned, to be replaced by the Whig-Liberal Lord John Russell. Yet the decision was popular overall, and to future generations Peel would be known as "the Prime Minister who repealed the Corn Laws."[1]

Thomas Carlyle sent the prime minister a letter, along with a complimentary copy of *Cromwell.* "Labour . . . may claim brotherhood with labour," he wrote Peel, viewing the two of them as toiling in similar vineyards, though he tactfully contrasts "this poor labour of mine" with the "late great and valiant labour of yours." Despite his famously low opinion of everyday politics, he acknowledged the rare accomplishment: "[H]ere has a great veracity been *done* in Parliament, considerably our greatest for many years past; a strenuous, courageous and manful thing." His expression of kinship with Britain's leader indicates a firm sense of achievement. He was confident enough to tell Peel that he hoped he would "find leisure to read and master" his Cromwell, "the noblest Governor England ever had." Known for responding personally to all who wrote him, Sir Robert Peel sent back a gracious reply. Nonetheless friends kept remarking on Thomas's savage moods, a mysterious degree of savagery, it might seem, given these favorable circumstances.

A few pleasures were in store this June. Able now to afford it, Thomas undertook the expense of hiring a carriage (his horse Bobus had not yet been shipped off to Scotland to be sold). He and Jane could travel the streets of their Chelsea neighborhood as well as the leafy lanes of Surrey for the benefit of their health. Jane made plans to host a breakfast in honor of the Countess Ida von Hahn-Hahn, a German novelist visiting London, issuing invitations to Anna Jameson, Robert Browning (she was not yet acquainted with the poet he loved, Elizabeth Barrett), and others. She wrote about her party preparations to Geraldine, who understood the difficulties of carrying off such events when one had "a small establishment." Although Hahn-Hahn had a faux husband trailing after her—the pair were spoken of as "adulterers"[2]—Thomas appreciated the woman's natural manner. She expressed herself simply and sincerely.[3]

But this sudden overlooking of adultery could not have reassured Jane. Amused, Geraldine wrote from Manchester, "Carlyle putting up with her is the most wonderful thing possible; I thought he was of a real Scotch strictness in those matters, and could not stand 'George Sandism' in theory, let alone practice."[4]

A sickening heat wave swept over southern England this June. Unbearably hot weather persisted day after day with temperatures rising as high as 96 degrees F in the shade, 105 in the sun. London became a boiling cauldron with disastrous results. There were reports of laborers expiring of sunstroke and heatstroke while at work outdoors, and outbreaks of typhus.[5] In the middle of the heat wave, the Carlyles made an unhappy weekend visit to Addiscombe. From the first moment of their journey, plans went awry.

"You know what a day of heat Sunday was," Jane wrote her cousin: "—well we first stewed about an hour in a crowded Steamboat." They just missed one train and while waiting on the platform for the next, they had to "hang about on our legs in the burning-sunshine." When they arrived "at the Croydon Station no *fly* was procurable to take us to Addiscombe and Carlyle was quite desperate so I declared magnanimously I could *walk*." Walk she did in the beating sun (it would have taken perhaps twenty minutes). When Jane made it to bed, she collapsed, remaining there "till next morning with a splitting headach—without sleep—the most wretched of mortals—for I fancied myself *taking a fever*—and Lady Harriet has '*a perfect terror of infection.*' Why had I not stayed at home?—I did get home": here the sentence breaks off, the rest of the letter perhaps intentionally torn away.

In the face of the typhus scare, Lady Harriet must have dreaded the thought of illness contaminating her household. Yet Thomas Carlyle's description of her, "all sunshine of the hottest," comes to mind, for in addition to the choking heat, Jane apparently felt scorched by disapproval. Communication between the women was impossible. The visit marked another significant turning point in Jane Carlyle's anxieties about Harriet Baring.

Whatever she wrote Geraldine, her friend replied that she was sorry to find her "in such an unsatisfactory state!" Jane had made plans to visit Seaforth House again. Knowing this, Geraldine declared, "All those grand people may be very well—a great privilege to know, and all that—but just now you want to be out of the hearing of 'wits,' and with somebody that loves you, and to whom you can speak."[6] She meant herself—she was going again to Seaforth—and Betsey Paulet.

•

"CERTAINLY WE NEVER before parted in such a manner!" Thomas Carlyle wrote those words to his wife just after they quarreled, when she had reached the Paulets' refuge on the banks of the Mersey, seeking solace. His letter of July 6, 1846, contains what we know of why they had parted in anger.

Regarding what Jane wrote this summer, Thomas's nephew and heir Alexander Carlyle, according to the editors of the *Collected Letters*, "withheld several of the original [presumably complete] letters written at this time, which have still not come to light."[7] Although Jane told Giuseppe Mazzini about the quarrel, underscoring its seriousness, her letter to him does not survive either. The gaps in her story must be kept in mind, in addition to what everybody understands: any marriage is a complex dynamic and whatever transpires in some way takes two. And it is more interesting to explore what happened, with all the nuances, than to belabor whose fault it was. But as this is the story of Jane Welsh Carlyle, the particular interest must be to discern how events affected her, even if that requires some speculation because of the lamentable lacunae in her correspondence.

"My Dear," her husband wrote in the letter he sent after her, "I hope it is only displeasure or embarrassed estrangement from me, and not any accident or illness of your own, that robs me of a Note this morning . . . . Certainly we never before parted in such a manner! And all for,—literal[l]y,—Nothing!" Uncharacteristically, Thomas evoked God. Time and distance would show them both "more clearly what the God's Truth of the matter *is*: may God give us strength to follow piously and with all loyal fidelity what that is!"

In some manner, the Carlyles had argued over *what the truth was* concerning Lady Harriet. Thomas confessed that since Jane had left Chelsea, he had been "in miserable enough humour, the saddest I think I have been in for ten years and more." (A decade before he had been striving to gain a foothold as an author.) Yet he retained enough presence of mind to work each day on a draft index, provided by his assistant John Christie, for an American edition of *The French Revolution*.

When Jane, probably from Seaforth House, wrote her brief letter to Giuseppe Mazzini concerning her feelings about the quarrel with her husband, he echoed her words: "Your life proves an empty thing, you say?" Giuseppe's very important letters to Jane— he wrote two of them this July—reflect back some of what she had told him, and show the limits of his loyalty.[8]

In the first he spoke mysteriously of "those yearnings after happiness, that are now making us both unhappy." His use of *us both* might imply that their warm, close friendship had serious romantic overtones. And / or it could refer to his decision to stay married to the Revolution, which prevented him from pursuing a permanent relationship with any woman, or letting romantic love overwhelm him; implying, in other words, that his was a parallel unhappiness to Jane's.

Whatever the truth, he plunges into an unromantic screed on duty. "Your few words sound sad, deeply," he writes. As a close friend, as a brother, he perceives she is undergoing a true crisis. He is attuned. He has heard her. But he adds, "It is only you who can, by a calm dispassionate fair re-examination of the past, send back to nothingness the ghosts and phantoms you have been conjuring up." As he goes on, however, he acknowledges that more than ghosts and phantoms are involved: "whatever the *present* may be, you *must* front it with dignity, with a clear perception of all your duties, with a due reverence to your immortal soul, with a religious faith." Doing her duty will make her life not happy "but earnest, sacred, and resignated [sic]." "Empty!" he admonishes Jane: "do not blaspheme; have you never done good? have you never loved? Think of your mother and do good." He adds, speaking either of God or Thomas Carlyle, "Can't you trust him a little longer?"

Giuseppe also chides Jane for her stance toward life. He disagreed with what he saw as her ironic worldview, when irony formed the sparkling diamond at the heart of her writing talents. "It is not as a mere piece of irony," he tells her, "that God has placed us here; not as a mere piece of irony that he has given to us those aspirations, those yearnings after happiness, that are now making us both unhappy." A few days later when Giuseppe writes again, he worries she has become too isolated and unbusy: "Get up and work; do not set yourself against us. When the Evil One wished to tempt Jesus, he led Him into a desert."[9]

It was Giuseppe Mazzini's true voice, reverberating from his Catholic upbringing, however unconventional that may have been. Yet wittingly or not, his advice resembled what Thomas Carlyle had to say during this crisis, which means that, in effect, she was quarreling with and estranged from the two men closest to her.

Their reactions follow an all-too-familiar Victorian scenario, the squelching voice of patriarchy, frightened by a woman's hysterical outburst, rushing self-servingly to characterize it negatively, insisting on adherence to duty, mother, god, the Bible, rationality, and acceptance of one's lot. It shows a preternatural sensitivity to the first creak of a Pandora's box opening; the eternal question of how to handle *the troublesome woman* when it looks as though she might be about to go out of bounds, the problem quickly assuming mythic dimensions. If she is allowed to continue in such a nonsensical manner, won't she end by disrupting the Natural Order of Things?

•

AT SEAFORTH HOUSE, Jane Carlyle woke on her forty-fifth birthday after a miserable night, unhappy and lonely, in "a bitter mood of disbelief and morbid sorrow." Though anniversaries always brought nostalgic memories, none had been so painful as this. She had received no acknowledgement of the day from her husband. Before she finished dressing, "*two hours before post time*," a mysterious packet arrived at the door of her upstairs bedroom, but it had been mailed from Cambridge, not London.

Wonderingly she opened it. *Amely Bölte* had remembered her birthday. The governess had written to Jane and sent her the gift of a "beautiful little collar and cuffs" she had fashioned herself. As Jane prepared to go down to breakfast with the Paulets, she added the pretty adornments to her dress, "a sort of *charm* to mol[l]ify Destiny towards my new year." Amely's thoughtfulness and generosity surprised Jane into a new respect. In dismay she recalled her irritated, dismissive words to Amely in March, now calling them "all my cruelties to her!" In a thank you for the letter, Jane conveyed her gratitude to Amely for "the real *good* it did to my soul." She continued philosophically, "with true respect have I seen your struggle to make your life useful to others and honourable to yourself—and to find *there* a cure for your individual sorrows—God speed you in this course and enable *me* to do likewise!" It was a moment of insight and empathy.

Later on her birthday, she, Geraldine, and Betsey Paulet walked to the post office only to discover the postmistress still had nothing from Chelsea for Jane. As she eventually revealed to Thomas, when told again there was no letter from him, "I did not burst out crying—did not faint . . . but I walked back again without speaking a word, and with such a tumult of wretchedness in my heart as you who know me can conceive—And then I shut myself in my own room to fancy everything that was most tormenting—Were you finally so out of patience with me that you had resolved to write to me no more at all?—had you gone to Addiscombe and found no leisure *there* to remember my existence?"

The packet had been overlooked. When the postmistress realized her mistake, she notified the Paulets' footman Robert, who promptly delivered it to the house. Thomas had sent his wife a birthday letter after all, and the gift of a card case. "I wonder what *love-letter* was ever received with such thankfulness!" Jane wrote back. Her anguish and relief reveal the strongest weapon in the Carlyles' marital arsenal: the refusal to write.

Her warm response to his letter and gift suggest their quarrel will soon be over. Just before Jane's birthday, Amely had visited Thomas Carlyle in his back garden and found him in an unruffled mood, which boded well. "I saw him the other day," she reported to Varnhagen, "sitting in the garden behind his house smoking a pipe, leafing through magazines. I brought him the *Hamburger Zeitung*, several editions containing literary notes that he always mocks. He calls them watery stuff, but that is why he loves reading them so much."[10]

Thomas's answer to Jane, July 18, made a quick resolution seem a certainty. He told her nearly everything she had been longing to hear. He had paid the Barings a visit in London. The conclusion: he would go to Addiscombe neither "today nor tomorrow, nor indeed for an indefinite perhaps infinite time to come!" He added, "To the Lady I have of course told nothing, except that you are very unwell; but she seems to have discerned pretty clearly for herself that our intercourse is to be carried on under different conditions henceforth, or probably to cease altogether before long; to which arrangement she gives signs of being ready to conform with fully more indifference than I expected,—with no unkindness at all, but with no discernible regret either." He complimented the lady's good manners, saying that he too could "adopt and accept." Yet a loophole remained: "An opening is left for my meeting them about Carlisle or Edin*r* on their Scotch Tour; but it seems to be with little expectation on either side that it will take effect."

Thomas Carlyle was promising—almost—to stop seeing the Barings. At least not on the old terms. No more forced marches to Addiscombe. It confirms that arguing over the import of that sweltering June visit and Lady Harriet's intentions had been the immediate cause of their quarrel.

Jane had been exercising the powers available to her as a Victorian wife married to a fairly reasonable man, not a Bluebeard, to bring about the conclusion she desired. Arguing. Pleading. Showing how deeply hurt she was. Asking for changes. Departing on a visit to friends to allow matters to cool down.

She appeared to have been successful.

Her July 19 letter is either a direct response to the good news from Thomas, or in anticipation of a happy resolution. Staying overnight for a lark at Speke Hall, an Elizabethan manor house a short distance from Seaforth, she writes her husband a fun, friendly, bubbly letter about gothic heroines, ghosts, secret passageways, and screech owls behind the tapestries—mocking the gothic novel. Her good spirits have been released. "[I]t would scarcely surprise me when a door opens if the Maiden Queen and all her court should walk in in their winding-Sheets and seat themselves on the high backed chairs to have 'a little comfortable talk' with me about the other world." With Thomas planning to join her soon at Seaforth, she adds, "I need not say how glad we shall be to pick you up at the Railway whenever you desire it."

As far as is known, no letters from Jane to Thomas were kept for the next twenty-four days. Part of the time they were together in Seaforth, so there would have been none then. But before he arrived, Geraldine, writing to Amely while Jane was at Speke Hall, reported that she had been keeping up a daily correspondence with Thomas, more dutiful than anything: "A daily letter to her husband is the utmost she gets accomplished & I think she rejoices in her heart when Saturday comes [there was no Sunday post] in order that she may abstain from *that* with a clear conscience—"[11]

Her women friends had gathered around in support, but it is hard to tell just what they knew. Usually they speak as if Jane were only physically ill, Geraldine telling Amely, for instance, that she hoped Mrs. Carlyle really was in good health. And Jane later wrote that during this visit "Betsey with her fixed idea of my 'liver-complaint'" had kept hovering, speaking of how wildly ill she looked, "reminding her now of 'Nodes [Betsey's brother] after he had taken poison,' now of 'Marianne before her brain fever,' now of 'old Nannie in her last illness.'" Jane's wry sense of humor did not desert her.

When the next letter arrived from Thomas, however, an ominous tone had crept in. He had been to see the Barings again: "[A]ll is handsome and clear there; and nothing is wrong, except *your* and my ill-genius may still force it to be so a little!" And he again speaks again of the lady's *altered manner* toward him.

Lady Harriet who knew how to send meaningful signals with her eyes when flirting with Giuseppe Mazzini would surely have known how to turn a cold shoulder to Thomas Carlyle if she inwardly disapproved of what he had said about seeing her less often. Her altered manner, along with that earlier show of indifference would doubtless, on reflection, have scared him. How could he bear to lose his exciting friendship with the queenly, commanding Lady Harriet, she of charismatic presence and strong intellect, who had such special, ennobling feelings for him?

Insisting to his wife that Lady Harriet harbored no ill will, Thomas now suggested that Jane ought to write her. His change of emphasis is unmistakable: "Her intents towards you and towards me, so far as I can read them, *are* charitable and *not* wicked: my relation to her is by a very *small* element of her position, but by a very just and laudable one; and I wish to retain that if I can, and give it up if I cannot, voilà tout. O Goody dear, be wise and all is well."

I wish to retain that if I can.

Jane's anguish must have gone deep, as if a wave had crashed over, composed of disbelief, morbid sorrow, and tumults of wretchedness, leaving her with a sense of life having become, suddenly, empty and useless. All seemed chaotic and unclear. She hardly knew, now, what to do, or try.

•

AFTER HE HAD joined Jane at Seaforth House, Thomas wrote a private note to Lady Harriet calling her "O Daughter of Adam most beautiful." He and Jane, he told her, have "talked of you: do not suppose that she does other, or ever did other, than respect and even love you,—tho' with some degree of terror. Baseless, I do believe." This was a far cry from the loyal "To the Lady I have of course told nothing." He concluded, "Adieu dear Lady mine,—*mine* yes, and yet forever no!" And made it clear that he had decided he would, after all, accompany the Barings on part of their upcoming tour.

Though Thomas does not forthrightly say so, this was going back on his word to Jane. Rather than admit it, he begins to gaslight her—to use the twentieth-century "Victorian" term from the eponymous film, where a devilish husband tries to convince his wife that she is losing her mind by denying the reality of what she perceives. The gaslighting in Thomas Carlyle's case was not necessarily coldly intentional. All of them were caught in a vortex of passions, saying what came to mind. In his letters to Jane he often sounds as if he had convinced himself that nothing improper was going on, that the problem lay solely in his wife's imagination—what Giuseppe Mazzini had called her ghosts and phantoms.

As posterity discovered, able to read Thomas Carlyle's notes to Lady Harriet Baring, their heady romantic friendship was not some delusion of Jane Carlyle's. But to prove to his wife that she was the irrational one, he sent a barrage of distracting, accusatory words her way, abetted, if unwittingly, by Giuseppe Mazzini. Her notions were chimeras, delusions, black confusions, brain webs, black spider webs, the devil's work (the temptations of Satan). She was daft and jealous. It was all "Nothing." She had a sickly imagination. Why could she not get a grip and be reasonable?

The all-too-real tidal pull of obedience for a Victorian wife might be hard for a modern reader to comprehend. To be obedient was an admired, in fact a highly desired trait. Through upbringing, conduct books, and moral fiction girls were trained to obey even the irrational demands of their parents, as a model for how they were later to behave toward their husbands. Despite some countervailing trends, it was generally thought that such behavior preserved the intrinsic angelic goodness of the pure, uncorrupted feminine character, surviving all trials to serve in society as a beneficent moral force. Acting obediently could make a Victorian girl or woman feel on the path of righteousness. In just a few months Dickens' *Dombey and Son*—really "Dombey and *Daughter*"—began appearing in one-shilling segments, which Jane read. In the novel, a good girl's obedience to her cruel father approaches the pathologically masochistic.

In her own life's drama, Jane soon grasped the obvious. Her husband intended, after all, to retain his relationship with Lady Harriet. As a doted upon only child, Jane had held a secure, important position in her family. For the most part, a sense of specialness had flourished during her marriage to Thomas. But now Lady Harriet—it is hard to imagine a more formidable rival—threatened subordination and displacement. All the evidence indicates that Jane feared and detested this.

Yet in addition to the contradictions inherent in the situation—such as the lady's array of admirable qualities, which Jane was forced to acknowledge—the gaslighting engendered a great deal of confusion. As any vulnerable being subjected to it knows, this can all too easily happen to someone uncertain and insecure. He sounds so *convinced* she is being unreasonable. *Is* she imaging things? *Has* her mind been affected? Profoundly puzzled, Jane sometimes buys into the criticism, admonishing herself to be sensible to the point where she admits to being beset by devilries—as when she says, "I have no 'liver-complaint' whatever other devilries I may have."

On August 4 Lady Harriet sent Thomas Carlyle details of their forthcoming itinerary, indicating she expected him to join them for a couple of days in Langholm, north of Carlisle. "O my Friend, my Friend," he wrote back, picturing her there in his imagination, "how strange an element are *you* in these old Langholm moors to me!"

Lady Harriet rarely writes in a charged tone to him, with a few exceptions. On the whole she is a more conventional writer than the Carlyles. Her extant letters are often careful and minimal. But now and then, especially in these first years of friendship, she expresses herself more freely through her love of nature. For instance on this occasion she writes back, "Langholm is just what I want to stay quietly in. Green hills & moorland and nothing to take the *trouble of going* to *see*—as if every portion of God's earth left alone wasn't worth looking upon." During their time together, she anticipates, a contemplation of the green and quiet moorland would be preferable to hurrying about as tourists, staring at columns and statues.[12]

When Thomas left Seaforth for Dumfriesshire, the impetus being his plan to meet up with the Barings, Jane employed the ultimate weapon. She refused *on purpose* to write her husband. And made a sudden decision to travel on to Manchester.

From his mother's home, Thomas wrote his wife anxiously, "I do not remember a more miserable set of hours for the most part than those since I left you.—But we will *hope* for a good issue out of them too; nay believe in it, and manfully strive with our best strength for it! . . . O my Dearest, how little I *can* make thee know of me; in what a black baleful cloud for myself and thee are all our affairs involved to thy eyes at this moment; threatening shipwreck if we do not mind!"

Threatening shipwreck implies separation or divorce, but for Jane Carlyle as a middle-class woman during the first half of the nineteenth century, divorce, as a practical matter, was out of the question. She had no legal standing. Upon marriage her property had officially become her husband's. So rare as to be basically nonexistent, divorce required a private act of Parliament and a great deal of money. Worse, it involved the woman in shameful, scandalous publicity. Separations did occur. Jane's friend Anna Jameson, for instance, who had an income from her writing, had separated from her husband by mutual agreement. But in Jane Carlyle's case, if she even contemplated separation seriously, where could she go? Certainly not to her beloved uncle's crowded, odoriferous Liverpool household, the site of "roast meats and proprieties."[13] Moreover, her public status was ever more closely wrapped up with her husband's. The Carlyles as a pair were on their way to becoming a literary fixture in London, almost an institution.

There is not the slightest suggestion that Thomas Carlyle entertained thoughts of divorce. He wanted his wife, Jane Welsh Carlyle, and he wanted the freedom to pursue his friendship with Lady Harriet Baring. If Jane could see her way to becoming a frequent presence at the Barings' house parties, part of the scene, so much the better. The most cynical interpretation is that Jane's participation would give cover to the romantic liaison between Thomas Carlyle and Lady Harriet Baring, but we do not know if either of them consciously planned such a dark ploy. For Thomas a more likely interpretation is that he wished Jane to join him on his adventure in the higher social realms—on his terms.

He seemed sincerely committed to the institution of marriage. In 1834 when he had written his wife about the house he found for them in Chelsea (Jane was then in Scotland), he told her he wanted her to "have a vote" in the decision, adding, "The sweet word, *Ours!* The blessed ordinance . . . by which all things are forever one between us, and separation an impossibility!" Intriguingly for twenty-first-century readers, he thought the blessed ordinance, in some manner, ought to be extended to men, writing (in 1833) the author Leigh Hunt, who disagreed with his advocacy of traditional marriage, "I would stand by my argument that the Covenant of Marriage m[ust] be perennial; nay that in a better state of society there will be other pere[nnial] Covenants between man and man, and the home-feeling of man in this world [of] his be all the kindlier for it. For instance, could two Friends, good men both, declare themselves Brothers, and by Law make themselves so! Alas, Friendship were again possible in this Earth; and not as at present only Dining-together."[14] He sidesteps the possibility of women declaring themselves Sisters and making a legal covenant; though single women, encouraged to stay in their domestic sphere and conserve their families' resources, might make a home together without causing raised eyebrows.

As Jane continues her silence, Thomas confides to Lady Harriet, August 9, that his wife who is "rather worse again . . . is, as you may fancy, the weightiest item of my cares at present." He tells the lady he will soon be "in Carlisle waylaying you." And pronounces enigmatically, "The gods are great; and so are the devils," before adding, "Your little Note was beautiful, in its words and in its silences. You are all good and beautiful; and I am bound to be forever grateful to you. *Bound*; and do not need much binding."

Jane and Thomas Carlyle were, nevertheless, at this moment—as always—highly invested in their correspondence with each other:

> Thomas in Scotsbrig: "Dear Jeannie, what am I to make of this continued silence? No Letter this morning still! . . . Write to me as briefly as you like, but write. There can be no propriety in punishing me by such feelings as *these* are. . . . If I cared less about you, the punishment would be less! It is not fair, nor right . . . . O my darling, if you could look into my heart of hearts I do not think you could be angry with me, or sorry for yourself either."
>
> Jane in Manchester: "In the first day or two after your departure I *could* not write any Letter that you would not have found worse than none,—and—so you got none!"
>
> Thomas in Scotsbrig (not yet having received the above): "I said to myself, last night, while tossing and tumbling amid thousandfold annoyances outward and inward, 'It is not fair all this; really it is not fair! I wanted to do none any injury.'" But he adds, quite harshly, "The annals of insanity contain nothing madder than 'jealousy' directed against such a journey as I have before me today [meeting up with the Barings]. . . .To the deepest bottom of my heart that I can sound, I find far other feelings, far other humours and thoughts at present than belong to 'jealousy' on your part! Alas, alas!"
>
> Jane in Manchester: "My dear Husband—I am very grieved at all this uneasiness you have had for want of Letters. To punish you was far as possible from my thoughts. Often as I have pained you, first and last, I *never* caused you *intentional* pain, so far as I remember."

Both were quick to say they had not intended to injure the other. But Thomas's accusation of mad, baseless jealousy had been thrown into the open. He and Jane had recently seen with their own eyes where such emotions led. The context was that raving mad woman in the attic Charlotte Sterling (two years before *Jane Eyre* immortalized Bertha Rochester in the role), and her pale shadow, Bessy Helps. At worst, strait waistcoats and confinement to a cell at the back of the house, padded with flocked wallpaper. At best, the jealous woman becomes a figure of fun, mocked by the world.

A woman's jealousy, as Jane Carlyle had understood and commented on, could be exacerbated if she had no purpose, no mission in life, no hard work to do. She had noted that Charlotte Sterling had read too many novels, shorthand for a wife of leisure who remained an ornament. Not having real work could leave a woman all the more vulnerable, defenseless, and susceptible to the green demon. But in this case the jealousy was not insane or fanciful. It had a cause.

•

THE GREAT CITY of Manchester, linked to the rest of England by railway only in the last decade and a half, was a fast growing, smoke belching, boisterous place. It was illustrative of the best and worst of industrial capitalism, notorious as the site of the Peterloo Massacre of 1819, when a huge crowd advocating for parliamentary reform had been viciously suppressed. In this booming center of the cotton trade, new mills and factories, industrial inventions, and slums for the laborers streaming in from the countryside in search of work had tumbled into being at a furious pace. In a hundred years, Manchester had gone from swampland to "the most densely populated strip of country in England," as Friedrich Engels, who lived there managing his father's factory, had written in 1844.[15] Political radicalism flourished, along with a hunger for knowledge, culture, and social reform.

What happened to Jane Carlyle in Manchester this August surprises, yet follows a pattern revealing of her resourceful character. At another dark moment, she was able to take a decisive step to help herself, accepting Geraldine Jewsbury's invitation to stay with her at her brother Frank's house, located in a half-town / half-country area. It would turn into a two-week stay. The summer before a pastoral respite had revived Jane. This time she responded to the stimulation of an urban center.

In Manchester she saw and heard, fascinated, all the commotion of a British manufacturing city, and it slowly reawakened her zest for life. Geraldine provided a clean, quiet, well-run home base, from which she took Jane to see the sights: cotton mills, printing mills, warehouses, factories, and foundries. All dressed up, bedecked with broaches and bracelets, the two friends visited Samuel Bamford, warehouseman, weaver, poet, and witness to Peterloo (he had been jailed for attending the demonstration). Jane who found him to be "a fine sturdy old fellow" had recommended to others his acclaimed book, *Passages in the Life of a Radical*. She also met and admired the mechanical engineer Joseph Whitworth, "inventor of the besom-cart [for street sweeping] and many other more wonderful machines," observing that his face looked "not unlike a baboon." And she made the acquaintance of a beautiful-looking young man from Corfu, Stavros Dilberoglue, a protégé of Frank Jewsbury's, who represented a Greek trading firm. Unexpectedly, she and Stavros fast developed an affinity for each other.

Jane often got out into the fresh air near Frank Jewsbury's house, reporting once on "having walked four or five miles thro' the fields last night *after dark*." Her approving sum up of the visit: "[M]y mind has been kept wide awake." What she had seen and done "would fill a volume and . . . the amount of exercise of body and mind I have gone thro has astonished myself . . . Geraldine no sooner perceived that I took interest in the practical activity of this place than she applied herself to getting me admission into all sorts of factories, and day after day has passed for me in going up and down in '*hoists*' and thro forests of machinery for every conceivable purpose—I have seen more of the condition of my fellow-creatures in these two weeks than in any dozen years of my previous existence."

Jane wrote these observations of Manchester to her husband, aware that he had penned an eloquent paragraph about the city in his *Chartism* essay (1840). Angry though she was, she knew how to capture his interest and show that she, also, could depict a great industrial city.

Might this newly discovered fascination lead to work she could do? Although her style and approach to life differed radically from her friend's, which is probably why they had no chance of bringing it off, Geraldine, as she had often done, pressed Jane to collaborate: "Do, I beseech you, keep up your good intention about one book, *our* book!"[16] Or perhaps Geraldine meant she required Jane's editorial assistance with her current novel-in-progress, *The Half-Sisters*.

Jane was learning enough to fill a shelf with pamphlets. "[I] shall return to London quite as well qualified to write *little books* on the 'manufacturing districts' as either Camilla Toulman or Arthur Helps—" (authors who wrote about labor and the poor). Possibilities were thrumming all over England. Elizabeth Gaskell, author of *Mary Barton: A Tale of Manchester Life* (1848), and other Victorian women writers would find in these industrial centers vital sources of inspiration, creating lasting works of fiction based upon them.

Geraldine, as Amely had recently done, rose in Jane's estimation. She described her friend's qualities for her cousin: "This noiseless well-ordered little house of hers—the very pink of Martha-Tidyism—is so calming-down after Seaforth. [A]nd herself so good and *quiet* and *sensible*!—I should like to see the perfectly *rational proper* Mrs Ellis of a woman that could have managed as well with me as this poor little Authoress of a questionable *Zoe* has done." Jane praised "all the intelligent sympathy and real practical good" that lay in Geraldine. She was grateful, also, to the Jewsbury brothers, Frank and Tom, for treating her during this visit like a sister.

As if poetic justice were at work, or his conscience, Thomas Carlyle had a miserable time with the Barings. The weather would not cooperate. He could not sleep. He made a point of telling Jane, "During rain we had to sit in a little room, where neither fire in the grate nor the smallest chink of ventilation otherwise could be permitted; one grew half-distracted naturally in such an element, and prayed for fair weather as the alternative of suicide." A criticism of the ideal lady had registered. When it rained, Lady Harriet, with a strange liking for being indoors and airless, became quite surprisingly tiresome. Briefly he glimpsed *her* as a wife, prompting sympathy for her husband: "The brave Baring's cheerfulness and calmness never failed him for a moment." In other words, Jane had missed nothing by refusing to go on this trek and there was no cause for jealousy.

While with the Barings, Thomas sent Jane a sealed note from the lady herself, written August 18. It should "keep your fancy quiet," he admonished. Jane opened it— with what trepidation?—to discover a piece of unsolicited advice.

It is an opportunity to hear the voice of the third party in the triangle. "The only check to our felicity," Lady Harriet writes Mrs. Carlyle, "has been the missing you; and more, the accounts he gave of the little permanent good Seaforth had as yet done you." It becomes an excuse for scolding. "You are very, very foolish to go on without some trial, at least, of advice and remedies. I *am sure* your headaches could be very much mitigated; and cough and all kinds of derangement will come upon neglect. Whatever one's own belief and feelings in the matter, it is a thing one owes to those who are anxious and careful, to neglect no reasonable care for one's health and life. And you are really trifling with the first." She hopes that Jane is better and urges her to spend the month of November with them at Bay House—again.[17]

If Thomas had read Lady Harriet's letter, he would doubtless have found much to admire. To his wife, listening from a different dimension, disturbing notes were struck. The only check to our felicity. You are very, very foolish. Those alleged headaches might so easily be mitigated. In trifling with your health, you are neglecting yourself and becoming an imposition upon those who are anxious for you.

Do pull yourself together.

Jane commented dryly that the note "did not seem to want any answer," yet some days later dutifully roused herself to write a "longish" and "*amusing*" reply.

No wonderful resolution to this particular quarrel took place, but slowly it began passing out of the most dangerous shoals. Thomas's friendship with Lady Harriet did not diminish, nor did shipwreck occur. Partly, perhaps, to give his marriage space, he resolved on a short dash to Ireland to visit Charles Gavan Duffy. Before leaving, he wrote Jane (who would return to Chelsea after a brief stay with the Welsh family): "remember one thing: to write a little oftener to me. And as near the old tone as you can come before the 'spider-webs' got upon the loom at all! In me is no change, nor was, nor is like to be. Alas I do not much deserve to be loved by anybody,—not much or at all: but I am very grateful if anybody will take the trouble to do it. God guide us all; for our pathway is sometimes intricate, and our own insight is now and then very bad!"

The admission was significant—and rare—as was the confession that he was grateful to anybody who took the trouble of loving him, implying both women had done so. When Jane was back home September 5, he wrote again from Dublin pleading, "O my own dear Jeannie, wilt thou never love or trust me any more?"

Perhaps touched by these words, she wrote a chatty friendly letter, rattling off, though thinly and superficially for her, the names of friends and acquaintances she had been seeing or thinking about: Giuseppe Mazzini, Elizabeth Pepoli, the Sterlings father and son, Robertson, Chapman, Darwin, Fleming, Mrs. Buller, Harriet Martineau, Geraldine—and her new young Greek friend, Stavros Dilberoglue. Although the letter has not her usual energy, it is as if, by naming her friends as touchstones, she can signal she is back inside known life again.

Her husband approved. The letter was "good-morrow to a weary heart." Yet much remained unsettled.

On September 12, in what could have seemed an ironic coincidence of timing to Jane, Robert Browning married his sweetheart Elizabeth Barrett. Romantically in love, the two poets soon left for Italy, to live—as the fairy tale went—happily ever after. Once he returned to Chelsea, Thomas reported to Edward FitzGerald that Browning "is just *wedded*, as his card testifies this morning; the M*rs* Browning still an enigma to us here." To his brother he brusquely described the enigma as "a Miss Barrett, *Poetess*, who lay lamed on a sofa for many years, but is now suddenly on her feet again."

Soon after Jane told an Edinburgh friend regarding her own marriage, "When I married Carlyle I was content with feeling *perfectly sure myself* that he was a *man of genius* and never troubled my head with wishing that the world would recognize it along with me[.] And now that the world *has* recognized it; I often think that its recognition has been of small service either to him or me."

She issued an invitation to Helen Welsh to come to Cheyne Row for a long visit. (Her cousin would arrive late November.) This was consciously done to provide a buffer between husband and wife, an idea she expressed bitterly to Thomas: "I might take my Cousin Helen back with me for a while as a social restraint in a small way, and to leave you more at liberty from the fret and responsibility of me." They both understood some space between them, whether physical or psychological, was essential.

A little of Jane's sparkle had subsided. Thomas told his mother this fall that his wife had become more *serious*. And he made a curious comment to Amely Bölte. When discussing the work of Countess Ida von Hahn-Hahn with the governess, he objected to the "tender sentimentality" of Hahn-Hahn's "idea of some life-long romantic love—that so many women seem haunted by."[18] Possibly he thought his wife's problem was an unrealistic desire for life-long romantic wedded love. And that however strong his feelings for her might be—they were undeniably strong, at times even tender, especially when they were separated and writing letters—they no longer involved the *romantic*. That was something for a different realm.

In her old amusing fashion, Jane wrote her cousin Helen about the kind of wife her husband evidently needed. "C should have had 'a strong-minded woman' for wife, with a perfectly sound liver, plenty of *solid fat*, and mirth and good humour world without end—men do best with their opposites. *I* am too like himself in some things—especially as to the state of our livers. [A]nd so we aggravate one anothers tendencies to *despair*! But there is no altering of all that now—nothing to be done but make the best of it."

Good humored, strong-minded, fat: we know whom those epithets call to mind.

Jane spoke of not knowing what their immediate plans were regarding Lady Harriet, and of being "down at *Zero* again." To keep her spirits up, she set herself a regimen to improve body and soul, taking daily cold baths, the water-cure remedy doctors recommended; eating as much as she could manage to; drinking "*bottled porter*"; keeping busy; and going on long brisk walks—"six and seven miles in the day on an average!"

However often the two women were to see each other socially, however much they would make attempts, sometimes considerable, to get along, Jane Carlyle's view of Lady Harriet had undergone some kind of permanent shift. She might recognize and even pay tribute to the lady's impressive personal and social qualities. But hope of a warm, sustained friendship between them had now diminished to almost nothing.

•

IN NOVEMBER, AFTER hiding the Cheyne Row silver, a precaution taken to prevent theft, Jane Carlyle found herself at the Grange in Hampshire. Seeing the place for the first time, she described that shockingly enormous Greek temple, without exaggeration, as "'a country house' with a vengeance!" And spoke of her hostess as "clever to death." "I feel to have got out of my latitude," she wrote her cousin, "—as much as if I were hanging on the horns of the moon!" Regarding Lady Harriet, Jane said she now felt "in a *false position*—and find it very difficult to guide myself in it." She had lost previously held illusions, even, as she had put it the previous May, some of her "most reasonable hopes." Forced to grow up, she was now watching the world with a colder eye.

That no one at the Grange appeared to notice her difficulties helped; "except C—who since I make no noise about them is bound to recognize them with respectful toleration." It was their current truce. He would tolerate her reluctance to be part of these visits and would not berate her for her private opinions. He himself understood the fatigue of countless "champagne dinners with plate-services and a regiment of valets!"

And she would attempt to complain less, or *make no noise*. Although she would participate in the Barings' house parties, she did not have to like them.

But where was all of this leading?

As for Thomas Carlyle and Lady Harriet, a strange silence now arose between them, hinting of tensions they had begun to experience. He told his brother that during this stay, "Lady Harriet lived mostly in her own apartments, dined at another hour than we; and except at breakfast and tea did not much appear." He hardly saw her. She did sometimes choose not to dine with her houseguests, but the fact that he comments on her absences indicates he was struck by them. There are, furthermore, no extant letters from Thomas to the lady between August 9 and December 16.

Now and then, she had sent him a note. Back in August, writing from Bay House, Lady Harriet had written "Mr. Carlyle" some soulful words. Referring to her father-in-law Lord Ashburton's sailboat, moored in the harbor, she had used a surprisingly sensuous image: "I have often wished for you as our little vessel lay quite down on her side in the water, with the bright waves curling over & dashing up the deck, & springing on thro' the foam as *we* shall when we have those wings—which you will only think of as means of *quills*. Alas indeed!"[19]

Had Jane come across this letter and read with pain the words "I have often wished for you"? If so she might have wondered what the writer meant by "when we have those wings." As if Lady Harriet had been dreaming of a time when she and Thomas Carlyle would become angels together? "Springing on thro' the foam" is a romantic image of freedom. No matter that wings, to Thomas, implied quills for pens.

After a long silence, on 16 December, Thomas Carlyle confessed to Lady Harriet in a rather cryptic fashion, "I do not write to you in these weeks; I cannot write. Some Fate seems to prohibit me, to say I ought not. In truth, the element I have lived in is very dark, this long while; and I would not complain of it. . . . You know well, I suppose, that it is not my *blame*,—alas, no, not my *blame*! And for what you understand of me, and for what you do not understand, I trust always to your goodness, and nobleness of mind; to your divine benevolence for me, which indeed has, and had always, something of *divine* in it, I think?"

He went on to talk in a mundane manner of his wife's being ill with a cold. He had been "pasting up crevices" to make "a summer temperature for the poor Patient," and also spoke of servant problems they had been having (discussed in the next chapter). As for plans to visit the Barings at Bay House this winter, it was difficult to know. "My Wife clearly cannot come; at least I do not expect it: but as for myself—Well I will hope!"

Did Lady Harriet somehow hear in this that if she wished for his company, she must do more to placate his mate? As if picking up the cue, in her reply she writes carefully and solicitously of his wife. She recommends bitter ale or wine as remedies for Mrs. Carlyle's ailments; advocates Bay House with its sea air for convalescence; and issues a specific invitation: "She must choose her own day." She continues, "Please let me have a line to say how y*r.* poor invalid is."

But Lady Harriet's eloquent conclusion to this letter connects a difficulty with her writing materials to a larger point she wishes to convey but cannot speak of outright: "My paper is greasy, my pen infamous, the ink a jelly of the most strengthening kind, such as y*r.* patient sh*d.* eat; and what this letter has cost me no words can tell."[20]

Thomas signals he understands: "[Y]our Letter first of all . . . in spite of the *thick ink* and other difficulties, is as good as ever! 'All suns,' as the Roman Proverb says, 'have not set': there will better days dawn by and by."

At the start of the new year, from his tiny dressing-room study, he again wrote to the lady: "Mrs C. is still very feeble; never ventures even downstairs: we live in the Library place, which is only a step from her own room and fire; I have banished myself aloft to a little dressing-closet, about 8 feet square, in the rear of the house; where I sit, with fire-screen and desk, extremely quiet; hearing only the distant groan of

London and the world; looking out over little gardens, sooty trees, chimney-tops and smoke, in the distance . . . nothing but St. James's steeple in Piccadilly and the cross of the top of St. Paul's. . . . Of you I think as of the beautifullest creature in all this world; divided from me by great gulphs forevermore."

However acute her husband's perception was of those great and permanent gulfs, it was clear that Jane Carlyle, who had succeeded in making her unhappiness felt and her wishes known, had *not* won this round. (Other rounds were to come.)

Though it is hard to pinpoint precisely or describe, what Jane had gone through this summer and fall had altered her in some fundamental way. The man who eventually became Thomas Carlyle's biographer, James Anthony Froude, when he met her just a couple of years later, thought he "had never seen a more interesting-looking woman" and was the first to notice the "dangerous light" that had appeared in Mrs. Carlyle's eyes.[21]

CHAPTER THIRTEEN
BREAKING OUT

"[T]o be made a Lady of all on a sudden does not fall in one's way every day!"

—JANE WELSH CARLYLE, 25 September 1846

"As to that Miss ______, I loathe her heartily from your description. I have no patience with theoretical profligacy."

—GERALDINE JEWSBURY TO JANE WELSH CARLYLE, 19 October 1846[1]

WHEN JANE CARLYLE WAS LITTLE JEANNIE WELSH IN HADDINGTON, she had been transfixed by a mysteriously sealed door in the family dining room. In 1859 Jane talked of this door in an enthusiastic letter of thanks to George Eliot who had sent "Mrs. Carlyle" a presentation copy of her novel *Adam Bede*. (Jane did not then know that the author was Marian Evans Lewes, rather than a pseudonymous clergyman.) Reading the novel—"In truth, it is a beautiful most *human* Book!"—had prompted Jane to recall the potent image of a door from her childhood.

"What *did* that door open into?" she wrote George Eliot. "Why had I never seen it opened? Standing before it, 'as in presence of The Infinite,' I pictured to myself glorious possibilities on the other side, and also horrible ones! I spun long romances about it in my little absurd head! I never *told* how that door had taken hold of me . . . . But I lay in wait to catch it open some day; and then I somehow—forgot all about it!"

In the fall of 1846, just when parts of her own life seemed to be closing down, Jane had experiences with two very different women for whom the door of possibilities was opening: her maid Helen Mitchell and the American author Margaret Fuller.

For the Carlyles' Scottish maid-of-all-work, whom they habitually described as petite, ugly, able, foolish, literate, and almost preternaturally bright and intuitive, a wholly unexpected opportunity presented itself one late September afternoon. Her younger brother, John Mitchell, "a flustery incredible sort of man—and very selfish with the two black eyes set close together in his head!" stopped by Cheyne Row to invite his sister to become mistress of his household in Dublin. He had recently established a factory there to make bell-rope, coach fringe, and similar small products, employing some two hundred women to do the work. Decorative fringe or carriage lace, as Jane explained it, was now needed in great quantities, "thanks to the imme[n]se consumption of that article on the Railways!"

Success having made John Mitchell a gentleman, he had need of a housekeeper.

If Helen accepted her brother's offer, she would be able to manage his household with the help of servants of her own. Should he marry and his wife take over the duties, he promised that Helen would not be left stranded in Ireland; he would make an adequate settlement on her. As Jane warily observed, this brother had previously paid next to no attention to his sister. Yet chancy as the venture seemed and wrenching though it would be to part with Helen, Jane saw the drama and excitement of the story: "She is going to be made a sort of a *Lady* of!" To a cousin she exclaimed, "insignificant as she looks she has *a Destiny*!—is liable to great Events!—and what is most extraordinary of all is going to be an exceptional instance of *virtue* really *getting* its own reward! At least one hopes so!" It was as if fairy dust had been sprinkled over the maidservant's life of drudgery—a Cinderella story.

Helen wept at the thought of leaving Mrs. Carlyle, yet could not keep from breaking into smiles. She gave her employers notice and in two months time would depart for a new life in Dublin.

Jane had painstakingly trained Helen and would sorely miss her despite the trouble of caring for her during her rare but hideous drinking binges, when the Carlyles would lock Helen into a cellar room, probably the back kitchen or larder, to sober up—if they could catch her and drag her into it. Jane claimed that Helen would roll on the floor, turning into a wild and sooty tiger. Thomas Carlyle once referred to the maid as an animal of another sort, apparently quoting back to Lady Harriet, who had been startled by the sight of her, some words she had used: "our poor little Helen the 'white-bearded Ape' whom you have seen." But the drinking episodes had fortunately not occurred for a long while.

For the better part of a decade, the third resident of the house on Cheyne Row had been a vivacious presence. A hard worker, Helen had ably undertaken the many tasks associated with keeping a multi-storied house clean and tidy. Mistress and maid had attained a fairly steady, reasonably warm relationship that survived their occasional arguments and threats to part company.

Over tea at the end of the day, Jane liked to tell Thomas funny things Helen had said. She wrote down several of these sayings in a notebook. For instance, after hanging up clothes during a dry spell: "I am sure it must have been quite a *treat* to *the flannels* to get one day of drought." And on the nature of empty, innocuous personalities: "I would rather live single all of my life than be married to a *saft taty* (*Anglice*, soft potato), as sae mony [so many] men are, and women, too,—nothing in the worl'[d] in them but what the spoon puts in!"[2]

Years later, attempting to get at the essence of Helen Mitchell, Thomas struggled to describe. After praising her work and Jane's supervision, he remembered how the maidservant had "been even cured from a wild habit of occasional drinking, and tamed into living with us, and loyally and faithfully serving us for many years. She was one of the strangest creatures I ever saw; had an intellectual insight almost as of genius, and a folly and simplicity as of infancy: her sayings and observations, her occasional criticisms on men and things translated into the dialect of upstairs [vs. downstairs], were by far the most authentic table wit I have anywhere heard! This is literally true, though I cannot make it conceivable." In high Victorian terms, he acknowledged his wife's re-creation of Helen's wit in her stories at the end of the day: Jane was "the 'beautifully prismatic' medium that conveyed it to me."[3]

Jane now told an Edinburgh friend that Helen had "been growing, like wine . . . always the better by keeping. So that at no period of our relation could I have felt more regret at losing her." She continued to doubt the brother's reliability, and Thomas shared the apprehension: the Dublin manufacturing business, he feared, was "all upon float."

As numerous nineteenth-century advice books make clear, including Mrs. Isabella Beeton's well-known *Book of Household Management*, locating and overseeing a new maid servant was the wife's responsibility, a division of labor the Carlyles did not question. Regarding the business of training a replacement, Thomas spoke of himself as "*I*, who am little concerned," indicating he wished to remain "obstinately quiet, contracted into the narrowest compass." While change-of-servant chaos erupted around him, he hoped to keep out of the way till all was running smoothly again.

The loss of her maid came at a vulnerable moment for Jane, yet her letters indicate that despite her heartrending troubles over Lady Harriet, sorrows and anxieties that had *not at all* gone away, she could summon resilience. She had been appealing to various friends in Scotland, determined to hire another Scotswoman; and when she tells her Edinburgh friend that "of late years" she has been "ever ailing—ever depressed in spirits," it is partly to explain why she had not written until she needed something. In fact Jane was going briskly about her business—this, after all, was part of her *work*.

She gave careful thought to the terms of employment, spelling them out. She would pay a new maid the same wage, twelve pounds a year (slightly better than average), with another pound or so for tea, sugar, and beer. A washerwoman might be brought in to assist on heavy laundry days, except for the servant's own clothing, which she would wash herself and hang up to dry on the clothesline behind the house. (Extra help had to be chosen with a discerning eye: a washerwoman was said to have been the first to ply Helen with liquor.) Londoners gave new servants a month's trial, but Jane would stick to "the Scotch principle of having to stay six months," which provided extra time for mistress and maid to get used to each other. At the end of that period, either might terminate the arrangement. If the maid left before a year was up, half her traveling expenses would come out of her wages. But Jane could not bring herself to adhere to what she called the London Rule of No Followers, that is, no male visitors—too cruel a restriction for a maid in a single servant household.

When Jane wrote family friend Mary Russell for help, she detailed further requirements, describing herself and her husband rather oddly: she wanted a maidservant "to do every thing in a house that two quiet, philosophical people require—she would need to be up to *cooking* 'in its simplest expressions'—to washing—and cleaning rooms—and I should like her not to steal or drink, or fly into rages[;]—what is called 'a very good temper' I am not particular about—but *explosions* hurt my liver which is bad enough at any time—"

In late November 1846, within the space of a few days, life at Cheyne Row underwent a great change. Jane's pleasant, determinedly ladylike cousin Helen Welsh came from Liverpool for that long-planned visit arranged to alleviate tensions between husband and wife. Helen Mitchell departed for Ireland. And her replacement, recommended by Jane's childhood nurse Betty Braid, arrived from Edinburgh with her trunk after "a rough and tedious passage" on a steamer.

•

ENTER ISABELLA. IN voice and appearance she was respectable and presentable, a great contrast to the "little ugly *dottle*!" She did not find herself alone in London; she had friends in service there, as well as numerous cousins. The outlook was promising. "She is soft and slow—but on the other hand methodical and orderly." But Isabella (no last name is given) turned out to require a great deal of training.

As Jane reported to her Edinburgh friend, "I am mercifully pretty well just now—and I *can* work like a house on fire when I can keep my feet, and am *obliged* to do it. . . . But oh dear," she continued in the mock epic style she liked to employ when describing housework, "—after the easy life as to household matters which I have been leading of late years I feel it monstrously tiresome to be running for ever 'up stairs, down stairs, in my Lady's chamber['], and explaining to this Novice the simplest rudiments of things! In fact ever since she came the house has been like a sort of battle of Waterloo—and when I lie down at night it is with something of the same feeling Napoleon must have had when he went to sleep (I forget where) under the fire of the Enemy's cannon!"

For her friend's amusement, Jane wrote out a back and forth she had with Isabella. The new maid had complained: "no one woman living could do my work." It was ruining her hands. And no one had told her she was expected to do the washing! When Jane snapped in reply that Helen Mitchell had done it all and done it well, Isabella retorted, "Oh yes there are women that *like to make slaves of themselves*, and her you had was of that sort but *I* will never slave myself for anybody's pleasure."

Before ten days transpired, Thomas was telling his brother that Jane had caught a cold and Isabella was poised to depart. With his wife ill, he stepped in, after all, to participate in the domestic kerfuffle, voicing his opinions in no uncertain terms. Isabella, he said, was "one of the most perfect *Ploots* [Rustics]; can do nothing of her work at all in a complete manner; has a bad discontented temper too; —and indeed, on the whole has, this very day, much to my satisfaction, come to the mutual conclusion with us that she is to go about her business at the end of the Month."

But just after his birthday—he was now fifty one, starting to feel old, and taking notice of his graying hair—he wrote his mother that their end-of-December agreement in which Isabella and the Carlyles would share the cost of her voyage to London had failed to hold, and they had finally given in, agreeing to pay all. He continued, "This satisfied the poor trailing smearing gomeral [fool] for a day or two, and we tried to put up with her miserable ways without criticism; but yesternight she took suddenly to 'fainting,' or threatening to faint."

With Isabella wailing that she could not take it any longer, the Carlyles lost all patience and dismissed her at once. With Jane looking scornfully on, the maid waltzed cheerfully out the door to stay with a cousin. She made the acid comment that Isabella had left decked out "like a street walker."

"I have not in all my days seen a worse human subject than that unfortunate creature," Thomas pronounced, summing her up as "insolent, mutinous, impotent; in every way *base*, and to be avoided by rational creatures." He nicknamed her Pessima, The Worst. "I have not had such an inclination to cuff anybody's *haffets* [cheeks] these thirty years, as I had in giving my brief final address to that miserable slut [in the sense of slovenly] this morning."

Exit Isabella.

•

ONE WONDERS HOW the maid reacted to that final address. On Isabella's behalf, when Jane's doctor had first caught sight of her, he suspected that she was suffering from "*the greensickness*," or anemia. After her dismissal he concluded, harshly, that Mrs. Carlyle was "well rid of her." The cruel truth was that few employers wished to take care of sick servants, most especially ones they hardly knew. Isabella, perhaps cleverly, had played on those fears, threatening that if the Carlyles did not let her break the trial agreement and leave at once (as Jane reported it), she "*would take fits* and be *laid up in my house a whole year* as happened to her once before in a place where the work was too hard."

An unexpected irony was revealed: Jane's paternal aunts Ann, Grace, and Elizabeth Welsh who lived in Edinburgh (there were Welshes, unrelated, on both sides of the family) had helped to shape Isabella's views. Jane for the most part considered these aunts tiresomely rigid Christians and did not often see them; but Isabella, she discovered, had been their protégée. As she explained to Mary Russell, the maid had "been selected [to work for the Carlyles] more on account of her pretentions to '*free grace*' [part of the newish Free Kirk or Free Church orthodoxy] than of any '*works*' she was capable of—in fact my Aunt Ann it turned out had had a hand in her education— If I had only known *that* sooner; she should never have sailed to London at *my* expense!" In the end Jane was out two guineas.

Isabella exacted her revenge. She told the people they knew in common of the pious shock she had suffered upon discovering that Mr. and Mrs. Carlyle violated the Sabbath—to the extent of entertaining visitors on the sacred day. Such heathenish behavior, she implied, explained why she had felt obligated to leave their employ.

By now Jane was seriously ill in bed, "taking tartar-emetic and opium every two hours!" for a severe cough and chest inflammation. Her cousin Helen Welsh, for all her fine young lady ways, kindly intervened to help manage the household, undertaking some of the servant tasks herself. Jane had been hoping to show her cousin a few London sights but that was not to be. Helen Welsh spent most of her Cheyne Row visit cooped up inside. As far as is known, she did not complain. It was certainly a household of curious comings and goings.

On top of all else, the Carlyles had been involved in learning how to cook and eat Indian corn, or maize, a food they had barely heard of, as a substitute for potatoes. After Thomas described a porridge they had managed to make by boiling the stuff many hours, he wrote his brother that they had been able to get "a small loaf of bread from Indian meal today: very yellow and strange, but not unpleasant to eat, tho' much inferior to good wheaten bread." They had as yet no word for cornbread.

The Carlyles' struggle, with an unreliable servant, to figure out how to cook and eat a strange new food underscores the difficulty that Irish peasants had, if they were even able to obtain it. Improperly prepared Indian corn was impossible to digest and could only contribute to their misery. A Labour Rate Act, passed in August 1846, involved the creation of public works projects in Ireland to be paid for by assessments on landowners. The purpose: to create badly needed jobs for the working poor. Since such projects were expected to address consequences of the famine, the new Prime Minister, Lord John Russell, bowed to pressure from those who demanded no free trade interference and refused to import the quantities of Indian corn needed to feed the starving Irish. Yet if huge quantities of maize had been widely distributed with proper instructions for cooking and consuming, some of Ireland's desperate need might have been alleviated. When landlords could not or would not pay their assessments, and the Labour Rate Act failed, millions continued hungry. Hundreds of thousands perished. In this context, the government's refusal to distribute maize defies comprehension.

On his brief trip to Ireland in September, Thomas had observed the "black potatoe-fields" and wondered if the crisis might possibly lead to transforming change. He had been a little encouraged by Young Ireland, Charles Gavan Duffy and friends, yet did not then grasp the full scope of Ireland's destitution. In the coming months he would obtain more information, and during a second trip to Ireland in the summer of 1849, the country's agony would become seared into his imagination. But this December with his own travails on his mind—the quarrel with Jane and his possible estrangement from Lady Harriet—along with the woes he had witnessed in that benighted country, he wrote Ralph Waldo Emerson, "Ireland was not the place to console my sorrows. I returned home very sad out of Ireland."

•

FOR SOME THREE weeks, Jane lay ill. On top of catching a cold and fighting subsequent infection, she had used up her emotional reserves in coping with the aftermath of her quarrel with her husband and the loss of her maid. During the best times, she and Helen Mitchell had enjoyed each other's company. At the worst, they were at least deeply familiar with each other's ways. When Jane failed at training Isabella, after priding herself on her knack for training servants, it was a blow too many to her faltering esteem. An aura of nervous collapse surrounds this particular illness, with Jane acknowledging that she might have taken better care of herself had she not become so upset by Isabella's recalcitrance.

The opium Jane was using caused increased distress. Victorian doctors routinely prescribed the drug, whose effects were not well understood, for coughs and colds. But it could produce vivid bad dreams. The following spring, Jane related a nightmare she had experienced to Caroline Fox, the young Quaker woman who kept a journal wherein she recorded visits to the Carlyles. Jane's dream illustrates how scary opium visions could be, yet conveys, too, a sense of her storytelling powers.

According to Caroline, Mrs. Carlyle dreamed that she had "a miserable feeling of turning to marble herself and lying on marble, her hair, her arms, and her whole person petrifying and adhering to the marble slab on which she lay. One night it was a tombstone—one in Scotland which she well knew. She lay along it with a graver in her hand, carving her own epitaph under another, which she read and knew by heart. It was her mother's."[4] Guilt lingered that Jane had not been a good enough dutiful daughter to her sometimes-provoking mother, whom she had loved and continued to miss.

On behalf of his sick wife, Thomas wrote to John Forster, famous for his well-stocked library, and begged him to send Bulwer-Lytton's *Lucretia: or, Children of the Night*, or some other new novel to amuse her. Jane did have the first installments of Dickens' *Dombey and Son* to keep her company. Mr. Dombey, having been deeply invested in a son who died young, loathes his remaining child, a daughter named Florence, with a misogynist ire. Reading about this much-put-upon girl child, Jane might have concluded something like what she had written to her cousin from the Grange earlier this fall. Hearing talk there of the secret trials of aristocratic women—for instance, the burden of having to conceal a husband's drunkenness from the servants— she had wryly concluded of her sex: "Every mortal woman I fancy is born to be made miserable thro one cause or other."

Being confined to her bed did have a few positive effects. It provided a much-needed respite for body and soul. And forestalled for the moment further visits to the Barings.

As a stopgap measure, the Carlyles hired an older woman they nicknamed Slow Coach, who performed her tasks with a lumbering dignity. When they placed a newspaper advertisement for a permanent maid, an applicant appeared named Anne Brown. Jane described her as "a cheery little *button* of a creature with a sort of cockney resemblance to Helen—" Although Anne was English, the welcome resemblance to Helen was enough. She was quickly hired. Jane considered herself lucky to have obtained such a promising servant "out of the great sink of London."

Feeling better, finally, and appalled by the mess her household had fallen into, Jane pulled herself together yet again. She dispatched her cousin back to Liverpool, rolled up her sleeves, and prepared to devote herself to training the new maid, who was set to arrive the last day of the year. (Anne was to stay with the Carlyles for about a year and a half.)

This time Jane was determined to succeed at the job of servant training. "Carlyle," she wrote Mary Russell, "has been giving signs of having reached the limits of his human patience—and if he do not soon have a pair of shoes cleaned for him and his Library swept he will also 'take fits.'"

•

IN OCTOBER, IN the midst of the servant crisis, Jane Carlyle encountered one of the nineteenth century's most extraordinary women, Margaret Fuller, the American journalist, critic, and educator. Having recently sailed to Liverpool, Margaret was at the start of a European journey that would open the door of possibilities for *her*.

Her recent book, *Woman in the Nineteenth Century, and Kindred Papers Relating to the Sphere, Condition and Duties of Women* (1845) —pronounced *Beautiful!* by Harriet Martineau who had met her on her trip to the United States[5]—guaranteed Margaret entrée to writers and political figures in England and on the Continent. A friend of Ralph Waldo Emerson, she brought letters of introduction from him and other Transcendentalists.

Helen Mitchell had broken out of her social stratum to become a lady-housekeeper with Jane Carlyle's support. In Margaret Fuller she experienced a very different form of pattern breaking and was unable to summon sympathy—though to picture Jane's encounter with Margaret takes some reading between the lines. From the vantage point of our time, it can seem as if Jane had to entertain a visitor from the future.

An idiosyncratic individual, Margaret Fuller was also, to borrow a phrase of eighteenth-century feminist foremother Mary Wollstonecraft, *a new genus*. That is, she was in the process of becoming an intellectually accomplished, self-realized woman of a sort rarely seen. Although Margaret had numerous friends, there were women on both sides of the Atlantic who, despite holding ideas enlightened for their time, thought her puzzling, supercilious, and contradictory in ways hard to analyze. It could be very difficult to place her.

Before learning to respect and admire Margaret, Harriet Martineau's impression had been that she was haughty and a pedant.[6] The very subject matter of her current book made some uneasy. Elizabeth Barrett Browning, once she had met Margaret in person, "felt strongly drawn to her" and thought of her as a friend.[7] Yet she too had had a negative first impression, based only upon hearing of *Woman in the Nineteenth Century*, which she confusingly lumped together with conduct manuals like *Wives of England* by Sarah Stickney Ellis. Elizabeth Barrett told Robert Browning that the book was by "a Mrs. or a Miss Fuller—how I hate those 'Women of England,''Women & their Mission' & the rest. As if any possible good were to be done by such expositions of rights & wrongs."[8] Margaret had reviewed the work of both poets, but when she wrote to Miss Barrett asking to meet her in London this season, Elizabeth confessed to Robert how much she wished to avoid the American. And avoid her she did—because of the couple's elopement to Italy.[9]

When Margaret arrived in London, she was recovering from a romantic disappointment. She had been in love with a German businessman who she had hoped would join her on her travels in Scotland. Although she had known of his philandering nature, it was a painful shock to receive a letter informing her that he had become engaged to another. Margaret was, therefore, all the more grateful for having company on this trip, the American Abolitionists Marcus and Rebecca Spring. They, along with their son Eddie who was about nine years old, were her traveling companions. In fact the progressive-minded Springs —he was a successful businessman and she the daughter of anti-slavery Quakers—had initiated the idea of the journey, which would turn out to be a life-changing one for Margaret.

She was also grateful, once their party reached London, to find herself caught in a whirl of activity. With the city as her base, Margaret visited such places as Hampton Court, the Dulwich and National Galleries,

Giuseppe Mazzini's school for impoverished Italian children, and the Greek and Egyptian rooms of the British Museum. She saw "the Vandykes, at Warwick" and devoted a full day to a private collection of J. M. W. Turner's misty, beautifully colored works, telling a friend she was in the process of discovering what paintings were now to mean to her.[10] Margaret met numerous people of talent, took copious notes, and attended theatre performances, including John Westland Marston's *The Patrician's Daughter*. She had reviewed a published version of the play for *The Dial* (1844) but found the stage production more contemporary and effective.[11] It had audience-pleasing attributes of "a knightly exploit" with "manly expression," as she wrote in a note to Thomas Carlyle, knowing he would likely approve such sentiments.[12] Yearning for extra energy to enjoy all this varied life, Margaret exclaimed to a friend, "O, were life but longer, and my strength greater! Ever I am bewildered by the riches of existence, had I but more time to open the oysters, and get out the pearls."[13]

Thomas Carlyle called on Miss Fuller where she was staying at 17 Warwick Court and invited her and the Springs to Cheyne Row. After they had visited the Carlyles October 7, he described the thirty-six-year-old woman to his brother as "a strange *lilting* lean old-maid, not nearly such a bore as I expected: we are to see them again."

He was referring to a dinner party that he and Jane had decided to give, which took place Wednesday, October 14, 1846. George Henry Lewes, a young literary man, attended also. (This was several years before he met Marian Evans, who in time and with his encouragement became "George Eliot.")

What did Margaret Fuller think of Jane Carlyle? "I had, afterward," she wrote Ralph Waldo Emerson, "some talk with Mrs. C., whom hitherto I had only *seen*, for who can speak while her husband is there? I like her very much; —she is full of grace, sweetness, and talent. Her eyes are sad and charming."[14] It was discerning of Margaret to note Jane's sad expression—it accords with all she was then enduring. But we may smile at the phrase *full of sweetness*. Few in Jane's lifetime accused her of that.

While Margaret did not notice any dangerous light in Jane's eyes, they must have been glittering that evening. Jane's letter to Geraldine about Margaret Fuller does not survive, but what her friend wrote back indicates her view had been harshly negative. Geraldine provides a picture of the clash and shock of meeting a new woman in person. No longer is she just an idea, or the protagonist of a work of fiction, or a legendary literary figure dwelling safely across the Channel in France. She is, suddenly, very present and very real.

After praising what Jane had written about a street sweeper who *knew his place in the order of things*, Geraldine takes off, echoing certain words and phrases of Jane's. "As to that Miss [Fuller], I loathe her heartily from your description. I have no patience with theoretical profligacy. . . . She must be . . . a hypocrite, if she be tempted to death to live 'a free and easy life,' and yet keeps herself straitlaced up in practice to keep in with Emerson & Co.! I am extremely charitable towards people who honestly work out their own inclinations, but it makes me very poorly to see them putting on a grand fancy dress or transcendental philosophy to dignify their inclination! . . . And then those doctrines from an irredeemably ugly, uninteresting woman are really 'damnable.'" In an about-face, Geraldine continues, "Somebody was talking about that woman here the other night. If she comes to Manchester I shall see her."[15] The American intellectual had clearly aroused Geraldine's curiosity.

In Margaret Fuller's possibly unconscious disregard of how Victorian women were expected to comport themselves, she must have appeared odd, perhaps threatening. A Miss Fuller who constructed theories or damnable doctrines and put "on a grand fancy dress or transcendental philosophy" did not, as Jane had apparently indicated, know her place. The vehemence of the British women's dislike seems to have gone beyond whatever personal characteristics may have offended—Margaret's having acted, perhaps, in a queenly or pedantic manner. The word *uninteresting*, however, convinces not at all. Jane and Geraldine's recoiling at the idea of Margaret might indicate the disturbance and unease that can presage the breaking up of preconceptions, the signal of a mind in the process of change, first abhorring something new and strange that it will come to embrace.

Margaret Fuller wrote to Emerson, struggling to portray Thomas Carlyle the way she had hoped to find him, noble and great. But even during that first Cheyne Row evening when he had been on fairly good behavior, she had experienced irritation. "I admired his Scotch, his way of singing his great full sentences, so that each one was like the stanza of a narrative ballad. He let me talk a little now and then, enough to free my lungs, and change my position, so that I did not get tired."[16]

Margaret complained that during every visit Thomas had mostly prevented others from interrupting: "To interrupt him is a physical impossibility; if you get a chance to remonstrate for a moment, he raises his voice and bears you down."[17] As for George Henry Lewes, who was entertaining and full of fun—barely thirty years old, widely read, a talented mimic, and a fluent talker—Margaret reported him to be, at the dinner party, all "sparkling shallowness."[18] Though he *was* now and then allowed to interrupt. After a later visit that Margaret Fuller made to England, Lewes claimed that when she spoke, others, Thomas Carlyle included, fell silent, indicating that she at least *became* a woman who could more than hold her own in conversation with prominent men.[19]

Thomas's famous diatribes could end in helpless laughter all around, and Margaret did appreciate his sense of humor. Even at his most exaggeratedly outrageous, if they could get a word in edgewise, there were women in those years who had the experience of taking Thomas Carlyle on, despite his proven ability to physically overpower opposition through loud and constant talking. On the list of female writers who engaged him in verbal combat and lived to tell the tale were Margaret Fuller, Sara Coleridge (daughter of Samuel Taylor Coleridge), Martha Macdonald Lamont, Amely Bölte, Anna Brownell Jameson, and Harriet Martineau.

Two of Thomas's monologue topics especially provoked Margaret. The first was a typical harangue against poetry: "Tennyson wrote in verse because the schoolmasters had taught him that it was great to do so, and had thus unfortunately been turned from the true path for a man. . . . Shakespeare had not had the good sense to see that it would have been better to write straight on in prose."[20] Not even the beloved Robert Burns escaped, despite the fact that in 1828 Thomas had written an appreciative, touching, though critical essay about the Scottish poet (a little book that became one of his most frequently reprinted works). Poetry had there received Thomas Carlyle's praise: "For Poetry, as Burns could have followed it, is but another form of Wisdom, of Religion; is itself Wisdom and Religion."[21]

A far more disturbing topic, Margaret reported, was his "defence of mere force,—success the test of right;—if people would not behave well, put collars round their necks;—find a hero, and let them be his slaves, &c. It was very Titanic, and anti-celestial." What he said shocked her, yet she continued to insist he had a great and noble nature, like that of an old Norse king.

As she continued, Margaret made an intriguing comment about his contribution to Victorian society: "I never appreciated the work he has done for his age till I saw England. I could not. You must stand in the shadow of that mountain of shams, to know how hard it is to cast light across it."[22] It is difficult for us, well over a century and a half later, to comprehend what it was like to live under that shadow, or even to grasp what Margaret experienced on her three-months-long trip to Scotland and England that led her to the phrase. But it must have had to do with the thick ubiquitous layers of Victorian piety, sentimentality, convention, hypocrisy, and euphemism, what Thomas Carlyle called (see below) "*sweetness* of sugar-of-lead." Manly energies, Margaret Fuller more than once suggested, were required to contest the mountain of shams.

Despite finding so much to disagree with, she later wrote of Thomas Carlyle in a *New York Daily Tribune* dispatch: "His talk, like his books, is full of pictures, his critical strokes masterly; allow for his point of view, and his survey is admirable." This was very generous, considering his views on slavery. She summed up astutely that his power was "rather to destroy evil than legislate for good."[23]

In November Jane and Thomas saw Margaret once more, at a tea party. Also present were the Springs, their child Eddie, and Giuseppe Mazzini. Margaret had quickly become enamored with the hero Mazzini—it meant she was fast falling in love with the entire Italian revolution. (After she grew deeply involved with socialist thought and ideas for reform, she would turn somewhat critical of him.) She wrote Emerson that Mazzini was "a beauteous and pure music" and went on to say, "he is a dear friend of Mrs. C.; but his being there gave the conversation a turn to 'progress' and ideal subjects, and C. was fluent in invectives on all our 'rose-water imbecilities.' We all felt distant from [Carlyle], and Mazzini, after some vain efforts to remonstrate, became very sad. Mrs. C. said to me, 'These are but opinions to Carlyle; but to Mazzini, who has given his all, and helped bring his friends to the scaffold, in pursuit of such subjects, it is a matter of life and death.'"[24]

During the tea, Rebecca Spring directly challenged Thomas Carlyle on the subject of slavery. Jane was present at the scene, which Rebecca later depicted: "Margaret was standing before the open fire, looking amused; Massini [sic] was walking, with his hands behind him, looking annoyed; others grouped about. I heard Carlyle say, 'If people consent to be slaves, they deserve to be slaves! I have no pity for them!' As I started towards him, Margaret laughed, 'I have been wondering how long Rebecca would bear it!' I told him of the severe slave laws against teaching slaves to read, and yet they contrived to learn. What wit and skill they used in escaping, often running a long way on the railroad track until they saw a train approaching, which passing over would obliterate the scent, and thus they would escape the bloodhounds. I told him of many things. Carlyle listened, frequently commenting, 'I am glad to hear it! I am glad to hear it!'" According to Rebecca, he seemed abashed. Yet hearing Rebecca Spring's information and being glad to hear it did not alter his views.

Toward the end of the evening, he settled down and kissed little Eddie good night before the child was put to bed. Mr. Carlyle then, said Rebecca, "was charming, and we all sat around him, the delighted listeners to his picture talk."[25]

A month or so after the tea, Thomas Carlyle gave Ralph Waldo Emerson his version of encountering Margaret. "Miss Fuller came duly as you announced; was welcomed for your sake and her own. A high-soaring, clear, enthusiast soul; in whose speech there is much of all that one wants to find in speech. A sharp subtle intellect too; and less of that shoreless Asiatic dreaminess than I have sometimes met with in her writings." (By that phrase he perhaps meant the vague evocative spirituality of some of her work.)

Thomas admitted to behaving badly. He related a tirade he had given on Christianity from Margaret's point of view: "But, on the whole, it could not be concealed, least of all from the sharp female intellect, that this Carlyle was a dreadfully heterodox, not to say a dreadfully savage fellow, at heart; believing no syllable of all that Gospel of Fraternity, Benevolence, and *new* Heaven-on-Earth." He had treated all that "as poisonous Cant,—*sweetness* of sugar-of-lead,—a detestable *phosphorescence* from the dead body of a Christianity, that would not admit itself to be dead, and lie buried with all its unspeakable putrescences, as a venerable dead one ought!" And he concluded, "To all which Margaret listened with much good nature; tho' of course with sad reflexions not a few."

Allowance must be made for the subjectivities at work in these encounters. No one was at his or her best. The Carlyles had their marriage problems. Jane, still uncertain of her mission in life, was facing her servant crisis and about to leave on a dreaded visit to the Grange and Lady Harriet (discussed in the previous chapter). Thomas was in a months-long post-Cromwell phase of being unable to write. Margaret was suffering her romantic disappointment and might have been nervous about the impression she was making on Emerson's friend.

Sadly, four years later, on her way back to America from Italy, Margaret Fuller met her untimely death, drowning with her partner, Giovanni Angelo Ossoli, and their small son in a shipwreck off Fire Island. But her all too brief life, whether or not she came to experience it as a happy one, had been fully lived. In 1852 Thomas Carlyle, reading through a volume of reminiscences, *Memoirs of Margaret Fuller Ossoli*, echoed words of hers that were quoted there (and above): "O, were life but longer, and my strength greater! Ever I am bewildered by the riches of existence, had I but more time to open the oysters, and get out the pearls."

Ralph Waldo Emerson, one of the book's editors, had written, "Margaret occasionally let slip, with all the innocence imaginable, some phrase betraying the presence of a rather mountainous ME." Thomas Carlyle echoed that, "Her 'mountain *me*' indeed." But he also said, "Such a predetermination to *eat* this big universe as her oyster or her egg, and to be absolute empress of all height and glory in it that her heart could conceive, I have not before seen in any human soul."[26] For him, it was a generous salute to Margaret's ambition. Surprisingly he seemed to tolerate this new genus better than his wife did.

Time and thought were needed to perceive a new kind of woman rightly. Half a year after meeting Margaret, having by then very likely read her *Papers on Literature and Art* (1846), Jane Carlyle acknowledged to Caroline Fox that the American woman had "written some beautiful things"—this even though Jane was in one of her phases of warning about the perils of over educating women, which more than anything expressed her own intermittent frustrations over the discrepancy between her talent and accomplishments, and worries over finding the right work for herself.

According to Caroline's account, nothing was said about ugliness or hypocrisy. Mrs. Carlyle informed her that Miss Fuller, who yearned for a freedom beyond the norms of straitlaced New England transcendentalists, held a discerning view of Emerson "of whom she speaks with more love than reverence."[27] Always impatient with airy-fairy transcendentalism (what she had found in the utopian, vegetarian Bronson Alcott), Jane would have endorsed such a sentiment. Caroline observed that she went beyond it: "Mrs. Carlyle does not see that much good is to come of Emerson's writings"! When Emerson, "the Yankee-Seraph," visited the Carlyles a year later, Jane wrote in fun, "We have seen him 'face to face and (over-) soul to (over-) soul'! [F]or two days I have lived on the *manna* of his speech, and now I have escaped to my bedroom to *bathe my head* in *cold water*."

After her weeks in London, Margaret Fuller traveled on to Paris where she met two other great nineteenth century women, the French-Jewish actress Rachel and that legendary literary figure George Sand. She said of Sand, "I never liked a woman better."[28] Margaret was to have many broadening, life altering experiences in Europe, especially in Italy. Italy was her destination; and Italy and its revolution would be her destiny. There she found love, bore a child, and discovered radical politics. Elizabeth Barrett Browning believed that the book Margaret had been writing about Italy, an unfinished manuscript lost with her when she drowned, would have been her best. Elizabeth, however, who did not share Margaret's politics, feared that the "blood colours of Socialistic views [if published in her book] . . . would have drawn the wolves on her, with a still more howling enmity, both in England and America."[29] Yet Margaret Fuller might have been just the woman to handle the howls of the wolves of the western world.

On the small but brightly lit stage of London society, it was as if Margaret had slipped the bonds of sisterhood. Neither Jane nor Geraldine could envision her as one of them, viewing her as a theorizing intellectual striving to hold forth with the men, over-focused on the question of when she might get to interrupt and participate. A Boston friend who later changed her mind about Margaret admitted that she and others had originally thought of her as being on "intellectual stilts."[3]

•

WE HAVE SEEN that Jane Carlyle came to characterize her own views on women and marriage as *too much in advance of the Century*. There is quite a lot of truth to that. But tradition and modernity contend very differently in individuals. One side usually pulls on a person's character more strongly than the other.

For all her subversive irony and genuine curiosity about the new ideas of the 1840s, Jane had a true respect for tradition in several senses. Literary tradition: in her mock epic passages and parodies, Jane's artistry involved playing off traditional genres. The traditions of communities of people over time: making use of "coterie speech," she wove a great many memorable sayings of others, past and present and from all classes, into her own writing. Family traditions: they were expressed in her Scottish values, as well as in the furniture and objects that she carefully collected and used in the decoration of her London home. Jane's attitudes toward *English conventions*, though, were more negative.

In ambition, training, and passion for a public presence, Margaret Fuller drew far ahead. As a new genus, or the prototype of one, she was unsettlingly breaking a feminine mold. Even though novels and conduct books of the 1840s explored male and female characteristics and obligations, and attempts were made to define the nature of manliness and womanliness, it would have been unclear in 1846 what Margaret's futuristic behavior might portend, or where it might lead.

As Margaret crosses the threshold and turns from view, her skirts whisking after her, she seems always ahead of us, a little beyond our ken. It was—it may still be—hard to perceive her rightly.

•

THIS FALL HELEN Mitchell and Margaret Fuller each gave Jane Carlyle the experience of watching a woman breaking out of an established category. In becoming a lady, Helen gained Jane's sympathy, while she remained skeptical that her Cinderella story could turn out well. (Helen did eventually have a falling out with her brother and returned to work for the Carlyles.) From these instances, the upsetting of gender expectations appears to have been more unsettling than the change in class status.

In her 1859 letter to George Eliot, Jane spoke of that sealed door of her childhood as one of her lost illusions. As a young girl, after a magical year of pondering the wondrous door, which Jane refers to as *door-worship*, it smote her "like a slap on the face" that "It was a door into—*nothing*! Make-believe! *There* for uniformity! Behind it was bare lath and plaster; behind *that* the Drawing-room with its familiar tables and chairs! Dispelled illusion no. 1!"

Despite the adventurous examples of her maid and Margaret, Jane Carlyle had recently endured an entire season of dispelled illusions. Furthermore, something new was afoot between Thomas and Lady Harriet, and pressure was on Jane to pay a country house visit—yet again.

CHAPTER FOURTEEN

"SUCH SHIFTING SCENES—SUCH INCONGRUITIES"

"My mind at all events keeps on the even tenor of its way—always with more *weight* on it than it can well bear always envelloped in London fog (figuratively speaking) burn this letter of course—"

—JANE WELSH CARLYLE TO HELEN WELSH, *from Bay House / Alverstoke /* January 20, 1847

DURING THIS PERTURBING TIME, IT WAS DIFFICULT FOR JANE CARLYLE TO discern from one day to the next just who she was. "My views of myself are a sort of 'dissolving views,' never the same for many minutes together," she wrote, using an image she liked from magic lantern shows where one scene dissolved into the next. What a sketch of herself might contain, she said, depended on how she had slept the night before.

Though she lightly tossed off the comment, she was standing on very uncertain ground, finding it hard to discover precisely what was on her husband's mind regarding Lady Harriet, and what she could do at this point about the triangle she found herself locked into against her will. Once again a crisis was brewing in the Carlyles' marriage.

After refusing pressing invitations to join Lady Harriet at Bay House, claiming illness, Jane all at once changed her mind and agreed to accompany her husband there. They would depart January 18, 1847, and be gone a month.

Her current ailments, which Jane spoke of as both physical illnesses and soul sickness, had been keeping her confined to two suffocating rooms in the Cheyne Row house, shut up against the winter weather. Giuseppe Mazzini, ever more public and preoccupied, was not as frequent a visitor. More to the point, his charm for her had diminished considerably since his refusal to firmly take her side in her quarrel with Thomas. Restive, bored, too often alone, she recognized more clearly than ever what a blow the loss of her maid Helen Mitchell had been, with the subsequent damage to her household routine. Not only that, she missed the living, breathing presence of the odd, tiny Kirkcaldy woman whose caprices she had become so well accustomed to. Besides, all that confinement to stuffy rooms had not made her well, so why not, she reasoned, try "rashness" instead and a change of scene?

Another explanation Jane gave for traveling to Bay House was more disturbing. At first she had encouraged her husband to go there alone. He had just sent Lady Harriet the third edition of his *Heroes and Hero Worship* as well as an eighteenth-century copy of *Cicero's Life and Letters*, writing her that she was the "beautifullest creature in all this world." His use of superlatives implies, repeatedly, that the lady is his favorite (though surely Jane did not see these letters). And he seemed more than willing to journey down to Alverstoke on his own.

However a note arrived from Lady Harriet that gave both Jane and Thomas a jolt. "There is y*r*. room," she wrote him after being informed his wife could not come because of illness, "—& welcome—ready, if you will, but if you come alone you must go on Tuesday when Bingham goes up for the meeting of Parl*t*."[1] That is, Thomas could not stay by himself in the house with her, the large corps of servants notwithstanding. Unless Mrs. Carlyle accompanied him, it would not look right if he were to be present when Lady Harriet's husband was absent. Had she grown alarmed by talk about the two of them? Had Bingham Baring been embarrassed by murmurs behind newspapers at his London club? Her worry over appearances suggests that Society had begun to engage in serious gossip about Lady Harriet Baring and Thomas Carlyle.

As Jane explained things to her cousin, "[J]ust when I was beginning to feel less fussed came [a] new invitation from Alverstoke exciting all manner of agitations." Lady Harriet "could not have C to stay with her alone by their two selves without *me*—and when she gave him so to understand he made a sort of point of *my* going—and I was too *proud* to stand in the way." She added, "But for the idea that it would have been a grievance had I refused to come when *he* could not get [there] without me I should not have dreamt of leaving home in such a state."

But leave home she did. The day of their departure the Carlyles hired a fly to take them to the railway station where they caught the 12:30 p. m. express train to Gosport, Hampshire, on Portsmouth Harbor. Although the train car was wintertime cold—no steam heat, toilets, or dining cars yet existed—Jane had come prepared. She kept her bonnet on, wore a close-fitting wool jacket over her dress, and on top of that a coat she had made from thick Scotch plaid blankets dyed a subdued and stylish black. We know the details from the conscientious letters that Jane and Thomas wrote their families. In those perilous times, all were highly solicitous of each other's health and liked to hear that ample precautions had been taken.

To keep her feet warm, Jane had what railway passengers often used, a bottle of hot water, and Thomas wrapped his up in a piece of horse cloth. She also brought along a respirator. Earlier Jane had written of this gadget, "the wonderfulest of all my acquisitions is a thing made of black silk with a *quarter of mile* of brass wire in it which clap on the under part of my face when I go out, and which is precisely like the muzzle on a mad dog—but has the property of making all the air that goes down one's throat as warm as summer air—" (*The Oxford English Dictionary* quotes her description to illustrate the term.) The surreal-looking respirator kept out grime and coal dust as well.

As the train rocked along the tracks, down through the Hampshire countryside, Thomas Carlyle took note of facts like a good Victorian—what time it left the station; how long it took to reach various landmarks—while an exhausted Jane, having suffered such agitation at the prospect of this visit, was unexpectedly lulled to sleep. She enjoyed a long nap as they journeyed toward the sea.

•

THE TRIP OF eighty-eight miles, in this quick new mode of travel, took a mere two hours and twenty minutes, which pleased Thomas, who wavered between being impressed by the latest railway advances and bemoaning their destructive effects on the harmony of rural life. As the train slowed to its destination, we can imagine him taking out a pocket watch and noting the time with satisfaction. Lady Harriet's brougham, awaiting them at Gosport, conveyed the couple directly to Bay House.

On their arrival the lady ordered the servants to provide the travelers with a tureen of hot soup in the dining room, even though an extravagance like that at an odd hour was counter to the well-regulated Bay House routine and would annoy the servants. And she decreed that Jane was to have a larger room than on her previous visit (again, one separate from her husband's). The room contained a "magnificent Canopy-bed," but unlike Jane's own red bed, it had no curtains. One would have to lie upon it exposed to the servants, she noticed, "exposed to the whole world."

By now Jane had become consistently cautious, wary, even fearful of Lady Harriet's intentions. And very unsure of her own role: as Mrs. Carlyle, what social duties was she expected to perform? She did not want to be looked upon as a bad wife, or to be thought in the wrong, when her husband was the one in the wrong. And when all was said and done, did she desire to participate on this exotic stage along with him—or not?

She knew many would envy her good fortune in being invited to Bay House at all. It remained the same fine new dwelling as on her prior visit, with the same extraordinary bank of windows facing the large expanse of water, plied by steamers and skiffs. There was now talk of a royal residence that Queen Victoria and Prince Albert were building across the Solent on the Isle of Wight, a new Osborne House in the style of an Italian palazzo. The prospect of having the Queen so close by during summertime holidays contributed to the fairytale sense of specialness that characterized all the Baring / Ashburton residences.

•

UNQUESTIONABLY JANE FOUND herself in an elevated realm. Bingham Baring was to travel down from Parliament on Saturdays—he was M. P. for Thetford—bringing colleagues like Charles Buller and Richard Monckton Milnes, along with the latest political news. A string of upper echelon visitors had been invited: the Marquis of Lansdowne; the Earl of Clarendon; Edward Ellice, a Highland laird; Lady Anne Charteris; and the four unmarried daughters of the Marchioness of Clanricarde, whom Jane found to be "very dowdy young ladies."

No one would claim the British aristocracy was uniformly peopled by glamorous, scintillating individuals, but their status, especially when coupled with great wealth, placed them in an undeniably rarified sphere. Certain sharp contrasts brought the vast disparity directly home to Jane. She shared a Haddington connection with Frank Charteris, at the moment residing nearby with his wife Anne. His aristocratic family's lands, the Wemyss estates, so close to where Jane had grown up, comprised nearly 57,000 acres. (Charteris, to be elected MP from East Lothian in July, would eventually become the eighth earl of Wemyss and the sixth earl of March.[2]) Jane Carlyle readily accepted people as just people. When she later met Lady Harriet's mother, Lady Sandwich, a supposedly terrifying peeress, Jane felt warmly toward her and thought of her as a friend. Yet, democratic-minded in these matters, she was proud of her own comparatively modest background and unpretentious style of living.

Soon after her arrival, perhaps to establish a sense of balance, she sat down at a desk in her room and straightaway composed a letter to her paternal uncle's widow, Margaret Welsh, who was working as a governess in Ireland. She told Mrs. Welsh that in Bay House it was "as tho one were living *on* some magnificent Cleopatra's barge—there are so many windows in it looking out on the sea and mirrors reflecting the prospect from these windows, so that wherever one turns there is always sea sea."

With her tallish slender figure, Jane dressed simply, sometimes in puritanically dark clothing. She must often have stood silhouetted at those Bay House windows looking out upon "sea sea," watching the endless splash of wavelets on the beach. And she must have gazed down upon the docks where the boats were anchored, unknowingly seeing what Lady Harriet had described to Thomas when she wrote to him, "I have often wished for you as our little vessel lay quite down on her side in the water, with the bright waves curling over."[3]

In her letter to Mrs. Welsh, Jane noted, "one has all . . . that money and taste can do for one—to read here of the starving Irish or starving anything is like a fairy tale." Writing to a woman busy earning her living in Ireland, Jane made a point of addressing the social disparities. A moral seemed in order. She drew a comparison to the homes that she and Mrs. Welsh had grown up in: "The longer I live the more deeply do I feel convinced that *money* beyond what gives the bare necessaries of life does good to no one and to many great harm—I suppose there is not a servant in this house who has not every day more luxuries of all kinds than you or I ever had or dreamt of having in our own houses—and see what they make of it! greedy, selfish, stupid! looked upon as necessary evils—looking upon their employers as their natural enemies—a Scotch Byrewoman [cow woman] with forty shillings a year who had a respect for her mistress and a love for her beasts was better off than these."

Jane was conveying ideas about the poor relationship between masters and servants in England that she, Betsey Paulet, and Geraldine Jewsbury had talked over at Seaforth House, where the Paulets were attempting to establish a more humane regime, although all three women valued "knowing your place" in the scheme of things.

Yet the Castle of Indolence, as Thomas termed Bay House, after a satirical poem by the Scottish poet James Thomson, had undeniable appeal. Guests like the Carlyles, having left behind their dull sublunary lives, became enhanced through mere association. The balmy, sunshiny weather. The spaciousness. The service, food, and (sometimes) witty conversation, with bells signaling when guests should dress for dinner, a formal, elaborate affair. In the evenings they read aloud to each other from the latest literature, though on this occasion the other guests refused to listen to Thomas read from his presentation copy of Ralph Waldo Emerson's new book of poems. Instead he read them to himself, later telling the poet, after a ritual admonishment to return to prose, that they were "*thin* piercing radiances which affect me like the light of the *stars*."

Thomas, for the most part, despite the acknowledgement of indolence, appreciated his sojourn there. Jane, however, resisted the grandeur and entertainment, a resistance she thought Lady Harriet regarded as "taking reactionary turns." For Jane her own Chelsea home was anchor and center, the place where she could be calmer and more productive. She told correspondents she would rather be there training her maid Anne Brown than languishing week after week at some idle house party. For a short time she hovered on the verge of packing her bags and returning to London. At one point, when she had come down with a virulent sore throat that had been going around the household (Lady Harriet had suffered from it earlier), Thomas believed he would have to escort her back to Chelsea.

A guest who fell ill at Bay House was in trouble. Outside the strictly ordered routines, it could be difficult to obtain something as simple as a cup of tea. "So long as you can keep on foot, and play your part as an agreeable—at lowest a *not boring* member of society you are treated with courtesy," Jane told her husband's sister; ". . . but fall ill—have to take to bed—and you are lost!—The Lady never comes near you—the housemaids do not find it *in their department* to look after sick visitors—you are like an unfortunate toppled over in the treadmill [a device associated with prison labor]—in danger of perishing there while the general business—or rather I should say *amusement* of the house rushes on over your body!"

One day despite repeated pleas no tea arrived. Finally a footman entered her room with a tea tray and deposited it near her supine and exposed body. (When no female servant could be found to do the deed, Thomas had successfully harassed the man into helping out.) The intrusion prompted Jane to exclaim, "How ridiculous my life is as a whole! such shifting scenes—such incongruities,—material splendour alternating with material squalour—one time unable to get a cup of tea without two or three men-servants mixing themselves with the concern—another day advertising in the Times for a Maid of All-Work—and thankful to get one who can boil a kettle!"

She recovered quickly, though, and before long was chatting with guests, playing chess, and taking walks on the pebble beach. She could even say, "I shall go back much stronger than I came." Her renewal of strength might have had something to do with confronting and handling the confusing reality of Lady Harriet once again.

Lady Harriet continued ever opaque and mysterious, to the point where a baffled Jane wrote her cousin, "I cannot make out what Lady H is after—but to look at her one would say she was systematically *playing my cards for me*." She added, "Please do not read *that* aloud—."

Jane found it mystifying that Lady Harriet now appeared to be purposefully altering the nature of her friendship with Thomas Carlyle. She had acquired a parrot as a pet, which the Carlyles nicknamed the Green Chimera. While Thomas joked about the bird, he seemed genuinely to loathe it because of the way the lady perpetually fussed over the creature. Furthermore the parrot (unlike Margaret Fuller, we may remember) was allowed to interrupt the Sage of Chelsea during his holdings-forth whenever it pleased.

Green chimera of course connotes jealousy. Thomas was meeting "with other little contradictions" from Lady Harriet, which Jane said she could not "pretend to be sorry for—" The lady decided to give up her intimate sessions of reading German literature with Mr. Carlyle, wherein the classic, romantic mentor-pupil relationship had flourished, in favor of spending more time with her other company. She claimed her better health these days meant she had now no pretence for neglecting her other guests.

"By Heaven," Jane decided, "she is *the very cleverest* woman I ever saw or heard of—*she can* do what she wills . . . I am perfectly certain there is not a created being alive whom she could not gain within twenty four hours after she set her mind to it— Just witness myself—how she plies *me* round her little finger whenever she sees I am taking a reactionary turn—" The moment Jane got well, Lady Harriet began behaving toward her in an exceedingly gracious, if manipulative, manner. "[S]ystematically or involuntarily she has *staved off* a deal of vexation from me," Jane wrote her cousin, "which might easily have attended my visit and made it very wretched." With Lady Harriet at her diplomatic best, distancing herself from Mr. Carlyle and bestowing graciousness and benevolence upon his Mrs., Jane in true wonderment, admiring yet suspicious, watched herself being played. Whether Lady Harriet was doing this systemically or involuntarily Jane could not make out.

Was Lady Harriet a master chess player making complicated moves just out of sight? She had possibly feared a crisis building ever since Thomas had suggested in late autumn that they ought not to correspond at all. In addition to her worries over what Society might be saying, it had proven tricky to secure the attendance of Mr. Carlyle without his wife's cooperation. Having already exercised her skills in efforts to placate Mrs. Carlyle, she had, on this occasion, gone to even greater trouble, with the result that Jane found the visit far smoother than expected. But the strain on the Carlyles' marriage continued.

Living in a larger world would have given Lady Harriet a very different frame of reference. There was a built-in imbalance. The aristocratic woman traveled to other countries, ran a salon, existed within powerful networks of family and friends, and oversaw a string of establishments with large staffs of servants. Both women lived within Victorian constraints. Both experienced rivalry with each other. But Jane Carlyle was caught in the far more confining circumstances of a middle class housewife. She in no way loomed as large in Lady Harriet's life as the lady loomed in hers.

•

BACK IN THEIR Chelsea home after the month in Hampshire, Thomas reported that Jane, improved in health, was out strolling in the early spring sunshine, doing business with local merchants, and training her maid. Anne Brown, a sleepyhead, required her mistress to ring her awake in the morning and could be a bit tardy in getting her duties done. Mostly, though, Jane complimented the little cockney woman, nicknaming her Tadpole, and considered her overall "the nicest tidiest activest cheerfulest little thing—cooks 'like an Angel.'" Unlike Isabella, Anne made no fuss about washing dishes or cleaning the grate on the Sabbath. And she expressed affection and admiration for her mistress who could "stuff chair-cushions and do *any*thing that was needed and be *a Lady* too." Anne was not socially isolated, often seeing her best female friend and keeping company with the butcher's assistant. The young couple, Jane believed (correctly), would not marry until he had the prospect of a business of his own. "[M]eanwhile," she said with a touch of wistfulness, "it rather pleases me to know of a little *decent* love-making going on in the house—"

As Jane recovered her health, her thoughts turned outward. Giuseppe Mazzini was holding a bazaar this spring to raise money for his Italian Free School. Despite the alterations in their friendship, she wished to help. He was living in an ever-widening world, far wider than Lady Harriet's. This year, 1847, it included a Europe hurtling toward change. Corresponding with comrades and sympathizers in many countries, Mazzini kept an eye on all the intriguing developments.

The Ten Hour Bill, or British Factory Act, passed in England this year, reducing the working day for women and children. Reform Banquets, a way to enable large numbers of people to assemble legally, were being held in France, calling for universal suffrage for men and parliamentary reform. Many varied factors were propelling the engine of change, which would erupt, in 1848, into a European Spring.

Forging Italy into a unified nation was Giuseppe Mazzini's driving endeavor, but he was also an internationalist, organizing this spring a People's International League, gathering together friends like the Chartist wood engraver and landscape painter William James Linton, who had supported him during the post office affair; the novelist Charles Dickens; and the journalist Douglas Jerrold. The League was a British organization formed to advocate the sharing of information and understanding among countries; and to encourage freedom, progress, and national self-governance. Yet Giuseppe Mazzini dreamed of more. He wished to turn it into a European confederation, composed of delegates representing different countries.[4] It is not far fetched to say that in a small way his conception of the League (which was short lived, overpowered by the 1848 uprisings) anticipated the League of Nations, the United Nations, and the European Union.

With fellow Italians in exile, Giuseppe Mazzini had also formed his Committee for the Direction of the Bazaar to solicit handmade items from well-to-do English women to sell at an event scheduled for the afternoon of May 22 at the home of Mrs. Arethusa Milner-Gibson, a firm advocate of Italian liberty. Jane decided to make a silk purse for the bazaar and wrote her Liverpool cousins, including her deft-handed youngest cousin, urging them to donate their famous handcrafted pincushions. Closer to the date, she told them the need was less urgent: "he has got many Ladies working for it with enthusiasm—M*rs* Milner Gibson alone has made 'a hundred and fifty small objects.'"

No detail was too small to interest the remarkable Mazzini as he concerned himself with pincushions one moment and warships the next, whatever might benefit the cause.

Jane now summed up his less-isolated circumstances: "Mazzini is pretty well—very busy as usual with his benevolent schemes—not so solitary as he used to be." No longer was he a black-garbed stranger pacing the crowded yet lonely streets of a foreign city, greatly in need of her companionship and attentive concern. He had made new friends. He was "up to the ears in a *good* twadly family of the name of Ashurst —who have plenty of money—and help 'his *things*' [projects] and *toady* him till I think it has rather gone to his head—A Miss Eliza Ashurst— who does strange things—made his acquaintance first—by going to his house to drink tea with him all alone &c &c!!" (That of course being quite *improper*.) Jane continued, "[A]nd when she had got him to *her* house she introduced him into innumerable other houses of her kindred—and the women of them [four sisters] paint his picture, and send him flowers, and *work* for his bazaar, and make verses about him." The father, a solicitor, provided encouragement and capital, and joined the People's International League. Wholly dedicated to the cause, the Ashursts, their mother included, were honored and thrilled to become intimate with him. Fondly, they called him Mazz or The Angel.

Jane turned a sharp eye on the Ashursts, and if she wrote with an extra dollop of satire, it was perhaps because now that she and Giuseppe were drifting apart she was experiencing a twinge of envy. A portrait of Eliza Ashurst shows a neat, plain woman with smooth, full dark hair framing a sweet, bland face. Yet plain as she was, Eliza had enchanted not only Giuseppe but also Geraldine Jewsbury. Geraldine had just sworn eternal friendship with Eliza in the same annoying (to Jane) way she had done with the actress Charlotte Cushman. This April and May, Geraldine and Eliza, who had in common a passion for the work of George Sand, in addition to the liberation of Italy, were making enthusiastic visits to each other's homes. Jane, however, was becoming more philosophical about Geraldine's infatuations: "I know her ways now, and can let her take her swing sure that she will right herself at last."

•

JANE DID SEE that Giuseppe's friendship with Eliza differed in significant ways from their own. And understood that Eliza, the eldest and only unmarried Ashurst sister, "would *marry him* out and out with all the joy in life—but *that* is not Mazzinis way." Jane knew her man. Giuseppe Mazzini was determined to stay married, as it were, to the revolution. He was certainly not going to tie himself down to Eliza Ashurst. One of her sisters later confirmed Jane's perceptions, writing: "That such a dream could ever be fulfilled was, Mazzini knew, impossible. . . . [T]here lay in the background of his life a love that exacted the utmost of his powers, and his entire loyalty: Italy, the Niobe [or most unfortunate] of nations."[5]

In friendly letters, Giuseppe tactfully but firmly turned Eliza away from romantic ideas about him, because of his revolutionary obligations. In the charmingly idiosyncratic English that Jane could so deftly capture when describing his talk, Giuseppe wrote Eliza, "Next year, most likely, I will vanish out of England into the space." "Be good and kind and friendly and sisterly, if you can and if I deserve it . . . but leave future in the dark and never attempt to lift its veil." "Are we not brother and sister? Or, if you, like Zoe [Geraldine], do not like these names, which I am fond of, are we not friends?"[6]

He had used the sister / brother approach with Jane, and she had accepted the formulation, possibly as a way to handle whatever romantic, affectionate feelings existed between them. But now the intensity of their friendship was over. The Ashurst women had taken her place. In Giuseppe Mazzini's letters of 1847, an important political year for him, there is a dramatic diminution in letters to or about the Carlyles.

He needed close female friends and seems always to have had them. He supported education for women and this summer would accept a position as a vice president of the Whittington Club, founded by Douglas Jerrold, which admitted women members with full rights and privileges.[7] Amely Bölte, for one, was excited by the concept of the club and applied for membership, saying it was "somewhat modeled after Communist ideas, [and] tastes a little bit of emancipation for women." But when Amely actually visited the place, she found herself seated in a large room "where I sat on my own with one hundred gentlemen." She hinted that Thomas Carlyle had goaded her into going, ostensibly to "read all the most recent newspapers," which she longed to have access to, after an argument they had had over the rights of women. "Carlyle's determination drove me to the Whittington Club," she said. "I don't thank him for this."[8] Amely, who wished to be a free thinking woman *and* a respectable lady, had found herself extremely ill at ease among all those gentlemen. Visiting such a club was not a comfortable thing to do, not even for a Victorian bluestocking.

The Ashurst family continued faithfully to support their Italian hero. In this period Thomas Carlyle and Giuseppe Mazzini were both attracting disciples only too ready to provide slavish assistance, along with doses of over-the-top adulation.

Jane's behavior with Giuseppe had been very different. Both of them paid tribute to values like Mission and Duty, but her irony and skepticism balanced his sentimentality and religiosity. He brought out her warmer, more liberal side, and she proved a witty, bracing companion for him. Importantly, however diminished their involvement with each other, they would remain friends.

•

AMELY BÖLTE WAS calling on Jane Carlyle frequently this spring, but after an unpleasant encounter with Thomas one day, she wrote in exasperation to Varnhagen that compared to him, Mr. Carlyle would shrink "to the size of a pygmy." Amely's letters reveal that overall she regarded Thomas as a special being, an original, who fascinated and even dazzled her. When she annoyed him, he sometimes fled upstairs to avoid her, but he also enjoyed their talks about German politics and literature, and liked hearing news of Varnhagen and his circle. Amely believed that he tolerated her company most easily when she was compliant, though there is a zest to her descriptions of their verbal contests. But she experienced him as a friend one day and an antagonist the next—Amely gives a sense of shifting scenes as well.

After her most recent unpleasant encounter, she gave Varnhagen her analysis, mincing no words. Thomas Carlyle's books, she told him, "are everything and their author nothing. I cannot recognize in him one virtue or any sense of beauty or goodness. He writes for mankind, but a human being is nothing to him. He hates the aristocracy and adores an aristocrat. He speaks of the liberty of nations and would like them to be ruled by the sword. One cannot discover anything clear or definite in him; one cannot get a hold on him. . . . It is always paradoxes he creates, and . . . since no one contradicts him, he will always remain one-sided. His conversation is like clockwork that needs to be wound up in order to keep going. . . . He often tells me, 'I do not like people who talk, but who make me talk.'" Tellingly Amely added, "Only with his wife is he taciturn and in a foul mood. Generally he does not talk to ladies at all, except to some peeresses."[9]

That foul mood oppressed his wife and had a detrimental effect on the atmosphere of their household. To understand better what Jane Carlyle was facing, it is necessary to probe a little more into what might have been troubling her husband at this moment of his life.

Something seemed deeply the matter. At fifty-one (older of course in the nineteenth century than it seems now), conscious of his graying hair and the limited time before him, his savagery continued. It was gathering force and pressure, seeking an outlet in some new writing project. Though considering several ideas and telling people his next book would be *dreadful* or *frightful*, he had as yet no set plan.

His letters indicate a growing irritation with the religious tradition of his family. When visiting Scotsbrig later this year he complained, uncharacteristically, of his mother. Her presence curtailed conversation, "for my Mother is terribly sensitive on *the Semitic* side of things, which mostly excludes speculation." In his denunciations of Hebraic Calvinism to other correspondents, he used phrases like Hebrew "rags" and "the dreary abyss of Old-Jewhood and Old-Genevahood." On one occasion, aware of how extreme he sounded, he told Jane, "It is positively very wicked and base to write all this, even to thee; and I charge thee speak of it to no mortal whatsoever."

Yet he had already written Ralph Waldo Emerson of his need to peel off "fetid *Jewhood* in every sense from myself and my poor bewildered brethren." By Jewhood he seemed to mean the Old Testament, but the New did not escape. As Emerson wrote his wife Lidian (after his autumn 1847 visit to Cheyne Row), Thomas Carlyle's virulence took the form of "the utmost impatience of Christendom and Jewdom, and all existing presentments of the good old story. He talks like a very unhappy man."[10] All this suggests inroads into whatever remnants of faith he had left; and an increasing, if unwelcome, skepticism.[11] A possibly apocryphal story attributed to Alfred Tennyson suggests that, strangely enough, Thomas Carlyle equated the outworn "old Jewish rags" with a belief in a hereafter—that he could no longer imagine.[12] Though Thomas continued to console family members with generic Christian sentiments, he, too, found himself on shifting, uncertain ground.

The plight of Ireland weighed ever more heavily. He understood now that tens of thousands would perish, writing Lady Harriet, "There never was, surely, under the Sun such a spectacle as that wretched Island now exhibits." Edward FitzGerald complained to a correspondent that Gurlyle—his and Thackeray's nickname for Carlyle—was busy foaming about Ireland.[13] Thomas had written Edward, "Ireland is a perpetual misery to me; lies like a kind of nightmare on my thoughts, little as I personally have to do with it."

He related a terrible detail of the desperate Irish poor to his brother Alexander in Canada: "they *wall* themselves into their cabins (for *burial* is not always to be had), and there silently lie down to die!" It had been reported that some peasants, unemployed, starving, ashamed, and rebellious—refusing to work for nothing—had seen no alternative but to die in this very private, walled-up way with their children. Where was the religion that could give meaning to misery, starvation, and death on such a scale?

He blamed feckless landlords and supported those raising money for Irish relief, yet believed in a kind of creative destruction: if all fell to pieces, would that not force into being new solutions? He sometimes thought his Young Ireland friends, in the unlikely event they survived their trials and tribulations as political activists and took over, would prove more competent administrators. Was that slim ray the only hope? Otherwise he was staring into an abyss, pained but paralyzed. The most baffling, intransigent political problem of a lifetime.

Oddly, when he wrote Charles Gavan Duffy about Ireland, he used a marriage metaphor, linking the outer crisis to his inner one. Repeal of the union between Ireland and England, he argued, was out of the question according to "the laws of Nature": "We are married to Ireland by the ground-plan of this world—a thick-skinned labouring man to a drunken ill-tongued wife, and dreadful family quarrels have ensued!"

Believing marriage to be a sacred contract, Thomas had no intention of seeking repeal of his union with Jane, however much he might at the moment have been experiencing it as an unhappy ironclad bond. Because he was, overall, discreet on the subject, we cannot be certain how powerfully he was drawn to Lady Harriet. That is, we do not know if he suffered from their inability to pursue a physical relationship, or if he even desired that. Or to what extent frustration on any sexual front contributed to his state of mind.

Lady Harriet continued to play her game of hard to get. This March she traveled to Paris to look after her ailing mother and did not inform him. Thomas went to Stanhope Street one day with the expectation of seeing her, only to be told, "Her Ladyship is gone to Paris, sir; not to be back till after Easter, sir!" She who had once written intimate, sensuous notes about nature to him would no longer do so.

In the process, as her friendship with Mr. Carlyle shifted and changed, seeking to find a way, she may have experienced a certain sourness setting in, turning the rejected sensuous into the rebarbative sensual. When on March 31 she finally writes to Thomas Carlyle from the Hotel Meurice, Rue de Rivoli—her mother is recovered, but now Lady Harriet has become sick with a cold—she begins "I have nothing to tell you," and praises, as always, the sunshine. But surprisingly she transitions into his own misanthropic, apocalyptic style: "I walk ab*t*. with my pocket handkerchief steeped in vinegar," she tells him, "from the effluvia which greets one in the thronged streets & I must say a moral antiseptic would be equally assailable had one made such a discovery. The people—and their habits and pursuits—& interests are all loathsome—degraded—sensual and venal. What can come of them? The public spirit of those who effect it is mere fanfaronade & I quite agree with L*d*. Ellesmere who said he expected on turning around to see a great lake of fire & brimstone and nothing visible but the Dome of the Tuileries to mark where

Paris had been—" Lady Harriet concludes, "So much for the centre and head of all civilisation."[14]

During the next many months she was hardly to write him at all.

•

On February 20, 1847, Thomas Carlyle, man of paradox and incongruity, wrote to a Dr. Thomas Chalmers in a very different tone. A theologian and church leader, Dr. Chalmers had sent him his review of a book about speculative European philosophy. In response, Thomas put forth his own thoughts in unusually clear terms for this period. His phrases ring with authenticity, as opposed to the contrarian harangues his friends were forever complaining about. He calls what he is writing *an article of faith*.

German transcendental metaphysics, when Thomas Carlyle encountered that body of thought as a young man, had driven out the dry, over-reasoning, Scotch-French skepticism of the Enlightenment, a large part of his university education, which had come close to annihilating him: "I had nearly lost my life." After being raised in his strict Calvinist family of peasants and stonemasons, he had, as a student at the University of Edinburgh, begun to doubt the religious tenets they held dear. But reading Goethe and the German romantics revived his flagging spirituality. After that, he was able "by Heaven's unspeakable mercy" to "look abroad with my own eyes over the *real Universe* once more, and *see!*" He all but said, "I was blind but now can see."

"Since that," however, he tells Dr. Chalmers, "I have more and more decidedly kept clear of all such speculations." Speculation was too often unhealthy and diseased. He describes, in contrast, the glory of the past: "in all ancient healthy ages, men *have* used their intellect not for looking into *itself* (which I consider to be naturally *impossible*, and a mere morbid spasm), but to look out, as an *eye* should, over the Universe which is not we, and *there* to recognise innumerable things, and to believe, and do,—and *adore* withal."

In olden times, humans did not over-examine themselves or their world: "Since the first Norse *Thinker*, Odin or whatever his name, sank prostrate at the Unutterable Spectacle of Earth and Sea and Air, of the Stars and the Graves, of the Lightnings and the Azures, of Life and of Death; and, with his brow in the dust, said awestruck 'It is a God!'—from this first Norse Thinker with his eyes and his worship, onward to the last German one with his telescopes, crucibles, 'immense practical utilities,' accredited sentimentalisms, and 'love of the picturesque,' what a way have we travelled!"

His appeal to the many who revered his spiritual autobiography *Sartor Resartus*—and Jane was one who strongly admired it—can be glimpsed in that passage. It is the "early" Thomas Carlyle, whose voice is nearly lost today. He utters a poetic outcry against the deadness, artificiality, and mechanization of industrialization; against lifeless rituals of institutionalized religion; against university-educated logicians who would talk life to death. His is the world of wonder as it appears to a child, to a primitive person, at times terrifying but fresh and amazing, calling forth gratitude and adoration for the sheer gladness of being alive on this rotating earth. For those in our own self-absorbed era, the exhortation to look out "as an *eye* should, over the Universe which is not we, and *there* to recognise innumerable things, and to believe, and do" can still inspire.

He can make us wonder if we can recover what we have lost growing up in a modern capitalistic era. He allows a romantic hope. The world around us brightens. However, if he believes that people cannot also use their intellects for looking into themselves (shocking to all who think the examined life is worth living); if that is considered "naturally *impossible*, and a mere morbid spasm"; how are people to know themselves? And if unfathomable to themselves, will they not inevitably be mistaken in their views of others?

Curiously, two of his friends, Erasmus Darwin and Ralph Waldo Emerson, spoke of Thomas Carlyle this year as a child. To Emerson the Transcendentalist (who told it to Jane in confidence), he seemed at heart, despite everything, "a good Child." Darwin, scion of a sterner tradition, said, "Carlyle's ferocity is like a child's so that really one hardly cares [about] it . . . unfortunately he has no Ma to carry him off cursing and swearing."[15] Thomas Carlyle's letter to Chalmers allows us to imagine for a moment a wondering child trapped inside this self-tortured, aggravating mystery of a man.

•

JANE CARLYLE, THIS spring, was sewing. Never anything like a consistent journal keeper, she wrote only a single entry in her notebook for 1847, a short passage about the funeral of Dr. Christie's wife. There were no interesting attempts to express herself in a different genre, though possibly she wrote pages she later destroyed. The literary standard this year was set spectacularly high. Novels that we continue to read were published by the Brontës, Dickens, and Thackeray: *Wuthering Heights*, *Jane Eyre*, *Dombey and Son*, and *Vanity Fair*—with Jane Carlyle saying of the last, "Very good—indeed—beats Dickens out of the world—"

For the time being, the needle had taken precedence over the pen. After making that silk purse for Mazzini's bazaar, she was sewing curtains and covers galore for the furniture of the ground floor parlor, using "rather dashing chintz at 8*d* a yard," or "*glazed calico*," rendering the room "much brighter than its mistress." Jane was also making fresh straps for the Venetian blinds and giving each slat a coat of linseed oil. Always appreciative of her frugality and household improvements, Thomas told his mother that his wife was "a top needlewoman."

Geraldine humorously warned her friend of the disadvantages that accrued to "women who take to sewing and female employments." She herself had just finished making a habit shirt—a chemisette with a linen collar that could be worn under a riding habit—on the strength of someone's well-intentioned advice to use her needle for her betterment. Instead, Geraldine told Jane, "every day I am getting more and more like a lump of sugar that is melting away at the bottom of a cup of weak tea, and all the sewing in the world would not revive me."[16]

Richard Plattnauer, with his air of grave dignity, was visiting often. With Thomas in a tortured mood and Giuseppe busy with politics and the Ashurst women, Jane no doubt relied on Richard's affection and intelligent conversation. "He gives no signs of derangement *at present*," she noted; "unless his almost superhuman insight and elevation, can be called *derangement*. . . . [I]t does me good to talk with him—" She told her cousin, "they may all say what they like, the *madness* is lying in him all the same as ever, only deep down—ready to burst up any day—*That* I know—but I also do not mind it."

Caroline Fox visited, too, and in a diary entry for May 20, 1847, the young Quaker recorded an account of a long visit with Mrs. Carlyle who detailed a morbid opium dream (recounted in the previous chapter) and informed her, "I often wonder what right I have to live at all." Jane spoke to Caroline of "the world's hollowness," her own supposed over-education, and the deaths of parents and friends.

In this July 1854 photograph by Robert Scott Tait, Thomas Carlyle looks much the same as he did in the 1840s. It was considered an excellent likeness.

Giuseppe Mazzini, Italian hero, famed throughout Europe. From the late 1830s through the 1840s he was close to JWC, calling her "the woman I value the most in England."

Erasmus Alvey Darwin, older brother of Charles, was an independently wealthy London bachelor. Since he and the Carlyles saw each other often and rarely saved each other's notes, the written record does not reflect the depth of their enduring friendship.

Prolific author Harriet Martineau, famously deaf, has her hand cupped to her ear.

In her graceful handwriting, JWC copied a nearly illegible flower poem by the Carlyles' friend Richard Monckton Milnes. It concludes: "How the vividest remembrance / Does not rest in noisy wonder / In the ocean in the Thunder, / But in Nature's tiny dot— / Littlest Forget me not!"

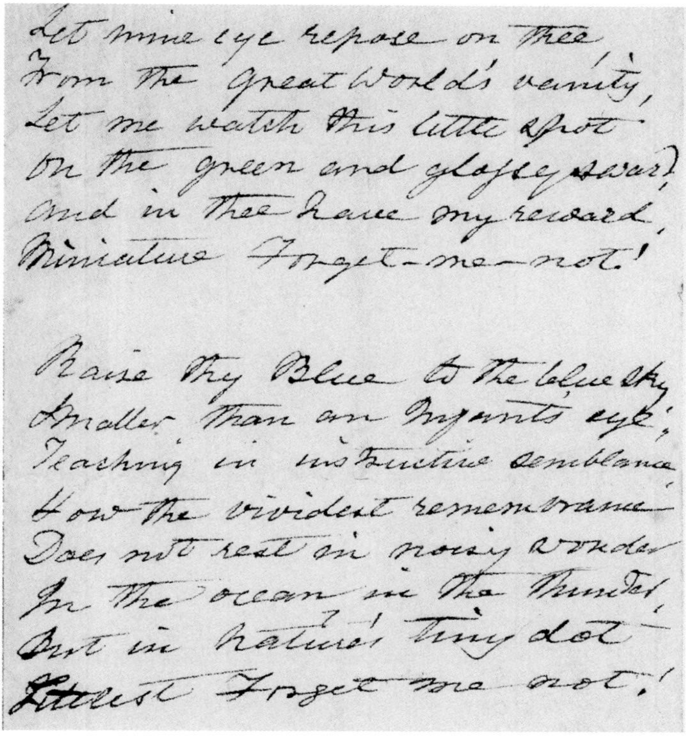

Let mine eye repose on thee
From the Great World's vanity,
Let me watch this little spot
On the green and glossy sward,
And in thee have my reward,
Miniature Forget-me-not!

Raise thy Blue to the blue sky
Smaller than an Infant's eye;
Teaching in instructive semblance
How the vividest remembrance
Does not rest in noisy wonder
In the ocean in the Thunder,
But in Nature's tiny dot
Littlest Forget me not!

"Charles Dickens Reading 'The Chimes'" by Daniel Maclise, 1844. Dickens asked that JWC be part of the group—a rare invitation for a woman to receive—but she did not attend. At the far left: the Carlyles' close friend, editor John Forster. He hosted the event in his chambers. TC sits to the novelist's right, hand to head.

"Paul Pry at the Post Office," a Punch *cartoon from June 1844 after it became known that, scandalously, Home Secretary Sir James Graham had presided over the secret opening of Giuseppe Mazzini's personal mail.*

The formidable Lady Harriet Baring (later Lady Ashburton), from a Francis Holl lithograph. She was a dear friend of TC and a challenging, sometimes threatening, psychological puzzle to JWC.

An early image of the Grange, the vast Greek-style country house of the Baring/Ashburtons in Hampshire. When visiting, the Carlyles would stand out on the huge columned portico to talk and take in fresh air. Its impressive ruins can be seen today.

In this sweet, slightly sensuous Victorian cameo, Jane Welsh Carlyle is wearing a dark lace mantilla. The portrait was commissioned by her cousin Jeannie Welsh and painted by Italian refugee artist Spiridione Gambardella in 1843.

This sophisticated image of Jane Welsh Carlyle, commissioned by governess and author Amely Bölte, is based on a crayon and watercolor sketch made by German refugee artist Carl Hartmann in 1849.

Jane and Geraldine together: Robert Scott Tait took this photograph in April 1855—a rare image, in this period, of JWC with another person. From the Carlyles' albums. Carefully dressed in their lovely best, JWC is standing, GEJ seated. Despite ups and downs, their friendship endured: "best friends forever."

She then made an intriguing comment on her marriage, as if she had been thinking through whether she and her husband (in another world) might have formed a less conventional liaison, one more independent and companionate. She told Caroline how her tutor Edward Irving had introduced them when she was living with her mother in Haddington. During their courtship years, she and Thomas "had a literary intimacy, and she would be writing constantly and consulting him about everything." Caroline then quotes Jane directly: "and so it would probably have always gone on, for we were both of us made for independence, and I believe should never have wanted to live together, but this intimacy was not considered discreet, so we married quietly and departed."[17]

•

IN THIS TIME of dissolving views and shifting scenes, Jane had been rethinking her life and her marriage. She and her husband could not just keep going on and on exactly the same way. *Something* different needed to be done.

CHAPTER FIFTEEN
A GREEN AND PLEASANT IDYLL

"The country in the neighbourhood of this village [Matlock] resembled . . . the scenery of Switzerland; but every thing is on a lower scale, and the green hills want the crown of distant white Alps. . . . We visited the wondrous cave."
—MARY SHELLEY, *Frankenstein*

THE CARLYLES' LIFE BECAME BUSY, PERHAPS RATHER TOO BUSY, AS THE summer of 1847 approached. They undertook a visit to Addiscombe in May. (This year they were to spend a total of two months with the Barings). At the Macreadys' London home they met the acclaimed singer Jenny Lind, just then making her London debut. Geraldine descended on Cheyne Row for a visit, creating a small splash in their social circle, and went out to the theatre accompanied by Dr. John Carlyle. He was completing his prose translation of Dante's *Inferno*, and Geraldine was in the process of finishing her second novel, *The Half Sisters*. Agitating thoughts of a possible match between the newly literary pair flared up in Jane's mind, then died away.

In June the heir to the Grand Duchy of Saxe-Weimar caused consternation when he arranged a formal visit to meet Thomas Carlyle in his Chelsea home. Jane dusted the trinkets, put Anne Brown into a clean gown, and changed the water in the flower vases. She then took herself off to spend the afternoon with Isabella Buller. Jane had left the premises because she refused to be subjected to royal protocol inside her own home, such as having to stand until invited to sit down in her own chair. But she was later fascinated to hear every detail about the distinguished man from her husband. Dignified though the royal personage was,

Thomas reported that in no way could he match the stately demeanor and erect carriage of Richard Plattnauer.

The heats of July were terrible, "disorganizing and demoralizing," which must have brought back memories of the scorching temperatures of the year before. On her 46th birthday Jane found herself weeping over her gifts, especially those from her husband, a cameo brooch and some pin money for transportation expenses, with a note reading: "For *Flies* thro' the year, / To my bonnie little Dear."[1] She wept over a tiny basket charm from Helen Welsh that contained a lock of hair and confessed to her cousin: "A *hat-box* from poor Bölte completed the overthrow of my sensibilities—it contained an immense bouquet of the loveliest flowers, in the middle of which was stuck—her picture!—in water-colours and gilt-framed." Jane enclosed Amely's note "that you may see Bölte in her best phase—People wonder always why I let myself be bored with that woman but with all her want of tact in the everyday intercourse of life she manifests a *sentiment* on occasions so delicate and deep that I should be a brute not to feel touched by it—" In the midst of planning a trip to Germany, the governess had paused to write Jane in her beautiful, educated script, "Egotism has prompted me to wish never to be forgotten by you . . . . I send you a little image of my own self, to remind you at times of one to whom you have been a God send and a saving in many evil hours. Let me have a little place some where about you, where your eye may fall upon me without looking particularly for it—unawares;—it will be a great consolation to me, when away from you, and more so while in Germany."[2]

The Carlyles were nearing a desperation point this summer. Not only had Jane been suffering in ordinary ways from the heat, she had started running a fever and could hardly eat or sleep. They went again a few days to Addiscombe, which at least had an abundance of shade trees. No letters that Jane wrote from there have survived. Was she again feeling hauled around for the convenience of others? It is likely the Carlyles quarreled, or at least that Jane again made known her profound unhappiness about their visits to the Barings.

"Jane needs, really *needs*, a little country air," Thomas told his mother. Each longed to escape the oppressive heat but it was hard to think of a place to go that would suit them both. Pressure to put their marriage on a better footing must have been an imperative, although they do not address that head on.

Thomas, too, was suffering from ailments. He experienced a bout of rheumatism or lumbago, felt in the back, making it a bit difficult to walk. Unable to visit the Barings' London home, he wrote Lady Harriet rather cryptically on August 3, "To Stanhope Street I clearly cannot come at present. Whether I shall see you again depends therefore on the favour of Heaven. Heaven, I believe, is favourable to those that *can* deserve it; but it is difficult, at times terribly difficult! Courage!" In the immediate sense he was referring to his back, but the note seems to confirm that Jane had once more objected to their constant intercourse with the Barings.

The Carlyles, as always, had trouble settling on precise dates and destinations for traveling. Then, quite suddenly, they came to an agreement: they would tour Derbyshire! For a modern reader that might bring to mind the romantic Pemberley, Elizabeth Bennett's stately Derbyshire home after her marriage to Mr. Darcy at the end of Jane Austen's *Pride and Prejudice*. But because Thomas and Jane both considered Miss Austen's work to be *washy gruel*, they were unlikely to have derived inspiration from that source.

Scarcely leaving themselves time to pack, they set off August 6, 1847, heading toward Matlock Bath, gateway to the Peak District, on the River Derwent. The village boasted mineral springs and steep hillsides offering multi-level views. Woods, waterfalls, cliff paths, and pastures abounded. George Gordon, Lord Byron, had visited the area and left part of a poem scratched on a piece of window glass.[3] In *Frankenstein* Mary Shelley had described the place as a little Switzerland. Long the site of healthful renewal, its reputation as a travelers' destination had been enhanced in 1844 when Queen Victoria made a second visit there.

The excursion was for the Carlyles alone, just the two of them. No visits to or with the Barings were included in their plans. In fun, parodying earlier travel literature, Jane summed up the journey for her literary friend Anna Jameson as "*The Pursuit of the Picturesque under Difficulties*," explaining it was "the first time in our married lives that we ever figured as declared Tourists."

New circumstances made such a holiday possible. Thomas now had a steady stream of income from frequent editions of his works, what he called *rent* from his books. Wherever they went, because of his celebrity, friends and acquaintances were eager to put them up or assist in some way. The railway was of course an important factor. As more and more tracks were laid down and train travel became less expensive, many middle-class Britons began taking their first summer tourist excursions to the hills or the shore. Though the passenger railway had not yet reached as far as Matlock Bath, it greatly eased travel from London to Derbyshire, a considerable advantage to such poor travelers as the Carlyles. As a matter fact, they traveled under fewer *Difficulties* than ever before.

Yet the last leg of the long day's journey was made an old way, via an uncomfortable omnibus. Two long facing planks held the crowded, jostled passengers, as a pair of work horses pulled the vehicle over the rough road leading away from the Ambergate station, the last stop by rail. If an old man had not warned of the distinction between Matlock Bath and Matlock, they would have stayed on too long and disembarked at the wrong place.

They found lodgings up the steep hillside on Temple Terrace, a pair of tiny bedrooms upstairs, with a small rustically decorated first floor sitting room. If Jane stood next to the writing desk and looked out the window, she saw a captivating view: a sheer limestone cliff face opposite, the river shaped like a crescent rushing by, the street at the river's edge way beneath her. She would have had to stand on tiptoes and lean out to see the pedestrians strolling on the street down below.

This river valley, with the pea-green waters of the River Derwent splashing through, was more like a chasm or gorge. When Thomas, out walking in the evening, gazed up from the low-lying street, he saw hanging from the hillsides modest houses that looked to him "like little birdcages" romantically candlelit from myriad tiny windows. "One of the strangest places in the world!" he exclaimed. It was like living in a dream. They both marveled at an area so different from anything they were used to. (Matlock Bath is recognizable today from their descriptions.)

Jane was soon writing her cousin, "We get on very peaceably here—walking eating and sleeping." Rest and health were the first considerations. Steep narrow stony footpaths wound up the rocky hill. Companionably they took walks together, which helped them to eat and sleep better. It is not known what they talked about on these walks, or whether they spoke much at all, but Thomas told his brother contentedly, "[E]very day [is] a day in which one can walk or sleep, and smoke or read or dream and dawdle at one's own sweet will."

Jane found the lodgings for the most part quiet and private, though a consumptive fellow lodger was present to take the waters for his health, and one day she witnessed a wedding in progress. At the town's mineral springs were fountains for drinking and tanks of greenish water for bathing. The soothing waters, said to aid rheumatism and digestive disorders, kept a steady temperature of 68 degrees F. The only real annoyance came from the numerous local residents who pressed their services upon them as guides.

The Carlyles' tour of Derbyshire would not have been a true Victorian holiday without inquiries into local factories and birthplaces of men of achievement. In close-by Cromford, Thomas was very taken with mills founded by Richard Arkwright, eighteenth-century inventor, famous for the cotton-spinning machine that had helped launch the factory system and the Industrial Revolution. Though he had died before he could reside in it, Arkwright had commissioned a castle home high on a hill, and Thomas noted it was still inhabited by a descendent. Not far off was the birthplace of an eighteenth-century builder of the impressive British canal system, James Brindley, another hero of industrialization, though Thomas found no one in the immediate area who had heard of him—a piercing lesson on the ephemerality of fame.

For Jane and Thomas it was pleasant just "to sit down anywhere, and look peaceably around." But after a week of unprecedentedly harmonious existence, the Carlyles, with their steadfast belief in the work ethic, and far too puritanical and nervous to luxuriate in such leisure, became restive. Thomas, who had written his sister Jean from Addiscombe with no discernable sense of irony, "I think when one is not working, one ought not to be happy; one ought to be very unhappy, *seeking* out work," now declared "our inaction has to cease." And Jane spoke longingly of returning home to Chelsea to clean the house.

In the midst of their mutual unease, Providence, as Jane humorously put it, arrived in the form of an energetic, capable, nearly thirty-year-old disciple, the son of a Quaker. Actually, they had had the foresight to arrange ahead of time for William Edward Forster to rescue them from the land of the lotus-eaters.[4] Tall, leggy, hairy, and rugged looking, he was given animal nicknames like the Crane, the Gorilla, and the Bear. Thomas Carlyle found him "a most cheery, frank-hearted, courageous, clear-sighted young fellow." Already a well-off woolen manufacturer, William Edward held enlightened ideas about the education and welfare of his employees. He was known for his involvement in anti-slavery campaigns, and also worked for Irish relief. The Prime Minister Lord John Russell thought highly enough of William Edward to ask, when he made a trip to Ireland, for his impressions of social conditions there.

The Carlyles' late beloved friend John Sterling had introduced them to the able fellow, who had an emotional, sentimental side, expressed in a sensitive look about his mouth and eyes. He felt true affection for the Carlyles, along with an opportunistic desire to lionize and take advantage of such a prominent connection. He revered Thomas Carlyle as "the deepest mind of the age." But according to William Edward Forster's late nineteenth-century biographer, he had "if possible, a still keener admiration for, and a truer sympathy with, Mrs. Carlyle. Only those who have heard him speak of that gifted woman, know how deep was the impression which she had made upon him."[5] He relished the prospect of spending extended time with the Carlyles, in fact saw it as a coup: "Catching such a visit is of course quite a trophy in life."

They were very much a pair to him, an important couple, perhaps parent figures. He behaved respectfully toward them both, and spoke of Jane not as the appendage of a great man but as someone in her own right. She did not have to remind *him*, "*I* too am here."

After their week alone at Matlock Bath, he met up with the Carlyles in order to accompany them, first on a tour of the northwestern section of the Peak District and then to his home in Rawdon, near Leeds, in Western Yorkshire, where he had purchased and modernized a hilltop mansion the year before. He offered to handle all details concerning transportation, meals, waiters, bills, and accommodations; and they gratefully accepted the help. According to Jane, he "guided us triumphantly thro' all the sights of Derbyshire." "Mrs. C.," Forster told a friend, was "like a girl in her delight at new scenes and situations."

Nothing made as strong an impression on the party as what locals called the Devil's Arse of Peak, based on the flatulent noises created as the waters drained out of the caverns. Though tickled by the old name, Thomas in good Victorian style called this extensive cavern "the Devil's apparatus" and used other euphemisms, even when writing his friend Richard Monckton Milnes, a collector of erotic literature. William Edward referred to this part of their tour as "performing the Peak

Cavern," and Thomas pictured the place for his sister Jean: "A huge Cave, runs 860 yards sloping down into the bowels of the mountain, has running waters, pools that you go over in a boat; now narrow vaulted like a tunnel, then expanding into great expanses like cathedrals."

His descriptions of all they saw, in letters to family and friends, constitute a colorful guidebook of the area, and he did not neglect the conditions of the very poor. He wrote his mother that they had come upon a solitary old woman who lived in a cave-like burrow carved out of limestone and the rubbish of kilns: "This poor old woman and her hut were all as tidy as a new pin, whitewashed, scoured &c; a most sensible haughty and even dignified old woman."

To Edward FitzGerald, Thomas Carlyle gave an idyllic overview of the Derbyshire scene, "a really interesting country" he was "well pleased to look upon." "Beautiful old grey villages, silent as churchyards; fresh green moors wild limestone cliffs and chasms;—and, above all things, a cleanly, diligent, welldoing population, in whom . . . one could trace the funded virtues of many generations of humble good men." Edward adored this as a depiction of old England and hoped—in vain—that it represented a new benevolent view of humankind, which would find expression in "Gurlyle's" future writings.[6]

William Edward found the Carlyles good company overall. He thought Mr. Carlyle "uncommonly good-humoured and accommodating," and, like so many, he praised his conversation for its "pictorial power," admiring "such a mind so completely at play." But he also tells a revealing story of a dinner at a first-class hotel in Buxton Crescent. He and the Carlyles were seated at a long table with random guests who had no idea who Thomas was, including "a tall, starched, gentlemanly Irish parson." Forster said, "For a time all went on easily in silent feeding or low grumbling, till at last Carlyle began to converse with the parson, then to argue with him on Ireland, then to lose thought of all arguments or *table-d'hôte*, and to declaim. How they did stare. All other speech was hushed; some looked aghast, others admiring." *How they did stare*, whether in admiration or horror, provides a rare glimpse of the response of ordinary people to Thomas Carlyle the man, unencumbered by fame.

After Forster had taken them to his dream-like hilltop home in Yorkshire with its views of "green heights, and their distant industries and steeple-chimnies," the Carlyles settled happily into the second phase of their journey. Their host went off to tend to his woolen worsted manufacturing business in Bradford, leaving them alone with his Quaker housekeeper and several well-trained maids. In this well-run home—a quality Jane always appreciated—and despite a few bouts of insomnia and headache, she became as content as she ever got. And Thomas, whose rheumatism continued to give him a bit of trouble, praised the vestiges they saw around them of their host's Quaker upbringing, "spring-well clearness and cleanness, and the divine silence." Thomas made a brief visit to Richard Monckton Milnes, who lived not far off at Fryston Hall, and toward the end of August reported that they were enjoying some of "the beautifullest bright autumn weather."

The Sabbath, though, emerged as a problem. In a burst of ill-judged enthusiasm for showing local sights, Forster took the Carlyles one Sunday to a Methodist meeting house service. The outcome was dismal. "It's little notion of a Sunday they have," he said of the Sabbath-averse Carlyles, adding, "I did catch it afterwards." A pair of preachers had prayed (or brayed) "at one another with all sorts of disgusting contortions," making "a burlesque of prayer." Jane and Thomas were audibly disgusted by such churchy cant and bombast, especially, of course, Mr. C.

Jane had help on this visit in managing her husband. According to contemporaneous letters, William Edward gave his problematic houseguest his conscientious attention. Although the young man was slowly moving away from his Quaker upbringing, he remained religious in some important way, taking his Christianity very seriously as he attempted to sort through what he thought and believed. Finding himself forced to listen to diatribes that might easily have wounded him, he discovered a way to handle his guest: "Of course he constantly utters shocks to all one's ideas and principles, sacred and profane; but it is no use arguing with him, as he takes no notice of argument, not even of a contradictory fact, so I wait the exhaustion of his fury, and then, if absolutely needful, content myself with a quiet, simple protest." To his surprise, he found that Mr. Carlyle's cranky, curmudgeonly monologues had inspired and stimulated his own thinking on religion.

Because Thomas Carlyle exhibited geniality and cooperation the rest of the time, William Edward convinced himself that the cantankerousness was a mask. Better qualities were somehow "shining through his assumed veil of misanthropy." Like all the Carlyles' friends he remarked on the "merciful safety-valve of humour!" Humor: that magic ingredient that made Jane and Thomas's daily co-existence possible.

One day the Carlyles and their host went into Bradford, "a huge huggermugger smoky Town" of "80 or 100 thousand spinners and weavers." Forster seated Mrs. Carlyle next to him in his two-wheeled open gig, with Mr. Carlyle accompanying them on horseback. On their way back home, with the steep hill to the mansion rising before them, the mare that was pulling the gig—a new horse William Edward had been trying out—became skittish. Thomas, coming up from behind, was warned not to get too close. He pulled on his bridle and stayed back a little, but it was too late. The nervous mare gave a violent jerk. The young man wrote his mother, "part of the kicking-strap gave way, so [the mare] managed to get one leg over the shaft, and as both the shafts broke, of course the gig fell forward."

Forster, who had been standing upright in the gig, holding the reins—he was a famously show-offy driver—got thrown out. Mrs. Carlyle tumbled out, also. Her husband came round the corner to see her "starting up from amid the rubbish with dust on her shoulder!"

Jane had experienced that all-too-common nineteenth-century calamity, an accident involving a horse. Luckily it was not serious. She had hurt her shoulder and their host had sprained his ankle. The gig had to be fixed and the horse sent back. But perhaps because of her marked improvement on this trip, she remained a good sport throughout and recovered swiftly. William Edward praised her for behaving "with wonderful presence of mind," saying that she had "turned her back to the horse, and embraced the gig, and so just rolled out."

To Anna Jameson, Jane described the event with aplomb: "The only time I have been reminded that I live in a conditional world, was two days ago when our young Host and myself were pitched heels over head out of a gig; but except bringing me back to what Carlyle calls 'the fact of things,' even this misadventure did me no harm; indeed I have felt rather better for the tumble." Like many a neurasthenic, she could rally when faced with a tangible external danger.

To Anna she also explained with the utmost clarity why she was having a wonderful time in Rawdon. As so often, Jane is telling a truth while laughing at herself: "I never enjoyed a visit so much before; and so far as I can dive into the secret of my contentment, it lies in the fact of there being no *women* in the house, except servants! So that I have as fine a time of it as *Beauty* in the Castle of the Beast!" She quotes a stanza from a poetic version of that fairy tale by Charles Lamb, "Speak thy wishes, speak thy will, / Swift obedience meets thee still." As an only child, she makes fun of herself for enjoying being catered to, while revealing exactly what it is that she wants and needs: to be first with someone and secure in the center of a domestic world. With that sense of security in place, she can face adversity and adventure with a surprising degree of equanimity.

She does not have to spell out what *no other women* implies.

•

DURING HER STAY in Yorkshire, Jane Carlyle grew closer in friendship with their host. One wonders if they attempted any analysis of her husband in private conversations. He later said of Mrs. Carlyle, "She was one of those few women to whom a man could talk all day, or listen all day, with equal pleasure."[7]

While under this umbrella of benevolence, Jane fell in love with a little black kitten. Not just any kitten, but an angry, scratching, spitting creature. When it was time to leave (she would briefly visit the home of Elizabeth Paulet's brother, then travel on to London; with Thomas going north to Scotsbrig via Manchester), Jane took the kitten with her in a basket.

"Mrs. C.," Forster wrote a friend, "has taken off a wild, furious, spitfire of a kitten, out of which she has been sedulously and most vainly trying to 'love the devil' *à la* Emerson." He had borrowed the phrase from the Carlyles' coterie speech. Loving the devil out of a naughty, fretful son or daughter was apparently the Transcendental approach to child rearing.

The kitten in its basket carrier survived the railway journey home. Back at 5 Cheyne Row, which Jane found in good order thanks to Anne Brown, she wrote a friend, "I am spending *my* time chiefly *loving the Devil out of* a—Yorkshire kitten! which I have adopted for its inexpressible charm of *tigerishness*." The way she speaks of the kitten hints at an embrace, temporarily at least, of her own fury and feistiness.

Jane had undertaken a month-long holiday with her husband in a peacefully green and pleasant land. With nothing said in her letters about the dark shadows that lay between them, she had been able to admire invigorating sights, rebound from an accident involving a horse, and bring home a delightfully angry kitten. This "perfectly black" kitten (black cats were thought to bring good luck to a household) grew to become more spirited than angry, even, in time, "caressing." The cat learned to jump up onto Jane's shoulder and ride about the house with her.[8]

Her health a bit improved, she had come away from her travels with a sense of accomplishment. Life seemed more in focus. A romantic-minded reader might wish to imagine that the Carlyles' trip had been a second honeymoon. But was it, and would it make a difference?

CHAPTER SIXTEEN

SISTER WOMAN / BROTHER HUSBAND

"[Women] are crushed down under so many generations of arbitrary rules for the regulation of their manners and conversation; they are from their cradle embedded in such a composite of fictitiously-tinted virtues, and artificial qualities, that even the best and strongest amongst them are not conscious that the physiology of their minds is as warped by the traditions of feminine decorum, as that of their persons is by the stiff corsets which, until very recently, were *de rigueur* for preventing them 'growing out of shape.'"

—GERALDINE JEWSBURY, *The Half Sisters* (1848)[1]

I

THE NEW IDEAS ABOUT WOMEN, LOVE, AND MARRIAGE WERE PULSING through intellectual, political, and literary circles in England and on the Continent in the fall of 1847. Intent on learning more about them, Amely Bölte had just gone off to Germany. The ideas, it should be noted, were cyclically new. There were echoes of Mary Wollstonecraft's 1792 *A Vindication of the Rights of Woman*, but that book (as mentioned earlier) had greatly declined in influence in Britain during the decades following the French Revolution. For Jane Carlyle, Geraldine Jewsbury, and Amely Bölte, it was an exciting, disturbing time. Although subject to the famous restrictions of Victorian England, all three women were affected, though in quite different ways, by what would later come to be called feminism.

A great deal was going on in the Carlyles' circle this fall. With her husband in Scotland for his annual visit, Jane was awaiting the manuscript of Geraldine's *The Half Sisters*, having promised to edit the final version "for decency." Ralph Waldo Emerson, on his way to England for a lecture tour, had been invited to be the Carlyles' houseguest in late

October. Giuseppe Mazzini was poised to depart on a semi-secret political trip to Switzerland and France to meet with members of Young Italy, the patriotic organization he had founded. It would be his first journey out of England in nearly a dozen years.

Fresh prospects were in sight for an uprising in Italy that might possibly lead to unification. Giuseppe wrote fellow nationalist Giuseppe Garibaldi about moving his Italian Legion troops from their place of exile in Montevideo, Uruguay, to southern Italy to be at the ready.[2] He also wrote an open letter to the Pope, asking him to take the lead in the struggle for a united Italy. A reforming pope, Pius IX (Pio Nono), had been elected the previous year. To Giuseppe that was a source of hope as well doubt—could the man be trusted? But gaining a pope's support would make their cause far more acceptable. Jane was fearful and skeptical of where Giuseppe's adventures were to take him, especially after he confessed to her that, truthfully, he would rather "*organize* and *lead* an expedition into Lombardy" than serve as "*an individual under the Pope*."

Though anxious about Giuseppe Mazzini, the Carlyles were also concerned with far more personal matters. On the family farm, Thomas said he was catching up on sleep, drinking lots of milk, and worrying about how frail and ailing his mother seemed. "[E]ver since intelligence began with me," he told a friend, "the frightfullest thought has been that of losing my Mother." From a very young age, he would have understood that mothers do not last forever: his father's first wife, mother of his half brother, had died young and lay buried in an Ecclefechan churchyard.

Having just experienced the close companionship of his wife in Derbyshire, Thomas found himself in a somber mood and complained of loneliness. He wrote to Jane in conciliatory tones and was, furthermore, going to great lengths to acquire a quantity of flavorful honey to send her as a special treat (though in the end a portion of it leaked into the clothing it was packed with). One of his letters concludes, "Good night, dear Jeannie, my own dear little Lifepartner, only the dearer to me for all the sorrows we have had together: if we had had *joys*, should we not have shared them! Adieu, Dearest: write, write."

Jane replies dutifully but does not match his tone. Why had their excellent holiday excursion not brought about a sounder reconciliation? Her current letters, written as she began her annual cleaning and fixing of their Chelsea home, indicate something held back. The warmth of Thomas's words can make one sway to his side and wonder why Jane was so withholding. An intriguing clue to Jane's reticence can be found in her reaction a few years before to a notorious trial, Fraser v. Bagley. How she viewed that trial could explain her ongoing reserve—in the context of her husband's continued friendship with Lady Harriet Baring.

The trial, which took place in February of 1844, forms a little story of its own. The Carlyles had been acquainted with William Fraser, an editor at the *Foreign Review and Critical Miscellany*, regarding him as something of a benign wastrel. But when he brought an unnecessary suit against his attorney friend William Bagley, they came to see him as brazen and outrageous. The charge he made was *criminal conversation*, the term for committing adultery with a married woman. The woman in question was his wife, Vivian Blair Fraser.

After squandering his own money as well as that which his wife had brought to their marriage, William Fraser had deserted her and their children, a month before the last was born. The heartbroken Vivian Fraser believed that he did so because of money troubles and to be with other women. In his absence, he asked his friend William Bagley, long a regular guest in their home, to look after his wife and help manage her affairs; but now (some two years later) he had turned around and accused this same friend of *crim con* (as the term was abbreviated), or having committed adultery with his wife.

The Carlyles, who considered Mrs. Fraser an earnest, industrious, blameless housewife, believed the suit to be without merit. As the trial unfolded, Jane became caught up in each detail: "*I* made it my own affair—from *esprit de corps* Carlyle says." She read the newspaper accounts and received reports from her brother-in-law John, who was regularly in the courtroom, ready to serve as a witness for the defense.

Servants instructed as to what they should say (so the Carlyles believed) acted as witnesses for the prosecution. With incredulity Jane repeated what a nurse in the home told the court to illustrate the cozy terms Mr. Bagley had been on with Mrs. Fraser. The nurse claimed that in the family dining room Vivian Fraser had once addressed William Bagley as "my dear" and asked him to ring for her maid, whereupon he, who had his feet propped upon her sofa, did as she requested, giving a yank to the bell pull.[3] What further evidence was needed of an inappropriate degree of intimacy?

The sensible jury acquitted Mr. Bagley (and by implication Mrs. Fraser) to hearty cheers from the courtroom and from the crowds of people awaiting the verdict in the streets. With the trial over, Jane paid a visit to Vivian Fraser (she was to remain on friendly terms with her), telling Erasmus Darwin that she would have done so whichever way the verdict had gone, despite knowing that certain acquaintances might consider such a visit a violation of propriety and cut her for it.

Jane Carlyle never forgot how tiny alleged instances of impropriety had brought this respectable woman into a criminal court case and to the brink of divorce. Later in a letter to John Forster, to excuse herself from visiting him in his rooms when he was ill, she capsulized the way Vivian Blair Fraser had been viewed, creating a picture of the tight grip that doing the proper thing had upon middle class English women. The trial, Jane said, had given a severe shock "to my '*Unconscious*' Moral Being which I have not recovered from to this hour!" She then quoted characterizations of Mrs. Fraser made during the proceedings, with which Jane identified: "For visiting one's Husband's friend *at his chambers*, or saying to him '*My Dear*' in the course of nature; a nineteenth-century married woman, it seems, tho 'well up in years,'—'notorious for her house-keeping tendencies' 'with no personal attractions to speak of,'—'always mending her own or her husband's clothes in the evenings' (my own *signalement* [description] to a nicety) may be dragged before a Jury of her Countrymen and narrowly miss getting herself divorced! This state of things weighs even on *my* insubordinate spirit, I can tell you, and clips my wings of impulse."

Jane valued her reputation for respectability, and to an extent the concept of respectability itself. In the context of the Fraser trial, she spoke of her "gratitude to Providence for having had my own reputation always mercifully preserved." Being Scottish she might so easily, unwittingly, trip herself up over petty English notions of gentility: "Merciful Heaven—what criminalities have *I* walked over the top of without knowing it!" In fact prevailing conventions *did* clip her wings. Jane would not visit John Forster in his chambers by herself. In the past she had resisted a friendship with John Stuart Mill's married friend Harriet Taylor, saying she was "engrossed with a dangerous passion" and (a bit ambiguously) it would not be "safe." Nor did she in years to come (though her views eventually softened) pay her respects to the novelist George Eliot whose work she adored, after discovering that the author was Marian Evans, the woman living with George Henry Lewes as his common law wife.

After the trial, prints of William Fraser as a notorious Handsome Husband sold like hotcakes on London streets. Despite the horror and shame the trial evoked and the genuine, profound suffering she endured, Vivian Fraser continued to pine after her man. Astonished and upset, Jane told Geraldine, "after all his diabolical usage and this infernal climax to it [the bringing of *crim con* charges], she is still *in love* with her own husband!" And added, "that sort of feeling makes a woman eternally irrevocably *a victim*."

To her cousin, she expressed herself even more strongly. When Mrs. Fraser heard after the trial that her husband had become ill, she confessed to Mrs. Carlyle that she longed to go and comfort him. Exclaimed Jane, "She loves the man passionately . . . after all the woe he has brought her!! And in this moral slavery lies the fearfulest prospect for her. It would make anybody weep to hear how she defends him."

In Jane's admittedly very different case, Thomas's current blandishments must have seemed nearly meaningless in light of his continued refusal to give in to her single demand: that he cease staying on such close, confidential terms with Lady Harriet. Worse, he was again insisting his wife was wrongheaded and unreasonable for objecting to that friendship.

With limited power in the matter, Jane had been forced to make accommodations. She was by now part of the Barings' circle, though not on such equal terms as her husband. She had repeatedly made efforts—all those country home visits. Yet feeling in general badly treated, and not having had that ill treatment even *recognized*, she could not, from pride and a sense of self worth, entirely capitulate.

In Jane's eyes, Mrs. Fraser had become the worst sort of female victim. Not only had she been treated abominably, she had thrown herself at the feet of her oppressor and kissed them. Not only had her husband degraded her; she had further degraded herself. Witnessing such behavior left a lasting impression. It must have seemed to Jane that keeping a certain emotional distance from her errant husband was helping to preserve her integrity.

Throughout the later nineteenth century and all of the twentieth, one of the most tenacious stereotypes clinging to Jane Welsh Carlyle was that of the victimized wife, miserably, helplessly put upon by an insensitive literary man. But as she withheld something emotionally, she was likely trying to *prevent* herself from turning into a hapless victim and moral slave.

•

WITH THOMAS STILL away in September, Lady Harriet began making overtures to Jane. Despite her grave doubts and suspicions, Jane had persisted in looking to the lady for signs of affection and respect. She was to cling to this hope a long while. (Was there a touch of moral slavery in that?) If Lady Harriet could be made to care for her in her own right, it might still make a difference.

Jane was busy de-worming a horsehair chair one day, a messy taxing business that involved standing over a hot cauldron and boiling the worms out of the stuffing material, then drying it and re-stuffing the cushion. Thomas had sent her a bank letter of seventy-five pounds to cover household expenses, and despite enduring a spell of ill health, she had undertaken a series of tasks, including having some extensive painting done.

Right in the midst of the de-worming process—Jane underscores the irony—an aristocratic invitation arrived. To enable Mrs. Carlyle to escape the noxious smells of paint, Lady Harriet was volunteering to send her carriage and whisk her away to Addiscombe Farm for some fresh air, any day she cared to name. "I accepted her offer at once," Jane wrote her husband defensively, "—as I always do every kindness she offers me." She chose a Saturday as the day she would like to go.

But late the night before—after a tired Jane had sat up in her parlor till nearly ten o'clock hoping to get John Carlyle and Giuseppe Mazzini to bring their lengthy discussion of Dante to a close and depart—Lady Harriet's friend and errand boy Henry Fleming arrived breathlessly with a note. The lady had just accepted an invitation to Baron Holland's home on Sunday—the famed Holland House, the great Whig center for discussion of arts and politics—and had therefore decided to put Jane's visit off.

Henry Fleming gushed to Mrs. Carlyle that evening that Lady Harriet was "the *dearest, playfullest, wittiest* creature! I *love her* beyond everything." Popular in the Barings' circles, a close friend of the younger Charles Buller and the lady's acolyte, he was said to wear make up. The Carlyles used a Scottish term for him, *Jenkin's hen*, meaning "a hen that never knew a cock," or an old maid.[4] "Lisping and prating," he said that the lady believed Mrs. Carlyle had brought her recent bout of ill health on herself by "unheard of imprudence." "Lady Harriet assures me that nothing was ever *like* your indiscretion *in diet*!" Jane reported Henry Fleming as saying, "—and that all these attacks proceed from *that* cause." (Possibly Lady Harriet thought Jane did not eat enough.)

When the lady pressed for another date, Jane reluctantly went off to Addiscombe with her but suffered from their strangely ascetic routines: no fires in the bedrooms and a stinginess about little things like offering guests a glass of wine. Lady Harriet on this occasion seemed in a high-spirited jovial frame of mind. Too downtrodden to be witty herself, and recalling the lady's accusations of *imprudence*, Jane not unreasonably concluded that Lady Harriet had typed her as a hypochondriac.

Jane's description of deprivation in an aristocratic household elicited a heartfelt cry of sympathy from Thomas's mother in Scotland: "That the puir craitur could na get a bit *fire*! . . . for a' their grandeur!" Margaret Aitken Carlyle sent her daughter-in-law a gift, a pair of missionary narratives. Perhaps in gratitude, Jane claimed that one of them, by Robert Moffat, a Scottish missionary sent by the London Missionary Society to South Africa (his daughter Mary had recently married the explorer David Livingstone), was the most fascinating book she had read in a long time.

As usual the Carlyles were writing back and forth as if to the tick of a metronome. Apropos of nothing, Thomas noted from Scotsbrig, "Terrible poisoning of Husbands and Wives still goes on everywhere, if we believe the Newspapers! What are the people coming to?"

Since March, when she had taken off for Paris without telling him, Lady Harriet had sent Thomas the odd clipping or book with marginal notes meant for his eyes, but had written few personal letters. Jane, however, told her husband she feared that the lady might have been receiving "plenty of letters" from *him*. He addresses her worry by saying, "I perceive, by one phrase in the last Letter, sad *doubts* still lingering: alas, alas," adding: "I think I could write upon a sheet all [the letters] she has got from *me* for a twelvemonth past!"

The game, or dance, continued. Thomas and Lady Harriet used Jane to send each other teasing messages about their non-correspondence, an odd, irritating, perhaps titillating thing to do. Their motive may have been to indicate all was in the open and harmless. It was not. As the fall went on, they now and then exchanged an illicit note. Later this year Thomas schemed outright, telling Lady Harriet to communicate with him by writing to Jane, and asked the lady not to acknowledge his current letter: "Do not write,—or rather do (when you have spirits for it) but not to *me*,—and *ignoring* this, never having *received* this!"

Cognizant of the difficulties plaguing their friendship, they were treading gingerly, keeping an anxious eye upon Jane. Recognizing that the recent Addiscombe visit had left something to be desired, Lady Harriet tried to compensate, managing at the same time a flick of the whip. She sent round a medicinal tonic, prepared by the Queen's personal physician himself, for the benefit of the self-neglectful, ever-ailing Mrs. Carlyle.

•

AFTER THOMAS CARLYLE returned to Chelsea, a Transcendentalist interlude took place. Poet and essayist Ralph Waldo Emerson, in Britain for a lecture tour, recorded in his journal late October 1847: "I came down to London, on Monday, &c, at 10 at night, the door was opened to me by Jane Carlyle, and the man himself was behind her with a lamp in the hall. They were very little changed from their old selves of fourteen years ago (in August) when I left them at Craigenputtock."[5]

Emerson had made a pilgrimage to the Craigenputtoch farm in southwest Scotland in 1833. Although he had stayed with the Carlyles little more than twenty-four hours, the visit had been meaningful enough to create a lifelong bond between himself and Thomas, maintained through correspondence that included offers of assistance for handling publishers in their respective countries. Emerson had first learned of Carlyle's thinking from British journals available in America. The ideas had resonated deeply; and when he embarked on a European journey, he resolved to seek out the little-known author.

At their remote farm, where the Carlyles had seldom if ever enjoyed the company of a foreign intellectual, Jane called the event "the first journey ever since Noah's Deluge undertaken to Craigenputtoch for such a purpose." They experienced that brief encounter with Emerson as the visitation of an angel. Both were enchanted and sadly missed him when he departed. The brevity of the visit allowed a measure of idealization to flourish on all sides.

For this second visit, the Carlyles promised the American a brotherly, sisterly welcome and designated a bedroom as his own. Jane got the house ready, telling Thomas she had been "in a pretty mess with Emerson's bed." At that point her husband was on his way back to London, and the maid Anne Brown had offered to sleep in *his* bed to take the damp out, a custom then. Jane accomplished the same purpose by keeping a fire burning in his bedroom fireplace. She sewed and mended furiously to fix up the guest bed: "The quantity of sewing that lies in a *lined* chinz [sic] bed is something awfully grand!" Expectations were high, Thomas imagining his friend Waldo as "among the truest I now have."

When the visit took place, the reality of living with a houseguest proved daunting. The three of them, thrown suddenly together, as a matter of fact hardly knew each other. "[T]alkee talkee" was how Thomas summed up what wore on them all. During the days spent in close quarters—October 25 to 29—they could not stop chattering and blamed each other for the sometimes over-stimulating, sometimes numbing stream of constant conversation. And their personalities clashed.

The Carlyles each gave an account to Lady Harriet. She and Jane were at last—or at least—no longer strangers, and Jane exercised her pen to make wits, telling the lady in confident coterie phrases that she hardly knew whether she liked their guest or not: "The man has *two* faces to begin with which are continually changing into one another like '*dissolving views*,' the one young, refined, almost beautiful, radiant with—what shall I say?— '*virtue its own reward*'! the other decidedly old, hatchet-like, crotchety, inconclusive—like an incarnation of one of his own *poems*!"

She was uncertain of her husband's opinion, since "he has had no opportunity of unbosoming himself to me on the subject, as we have literally not been *five minutes* alone together since Emerson arrived." Emerson rose earlier than they did and went to bed later than Jane—"as if I had got the measles," she rather mysteriously said.

The Carlyles did share reactions, though. Jane called their Yankee visitor "perhaps the most elevated man I ever saw—but it is the elevation of a *reed*." Thomas developed the metaphor in his note to Lady Harriet, "A pure-minded elevated man; *elevated* but without *breadth*, as a willow is, as a reed is; no fruit at all to be gathered from him." He would find his friend's London lectures, the following June, to be full of moonshine.[6]

For his part, Ralph Waldo Emerson was taken aback to discover that his host did not primarily seem like an author or scholar. Instead he found him to be "a very practical Scotchman, such as you would find in any saddler's or iron-dealer's shop." He was shocked, that is, by Thomas Carlyle's working-class demeanor, what others had called "rustic." Elaborating the point in his journal he wrote, "If you would know precisely how he talks, just suppose that our burly gardener, Hugh Whelan, had leisure enough, on the top of his day labor, to read Plato, Shakspeare [sic], & Calvin, &, remaining Hugh Whelan all the time, should talk scornfully of all this nonsense of books he had been bothered with, & you shall have the tone & talk & laughter of Carlyle."[7]

Though Emerson remained in awe of his host's powers of conversation —he said he could create word-pictures like sculpture—he complained about being trounced on for his inability to view the Puritan Oliver Cromwell the way Carlyle did.[8] As other friends had, he wearied of hearing many a sacred subject demolished: the Old and New Testaments, poetry, the railway, the Abolitionist cause. According to a perhaps apocryphal story (told later by George Eliot), Thomas walked his credulously optimistic American guest all over London, including to gin-shops and the House of Commons, pointing out instances of iniquity in order to force him to admit there was such a thing as the devil.[9]

At this juncture, the Sage of Chelsea and the Sage of Concord made a study in contrasts. One was curmudgeonly, argumentative, and attuned to the brutish, devilish side of human nature; the other serene, tolerant, and polite, able to see the best in everyone. According to one account, Emerson saw "man . . . still tending upwards" even among those who frequented houses of prostitution, a sentiment that allegedly provoked a horrified cry of indignation from Mrs. Carlyle.[10]

Throughout this trip, Emerson benefited enormously from the Carlyles' introductions. He met nearly every friend of theirs mentioned in these pages, and his fascination was profound. He saw Alfred Tennyson, Charles Dickens, John Forster, Monckton Milnes, William Edward Forster, Charlotte Cushman, Anna Jameson, Lady Harriet and William Bingham Baring, William Charles Macready, and Charles Buller. After leaving London, he stayed with Jane's friends Elizabeth and Étienne Paulet at Seaforth House, where they assigned to him the chamber that

Prime Minister George Canning had slept in when Gladstone's father owned the place.[11] He visited Geraldine in Manchester and Harriet Martineau in Ambleside. An outsider benefitting so greatly from their wide acquaintance, he was in a position fully to appreciate, as he put it, that "The Carlyles . . . have their own valuable circle."[12]

Ralph Waldo Emerson was much more aware of England's dark side than the Carlyles gave him credit for. As the weather turned wintry in Manchester and Liverpool, the poverty he witnessed in those cities was far worse than anything he had ever observed in New England. "I cannot go up the street," he wrote his wife Lidian, "but I shall see some woman in rags with a little creature just of Edie's [their son's] age & size, but in coarsest ragged clothes, & barefooted, stepping beside her." With a heavy heart, he distributed pennies to the children he saw "barefooted in the mud on a bridge in the rain all day to beg of passengers. But beggary is only the beginning & the sign of sorrow & evil here."[13]

During their visitor's stay in London, Jane had a burst of annoyance that brings to mind the feisty, scrappy black kitten she had adopted, and told her host, William Edward Forster, that he was worth "a cartload of Emersons." "I have seen him 'face to face & (over-) soul to (over-) soul' & (I may just as well 'speak the truth & chance the Devil[']) I do *not* like him the least bit! C. says he is a 'most polite & gentle creature—a man really of a quite *seraphic* nature'; & all that may be true." Jane tried to clarify what she meant: "his geniality is of the *head* not the *heart*—a theoretic systematic geniality that (as Mazzini would say) 'leaves me *cold*.'"

Mr. Emerson was too much of a gentleman to disparage Mrs. Carlyle, though one observer believed that on this trip his "admiration for her abated visibly."[14] He later appreciated her attendance at his lectures, however. And he commented in bemusement to Lidian that "Jane Carlyle suffers like all good women of my acquaintance from cruel headachs [sic]"[15]—an interesting remark that suggests, in a nutshell, the curious condition of a large number of talented nineteenth-century women attached to prominent literary men on both sides of the Atlantic, wives, daughters, and sisters with last names like Dickens, Thackeray, Bulwer-Lytton, Kipling, Twain, and Howells who were astonishingly prone to ailments, psychological problems, and / or invalidism. Their group portrait would make a fascinating study.

Ralph Waldo Emerson was to remain abroad some months more.

Irritations and disillusionment notwithstanding, his friendship with Thomas Carlyle would continue. Fourteen years later, it would survive, somehow, even their very different views on the American Civil War.

After his stay in Chelsea, Emerson offered his opinion of the Carlyles' marriage in another letter to Lidian, who had been curious about Jane, hoping to meet her if she and her husband should travel to America one day. He had scrutinized his hosts, taking note of the way they lived together at Cheyne Row. Despite all of the above, the rooms had often rung with laughter as the three of them wrote their letters at adjacent tables and shared meals and those endless conversations. He rummaged through the books in their library, pausing to read inscriptions. His conclusion, biased though it is toward the bright side, conveys truths about the Carlyles' often companionable literary marriage that existed right alongside their more famous stresses and strains: "Carlyle and his wife live on beautiful terms: Nothing can be more engaging than their ways, and in her book case all his books are inscribed to her, as they came from year to year, each with some significant lines."[16]

•

NEWS ARRIVED OF their friends' European travels. Amely Bölte was having an exciting time in Berlin, conversing with prominent thinkers. Giuseppe Mazzini sent a note about his safe arrival in Boulogne to Emilie Ashurst (a sister of the woman he had *not* become engaged to), disguising his handwriting for security's sake.[17] He was dodging the authorities, alarmed about his part in the revolution brewing in Italy. From Paris he wrote Jane Carlyle that he missed England and hoped to see her in London in December. In addition to attending secret planning meetings with members of Young Italy, he paid a visit to his friend George Sand. While in the novelist's presence, he thought of Jane. "There is not a single shadow of vanity or pride about her," he said of Madame Sand. "There is much of what you like and much of what I like, combined." Concerning Italy, Giuseppe told Jane he now sensed "the real awakening of a people to consciousness." Disturbingly he also said, "I feel hopeful, I could say confident, that before long I shall be enabled to die in and for my country, the best thing that can befall to me."[18] The Italian awakening was thrilling news, but that it could cost Giuseppe his life was exactly what Jane had always feared most.

In London as the season progressed a sooty, clammy, smelly miasma developed and hung over the city for days. Jane described it as "that extraordinary *substance* called *November-London fog*, which, not being *born* to it, I can never reconcile my mind to, any more than my body." Besides, she teasingly reminded John Forster, November was the month in which the people of England were most apt to commit suicide. As it happened, in letters of this time, Jane and Lady Harriet both joked uneasily about suicide, perhaps an indication of tensions the two women were under.[19]

One dark day Amely Bölte, just back from Berlin, hurried through the fog-shrouded streets of Chelsea to Cheyne Row to report on her trip abroad. Worried about Jane's health and wellbeing, Amely found her in her parlor with her husband and brother-in-law, "sitting comfortably by her fire, still pale, but improved."[20]

Amely Bölte had recently all but declared outright what she had long been hinting at: her love for Jane Carlyle. In a letter to Varnhagen she said that she adored Mrs. Carlyle "as the ideal of a pure heart." Enclosing for him some letters (evidently from Jane) that she had read and reread to lift her spirits, she told him, "You can see from looking at them how we feel about one another and how worried I must be thinking of her." She focused on the question of "what such a creature could do with herself and her life," echoing Jane's ongoing concern over what her mission might be. "I could love her, maybe passionately," Amely continued, "if she did not have two other women friends, whom she likes less, but prefers to spend time with [Geraldine Jewsbury and Elizabeth Paulet]. That does not agree with the pride of one's heart at all. But how could I live, if she did not like me any longer, I really do not know. If only I could save her. But how?"

Like many an ardent letter writer—like Jane—Amely was the star of her own drama. In her letters, the Carlyles, not unnaturally, revolve around her. She seems not to analyze why Jane, who when receptive appreciated her warm flattering attention and intellectual companionship, might have preferred being with other friends. Yet Amely did not hesitate to criticize Jane for behaving in an insufficiently loving manner toward her husband. When she heard Jane compare Thomas to Goethe in an uncomplimentary way (not further explained), she wrote Varnhagen, "It saddens me that she reverts to such jibes. It is the weapon of the weak and a small, ugly weapon." On that occasion, said Amely,

Thomas had turned to Jane and "measured her with an intense look and said nothing. If she loved him, she would not hurt him so deliberately." He had then left the house and gone into the back garden with his brother to smoke a pipe. She added, "You are right such people should not live with one another." Others would echo this sentiment, yet it was the opposite of what Ralph Waldo Emerson had just witnessed.

During her visit to Cheyne Row, Mr. Carlyle and Miss Bölte knocked heads over the topic of women. "He said we were only good for obeying men and sewing shirts for them," she related. "That was one of his new theories and I [said that I] wished God had taken a little break after creating man and left it right there [without bothering to create woman from Adam's rib]. He laughed and his brother laughed at this endlessly, and I joined in, even though I do not see what was so funny about it."

Thomas's contrary, provoking attitude especially dismayed the governess now, when she was bursting with news of her exciting discussions abroad. Jane reported that Amely had "returned from Germany all agog with *something* that she calls '*the new ideas*'—above all quite rabid against *marriage*. Varnhagen, Bettina [author Elizabeth von Arnim], all the *Thinkers* of Germany she says have arrived at the conclusion that marriage is a highly *immoral* Institution as well as a dreadfully disagreeable one and that the only possible"—

Here, Jane Carlyle's letter has been torn off.[21] We do not know who did the tearing, or when, but can guess that it was done to remove from the record some seditious words Jane had written.

II

THIS FALL AND winter Geraldine Jewsbury was putting the last touches on her novel *The Half Sisters*. Inspired in part by the works of George Sand and Germaine de Staël, she had set about capturing the current swirl of contradictory ideas about women. Her work was mainly addressed to the educated middle and upper middle class women who were the principal readers of such books.

For Jane Carlyle who had the job of providing a final edit, it was a critical moment. The novel caused a tumult of ambivalent feeling and thought to arise, raising questions close to her heart that were to pervade her entire life. Living in the midst of such ambivalence, it would have been impossible to see clear contours, especially when the questions touched her central dilemma: how to handle the tension between her respect for what was traditional, time-tested, socially proper, and sensible; and her desire for self expression and to be of use to the world. As a Scottish outsider, her genuine regard for tradition was mixed with anxiety about the fussy conventions of English gentility.

Her involvement with *The Half Sisters* would test Jane's marriage and also her friendship with Geraldine. For one thing, she was to be publically associated with the book: Geraldine intended to dedicate it to her friends Jane Welsh Carlyle and Elizabeth Newton Paulet. Further, it contained ideas about women and marriage that Jane had privately discussed and debated with Geraldine.

As with *Zoe*, Jane was to edit for decency. Geraldine wanted her help, admitting she had no fine sense of discernment, her excuse being the early death of her mother: she had never been properly taught. Jane's specific instructions were to "score out or alter any *exceptionable passages* as my own *great good sense* (!) should suggest."

It was a tall order. After returning from Derbyshire, Jane had confessed to John Forster that Geraldine's "huge brown paper parcel of M. S[.] lies like an incubus on my free spirit!" He was involved too, as Chapman and Hall's literary advisor: his task was to read the manuscript to determine if it was publishable, that is, fit for family-oriented lending libraries.

The two of them intended to undertake the job together in her Cheyne Row parlor, but delays ensued. Jane had her household responsibilities. John Forster, with Charles Dickens and others, was trying to purchase Shakespeare's birthplace on behalf of England (an effort that would prove successful). "[S]ympathy with my Sister-woman," Jane wrote her husband, required her to let Geraldine know of these delays as soon as possible, since she was "doubtless sitting in panting expectation of his [Forster's] verdict."

Yet Jane had deeper reasons for hesitating. As she faced the task of editing, her anguish was genuine, her worries long standing. Five years earlier, after reading pages of a Seaforth novel that Geraldine and Elizabeth Paulet were writing and had asked her to critique, she had expressed a similar vexation: how to balance respect for Victorian proprieties with a longing to hear about female aspirations and potential. The original plan back in 1842 had been for the three women to write a novel in letters. As Jane read through their Seaforth pages, she had found herself in awe of Geraldine's talent, praising her friend's genius and daring. Yet the pages ought *not* to be published, Jane decided, quoting the saying "decency forbids." In fact she backed out of the project altogether because of what she termed its *stormy* pages. (In time Elizabeth gave up also, and Geraldine decided to write *Zoe*.)

Jane believed her friends to be unconscious of wrongdoing—so what was she attempting to say? "I do not mean decency in the vulgar sense of the word," she told her cousin, "—[though] even in *that* sense they are not always *decent*!—but then their *indecency* looks so purely *scientific*, and so *essential* for the full development of the story that one cannot, at least I cannot get up a feeling of outraged modesty about it—nay I should feel as if *I* were the indecent person should I find anything to blush at."

If the so-called lapses were artistically necessary, it would be hard to explain her objections, yet Jane tried: "there is an indecency or want of reserve (let us call it) in the spiritual department—and exposure of their whole minds naked as before the fall— without so much as a fig-leaf of conformity remaining—which no respectable public could stand—which even the freest spirits among us would call 'coming it too strong'!"

Five years later, ambivalence remained. Abruptly this fall—late November 1847—Jane stopped work on *The Half Sisters*, too upset, as she told John Forster, to continue correcting the proofs. The excuse she gave: her husband disapproved. "C has got some furious objection to my meddling with them—even declares that I 'do not know bad grammar when I see it any better than *she* does'—that 'if I HAD any faculty I might find better employment for it' &c &c—So after having written to her [Geraldine] that I would do what you wished I must write again, that I am not permitted." In an angry tone, Jane repeated what Amely had said: "I do think there is much truth in the *young german* idea that Marriage is *a shockingly immoral Institution* as well as what we have long known it for an extremely disagreeable one—Please countermand the proofs—for every one that comes occasions a *row*."

When the Carlyles fought over Geraldine's proofs, Thomas's phrase about Jane—"if she *had* any faculty"—must have stung, for editing and critiquing her friend's manuscripts had for some time now been part of Jane's *work*.

What about the novel had so offended? Francis Espinasse, the young journalist who at Geraldine's request took over the job of correcting *The Half Sisters* (and decried Miss Jewsbury's overuse of dashes), believed that Thomas Carlyle's well-known puritanical dislike of fiction and *George Sandism* had caused him to object.[22]

In this period in a curious private writing on *phallus-worship*, something he associated with the work of George Sand, Thomas Carlyle ranted against the panting preoccupations in both society and fiction with sex and money: "a Phallus and a moneybag. . . . Such are the two Gospels preached to our poor Age." In considering great works of the past like Homer's epics and the Books of Moses, he put forth his belief on the place of romantic love for men *and* women: "Man's life is not there represented as made all or mainly out of Love. Love satisfying or not plays but a small due part in it [;] business, ambition, accumulation, loss, victory, defeat in thousands of other provinces fill up the life of man and woman there, and love comes in but as one fact among very many."[23]

It was an opinion that Jane knew well. Clearly there was a special place in his pantheon for the romantic, idealistic love of a knight for his lady. But for a long while now he seemed unable to find room for romantic love in marriage, the love of a husband for his wife. In recent years he sometimes appeared to regard Jane, always of the greatest importance to him, more like a live-in sibling, a family member one quarreled with, was annoyed by, counted on, intermittently felt a strong affection for, and could not do without. More idealistically, he regarded her as his fellow pilgrim on the road of life.

Regarding Geraldine's book, however, there was one very specific cause of alarm. With the proposed dedication to Jane, the novel would be associated in the mind of the public with his name.

To Jane Carlyle *The Half Sisters* was far and away the most important and fraught of Geraldine's novels. The essential story of the two sisters can be quickly told. Bianca Pazzi, the daughter of an Italian woman and the book's heroine, rises from poverty to become a famous actress with a career she loves. Her half sister Alice Helmsby Bryant, whose English mother had disapproved of serious education for girls (as Jane's mother had done), is an upper-middle-class wife, subordinate to her wealthy husband, an owner of iron works. William Bryant is portrayed as a well-intentioned but highly traditional man, consumed by his business.

The women embody sharp contrasts. While Alice sinks "under the weight of a golden leisure," Bianca, in her youth, is faced "with the prospect of the workhouse if sickness or accident should disable her" and prevent her from taking the small, varied parts that came her way as an apprentice actress.[24] In their stance toward life, the two sisters differ almost allegorically. One is Convention, the other Courage. Yet they share an English father (no longer living). Recognizing a portrait of her father in Alice's home, Bianca learns the truth but hides it from Alice. She fears it would upset her genteel friend to discover that she was the sister of an impoverished foreigner forced to work for a living. Although Alice feels an affinity for Bianca, she is never to find out that the Italian woman is her sister.

Their stories, for the most part, run on parallel tracks. Both women, coincidentally, fall in love with an attractive, weak-minded man, Conrad Percy. The strain of Alice's love for this man who is not her husband causes her great agony. When she is finally on the verge of *flying with* Conrad, her husband returns home unexpectedly, preventing their elopement. Though able to assure her devastated husband that he had not (yet) been *dishonoured*, Alice suffers severe spasms, falls into a decline, and dies.

Bianca, after becoming an acclaimed actress, at long last breaks free of her own attachment to Conrad Percy, who had rendered crucial assistance and earned her adoration when she was young. A new man takes the stage, the forward-looking Lord Maurice Melton, who loves Bianca. After necessary plot complications take the lord to Egypt and keep them separated for the sake of dramatic suspense, Bianca ends up marrying him. (Conrad, in reaction to his grief over Alice, joins a sect and becomes a religious fundamentalist—Geraldine's idea of perdition.)

At the novel's conclusion, Lord Melton's sister begs Bianca, now that she is part of their upper class family, to cease her work as an actress. Despite the vast amount written in the novel's pages about her devotion to her craft, Bianca at once complies. However, the author does provide Bianca (in a single sentence) with a new career: she will continue a school for the education of girls that Lord Melton's sister had established "and set up others on its model."[25] Considered far more respectable than acting, this second career allows Geraldine Jewsbury to promote a desperate need of the time, an improved system of education for girls. Bianca and her husband will also be blessed with several children.

In sharp contrast to many other artistic-philosophical women in the fiction of this period, such as Ludwig Tieck's Vittoria Accorombona, Bianca lives happily ever after while having it all, an astonishing ending for a heroine who had jousted with convention and won. Bianca is not punished for having had a successful artistic career, though she (disappointingly) gives it up upon marriage. The surprising message: a woman might dare without being doomed.

In *The Half Sisters* Geraldine had to acknowledge a reality of Victorian England: by the very nature of her career, an actress risked being scorned by good society. She might have had in mind conversations with Jane who had been shocked by that first sight of a ballerina displaying herself before an audience with her foot raised "Much *higher* than decency ever dreamt of!" Actresses were frequently associated with prostitution, a view articulated by Conrad Percy: "A woman who makes her mind public, or exhibits herself in any way, no matter how it may be dignified by the title of art, seems to me little better than a woman of a nameless class." A woman who wrote—like Geraldine—was bad enough, but an actress was worse, for she was "publishing both mind and body too."[26]

When Alice became acquainted with Bianca, she located a job for her as a nursery governess, considering that she was bestowing a great favor. The actress would no longer have to continue her "dreadful way of life." But Bianca turned the offer down, attempting to enlighten Alice: "The stage is to me a *passion*, as well as a profession . . . all my faculties would prey upon myself, and I should even be wicked and mischievous . . . if I were placed in any other position."[27] Mercifully not knowing how to sew, Bianca could not become a seamstress, the occupation forever posed as the respectable alternative to any self-flaunting career in the arts.

As an actress, Bianca managed to surmount the moral dangers of the theatre by remaining *perfectly respectable*. Genius counted, too: an exceptional woman might become an exception to the rules. Geraldine further enhanced Bianca's status by creating in the novel an anti-Bianca who met the stereotype, a talented but vulgar opera singer called La Fornasari, a woman of questionable morals. She was someone's mistress and had born a child out of wedlock. When Jane critiqued Geraldine's novel, she particularly objected to a loose and suggestive scene involving La Fornasari.

Geraldine Jewsbury made use of her own experiences as an author / artist and as a virtually motherless child. She incorporated those of friends like the American actress Charlotte Cushman, the "Egyptian" Charles Lambert, and the Carlyles (setting one scene in their recent vacation spot, near where Geraldine had grown up: Matlock in Derbyshire). Yet in no sense is the novel thinly veiled autobiography. It is an imaginative though melodramatic novel of ideas, questioning the proper role of women and containing back and forth debates on the subject. Conrad Percy utters conventional views in a most convincing manner, echoing Victorian conduct books. Geraldine puts her most advanced thoughts into to the mouth of the aristocratic Lord Melton, a clever tactic, utilizing gender and class to bolster her cause. Lord Melton is an attractive persuader.

Because Geraldine Jewsbury and Jane Carlyle talked about and argued over these ideas privately, there is no way to know precisely who said what. But Jane, moved since girlhood by extraordinary women characters depicted in novels, like Corinne and Heloise, nevertheless made it clear that she disapproved of throwing caution to the winds. She definitely would have kept more than a few fig leaves in place. Although Geraldine understood parameters were necessary in the real world and had *asked* Jane to edit her for decency, she heedlessly threw heart and soul into gaining more room and breathing space for women.

Though the two friends had so much in common, Jane, as we know, was more drawn to convention and tradition; Geraldine to testing the limits of what could be presented publically. When Jane pushed the boundaries, as she most certainly did, giving expression to her insubordinate spirit, it was through subversive satire, humor, and irony in her letters and conversation—an extended yet still private sphere.

The character Alice Bryant, an extreme case, is *not* Jane Carlyle, but shares a few qualities with her. Half imprisoned inside her claustrophobic world, the married Alice has "a morbid conscientiousness, which made her painfully anxious to do right, without ever feeling satisfied with any of her own actions," and "an immense power of passive resistance." Unlike Jane, though, Alice is isolated, bored, and nearly choked by the plethora of material possessions surrounding her, a situation that leads her to enter into an illicit romance as the way out. Like so many well-to-do women in this era, Alice had become an "ornamental appendage."[28]

Alice's inability to do anything without a social sanction, other than falling in love with Conrad, renders her without moral courage. Yet to Conrad who has a horror of professional women, Alice is a soft, delicate, childlike, half-opened rose who, as he puts it, realizes his ideal of an English lady. "Women ought to be taken care of, and kept in retirement," he believes; "they have no qualities which fit them to struggle with the world."[29] In the days of the British Empire, that view was sometimes referred to as *Oriental*. Alluding to women in the East kept in a harem, Harriet Martineau had used the word that way to describe the views of Geraldine's rejected fiancé John Robertson.

To Lord Melton, on the other hand, "A woman is a rational being, with reasonable soul and human flesh." Although a majority of women at that time were not well educated, he believed they ought to be for their soul's sake and to enable them to lead their own lives. He respected the several professional women he had known and believed woman's potential should not be "modified like the feet of Chinese women, to meet an arbitrary taste." Lord Melton deplored the sillier modes of decorum promoted by British conduct books.[30]

Geraldine qualifies Lord Melton's position. Whereas, regarding potential occupations for women, Margaret Fuller famously said "let them be sea captains if you will," Geraldine's lord insists, "I am not a stickler for the 'rights of women,' if by those you mean becoming a soldier, or a lawyer, or a member of Parliament." What he wanted instead was for women "not to have their lives and souls frittered into a shape to meet the notion of a 'truly feminine character.'"[31]

Geraldine included a reflexive Victorian paean to the maternal as woman's deepest instinct. And she genuinely accepted a woman's role as housekeeper: she and Jane both kept ship-shape homes. Surely with Jane in mind, Geraldine adds a touch of humor at the novel's end. She has Lord Melton and Bianca banter about the fact that the former actress, without a scrap of experience, has turned herself into an excellent household manager. Lord Melton to Bianca: "I have been wonder-struck at the prudence and dexterity with which you have adapted yourself to . . . a new order of things—the orderliness, the—what shall I say?—housekeeping qualities." Bianca: "You are like all the rest of men, and have no faith in a woman's genius, until it is shown in the practical manifestation of arranging your breakfasts, dinners, and servants."[32]

What Geraldine keeps returning to: women's natural talents and energies must be allowed to develop freely for the sake of their health and their souls. In Bianca's words, "I have had a definite employment all my life: when I rose in the morning my work lay before me, and I had a clear, definite channel in which all my energies might flow."[33]

Heartbroken over the end of her romance with Conrad, the actress utilized her distraught emotions in the service of her art, and thus worked through her grief in a natural manner. Geraldine's point about natural energies is generalized to include all humans. In a prescient reference to popular upsurges—the revolutionary year of 1848 was almost upon them—she wrote that if people are repeatedly stifled and held down, Nature will be forced to express itself, even "'*avec explosion*,' as the French dramatists say,—to the great relief of the social system."[34]

What Geraldine proposed was revolutionary. Lord Melton's practical sister, accusing her brother and Bianca of harboring unrealistic hopes, asks a very good question: "How, in the present state of society, are women to be employed? They cannot all work for their bread, and what is there for them to do? Women's employments are so limited." Where could women who wanted to change things even *begin*?

Geraldine offers a solution. The women of England, Lord Melton says, should go off on a retreat. "[T]hey should be alone, and have nothing to do but to sit down and consider what it is they have been taught all their lives, how much of it they really believe." They should examine what they care about and what they detest, and "strip off all the moral flannel-waistcoats, steel-collars, and go-carts, in which they have walked all the days of their life." And then emerge to "begin their life anew."[35] Put forward by an aristocratic male character in a novel published in 1848, the suggestion is prophetic of the women's consciousness-raising groups that arose in the late 1960s.

•

IN JANUARY JANE refused to join Thomas on a visit to Bay House, where a group had assembled. She kept Lady Harriet dangling for days—would she or would she not go in the end? As she temporized, she claimed uncertain health, knowing Thomas was sure to sympathize with that. But she did not budge, and in the end said no. And despite her husband's disapproval, she continued reading chapters of Geraldine's book.

Great God Jane wrote John Forster after receiving a new chapter, using her Scottish privilege of swearing. (Unlike her decorous English counterparts, Jane did now and then swear.) "Is not our young friend 'coming it rather strong'?" she continued. "More *actresses*! more 'hysteric seizures'!" She reminded him that Geraldine herself would be the first to confess she had "absolutely no *sense* of decency." Jane was also objecting, as we might, too, to her friend's hyperbolic tone and penchant for melodrama—a stormy style very different from her own.

A few days later after reading a passage she especially loathed, Jane uttered her harshest condemnation to John Forster. "This is worse than anything in Zoe . . . in fact perfectly disgusting for a young English woman to write—and from Chapman's point of view quite 'unfit for circulation in families.' I would not have such stuff *dedicated to me* . . . for any number of guineas." Jane's upset focused on a scene later cut that involved the opera singer with questionable morals, the anti-Bianca character, La Fornasari. We have only Jane's words, when she described the objectionable scene as "that feast of '*meats*' and *love* and *tobacco*, at the Fornisari's [sic]."

Then, unexpectedly, an early publication date was announced: Chapman and Hall were to bring out *The Half Sisters* in March. Panicked now about the dedication, Jane again leaned on the excuse of her husband's opinion. She told John Forster she wanted "to be guided by my Husbands authentic feelings in the matter—Knowing his dislike to be connected in people's minds, by even the slightest spider-thread, with what he calls 'George Sandism and all that accursed sort of thing.'" She had assured Thomas that the book would finally pass muster and begged Forster to confirm if that was truly the case. If the passages she so strenuously objected to had been left in, "not only would *he* detest a dedication to *his* wife, but his wife herself would detest it."

Though she might be forced to decline the dedication, Jane still hesitated to hurt Geraldine's feelings: "You see how I am situated—wishing *not* to give pain to Geraldine—still less to give offence to my Husband and least of all to promnade [sic] myself as an 'emancipated' woman."

When John Forster hastened to reply that Mrs. Carlyle had nothing to fear, she responded in tones of relief. With this assurance, her husband would not refuse permission. The manuscript went off to the printer's. The dedication remained as it was.

Months later, when Elizabeth Paulet's sister wrote "a note of female criticism on *the Halfsisters*," Jane enclosed it for Lady Harriet, saying it was "one small evidence that *all* my friends who think and write upon *woman* are not so entirely immoral after all!" She continued to distance herself from the work.

Geraldine well understood that a serious problem had sprung up between herself and Jane. Their correspondence lapsed. When they did write, irritation showed. Referring to her most recent letters from Jane, Geraldine complained about being treated badly. She had been "athirst for a word of affection" yet had "never received two such utterly, utterly, unsatisfactory letters from you since I knew you," adding "no one has ever made me suffer so much." Addressing the thorny issue between them directly, Geraldine wrote, "I sin against your notions of good taste very often . . . but I don't see how it [whatever was specifically annoying Jane] can be anything of a graver nature—anyway, I feel very innocent."[36]

The friends continued to see each other, though very infrequently, and both touched upon Jane's health as an excuse for her degree of disgust. By the time of Jane's July birthday, Geraldine had relented, wondering how many birthdays she and her best friend might have left to celebrate.

Over time, Jane came to change her views. She began to reflect favorably on this uncannily resonant book written by her sister-woman, and to accept her connection to it. In 1856 she told a dear friend, to whom she and Geraldine were sending a copy for her very own, that *The Half Sisters* was "the one of all her novels which I like the best. And it has bonafide arguments in it, betwixt her and me, written down almost word for word as we spoke them in our walks together."

Geraldine's new ideas about women took time to absorb. Jane would by no means endorse them all, yet it can be conjectured that, even so, her friend's portrait of a daring female artist was currently having an influence on her innermost self. Geraldine kept encouraging Jane to try authoring a piece of fiction, or perhaps words of instruction for women. She offered, as before, to collaborate on a project if Jane would like to do that.

But on the quiet Jane was thinking of some work of her own. In the year and a half to come, she would ponder her aesthetic and grow as a writer. She eventually attempted an experiment that turned into her best piece of non-epistolary prose—confidently written as if meant for a wider public. Slowly, surely she was becoming something of a Bianca in her own domain.

CHAPTER SEVENTEEN
CHANGES

"And what a time of Republics and Revolutions it is! The whole world, with hardly the exception of one Kingdom but our own, has started up into a kind of insurrection, and said to its Kings, 'Better Laws or—!'"

—THOMAS CARLYLE to his mother, 22 March 1848

I

AS THE REVOLUTIONARY YEAR OF 1848 DAWNED, THE CARLYLES BECAME keenly aware of events unfolding in Italy. Uprisings, riots, and demonstrations began to occur in such cities as Palermo, Milan, Venice, Parma, Livorno, Naples, and Genoa, helping to ignite flames of revolt and keep them burning. Protests against the Austrian occupation and for Italian independence took place, as well as tax revolts and pro-constitution marches. Although conflicts abounded among the different protesting groups, Giuseppe Mazzini was proud and hopeful to see such an impetus coming from the Italian people, and was making plans to travel to Italy to join them.[1] Jane Carlyle continued to take a lively interest in the cause of Italian unity.

The waves of revolt soon spread. More than fifty upsurges occurred during this European Springtime of the Peoples, many followed by quick and severe repression. Although Karl Marx and Friedrich Engels' *Communist Manifesto* was published this year, it was too late to have been a prompt for revolt. Rather, all was in response to the same underlying crises: hunger, unemployment, horrendous factory conditions, rural hardship, and the rising aspirations and disappointments of those who were taxed, repressed, and unrepresented. Famine meanwhile continued in Ireland, sending its destitute citizens by the hundreds of thousands into England, Scotland, Wales, and beyond: to North America, Australia, and New Zealand.

To keep up with the contagion of events, Thomas Carlyle, in a rare move, took out a subscription to the *Times* and shared with his brother the French *Le National*. He did not ordinarily need to consult newspapers, but the swift pace of history now demanded daily reports.

The Carlyles understood it was likely that their Chelsea neighborhood would remain sheltered from the storm. In fact, their day-to-day lives were not to be disrupted, not even by the Chartist demonstration that occurred in London on April 10. Yet metaphorically the momentous events of 1848 shook the rafters of the house on Cheyne Row, signaling that the world was changing around them at a great and bewildering speed. If they were never personally trapped behind a street barricade or caught in a crowd of shouting demonstrators, they were nonetheless provoked and inspired by events—Thomas especially—and led to utter some uncharacteristic views.

But shortly before an earth-shattering February revolution took place in France, Jane's attention was invested in a very immediate matter.

•

JANE CARLYLE AND her cousin Jeannie Welsh, her favorite correspondent, had become estranged. "[A] cheery bright little girl" was how Thomas described Jeannie, who had "ancient Scottish *golden* hair . . . the colour of a new guinea." Somewhat in the position of a niece or daughter, she was in need of her older cousin's advice—so Jane thought, as she put the blame for their falling-out on her bright-haired cousin's epistolary style.

The letters Jeannie was sending from Liverpool had become generic. "[N]o one word . . . seemed to have come out of any deeper source than your ink bottle," Jane scolded her. It was as if Jeannie had copied a stock advice-book letter "*from a young Lady residing in the Country to a female cousin in Town*." Letters like that were written to conceal, not reveal. Making the assumption her cousin was hiding unhappiness, she begged her to communicate whatever was in her heart, for who was better positioned than she to sympathize with any sorrows or disappointments Jeannie might be covering up?

A letter, ideally, Jane said, should be "*the real transcript of your mind at the moment*." That was her own approach, what she had trained and schooled herself to do, to pen an outpouring as if tipping her mind forward and letting it spill onto the page, a message sent directly from one heart and mind to another.

Beyond her current upset with her cousin, Jane had been pondering what made a good letter. A phrase she had previously used in a letter to Jeannie was "*splashing* off whatever is on my mind when I write to you, without forethought or back thought." And she had added, as if penning a novel, that she must "go on so . . . to the end of the chapter."

Jane was in the process of articulating her letter-writing aesthetic. The best letters were frank, free-flowing, and particular—and followed the caprice of the mind.

When Jeannie retorted that Jane's letters were less than frank, she had to admit her cousin had a point: "You may say my own letters are as little written out of the heart as yours—certainly—!" But she reminded her, "*my* inward life is connected with outward *facts* on which I am bound to be silent." Jane was of course referring to the ever confusing, tormenting Lady Harriet affair. If only she and Jeannie might go off somewhere for a long confidential talk—but in the meantime, knowing that letters sent to Liverpool would be read by others, Jane had to censor what she wrote. She might hint, allude, even now and then utter a brief direct complaint to her Welsh cousins, but anyone who knew her well had to understand there were hurtful incidents she could not give voice to.

Just this month Amely Bölte reported to Varnhagen that Thomas had been receiving numerous invitations for evening social events that did not include Jane.[2] The Bunsens, the Prussian ambassador and his wife, nearly always excluded Mrs. Carlyle. So, more painfully, did Lady Harriet. Complained Amely, "That's England for you!" Although the Bunsens did invite women to parties and Lady Harriet had certainly pressed enough country house invitations upon Jane, leaving the wife out of certain social evenings was a Victorian custom. Thomas often went out into society alone.

Without elaboration, Amely added that Jane told her she had "tried to write something, but wasn't able to get anything done that satisfied her."[3] As always in mid-nineteenth-century England, the literary bar was set spectacularly high. This was close to the time that Jane, after begging John Forster to send her anything he had on his library shelves by the Brontë sisters—any Currer Bell books—began reading Emily Brontë's *Wuthering Heights*.

Jane wrote family friend Mary Russell that she was feeling sensitive and irritated for other reasons as well. She was again taking morphine for a cough and for sleeplessness, even though her brother-in-law, in his family physician role, had warned her it "was 'very little better than arsenic' for a person of my constitution." Furthermore as she approached her forty-seventh birthday, Jane told Jeannie she had "been feeling more sensitive (from female causes)." If she had now begun menopause, it might have meant disturbing hot flashes and night sweats, temporarily destabilizing to the self, which would have increased her already-acute awareness of what she had called "shifting scenes and incongruities."

Giuseppe Mazzini intervened directly in the cousins' quarrel. On the verge of his most challenging political years, about to leave London for Europe, he took the time to tell Jeannie Welsh, whom he knew through Jane, to write more frankly and affectionately to her cousin, who was more in need of friendship than ever.[4] He might have been worrying how Jane would get along without him during his long absence, his perhaps *permanent* absence. In his note to Jeannie, Giuseppe tucked in information about a Friends of Italy & National Independence fundraising effort. Closely concerning himself with intimate details of his friends' lives and missing no opportunity to promote his cause: both were characteristic of this hardworking founder of modern Italy for whom the largest ideal and smallest deed were part of the same continuum.

When Jeannie next wrote, she apologized for what she assumed must be another short, disappointing letter. Jane, though, insisted what her cousin had sent this time was "real, genuine, authentic." Yet she could not resist a further piece of advice. It concerned crimes of penmanship, such as Jeannie's failure to join individual letters together, a matter Jane went on and on about. To drive her point home, in a fit of almost violent irritation, she cut samples of Jeannie's faulty handwriting out of the letter and glued them to the page. Jane's great anger is clear, the causes not entirely so.

In late March Giuseppe made an appointment to go to Cheyne Row to say farewell. He was headed for Paris again, this time with Italy as his destination: after seventeen years of exile, he was joining the Italian revolution on his homeland soil. Although Jane understood conditions were more dangerous than ever, she told her cousin she would be surprised to learn how tranquilly she was facing his departure.

Giuseppe and Jane had never recovered their former level of trust. She still could not forgive his failure to stand stalwartly by her when she had her greatest quarrel with Thomas over Lady Harriet. From whatever mixture of hurt and anger, she wrote Jeannie, "I take the prospect of his final departure with a *calm* that would surprise you. Whether it be that my *feelings* have got extremely chilled by years and suffering—or that *he* has worn them out—perhaps both causes have operated towards making me tolerably unconcerned."

Freely expressing the truth of the moment may have helped Jane to feel closer to Jeannie: the cousins were soon on good terms again.

•

ON FEBRUARY 24, 1848, a single action in France shook Europe to its core: a king had fallen. After his people rose in protest, the unpopular Louis Philippe abdicated, fleeing to England in disguise. On February 26 the Second Republic was proclaimed. From London Ralph Waldo Emerson wrote his wife Lidian that everyone in what he called the Carlyles' "valuable circle" was now "full of this astounding French Revolution." He described a gathering on March 23 at the Barings' home where "French politics are incessantly discussed."[5] Another friend reported that Mr. Carlyle had termed the "flinging out" of Louis Philippe a "beautiful radiancy."[6]

When hearing of this outburst of democracy, Thomas Carlyle exhibited a most atypical excitement: "All the people are in a sort of joy-dance over the new French Republic." He said further, "[T]his immense explosion of democracy in France, and from end to end in Europe, is very remarkable and full of interest. Certainly never in our time was there seen such a spectacle of history as we are now to look at and assist in." As he colorfully put it, "Louis-Philippe has gone out not like a King, but like a felon Coiner surprised by the Police. . . . *Bon voyage*, we will all cry after him." Addressing the issue that most concerned him—the vast numbers of the unemployed who could not find what he believed gave life its central meaning, *work*—Thomas added that the new government "and all Governments that can succeed it, *must* actually attack the 'Labour Question,' and either do something in it, or be blown in pieces, one after the other."

There was hardly a news-following person in Britain who was not riveted by the sheer spectacle unfolding across the Channel. Because Louis Philippe had neglected reform and increased repression, the February events galvanized and united most who had liberal, republican, or socialist sympathies.

But at the Barings' gathering, Emerson detected the fears of stately home owners whose palatial edifices he had just been visiting: "a certain anxiety to know whether *our* days also are not numbered, and whether the splendid privileges of these English palaces . . . are not in too dreadful contrast to famine & ignorance at the door, to last."[7]

That was indeed the great question for many in England's upper and middle classes: to what degree would such fervor spread to *their* shores? Riots did take place in Glasgow, and reports came of mobs roaming the streets of London. Most importantly, the Chartists now experienced a powerful resurgence. Thomas Carlyle encouraged Ralph Waldo Emerson to attend a March 7 Chartist meeting to experience first hand that working-class movement. At the meeting members heard the report back of a delegation they had sent to Paris to deliver their official congratulations to the new French Republic. "It was crowded," Emerson wrote of the gathering, which had resonance for him, "and the people very much in earnest[.] The Marsaillaise [sic] was sung as songs are in our abolition meetings."[8]

Author of the most celebrated book on the 1789 French Revolution, Thomas Carlyle wished to write about this historic recurrence, and expressed, at age fifty-two, a desire to become more politically engaged. As he had put it, it was "history as we are now to look at *and assist in*." After writing an unsigned leader for the *Examiner* on Louis Philippe, he spoke of starting his own newspaper or pamphlet series (his own name for what turned out to be a will o' the wisp project was Twopenny-Trash). Others spoke of sending him to Parliament, an idea he seemed receptive to. At the Barings' party, said Emerson, "Carlyle declaimed in this company a little in the style of that raven prophet who cried, 'Wo[e] to Jerusalem!' just before its Fall. But Carlyle finds little reception even in this company, where some were his warm friends. All his methods include a good deal of killing, & he does not see his way very clearly or far. The aristocrats say, 'Put that man in the House of Commons & you will hear no more of him.'"[9]

•

ON APRIL 10 THE Chartist demonstration took place in London, a grand procession to deliver to Parliament their petition or charter, listing the reforms they advocated, and signed by millions. Jane's friend Captain Anthony Sterling, who had volunteered to be a special constable, had been full of alarms about what might transpire; so for safety's sake she had taken herself off to Addiscombe Farm, where her hostess Lady Harriet was at least a known danger.

Thomas, who had stayed in London, stepped out that day in search of history in the making. He planned to send Jane a report. He walked from Chelsea to Hyde Park Corner, then into Green Park, noticing well-to-do Londoners had been frightened off: "not a single fashionable carriage was on the street; not a private vehicle . . . [except for] two surgeons' broughams." He saw a few omnibuses, street cabs, a mud cart or two, and some mounted guards, but no sign of the Chartist procession itself. When he reached the Burlington Arcade, he viewed an exhibit of satirical cartoons of key French figures, which had been making the rounds in Paris: Louis Philippe in the familiar shape of "a *Pear*, in various forms of ruin"; his detested Prime Minister Guizot; also the socialist Louis Blanc, a secretary of the new provisional French government; and poet and statesman Alphonse de Lamartine. Toward the end of his excursion, Thomas ran into a man he knew who had witnessed the march, and who told him at great length how it had gone.

Workers had arrived by railway from "Manchester, Birmingham, Rochdale, Liverpool, and other parts of Lancashire," as well as Edinburgh and Glasgow.[10] In an over reaction by authorities, tens of thousands of special constables—like Jane's friend Anthony Sterling—had been sworn in for the occasion, wearing white armbands, some carrying staves. Among them, astonishingly, was the nephew of Napoleon Bonaparte, Louis Napoleon, for the moment ensconced in England to bide his time politically.[11] The constables were standing guard all about London, along with cavalry, infantry, police, and other special forces. A motley, unprofessional crew, some constables appeared way too old or too short for the job. A few had spectacles perched on their noses and sported umbrellas. The crowds found them a great source of fun.

After gathering at various meeting places, the demonstrators marched in peaceful fashion over Blackfriars and London Bridges to Kennington Common, south of the Thames. Twenty to fifty thousand gathered there (estimates varied greatly). The multitude of men—and women, too, said to be "well-dressed" and "in numbers no less than usual"—represented the different trades. The colorful scene took on a holiday atmosphere. There were American, French, and Irish flags flying; rosettes, sashes for the marshalls, and streamers in the colors of the Chartist convention, red, green, and white; and slogans like "The voice of the people is the voice of God" and "Who would be a slave that could be free?" Other slogans indicated the demands of their ten-year-old People's Charter, such as universal suffrage for men and no property qualification for members of Parliament. The demonstrators were joined by some 5,000 Irish who were thereby, according to one of the speakers, taking the "first great step of identifying themselves with the body of the English democracy." At the front of the Irish contingent a green flag was held aloft, inscribed with a harp and the words "Irish Confederation" and "Let every man have his own country."

The focal point: two square canopied cars, each drawn by four "very splendid farm-horses." The cars held four or five huge and heavy bales of petitions in support of the Charter, destined for Parliament. The petitions had been signed by at least two million people; the Chartists claimed well over five million signatures.

The festive atmosphere changed abruptly, however. The weather turned dismal and rainy, and the planned procession back across the bridges to accompany the petitions to the House of Commons was forbidden by the authorities. Leader Feargus O'Connor decided that the protestors should disperse so as not bring down the violence of the state upon their heads. Some in the crowd urgently wished to press forward regardless. As people stood loudly debating what to do, according to *The Illustrated London News*, an eerie sound began mingling with shouts and arguments of the crowd, "that peculiar cry with which the young thieves of London signal to each other" (though it is not known what role any young thieves might have played). When some did push forth onto the bridges, the forces arrayed against protestors—police, soldiers, and special constables—drove them back, the narrow bridge passes making their job easier. Allowing themselves to become penned in south of the Thames turned out to have been a grave tactical error. Skirmishes occurred at the bridges as policemen wielded batons and protestors threw stones. Some heads got bloodied yet incidents of major violence did not occur.

Mostly the crowds did disperse, and it was reported that by 2 p. m. fewer than a hundred people were left on Kennington Common. At about 3 p. m., a delegation successfully delivered the weighty bales of petitions to the House of Commons.

After a now-rain-soaked Thomas Carlyle heard the report his acquaintance gave, he hurried back home to Cheyne Row, where he wrote Jane what he called a Private Historical Account, stating that "there is no revolution, nor any like to be for some months or years . . . the City of London is safe and quiet as the Farm of Addiscombe."

The protest did not lead to immediate results. Parliament roundly rejected the petition. The Chartist movement began, once again, to subside. But in the long run, the demonstrators and the articulation of their fair and just demands—most of which were eventually accepted—helped bend the arc of history toward justice. The Chartists' meeting on Kennington Common constituted a memorable moment, one *not* destined for Oblivion. Although he had not actually come across the march itself, Thomas well knew that private letters can be the eyes of history, and that what he wrote Jane was a tiny contribution to the record.

•

THE CARLYLES LEARNED that Giuseppe Mazzini had safely reached Italy April 7 and had been briefly reunited with his family. The great personal-political drama of Giuseppe's lifetime would occur in Rome the following year, and would be closely monitored by Jane.

Toward the end of April, eager to witness the Second Republic for themselves, several of the Carlyles' closest friends traveled to Paris. Betsey and Étienne Paulet rounded up Geraldine Jewsbury and William Edward Forster. Once there for a two-week stay, they met up with Ralph Waldo Emerson, Richard Monckton Milnes, Charles Lambert, and the young poet Arthur Hugh Clough. Like those of the generation before them at the time of the first French Revolution—William Wordsworth and Mary Wollstonecraft, for instance—they longed to experience what Wordsworth had called in *The Prelude* "the attraction of a country in romance."

Traffic across the Channel was heavy in both directions: Lady Harriet's mother had fled her Parisian residence for London, in fear of the aroused populace, and Frédéric Chopin had decided that Britain, with fewer revolutionary distractions, was better suited than Europe for his next concert tour.

Although the Carlyles did not appear to view a revolution holiday with distaste, there was no talk of the two of them, notoriously poor travelers whose spoken French was shaky, joining their friends. But the day before his departure, William Edward had tea at Cheyne Row; and upon his return he went straight to see Mr. and Mrs. Carlyle again. It is certain they heard lively first hand accounts.

Once in Paris the Carlyle's friends' political interests did not preclude them from behaving like ordinary tourists. As soon as they arrived, Geraldine and Betsey dashed out to buy bonnets. After a performance of *Phèdre*, the group saw the great French-Jewish actress Rachel wave the tricolor and chant, thrillingly, the Marseillaise, a deeply moving experience. They made a trip to Versailles, visited old tombs, and heard mass at various Catholic churches, though Geraldine was said to have rather quickly "exhausted her religion." During their late night walks in pre-Haussmann Paris, they admired "the old narrow streets, with their tall gable roofs, in the bright moonlight."[12]

The friends attended lectures and visited important national workshops, like the socialist Louis Blanc's tailor workshop that had put 1500 men to work—a form of social organization that greatly interested Thomas Carlyle—as well as clubs across the political spectrum.

One was the Club des Femmes. An active women's movement was burgeoning (while, on the other side of the Atlantic, the first women's rights convention occurred this same year in Seneca Falls, New York). The French movement brought forth a plethora of ideas and demands, discussed in newspapers like one called the *Voice of Women* (*La Voix des Femmes*).[13] William Edward purchased tickets for the Club des Femmes and once there (as he recorded in his diary) admired the "fifty to a hundred" attractively dressed young women seated in "an immense crowd of men." But part way through, some men began to jeer rudely in reaction to a speech from the dais about the *labor of free women*, choosing to interpret the phrase as referring to loose morals and prostitution. The jeering men caused such a tumult the event was broken up. "Ah! les bêtes," protested women sitting near William Edward—who believed that Englishmen would never have behaved in such a beastly, ungentlemanly fashion.

Jane wondered the following year why the warm-hearted, cheerful young man had not yet married, telling a friend that William Edward was "the sort of person that would have suited me very well!"[14] Revolutionary times were providing her with enticing examples of alternatives to her husband. If Thomas continued to be obsessed with Lady

Harriet, she might daydream about the affectionate, energetic men who enjoyed her conversation.

Paris exhilarated Ralph Waldo Emerson. "All France is bearded like goats & lions," he reported; "most of Paris is in some kind of uniform red sash, red cap, blouse [the blue workman's tunic] perhaps bound by red sash, brass helmet, & sword, and every body supposed to have a pistol in his pocket. But the deep sincerity of the speakers who are agitating social not political questions, and who are studying how to secure a fair share of bread to every man, and to get the God's justice done through the land, is very good to hear."[15] *Social not political* was the key distinction. It portended the chief fault line in the early unity. Moderate republicans favored a focus on political change to advance the rules and principles of democracy. Socialists and their working class allies wished to take the reforms further to improve the daily lives of ordinary people.

Emerson's opinion of the French—compared to the English, whom he had just been extolling in letters home—was rising by the minute. He liked seeing the whole city engaged in an open-air discussion: "Knots of people converse everywhere in the street, and the blouse or shirtsleeves-without-blouse becomes as readily the centre of discourse as any other, & Superfine and Shirt, —who never saw each other before,—converse in the most earnest yet deferential way. Nothing like it could happen in England."[16]

William Edward Forster jumped right in. He who had so much enjoyed his back and forth conversations with Jane Carlyle at his Yorkshire home discovered now among the stimulating Parisian street politicians a more robust form of talking. Geraldine Jewsbury told him, he proudly related, "it was as if I talked with my fists." (This love of speech would later lead him to a side career as a noted lecturer.)

Then came the fateful day, Monday May 15. It has been called the "European-wide turning point" of 1848.[17] As chance would have it, the Carlyles' friends were on the spot to witness events, and Emerson sent home the dramatic news: "[T]here was a revolution defeated, which came within an ace of succeeding."[18]

William Edward and Betsey Paulet set out that morning for a last look. It was to be their last day in Paris. (Through their shared experiences, the two of them, despite a dozen years discrepancy in age, were becoming very close friends, something that would later annoy Jane.)

Near the National Assembly, the Palais Bourbon, they came upon a huge demonstration in support of the liberation of Poland, then under the domination of foreign powers, where a recent effort at independence had been crushed.

Depending on one's point of view, the internationalism of the workers and socialists in France was a great source of fear (would they go rampaging into other countries to spread their values abroad?); or a great well of inspiration. Giuseppe Mazzini, the English Chartists, and supporters from countries all over Europe had led enthusiastic delegations to Paris in March to offer congratulations to the new republic.

Enthusiastic and international-minded, the demonstrators were now shouting "À bas [Down with] les Aristocrates!" and "Vive la Pologne!" A man on a rooftop began breaking twigs off trees and tossing them to the crowd—it was literally springtime in Paris. Betsey Paulet caught a leafy green branch and placed it atop her parasol. William Edward grabbed another branch, waving it dramatically with others in the crowd and yelling, "Vive la Pologne!"

He and Betsey, who were to meet up with Emerson, soon left, and only later comprehended what they had briefly been part of: the same marchers had gone on to pry bayonets out of the hands of guards, surge into the Assembly, and take over, demanding immediate action on behalf of Poland. Then and there, they had decreed a new Provisional Government.

In the subsequent confusion, the Paulets and Geraldine Jewsbury missed their train, and William Edward Forster put off his departure—Paris was too exciting to leave. Hearing that the new government had gone to the Hôtel de Ville, the city hall, to issue further decrees, William Edward rushed over just in time to see the National Guard moving in to arrest the radicals. Almost dizzy from the heady events, he recorded later in his diary, "Curious how the beat of the drum stirs the blood. I felt quite reckless." Here the crowd was chanting a *different* slogan, "À bas les Anarchistes!" When poet, novelist, and political leader Lamartine rode in on horseback at the head of a troop, William Edward, who had so recently shouted "Vive la Polgne" along with the workers and socialists, now reached up eagerly to clasp the hand of the man riding in to replace them.

Coup and counter-coup occurred swiftly. Moderate republicans were again in control. Like many, William Edward was amazed that so much had happened with "scarcely a blow." He was aware of his own contradictory position, caught between the *ouvriers*, or workers, and his fellow factory owners. Not the traitor to his class that Tory bankers and manufacturers in Yorkshire had accused him of being, he thought the best way to protect his business interests and prevent a bloody revolution against men like himself was to befriend the workingman and support his desire for just reforms. In his youth, at least, enlightened self-interest was the path William Edward attempted to pursue.

Two days later he was back in London telling his tales to the Carlyles.

•

AFTER MAY 15, divisions widened in the French Republic. General Louis Eugène Cavaignac took on a major role, and his participation colored how the Carlyles viewed what happened next.

They had cherished a friendship with the general's older brother, the late Godefroy Cavaignac, a republican and revolutionary during the 1830s uprisings in Louis Philippe's France (events immortalized in Victor Hugo's *Les Misérables*). Escaping prison after being condemned to death, Godefroy had fled to London, where he had met the Carlyles. Later returning to France under an amnesty, he had died of consumption (tuberculosis) in 1845.

The Carlyles loved revolutionaries far more than their revolutions and Godefroy had captivated Jane. A striking looking Byronic hero, he was swashbuckling, forthright, and impassioned. She described him romantically as "a man with that sort of dark half-savage beauty with which one would paint a fallen angel." He once chided her for speaking to him in some overly strained, witty, self-deprecating manner. For *him*, Godefroy told Jane, she had no need to "*make minced meat*" of herself. Impressed by his air of command as he advised her, Jane called what he said "*regal* words truly!" Possibly Godefroy reminded her a little of her handsome father, that dispenser of wise advice.

In January1849 Jane wrote a remarkable passage that conveys the intensity of her feelings for Godefroy. The burly John Robertson, Geraldine's one-time fiancé, after failing to lure Jane into a discussion of General Cavaignac's inferiority to his fiery revolutionary brother, informed her that the socialist Louis Blanc (by then in exile) was coming to tea, and that he had been the one to hold the dying Godefroy in his arms. Utilizing the romantic novel genre, positioning herself as heroine, Jane claimed that at those words, she "started as if he had shot me." She went on, "I had my boa gloves reticule &c in my lap, I flung them all violently on the floor—why. I don't know—I could not help it!" Later, learning that John Robertson had "been heard to speculate on [her] intimacy" with the French revolutionary, she loftily concluded: "Well! let him draw his inferences—it is no disgrace to any woman to be accused of having loved Godefroid [sic] Cavaignac. The only reproach to be made me is that I did not love him as well as he deserved—But now he is dead I will not deny him before all the Robertsons alive!"

In 1848 her love for his brother, ironically, encouraged Jane to view the general's harsh actions favorably. On June 20 the National Assembly dissolved the popular National Workshops that had been so badly needed in France and had put thousands to work, among them Louis Blanc's tailors. The Assembly instead made plans to draft the unemployed into swamp-draining regiments in the marshy Sologne in north-central France. With unemployment and hunger rampant in Paris, those actions provoked further demonstrations of laborers, artisans, and socialists. Tensions grew. Workers began erecting additional barricades in the streets of Paris—and were gaining ground. Some believed time was left to negotiate, but General Cavaignac, former dictator of Algeria and current Minister of War, was put in charge of suppressing those at the barricades and prepared his cannons. The result was a bloodbath.

Following the events, Jane and Thomas thought the general's bloody crushing of the uprising had been necessary, even though Godefroy had been a hero of the Thirties and their father, as a member of the National Convention in 1793, had voted for the execution of Louis XVI. As Thomas Carlyle explained, "Perhaps no man in all the world could have had so cruel a duty laid upon him, as that of cannonading and suppressing these wretched people, who . . . his Father and Brother and all his kindred had devoted themselves to stirring up."

The joy-dance in the streets had become a revolutionary upsurge —though not on May 15 very violent. But Paris now was the site of brutal oppression. One progressive club and newspaper after another was closed down. Under General Cavaignac's leadership, thousands upon thousands were killed, or jailed, or deported in convoys to Algeria, many dying along the way.[19]

A further irony: General Cavaignac who was a republican—though with his reputation tarnished by the killings of Bloody June—would lose the vote for the presidency the following December to Louis Napoleon. In 1852, despite various poses as friend of the people, Louis Napoleon entirely betrayed the spirit of 1848, putting an end to the Second Republic and getting himself crowned Emperor Napoleon III.

Jane Carlyle, sympathetic, often, to liberties but not to ideologies, saved her strongest feelings for individuals. Her friendship with the general's brother, as well as a tendency to agree in public with her husband's harsher views, caused her to approve the suppression wholeheartedly, writing her cousin: "The one earthly thing that I have been getting any real satisfaction out of has been . . . the wise and valourous conduct of General Cavaignac—and the admiration he has won from all parties—If I had been his Sister I could not have watched his progress with more interest."

Jane was definitely aware of—and condoned—some of the brutality committed under the general's leadership. Yet it is not clear what information she had been receiving. Most periodicals the Carlyles saw were not on the side of the workers and socialists. Rumors about *their* violence, some false or exaggerated, had been rampant. One of the papers Thomas subscribed to, *Le National*, interpreted the June events as a battle of Angels versus Animals: "[O]n one side there stood order, liberty, civilisation, the decent Republic, France; and on the other, barbarians, desperados emerging from their lairs for massacre and looting."[20]

For Thomas Carlyle, man of paradox, all was complex. His friends were forever trying, unsuccessfully, to get at the heart of his contradictions. Employing the word for lower-class rebels of the first French Revolution, Ralph Waldo Emerson called him a "sansculotte-aristocrat."[21] Thomas might rejoice in an uprising against corruption and sham. He had no special truck with kings, virtually none with Popes, and favored more just laws. But in this second wave of events, when republicans turned against workers and socialists, and vice versa, he, like many upper-and middle-class British supporters, found his enthusiasm for France waning.

A personal contribution to Thomas Carlyle's pessimism and disappointment might have been John Forster's rejection in March of a second article (possibly considered too progressive!) that he had written for the *Examiner*. In it, Thomas said, he had openly "*approved* of at least the *attempt* by France to do something for the guidance and benefit of the workpeople."

He continued to agonize over the widespread hunger and unemployment. From what he had experienced and witnessed growing up in Annandale, he of course comprehended the hardship of the poor. He also believed that famine or mob violence might expose corruption of "the Emperor has no clothes" variety and clear the field for something better. But in the end he considered the threat of chaos and anarchy too fearful: it had to be strongly suppressed. In no way did he trust the masses and their socialist leaders to sort things out, believing an iron hand was needed. As Ralph Waldo Emerson had put it back in March, "All his methods include a good deal of killing."

For both Carlyles the first half of 1848 was the most intense. Though Jane kept an eye on events in Europe, especially her friend Giuseppe's adventures in Italy, they were never central to her. Thomas continued to agonize over the issues, but his joyful exuberance of early spring had died away. During July, in disgust, he cancelled their subscription to the *Times*.

II

"CHOPIN HAS BEEN here!!" Jane wrote her cousin one day in July. Consumptive, fragile, and in the aftermath of his serious falling out with the novelist George Sand, with whom he had lived in Paris, Nohant, and Majorca, Frédéric Chopin had undertaken a tour of England and Scotland. His visit to Cheyne Row came after an entertaining week for Jane that had included one dinner party at the Macreadys and another at the home of Caroline Norton. Mrs. Norton famously and for good reasons lived apart from her husband—a jealous, often drunk, vindictive, and litigious man—which was enough to make her, socially speaking, one of the women on the margin who for Jane—when she comments favorably on them—signal a more open state of mind. "Well," she said of Mrs. Norton in fairly tolerant tones, "she is a beautiful witty graceful woman—whatever else." Part of the week's enlivening pleasure: Jane was able to attend two of Frédéric Chopin's concerts.

He and the Carlyles had a friend in common, the Scottish Jane Wilhelmina Stirling who had devoted herself to the musician, supplying money, assistance, and adoration. In turn, he had dedicated two Nocturnes to her and rumors were afloat that the two were poised to marry.

But as Chopin's correspondence makes clear, marriage was not his intention. (After his death in 1849, though, the Carlyles referred to her as the Widow Chopin.) Grateful for arrangements Jane Stirling and her widowed sister had made for his tour, he nevertheless found their attentions tedious. The endless efforts on his behalf could make him feel imprisoned. He knew he was very unwell: he often had to be carried up and down stairs. Yet despite his infirmities he was playing brilliantly. Those who wrote about him tried to convey the preternatural touch of his pale thin fingers on the keys that created such wondrous sounds.

Thomas Carlyle had discovered the musician's presence in England when members of Jane Stirling's circle asked him to send publicity announcements and reviews to editor John Forster for publication in the *Examiner*. A touch cranky and testy at having to impose on the editor (who had rejected one of his own articles), he did so, believing the musician's friends when they called him a "man of great modesty and moral worth." Forster was glad enough to include pieces in his journal, and he also obtained tickets for a July 7 Chopin recital, sending two of them around to Cheyne Row.

Thomas's denseness about music in general was well known, and the Darwin family had a story to illustrate it. One evening in 1845 at a dinner party at Hensleigh and Fanny Wedgwood's home, Thomas had insisted that Beethoven's sonatas were "nothing." This son of a stonemason had declared the sonatas were "like a great quantity of stones tumbled down for a building" that might just as well have been left in the quarry. Giuseppe Mazzini, present at the party and shocked, had called upon God to pardon him.[22] Friends said Thomas truly enjoyed only Scottish ballads and airs like those that Jane nimbly played for him on their (according to Amely) out-of-tune piano.[23]

Thomas Carlyle could not attend on July 7; he was leaving for his Stonehenge trip with Ralph Waldo Emerson (who would depart for America July 15). But by the time he departed, he had been able to hear Chopin play and complimented the music sincerely, adding, "what is far better, [he is] a truly delicate, interesting and excellent looking character. Sensitive, alas, tremulous as aspen-leaves, and evidently familiar enough with suffering."

When Jane Carlyle heard Chopin play, she was bewitched and deeply moved. In England he had various pianofortes at his disposal, including a Broadwood and a Pleyel, which sounded different from modern pianos. The keys were narrower; the lower and higher registers uneven in tone; the notes less sharp, rapid, and precise. The notes would ring and blend together (dampers on nineteenth-century pianos did not stop a sound so immediately), mingling at times to produce a suspended dissonance, delightful in its way. With the odd contrasts, from rough to tinny, there could be abrupt, stirring changes of mood. These were the pianos that Chopin played on and wrote for. In his London concerts, he included mazurkas, études, and nocturnes, as well as waltzes, scherzos, and his exquisite lullaby, the *Berceuse*.[24] Jane said that she had "never heard the piano played before—could not have believed the capabilities that lie in it." And she intuited rightly what music making must be costing him in his consumptive state: "I cannot fancy but that every piece he composes must leave him with many fewer days to live."

She sent Frédéric Chopin her compliments through Jane Stirling, enclosing a poem of praise that Captain Anthony Sterling, her escort to the July 7 concert, had penned right after hearing him play. It is laudatory doggerel: "The pale wizard's fingers / With magical skill / Make a music that lingers / In memory still," etc. But she asked that the poem be passed on to Chopin as a token of appreciation and suggested that Miss Stirling translate the verses into French.

Thrilled and honored though Jane was by the pianist's social visit to 5 Cheyne Row, neither she nor Thomas could communicate with him, a great frustration. Chopin could not speak English. He was fluent in French, which the Carlyles could read; but with whatever spoken vocabulary they possessed—Thomas said he had "lost the habit of writing or speaking even bad French"—they could not make themselves understood.

Instead, Jane expressed her profound appreciation of Chopin in her letter to Jane Stirling. She was again conveying her aesthetic, what she had been thinking through this year, her cousin's letters having provided one example of what it was not: the conventional, habitual, generic. "I never liked any music so well—," wrote Jane, "because *it feels* to me not so much a sample of the man's *art* offered '*on approbation*' (the effect of most music for me) but a portion of his soul and life *given away* by him—*spent* on those who have ears to hear and hearts to understand."

Here are echoes of what Jane believed letter writing should be: "a real transcript of your mind at the moment" and "the splash of the mind." Training, practice, and the achievement of artistry are in no way denied. But at some point the artist draws on it all with an effect spontaneous and natural: splashing the mind, spending the soul; the creator in sync with a responsive audience. A gift freely given. It is not a labored art offered up for approval, glancing slyly to see how it might be coming across, but rather a playful, generous expression from one living mind to another, in tones that might carry across the centuries.

When in full flight, the well-read, well-trained Jane Carlyle expressed in a natural manner not a naïve but a sophisticated exuberance. And she understood the ideal.

•

IN SEPTEMBER JANE again found herself in Hampshire at the Grange, that Grecian temple of a hundred-room mansion, this time for a five-week stay. Conditions, however, had changed. William Bingham Baring, whose father had died in May, had become the second Baron Ashburton, and Lady Harriet was now Lady Ashburton, sometimes Lady A., or Lady Harriet, still, in Jane's letters.

The new Lord Ashburton had inherited some sixty to eighty thousand pounds a year. Having to control and manage this vast fortune, including his father's properties, he was preoccupied with plans for investment and improvement. The new Lady Ashburton was assembling at the Grange a house party more splendid than ever, the illustrious company set to arrive in rotating shifts. Lords Lansdowne, Auckland, and Granville were expected, along with various ministers, politicians, literary men, and society ladies, as well as the ubiquitous Henry Fleming, close friend of Charles Buller, who was always a favored guest. Adding color to the scene, the Hampshire Yeomanry was mustered nearby. Amidst the grandeur and splendor, the Carlyles were well treated. Each had been given a two-bedroom suite, some doors apart.

Lady Ashburton's romantic friendship with Thomas had been wending its strange way, partly in but also partly out of Jane's sight. The lady was a great reader and her connection to Thomas had all along been strengthened through numerous exchanges and discussions of books as well as politics. The condition of Ireland was a current special concern of theirs. Still enamored, he had sent a complimentary note to the lady in June: "You too have eyes—O heaven!—God save the Queen,—my own Queen." And once he warned her not to acknowledge that she had received a letter from him.[25]

Despite that unresolved undercurrent, Jane's country house experience was different this time. From her rounds of such visits, she had been gaining social confidence. Back in April when Jane was at Addiscombe Farm (while Thomas was in London, hoping to witness the Chartist demonstration), she had seized on a way to make a unique contribution to her hosts and at the same time to connect with her own traditions. She had descended to the Barings' kitchens to teach the housekeeper how to make marmalade.

Grace Welsh had taught her daughter the art. She was a woman who kept her eye out for when "the *real* marmalade oranges" were in season, her secret ingredient being to double "the quantity of sugar to the fruit."[26] Jane, in turn, had become known for her own pots of Scottish marmalade, which made handy gifts. In an April letter from Addiscombe, Jane had told her husband, in a mock epic scene, that she first had to conquer the Barings' kitchen staff. Using images from the women of the Parisian barricades, she portrayed herself as "alone in that kitchen, —amidst the scowls of *women in pinafores* and suppressed cries of '*à bas la* [sic] *systeme*.'" Needing to win over the housekeeper, Mrs. Atchison, who had objected to the scheme, she joked it would have been easier to "lead 'a few brave men' against the Austrians."

The evening the job was completed, Jane took a spoonful of the hot amber marmalade in a saucer to her hosts in their dining room. They sipped it and pronounced it excellent. By that point, she said proudly, the kitchen maid would have gone "thro boiling sugar" for her, while Mrs. Atchison was "perfectly radiant . . . with 'virtue its own reward.'" The woman had even thanked Mrs. Carlyle for having taught her the skill. Lady Harriet had cooperated by making certain the right sort of oranges were brought to Addiscombe from London. What dear Democratic Jane (to use Betsey Paulet's phrase) did not realize was that putting herself in the position of head housekeeper in charge of the kitchens would not have raised her in the lady's estimation.[27]

On her visit at the Grange this fall, Jane apparently wrote only one real letter, to Jeannie Welsh. She acknowledged writing hardly any. A few now lost probably concerned her forthcoming change of maids—Anne Brown was to be married to her young man and a replacement found. With the exception of what she had written her cousin (and a note to a woman requesting Mrs. Carlyle's autograph, to which she replied she had done nothing bad or good enough to warrant one), no letters from Jane exist between 15 August and 23 October.

According to her husband, who wrote at least fourteen letters from the Grange, Jane fared better than he did. Thomas Carlyle was uneasy, his dissatisfaction perhaps stemming in part from the contrast of this solid bastion of the aristocracy to the current upheavals of the oppressed. He had been searching his mind for solutions to the massive unemployment, poverty, and starvation throughout Europe and Ireland, conditions that continued to fuel the uprisings.

The recent French experiment involving thousands of laborers, each paid a pittance and sent to clear boggy marshes of the Sologne under a strict system of rigid military discipline, had aroused his curiosity, and he wrote letters seeking to learn more.[28] Did the workers actually earn their pay; or, he worried, did they receive a stipend whether they worked or not? For a government to organize its labor force, the only plan he could envision involved huge regiments operating by "the method of command and obedience." He imagined this almost feudal corvée-type labor as a solution both for the French unemployed and the famine-starved peasants of Ireland.

In non-political reports from the Grange, Thomas acknowledged the pure Hampshire air; the opportunities for exercise (he rode horseback and Jane took walks); the solitude woody acres could provide; and the benefits to health if rich food and wine might be avoided. Leaning against one of the fat Doric pillars on the outsized portico cantilevered toward the lake and hillside, smoking his pipe, he could now and then share a relaxed moment with Jane. But searching more desperately for things to tell correspondents, he was driven to repetitive mentions of rooks heard and squirrels seen. At one exasperated point, he called the surrounding chorus of parlor chatter a "twaddle-deluge." Even more than usual, he lamented the do-nothingness, indolence, and incessant "making wits" in the drawing room. In some unknowable manner, his desire for harsh military enforcement of a work routine for others seemed to issue from a deep private terror of his own indolence.

As for Jane, now more used to the high life, she played her part successfully. Around her spun a fascinating whirl of activity. She met the Irish poet Aubrey de Vere and discovered the romantically named young man, then in his thirties, was one of the few she could address in an honest, straight-forward manner. He who was increasingly attracted to Rome (not of course in Mazzini's sense) talked reams of religion at Mrs. Carlyle (and in 1851 would convert to Catholicism). Stimulated by the varied company and her conversations with the poet, Jane had a more pleasant, rewarding time than on any previous visit to the Barings' homes.

But she kept her observant eye on everything. As recently as the previous April, Jane had drawn on the moral essay genre in a letter to Thomas's sister Jean: "The more I see of wealthy establishments . . . the less I wish to preside over one of my own—the superior splendour is overbalanced by the inferior comfort: and the only indisputable advantage of a large fortune—the power of helping other people with it—all these rich people, however good and generous their hearts may have been in the beginning, seem somehow enchanted into never availing themselves of."

In spite of her successes at the Grange on this occasion (and perhaps, after their quarrel, attempting to be more candid with Jeannie), she told her cousin that she had been experiencing a sense of suffocation. She added, "[I]t is wonderful how one gets used by long endurance to sufferings which in the first moments of them drive one beside oneself—To see me here nobody I am sure would suspect that I am not quite healthy and content . . . but the less one meditates on ones own miseries the better."

Amely Bölte objected to what she viewed as a self-destructive strategy Jane had entered upon during this phase, yet could not talk her out of it. She was mad enough to tell Varnhagen that despite her feelings for Jane, "some hiatus in our friendship must occur." Calling it "the path she has taken to bring harmony into her life," she claimed that Jane had resolved "to appear everything she is not. . . . She does not want to bother others with what pleases or saddens her as an individual." In other words, Jane had resolved to play a role. Donning such a mask exasperated the governess: "a person turns into a theatre puppet that recites the part she studied so well." Amely added, perhaps a touch jealous that Jane had heeded the advice of others, "So she may succumb for a while to the influence of those ladies who want to teach her the ways of the world and the result will show to what extent heart and soul will be satisfied with that."[29]

Those ladies instructing on the ways of the world had likely been counseling Mrs. Carlyle to relinquish her anguished, futile protests against her husband's friendship with Lady Ashburton. Neither he nor the lady was going to give it up—clearly. A worldly woman would make her peace with what she could not change and count her blessings the situation was not worse—after all it was said that the romance was platonic! As for keeping quiet and suppressing her I-ity to maintain social harmony, Jane herself had just said *the less one meditates on ones own miseries the better*. Concealing personal difficulties from others was the conventional socially acceptable way, and she was getting better at it. But for a woman who valued being free to say what she liked—and encouraged honesty in the letter writing of others—it was at the same time a terrible suppression of self.

During this spell at the Grange, Lady Ashburton fell ill and traveled briefly to London to see a physician who practiced gynecology. While there she caught a cold and on her return kept to her rooms, not dining with the others and seeing only female guests. Her prolonged retreat in the far reaches of the mansion might have contributed to Mr. Carlyle's dissatisfaction. Mrs. Carlyle, however, was admitted to the lady's inner sanctum. Feeling sensitive from her own female causes possibly gave Jane something in common with the lady: "I play chess and talk with her in her private sitting-room—which is the beautifullest room you can imagine and opening into a large conservatory with a glass door."

Jane made an interesting move on this visit. Lady Ashburton's mother, having left Paris because of the revolution, was visiting the Grange. The dowager countess of Sandwich—Mary Anne Julia Louisa Harriet Lowry-Corry—had a reputation "as the most insolent of English Peeresses." Yet Jane found her a "*very* agreeable and a good sort of woman to my notion tho her daughter can hardly endure her."

Surprisingly, Jane Carlyle and Lady Sandwich became friends. When in London, she was someone Jane could drop in on any time. Intentionally or not, Jane had formed a second triangle to counter the one that plagued her. On this visit to the Grange, she played the Good Daughter to Lady A.'s mother, who in turn became fond of Jane; whereas Lady A. remained, by default, the Bad Daughter. It must have provided moments of silent satisfaction (see how well I am getting along with your so-called insolent mother). Despite the formidable reputation of Lady Sandwich, Jane said that she was "precisely the only [peeress] . . . I have known with whom I feel entirely free to say what I like, and whom I can run in to with as little ceremony as I could do to any old woman living on a hundred a year."

Lady Harriet continued to find the mother who, in true upper-class fashion, had shunted her little daughter off to nannies and governesses to be very difficult indeed. It is not known whether she minded Jane's friendship with Lady Sandwich, or found it a relief that someone could keep her chatty, annoying mother occupied.

On this visit, a plan got proposed that horrified Jane. As she listened, her resolve to keep quiet for the sake of social harmony would have been sorely taxed. In looking about his great estate and contemplating improvements, Lord Ashburton and his wife happened upon the (to them) gladsome idea that Thomas Carlyle should have the use of a farmhouse on land surrounding the mansion. It was to be "fitted up" for him. Thomas had long been toying with the notion of finding some place in the country for himself and Jane—an idea that never had appeal for her. In fact in this very season, his family in Scotland had been inquiring on his behalf about the availability of specific Dumfriesshire properties.

Was a farmhouse on Ashburton property, then, to become the Carlyles' "very own" country residence? Acerbically Jane commented to her cousin that this was "no *poetical*-farm." Neither she nor Thomas would get a wink of sleep. Said farmhouse was situated in the midst of the estate's offices and an active farmyard replete with roosters, hens, geese, ducks, pigs, cows, horses, and carts—all harnessed in the service of the great mansion, which required a constant supply of meat, milk, fruits, and vegetables to be raised, grown, and transported by a sizeable troop of laborers.

Fortunately Jane did not have to break her vow of silence to vehemently object. On reflection Lord Ashburton discovered that he had, this first year of his baronetcy, too many "unexpected drains on his fortune—large as it is." The farmhouse renovation project was given up. "[I]t is much more agreeable for *me*," Jane said of her lucky escape, "that the project should sink away thus than that *I* should have put a veto on it or *he* for *my* consolation—" No matter how compliant she was schooling herself to be, the so-metropolitan Mrs. Carlyle, for more reasons than the pigs, ducks, and chickens, could not possibly have tolerated residing in a farmhouse adjacent to the Grange, playing milk-maid every summer to Harriet Baring's grand lady.

•

On her return to Cheyne Row, Jane suffered a small shock. "I was got so habituated to the vastness and splendour of the Grange," she wrote Helen Welsh, "and the luxury of all sorts; that for the first time in my life my own home looked excessively *small* and poverty-stricken." Not only had her Chelsea home taken on the appearance of an impoverished doll's house, the painting and papering done in her absence contributed to a further unsettling strangeness. At once she set about putting her books and pictures back in place, which helped, as did getting accustomed to some enticing improvements (presumably supervised by Anne Brown). She now had new "*regular* red stuff curtains with brass poles—only think!"

Jane was grateful "to get back to Chelsea again where I might find some work however humble." She continued her Employment Bureau tasks, as she would all her life. She had found a tutor for the Macreadys' son Henry and provided careful written reports on a whole series of scullery maids for a position that Lady Harriet's mother-in-law was trying to fill. She tried to help a distressed gentleman's servant (unnamed) who had a family to support to secure employment, and supplied Betsey Paulet's sister-in-law with "the very best nursemaid her children ever had."

Jane's old friend Isabella Buller suffered devastating losses this year, which gave her another form of humble work, nursing care. In May Isabella's husband had passed away and in November she lost a son. The radical M. P. Charles Buller, Jr., only forty-two, had minor surgery and was even given the new anesthetic, chloroform, to ease the procedure. But when unexpected complications developed, the still-young man so many adored had suddenly died.

Former pupil of Thomas Carlyle, a large, pleasant, clever fellow with easy, playful manners, had become a fixture at the Ashburtons' residences. Thomas wrote consoling letters to Lady Ashburton about the loss of Charles, who had brightened her circle more than anyone. Jane was aware of this particular round of their correspondence and, under the distressing circumstances, did not object. Thomas wrote an obituary of Charles for the *Examiner* and was present at his funeral. He observed that the severe blows Mrs. Buller had endured had rendered her "a poor thin old woman, wasted to a shadow."

In December, responding to Isabella's pleas—Charles' dear "lisping and prating" friend Henry Fleming, who had been comforting her, had to leave for the Grange to comfort the disconsolate Lady Ashburton—Jane traveled to the other side of Hyde Park to attend the older woman. On one occasion she spent three days there ministering to Isabella's needs. She wanted to view her as a benevolent mother figure, but worried that her friend was complicating her terrible grief by histrionically indulging in it and spending money recklessly at the slightest whim. The following March, Isabella herself passed away. Jane was with her just before she breathed her last—before leaving her house, she had "kissed her little cold hand."

The Bullers' wayward goddaughter Theresa Revis, according to Jane, had become so accustomed to their fancy style of living that she experienced the 250 pounds a year they had left her as a hardship. Lady Ashburton, always an astute observer of Tizzy, remarked that she was now "beyond all imagination something remarkable," acknowledging that her "'*Azure Devils*' [her eyes] are pretty!" But she claimed—in a forceful statement that conveys a sense of the lady's oomph—the girl had "not a trace any where of feeling for any of those that are gone! or feeling for herself that there is not now a soul on earth that loves her—or cares a straw what becomes of her but for the sake of those three coffins in Kensal Green."[30] Theresa's exasperated guardians finally shipped her off to India to live with her father, now a judge in Calcutta, and his reluctant wife.[31] Although the Bullers were not among the Carlyles' best or closest friends, they had long been woven into their lives. Their sudden absence left an unnerving gap.

The busyness, bustle, and charisma that had drawn so many to them—all was suddenly over, gone, no more. It was an instance of that too-frequent nineteenth-century phenomenon where most of a family could be wiped out at a stroke, sometimes from typhus or cholera or consumption. The actor William Charles Macready, in the 1850s, would lose a large part of his family to consumption. With life so very precarious, Thomas gave thanks that his family had not yet suffered that way. The Victorians lived with a sense of impending menace in the background: fear of the devastation sickness could bring to a family, never knowing when the blow might strike.

•

JANE'S PRINCIPAL DOMESTIC task this fall involved her change of maids. During the summer she and Anne Brown had survived some tiff concerning propriety. Anne had perhaps by accident (the word used) stayed out too late with her fiancé, although Thomas later recalled that the young man's sober habit of courting involved arriving "silently, and [sitting] two hours once a week."[32] Whatever the problem, it resolved itself after the maid told Mrs. Carlyle that she was henceforth "to regulate [Anne's] intercourse with her Lover" according to her "own ideas of *propriety*." Overall Jane admired and relied on Anne's quiet, reasonable, capable ways and was loath to see her go. But after a five-year courtship Anne was anxious to marry. She and her husband were to establish a home and manage a butcher shop on the Isle of Jersey.

In a coincidence of timing, the greatly missed Helen Mitchell became available—although the previous year she had annoyed Jane by writing from Dublin to boast of "her 'servants' and '*Country House*,' and 'housefuls of visitors.[']" Jane for the most part held conventional views on the question of *knowing one's place*. She had implied that Margaret Fuller did not, one of her problems with Margaret. It was an idea comprehensible only to those who believed in the inherent rightness of certain types of social stratification and the wrongness of *the mania for rising* into circles to which they did not belong. Jane's conviction, in fact, contributed to one sort of unease she experienced at the Ashburtons' aristocratic homes, where, so the logic went, the Carlyles had been unnaturally raised out of their proper sphere. When such a thing occurred, the Victorian Greek chorus would invariably, lugubriously groan in unison: "*and no good can come of it*." That is what Jane, implied, too.

Always wary of Helen's brother, Jane was not surprised to discover that she had fought with him and left Dublin for her former home in Kirkcaldy. There Helen had attempted to run a small shop, possibly a dram shop, with her sister. After the shop failed to work out, Helen Mitchell wrote to the Carlyles asking if she might enter service with them again. Jane found she could not say no to someone who had been such a close part of her life. On October 22 Helen returned to Cheyne Row, and during the brief transition sat hemming tea towels—and making odd, mysterious faces—as Anne Brown finished up her chores for the last time.

Concerned about Helen's taking to drink again, Jane took the precaution of preventing the potential bad influence of washerwomen (one of whom had originally plied Helen with liquor). She would send the laundry out. She was apprehensive about Helen's "strange half-witted look after the calm rational Anne," and worried that her more independent life in Dublin might have spoiled her. But although Helen had "great faults"—including a bad temper and moodiness—Jane concluded that she also had "great virtues." The tiny Scotswoman was probably the hardest working servant the Carlyles ever had in their employ. For the moment, mistress and maid were working in tandem again.

During this eventful year, Jane had followed revolutionary changes in Europe, entertained Chopin, and maneuvered her way through the Ashburtons' circles. After returning from the Grange, she got back to housekeeping, employment bureau work, nursing care, and supervising her change of maids. The humble work centered and grounded her and allowed her—as she put it—to once again call her soul her own "to a certain extent." Yet regarding work, she did still long for something more.

CHAPTER EIGHTEEN
A DASH AT THE WALL

"It may be a while before you see me again *climbing the Churchyard* Wall, but I am often there, for all that, in my *dreams* and in my waking thoughts too—"
—JANE WELSH CARLYLE, 23 November 1849[1]

I

AS THE 1840S WERE DRAWING TO A CLOSE, EVENTS IN ITALY TOOK AN unprecedented turn. Jane Carlyle became riveted by the happenings in that country when, for one hundred days, her friend Giuseppe Mazzini, as part of a triumvirate, was able to govern a Roman Republic. Desperate to know how he would fare in such a dangerous situation she had the newspaper *Italia del Populo* delivered to her each day: "you may fancy how anxiously I expect it every morning." It would at least let her know if Giuseppe were dead or alive.

A cluster of Papal reactions had opened the way for a republic. The once-popular reform Pope, Pius IX, torn between sentiment for Italy and allegiance to Catholicism in all forms, including the Austrian, behaved in a manner that greatly upset the many Italians who had placed their hopes for change in him. He drew back. He had intended only minor reforms. Popular protests underway in Rome began looking more and more like anarchy to him. After a minister of his was stabbed to death in a crowd and large numbers of people, including troops that the Pope had relied on, took to the streets of Rome singing "Happy the hand which rids the world of a tyrant!" he and his retinue fled south to the Kingdom of Naples.[2]

Margaret Fuller, now living in Rome and sending back dispatches to the *New York Daily Tribune*, witnessed events unfold. The news she reported was similar to what the Carlyles were hearing in London. Describing the Pope's absence in the first flush of excitement—after voicing a qualm about the violence that had precipitated his departure —Margaret wrote that people were saying, "The Pope, the Cardinals, the Princes are gone, and Rome is perfectly tranquil, and one does not miss anything, except that there are not so many rich carriages and liveries."[3]

On February 2, 1849, a Constitutional Assembly declared the official existence of the Roman Republic. On February 9 Margaret heard a deputy read the decree from a balcony of the Piazza del Campidoglio. The Pope would retain his spiritual leadership, but the Papacy had fallen, to be replaced by "a pure Democracy." The new republic would have relations "exacted by a common nationality" with the rest of Italy.[4] In one of their first acts, the deputies conferred citizenship upon Giuseppe Mazzini. When Margaret discovered he would now be able to enter the city as a full-fledged Roman citizen, she wrote to him saying that it seemed to her "almost the most sublime and poetical fact of history" she had heard of.[5]

After becoming head of the governing triumvirate, Giuseppe Mazzini instituted a series of progressive reforms. In the brief existence of the republic, censorship was lifted. Newspapers flourished. There was freedom to assemble. The death penalty was abolished. Certain buildings belonging to the Church were made over to housing for the poor. Despite rumors abroad to the contrary, the republic enjoyed a great deal of popular support. In addition to those realities of the evanescent moment, Giuseppe Mazzini, his fellow triumvirs, and the citizens of Rome were involved in something even greater. They were creating a myth, a symbol, a source of hope for future generations of the world's citizens that "these things shall be."

As had happened throughout Europe during this Springtime of the Peoples, in reaction to such popular uprisings and the constitutions and democracies that they were attempting to bring into being, a storm of opposition arose. In the very complicated story of the short-lived Roman Republic, the saddest betrayal came from France. To appease his Catholic base—and revealing his true colors—the so-called republican President Louis Napoleon Bonaparte sent invading troops. Soldier and leader Giuseppe Garibaldi's forces fought bravely but were outnumbered. After a damaging siege of Rome, Garibaldi had to face reality. A truce was negotiated, and he ordered his followers to quit the city and travel north. The time for a united Italy had not yet arrived.

Margaret Fuller, whose admiration and respect for Garibaldi had risen during the days of the republic, witnessed his heroic soldiers marching out of Rome. She wrote a heartfelt, idealized account for the *Tribune*: "Never have I seen a sight so beautiful, so romantic and so sad. . . . They had all put on the beautiful dress of the Garibaldi legion, the tunic of bright red cloth, the Greek cap, or else round hat with Puritan plume, their long hair was blown back from resolute faces; all looked full of courage; they had counted the cost before they entered on this perilous struggle; they had weighed life and all its material advantages against Liberty, and made their election; they turned not back, nor flinched, at this bitter crisis."[6]

Reluctant to give up, Giuseppe Mazzini was forced to comply with the inevitable. With the help of a friendly French sea captain—he counted a great many supporters among the French people—he was smuggled on board a vessel heading north to Marseilles, and escaped into exile. He would one day be back in London, and would remain—though in a far less intense way—on friendly terms with the Carlyles.

As she followed the drama of the Roman Republic, Jane found that her disappointment in Giuseppe—for not wholeheartedly siding with her in her quarrel with her husband, and for over-enthusiastically taking up the Ashurst family—was forgotten. Fondness and esteem had been restored. "Poor dear Mazzini," she wrote to her cousin Jeannie, taking aim at the hypocrisy of Louis Napoleon, "—all my affection for him has waked up since I knew him in jeopardy and so gallantly fulfilling his destiny—and not mine only—the public sympathy is fast going over to his side—under the atrocious injustice of the French—who one year ago loudly invited all nations to form republics and now procede [sic] to shoot lead into the only one that has obeyed the call." Once again, she understood the importance of her friend's role as a hero in history.

(A republican dedicated to his cause and in difficulty with various authorities till the end, Giuseppe Mazzini nevertheless lived to see a united Italy; and on the day of his funeral, thousands thronged the streets of Genoa.[7])

•

WHILE THE ROMAN Republic was being established, Jane had to confront a very personal crisis in her kitchen. But before she began telling that story to her cousin, Jane said she was about to continue "where I left off in *my life*—that is to say the history of my life—outwardly speaking." That intriguing comment clearly indicates that she saw letter writing as a form of autobiography.

The story Jane wanted to tell started with a brief pleasant visit she and Thomas had made to Captain Anthony Sterling's country place in Surrey. Having been the object of his mentally ill wife's wild-eyed jealousy, Jane had first politely requested and received permission from Charlotte Sterling, who remained in London, to undertake the journey. When Captain Sterling brought the Carlyles back home to Cheyne Row in his carriage on Monday, February 19, they knocked on their front door, which was locked, and rang and rang the bell. Where on earth was Helen Mitchell?

They were about to try breaking a window to get in when at last the door creaked open and "an apparition" appeared. "*There* stood Helen," said Jane, "—her mouth covered with blood, her brow, cheek and dark dress whitened with the chalk of the kitchen floor, like a very ill got up stage-ghost, her hair streaming wildly from under a crushed cap—and her face wearing a smile of idiotic self-complacency!"

Helen was drunk and chaos was come again. The fires in the house had been allowed to burn out and all was cold, dark, and dirty inside. They quickly summoned a neighborhood woman in to help, and Thomas dragged the highly inebriated Helen down the stairs where they locked her in her room, the back kitchen. But she later somehow managed to break the bolt and chain, and escape out the front door with "a bonnet and shawl on the top of her nightclothes" to purchase more liquor, consuming (said Jane) another half pint of gin, half a pint of rum, and a quart of ale.

Jane now decided that the odd facial contortions and half-witted looks she had been observing in the months since Helen's return must have meant the maid had been drinking secretly all along. There were even reports that while they were in Surrey she had held drinking parties in their house. No real understanding existed then of alcoholism as an addiction. At fault, most believed, was a lack of will power and self-control, or a naughty recalcitrance. Drinking was proof of a weak or bad character. In Jane's words, "all morality is broken down in her."

The Carlyles had given Helen a number of second chances. This time, despite her tears and beseeching pleas, Jane found herself at the end of her tether and dismissed the maid for good. She offered to pay to send her back to her sister's in Kirkcaldy, but Helen adamantly refused to return to Scotland. So Jane gave her two sovereigns and took her in a carriage to a reliable woman who knew Helen and would put her up in her home and supervise her. Before leaving, Helen stole an additional sovereign from Jane's purse. Thomas commented to his mother, "[M]ay it be usefuller to her than seems likely."

In the months to come, occasional reports surfaced that the maid had secured other positions. Jane once referred to her as "the nasty little beast . . . I never mean to set eyes on her again if I can help it." When asked for references, though, she detailed Helen's virtues—but if queried about her sobriety, did not lie. The following year a woman came to Cheyne Row, allegedly on Helen's behalf, and requested money for her. Her brothers (both in Dublin) were sending a little but not enough. The woman claimed that Helen had thrown herself into the Thames in a drowning attempt (for which she was said to have been put in jail for three months!), and also that she had spoken of wanting to take an overdose of opium. Believing in Helen's threats of suicide, Jane nevertheless responded, "Let her go into the workhouse and conduct herself decently there and then I would see what I could do for her." Every time she heard something of Helen, Jane said, "it vexes me for days . . . leaving her to her Destiny is against my feelings."

But she did, finally, leave Helen Mitchell to her Destiny. According to Thomas, Helen "at last was sent home to her kindred in Kirkcaldy to die. 'Poor bit dottle,' what a history and tragedy in small!"[8]

Geraldine reported that Jane spoke of Helen in later years with affection and regret.[9] Helen had taken very tender care of her mistress when she was ill with headaches, but Jane had hardened her heart to what she now considered a hopeless case. Amely sent a new candidate around to Cheyne Row to be interviewed, a nice-looking twenty-four-year-old from Devonshire, Elizabeth Sprague, who seemed promising, and Jane quickly hired her. But she would never again have a maid who could equal Helen's rare combination of qualities (when sober): her ability to do very hard work well; what Thomas had called "an intellectual insight almost as of genius"; and her capacity for affection.

•

JANE CARLYLE AND Lady Ashburton continued to juggle their difficult relationship at various gatherings, experiencing better times and worse, but there was a dimension beyond their own uncomfortable triangle.

Jane suffered in society, sometimes acutely, because of her husband's friendship. How intensely she could suffer came into sharpest relief at a dinner party given by Charles and Catherine Dickens on May 12, 1849.

The party took place on a grand scale at their Devonshire Terrace home near Marylebone Church and Regent's Park, just when the author's novel *David Copperfield* began appearing in monthly installments. Inside the eighteenth-century house, all was modern and splendid, decorated in the latest Victorian fashion with mahogany and rosewood furniture, oriental carpets, heavy crimson curtains, gilt-framed mirrors, and, reflected magnificently in the mirrors, numerous sparkling candelabra. In the ground floor dining room, five extra leaves for the mahogany table could be added to accommodate an overflow of guests. Although Charles Dickens had only leased the house, he had installed extensive indoor gas lighting—relatively new then in private dwellings—in hallway, staircase, and kitchen.[10]

Among the guests at the party was the novelist Elizabeth Gaskell. Jane had met and liked her, hoping that the celebrity following the publication of her *Mary Barton* (1848), which she and Thomas admired, would not spoil her. Also present were William Makepeace Thackeray, Lady Lovelace (the mathematician Ada Byron), Douglas Jerrold, John Forster, and the wealthy old poet and banker Samuel Rogers, long famous for the breakfasts he hosted for notables in literary and intellectual circles. Others joined the festivities later in the evening—all in all, an illustrious event. Thomas was reported to have worn for the occasion an unusually good-quality waistcoat.

In a letter to her cousin, Jane had fun comparing this dinner to a recent one hosted by the Ashburtons, who had displayed only "*four cowslips* in china-pots—four silver shells containing sweets, and a silver filigree temple in the middle!" Whereas the middle class Dickenses provided artificial flowers galore, and "such an overloaded des[s]ert!—pyramids of figs raisins oranges—ach! . . . . [T]he very candles rose each out of an artificial rose! Good God!" Quoting an old Annandale woman, Jane wondered if such "Ornament and Grander" was not "unbecoming to a literary man who *ought* to have his basis elsewhere."[11]

That letter provides a good example of the social-cultural record Jane Carlyle was leaving in her correspondence. She casually noted a change of custom at the Dickens' home: "The dinner was served up in the new fashion—not placed on the table at all—but handed round—

only the des[s]ert on the table." It was a new European fashion of dining called *à la russe*. Instead of most of the dishes being placed on the table as was the custom formerly (*à la française*), each course had been separately served, with only flowers and desserts on the table top, a style that became the norm for well to do families later in the century. Jane's letters contain in passing much information of this sort. Although well aware that great interest accrued to anyone or anything associated with "men of genius," she could not have foreseen how historically useful her letters would become. In the index of Janet Flanders' *Inside the Victorian Home*—to give one instance—Jane Carlyle is cited for references to bedbugs, coal consumption, daily routine, diet, dressmaking, fancy work, illness, meal times, and servants.[12]

Before dinner began at the Dickens' home that May evening, Samuel Rogers accosted Mrs. Carlyle, who quickly found herself trapped in a tête-à-tête with the sour, curmudgeonly eighty-six-year-old. She prefaces her account of their distressing conversation by saying that Rogers "ought to have been buried long ago, so old and illnatured is he grown."

In her drama in one scene, her dialogue reads like lines from a play:[13]

SR: (pointing to a chair beside him): Sit down, my dear—I want to ask you; is your husband as much infatuated as ever with Lady Ashburton?

JWC: Oh of course (*laughing*). Why shouldn't he?

SR: Now—do *you* like her—tell me honestly is she kind to *you*—as kind as she is to your husband?

JWC: Why you know it is impossible for *me* to know *how* kind she is to my husband—but I *can* say she is extremely kind to *me* and I should be stupid and ungrateful if I did *not* like her.

SR: Humph! (disappointedly) Well! It is very good of you to like her when she takes away all your husband's company from you—he is always there isn't he?

JWC: Oh good gracious no! (still laughing *admirably*) He writes and reads a great deal in his own study.

SR: But he spends all his evenings with her I am told?

JWC: No—not all—for example you see he is *here* this evening.

SR: Yes (in a tone of vexation) I *see* he is here *this* evening—and *hear* him too—for he has done nothing but talk across the room since he came in.

In her letter, Jane continues: "Very devilish old man! but he got no satisfaction to his devilishness out of *me*—." She then quotes the saying, "On Earth the living / Have much to bear."

In the 1830s Thomas Carlyle had met Samuel Rogers who, despite his prestige in society, struck him on first impression, even back then, as elderly and unpleasant. He described him in his journal as a "man with perfectly hairless head, with large clear, sagacious, sad, and cruel, blue eyes. . . . The head towers out hoary (from amid the black clothes) perfectly colorless except white; high; very queer-looking." Pondering the *why* of that rebarbative sight, he added, "Poor old man, thou hast perhaps none to love thee!"[14]

What Jane heard directly from the lips of the bitter old man at the Dickens' party was simply the gossip (however exaggerated) rampant in the Carlyles' circles and beyond. *She takes away all your husband's company from you—he's always there isn't he?* But she faced the humiliating conversation bravely. Overall this letter to her cousin was newsy and entertaining. As she acknowledged, "To *write* Lamentations has always you know been contrary to my ideas."

Jane held up her head and went on with the party. Having by now ample experience honing her social skills, she handled herself adroitly, painful though the encounter had been. Afterward, Mrs. Gaskell reported that she had sat next to Mrs. Carlyle after they had retired upstairs to the drawing room. Jane told her a story about an Annandale maid she had back in the 1830s, Anne Cook, who routinely bungled beyond recognition the names of men with titles: Lord Jeffrey, for instance, was an incomprehensible *Lorcherfield*. Mrs. Gaskell—noting in surprise that the maid had been "their only servant"—found Mrs. Carlyle to be a very amusing woman.[15]

By now Jane had lost any vestigial sense she might have had for the romance of marriage. While accepting marriage as a given and continuing to derive part of her identity, as well as many benefits, from being part of a couple—and retaining a variety of complex feelings for her husband—she had become even more cynical about the institution. What may have helped: she had discovered she was not alone.

When George Henry Lewes and his wife Agnes visited Cheyne Row this April, Jane observed them astutely (though she probably did not yet know of any infidelity—it was a year before Agnes gave birth to a child fathered by Thornton Hunt). When George, in the Cheyne

Row parlor, marveled aloud at the thought of young Julia Paulet's "dark luxurious eyes" and "smooth firm flesh," Agnes was sarcastic: "how did he know? had he been feeling it?" Jane who had once considered the Leweses "a perfect pair of love-birds always cuddling together on the same perch," now commented acerbically: "In the most honey-marriages, one has only to *wait*."

•

IN EARLY JULY Thomas departed on a journey to Ireland. Soon after he left, though busy thinking up plans for some trip of her own, Jane went in fun and secrecy to consult a phrenologist. Captain Anthony Sterling, in on the scheme, escorted her there and paid the guinea and a half that the visit cost. Desiring to know *who am I?* she was tempted to see if such a question could be answered by having her head examined, Victorian fashion. Phrenology and the practitioner she visited, Cornelius Donovan, were at the moment all the rage in London. Skeptical however, Jane made certain that the man did not discover her name, nor did she converse with him, so as to avoid unwittingly providing him with clues.

After examining her head and reading her character, he wrote up his summation. Of that report, she told a friend, "I find it as like *any* daughter of Eve as *me*—so my faith in phrenology has not risen." Certain items applied to her not at all. For instance, the man proclaimed her to be free of obstinacy. That occasioned one of Jane's exclamation points, as did another: he indicated that she had a good memory for historical periods—"I who can never remember so much as what year we are in!" Yet she was intrigued, and later sent the generic report to her husband for his amusement—and he *was* amused.

With the idea of *reading characters* so much in the air, she and Amely Bölte had played a game of comparing theirs, "to find out," as the governess put it, "how two such extremes" had managed to meet. *Two such extremes* is a good phrase for friends who were in key ways opposites.

Phrenologist Donovan in his report had pronounced Jane's head to be "truly effeminate," adding gratuitously that it was a pity when a woman did not look feminine: "the heads of women sometimes have a masculine type and this never works well."[16] Jane, though, had once called Amely "a fine *manly* little creature," a description the governess would probably have liked. Amely later claimed to be highly offended and angry upon hearing that Thomas had said she was looking more feminine than previously, and more like a lady.[17] Indications are that she enjoyed her manly persona.

Jane was a Scotswoman well educated for her time, Amely a European intellectual. Jane was a housewife with a private writing career. Amely was a governess and companion; also, by now, a translator and professional writer. Currently she was employed as governess or companion in the household of Sir Isaac Goldsmid, a Jewish financier who actively worked to advance Jewish civil liberties in England. And she had published a work of fiction called *Louisa; or, the German Maiden in England*, drawing on her job experience and daring to criticize certain upper-class English customs, such as preventing aristocratic young men from pursuing "frivolous" careers in music, and the failure to properly educate girls.

The women influenced and broadened each other's lives. Amely offered the latest radical ideas as well as stories about working for the wealthy. Jane had not only helped Amely find employment, she introduced her into circles to which she would otherwise have had no access. Amely, who liked taking care of people, helped ease Jane's life in small ways; and Jane invited her into the one parlor in London where she could be certain of finding stimulating conversation and a chance for heart–to–heart talks.

In May Amely boasted to Varnhagen (her letters to him contain something of a novelette about Carlyles) that she understood Mrs. Carlyle so thoroughly "I could present her to you in every fiber of her being." Jane, too, extols their mutual understanding in a note to Amely: "I think YOU *understand* me better than any *male lover* ever did—hang them all!" After the women had finished comparing their characters, Amely declared with confidence that the *two such extremes* had "agreed that each had been understood by the other completely."[18]

But Jane very much disagreed with *completely* and expressed a desire to write to Varnhagen herself to set the record straight. She made the perceptive comment that women like Amely and Charlotte Wynn, another who kept Varnhagen up-to-date on the Carlyles' doings, were projecting part of their own personalities onto her. As Amely put it, Jane thought that she and Charlotte, in their epistolary accounts, viewed her "with our own eyes and more or less added something of our own selves."[19] (Something doubtless true of even the most objective of biographers.)

The eyes of these friends were quite frequently fixed upon Jane. It was a rare thing for the wife of a literary man, who herself played no public role, to have become such a sought after / written about personality in her own right.

Although Jane was clearly Amely's favorite, Thomas came a close second, maddening though she often found him to be. The governess now and then depicts their ongoing serious quarrels over the nature and status of women as rowdy good fun. When she told him this year that emancipated German women were demanding "equality before the law," he responded true to form, "God bless me! First the women and next the dogs."

Amely retorted immediately to that rudeness, and pictured how he had looked that day "in a dressing gown with a high nightcap, sitting erect in front of me with a serious mien like the Dalai Lama." She said they had argued their fill, "during which time I laughed a lot and he was quite jolly—good heavens, if only you had heard us!!!" Amely then veers off into the absurdity of the moment: "Then he felt like singing. Nothing but Scottish songs, enough to drive you crazy and I could not help laughing in his face. He did not mind, only I was supposed to admire them, and since I could not, I said I did not care for anything so melancholy, so sentimental. My character demanded something stronger, more passionate . . . finally he started to sing a [Scottish] war song, the most beautiful his people possessed, adding, 'if that will not do for you, I have nothing more to offer.'" She ends: "the entire scene was so ridiculous that the whole evening was tantamount to a comedy." Jane is portrayed as sitting on the sidelines, keeping carefully out of the fray, her only comment being that she wished Thackeray had been there so that the two arguers could have wound up "as a caricature in *Punch*" (the novelist was a regular contributor to that magazine).[20]

It goes without saying the plucky Miss Bölte held forth in a generally disparaging environment. She had gotten over her fearfulness of appearing unorthodox, which had more than once caused her to be fired. By now she had learned when and where it was safe to state her opinions. But although she felt free to speak her mind in urbane circles, she knew women had no real power—that was her point. Every time she turned around, it seemed, some man, even a confirmed socialist like

Louis Blanc, was saying something like, "You know, it is not necessary for a woman to think."[21]

Jane and Amely talked excitedly about making a trip together to Berlin in the summer of 1849 but it did not take place (and would have been difficult to manage since Jane spoke neither German nor French fluently). After Amely had followed her life plan to live and write independently in Germany, moving to Dresden in the summer of 1851, she and Jane began to lose touch. But during these London years, notwithstanding the significant annoyances they voiced to others, they shared times of true friendship and intimacy across the divide of country and class.

•

THOMAS CARLYLE, OFF stage in Ireland this summer, was, among varied experiences there, viewing scenes of utter human devastation. He made a curious comment that throws light on an aspect of Jane's role in his life: "Dearest; I wish to Heaven thou wert here to screen me from myself and from all the world."

What he saw face to face, at its rawest, was perhaps the worst sorrow and degradation he had witnessed in his life. The best one can say of him, to his credit, is that he could hardly bear it. He wrote up his Irish travels, including the most horrifying scenes of starvation and poverty—they cut to the quick still today—but buried the pages in a drawer. (*Reminiscences of My Irish Journey in 1849* appeared posthumously in 1882). The experience did not open his heart to compassion. Instead it blasted his lingering hopes for humanity and brought forth an outpouring of scorn.

It is important at this point to recall the profound source of inspiration Thomas Carlyle had been to his generation, especially through his books of the 1830s, *Sartor Resartus* and *The French Revolution*, which served as a bridge from the Romantic to the Victorian era. Elizabeth Barrett had best captured what he meant to his contemporaries in that poetic image (quoted earlier) that she had written of expansion and light: "[H]e has knocked out his window from the blind wall of his century" through which they could behold "the new sun."[22] His intense apperception of infinity and eternity carried him beyond any religious dogma—almost to a sense of existential spaciousness. He had created a thrilling opening for nineteenth-century spiritual seekers, an arch through which they could pass.

These last several years, however, angers, terrors, and savageries had been rumbling and building inside of him, which could produce the sulphurish atmosphere in their home that made life difficult for Jane. At the end of this year, the Carlylean lava began erupting into print. Thomas wrote his darkest, most hostile, obnoxious, and prejudiced essay, his "Occasional Discourse on the Negro Question" (1849), which, along with his *Latter-Day Pamphlets* (1850), was to ruin his reputation for many in the future, especially after World War II. It is not possible to account for his depths of outrage and scorn, nor is it appropriate to offer any excuse. Could Thomas Carlyle have had any sense or prevision that a bright ambitious child at a British school in the mid twentieth century in, say, a country like Guyana might come across his "Negro Question" and experience the deepest personal pain? His rhetoric carried the weight and heft of his celebrity, as long as it lasted.

Yet soon after, as if he had worked the bile off his soul by publishing those hateful pieces, Thomas wrote his most loving and readable book, about a dear friend, *The Life of John Sterling* (1851). Caught in this period on the horns of his inner dilemmas, between his warring demons and angels, he relieved himself through writing and flung the results into the world.

Much more might be said.[23] But this is her story, not his. And she was about to make "a dash at the wall."

II

As WITH THE journal that had contained anecdotes for a possible book on "all the people who come about our house," Jane Carlyle, on a trip north in July 1849, again experienced a happy convergence of conditions that led her to try something in a different genre, this time a memoir essay. Modestly, she titled it "Much ado about Nothing." It is one of her finest achievements. The essay seems to be what Jane half consciously / half in the dark had been working toward throughout the 1840s as she searched for her mission in life: a sustained and polished piece of writing that went beyond the epistolary.

To trace the steps that led up to it: from July 13 to 23 she was at Rawdon in Yorkshire visiting William Edward Forster, having made the decision, finally, to head north for her summer excursion. Large and rugged as a bear, though still a rather slender one, the Quaker woolen manufacturer who had guided the Carlyles through the Peak District in Derbyshire and later hurried to tell them about his adventures in revolutionary Paris was again hosting Mrs. Carlyle.

Every indication is that Jane was just as glad to be away from her husband for a time. Thomas had by now reached Limerick, and when her visit to Rawdon ended, William Edward was planning to join up with him in Ireland.

Her stay in the young man's clean well-run house was not as peaceful as previously. She would have liked more time to herself and also more time alone with him, but the chatty, vivacious, only-too-sociable Betsey Paulet had arrived with her husband Étienne. (They were all combining this visit with a stay at a nearby water-cure establishment.) William Edward was again cheerful and encouraging of Jane, making it clear he appreciated her for herself and valued her company. But pretty Betsey Paulet was now a rival for his affections. After their experiences together in Paris, he seemed ever more captivated by the older woman, whose husband, whether oblivious, indifferent, or submissive, did not appear to mind their flirtation. As for Jane, she seemed ever *less* captivated by Betsey who was becoming more and more enamored of Hinduism and Emersonian thought; in Paris the poet Arthur Hugh Clough had found her "almost too Hindooish."[24] These were matters Jane had little patience for, and their friendship would soon begin to dwindle away.

But encouragement for Jane came from other directions as well. On her way north, she had stopped to see a German Jewish businessman and his sister in Nottingham. A lover of literature, involved with the Mechanics' Institute and other educational projects for workingmen, Joseph Neuberg was a great admirer of Thomas Carlyle (later volunteering to work as his amanuensis and translator). He had formed an acquaintance with the Carlyles, and by now he and Jane regarded each other as friends. When she wrote from Rawdon to thank him and his sister Rosetta for their hospitality, she enclosed a note from Amely Bölte.

"I send you one of your Countrywoman's *love-letters* to me," Jane told him, "which please to burn—I want you to tell me if this be a common style of female friendship in your country—I like it immensely—for the curiosity of the thing!" (His response is not known, nor is the fate of Amely's letter.) By *style of female friendship* Jane was surely signaling her understanding that Amely was some kind of Sapphist (or lesbian)—while pretending to relegate friendships of that tendency to Germany. When talking years later with the Sapphist Charlotte Cushman about "'swearing eternal Friendship,' like any boarding-school girl!" Jane told the actress she had felt "no misgivings about that somewhat german-looking transaction!" but "rather compliment myself on having so much *Life* left in me after all!"

Her inclusion of Amely's letter would not have seemed indiscreet; the passing along of the letters of others to aid communication was not unusual. Furthermore, passionate friendships between women were seldom looked at askance, even when sophisticated people—even in England—might intuit that erotic love was a motivating factor. It had long been evident that Jane valued Amely's love and attention, perhaps especially in letter form, and was proud to have others know she was regarded so glowingly. In notes Jane playfully bantered with Amely. After the governess had helped her this spring with a "little concern of a daily soreness" (something personal and private not further explained), Jane wrote: "Thanks for all your 'delicate attentions'—I rather wish you HAD been 'a man'; for if anything could rouse a spirit in one it would surely be the getting oneself '*eloped with*.'"

One day at Rawdon, Jane received a batch of eight letters, some forwarded from Chelsea, including one from a bookseller requesting that Mrs. Carlyle write for a forthcoming collection he hoped to publish. Believing her to be "favourable to emigration," he asked if she would—as she put it—"'contribute some pieces of poetry for that end!' *me*!" It was "a scheme to humanize the emigrant mind!" A laughably far-fetched request ("*me* entertain *opinions*!" she joked), it was nevertheless an invitation to pen a piece for a public audience. And would have been a reminder that, via rumor, she now had something of a literary reputation.

London gossip, based on observation or hearsay about her letters and conversation, often had it that Mrs. Carlyle was the author of this or that pseudonymous novel making the rounds. Such speculation in fact occurred later this year when Charlotte Brontë's *Shirley* was published under her pseudonym Currer Bell; and Jane said then, "I get the credit with certain CRITICS IN STYLE of writing these Jane Eyre books myself."

Her letters of this period indicate ongoing concerns about finding useful work, women's rights, and the continuing European uprisings.

On this visit to Rawdon, she went to nearby Bradford to participate in a protest against the French invasion of the Roman Republic, which had happened a few weeks before. Betsey Paulet, as another strong supporter of Italy, accompanied her. So, too, did a representative of Giuseppe Mazzini, a recent refugee from Perugia, the Italian patriot Ubaldo Marioni, who was there to address the crowd. On July 19, Jane informed her husband that she had just been standing on a public platform as part of a meeting for "Liberty—Roman." She then added for Thomas's sake the ironic skewer: "thank your stars it was not for 'the *rights of women*—.'"

On that subject, Jane remained divided. At some point (likely November 1847) she had received a ringing endorsement of woman's potential from Geraldine Jewsbury. Though the two women continued to quarrel and make up, and blew hot and cold, they were, overall, each other's best friend for life. While Jane's specific reaction is not known, Geraldine's letter is a brilliant example of the stimulating talk that she had been hearing close up during the latter half of the 1840s.[25]

The petite energetic strawberry-blond novelist writes the letter in her characteristic helter-skelter headlong manner, talking also of homeopathy, the Corn Laws, and redecorating her bedroom. But without warning, her rhetoric takes off and soars. "I believe we are touching on better days," she tells Jane, "when women will have a genuine, normal life of their own to lead." Marriage will no longer be obligatory; single women will no longer "feel their destiny *manque*"; and women "will be able to be friends and companions in a way they cannot be now." They will be able to have friendships with men "without being reduced by their position to see them [only] as lovers or husbands." She continues, "Instead of having appearances to attend to, they will be allowed to have their virtues, in any measure which it may please God to send . . . in short, they will make themselves women, as men are allowed to make themselves men."

That reads like a direct continuation of the late eighteenth-century *Vindication of the Rights of Woman* by Mary Wollstonecraft: "I shall first consider women in the grand light of human creatures, who, in common with men, are placed on this earth to unfold their faculties."[26] Whether or not Geraldine and Jane had read her book, they were acquainted with Mary Wollstonecraft's life and work through her husband William Godwin's memoirs.

Imagining this heaven-on-earth to be only a couple of generations away, Geraldine believes that in light of the hopeful trend, neither she nor Jane "are to be called failures. We are indications of a development of womanhood which as yet is not recognized." She goes on: "we have looked, and tried, and found that the present rules for women will not hold us . . . something better and stronger is needed." Since women of the future will be far more fulfilled, she regards herself "as a mere faint indication" of what is to come. Rejecting the constrained Mrs. Ellis-woman of Victorian conduct books, Geraldine foresees "a precious mine of a species of womanhood yet undreamed of." And explicitly encourages her friend: "the power and possibility is with you."

Moved by such sentiments, and fascinated, Jane was still not convinced. This year, 1849, according to Amely, she wanted "to read everything on the 'rights and position of woman.'" At the same time, the governess reported that Jane had found Margaret Fuller's *Woman in the Nineteenth Century* "disgusting" (not further explained, possibly she thought it too pedantic), and said they were both glad they had not written it![27] Jane was soon to tell the feminist-minded Martha MacDonald Lamont that she hoped a new book she had edited, *The Fortunes of Woman: Memoirs* (1849), did *not* detail "The rights of Women." "I am so weary of hearing about these *rights* of ours—and always to the tune of 'don't you wish you may get them'?" Women were of course not going to get them anytime soon. To refer again to one of the great inequities in Victorian England: upon marriage, husbands almost always became the owners of the property and earnings of their wives.

It is important to note that for all her ambivalence about women's rights in general, and with no known disagreements with her husband over the Craigenputtoch property she had inherited, Jane Carlyle in the 1850s would sign a petition for a women's property rights law. Early British feminists like Barbara Leigh Smith and Bessie Rayner Parkes spearheaded that particular effort to pass such legislation. The need for such a law had intensified as more careers for women began opening, with new opportunities for them to earn their own money, something that could affect women of all classes. In this petition, an analogy was drawn from the struggle against slavery on the other side of the Atlantic: if such a law were passed, women when they married would "no longer pass from freedom into the condition of a slave, all whose earnings belong to his master and not to himself."

The petition was circulated among "those most likely to take an interest in its success." Mrs. Carlyle put her name on the line along with Geraldine Jewsbury, Harriet Martineau, Anna Brownell Jameson, Elizabeth Barrett Browning, Charlotte Cushman, Mrs. Gaskell, and other women she knew. Signing the petition was a rare public act for Jane Carlyle—as standing on a platform for Italian liberty had been.

Close to three thousand "Women of Great Britain, Married and Single" signed that petition for property rights for married women; and on March 14, 1856, it was presented to the House of Peers by Lord Brougham and the House of Commons by Sir Erskine Perry.[28] A Married Women's Property Act did not pass, however, until 1870.

Ambivalent though Jane continued to be, the new ideas concerning marriage, rights, and liberties had come alive in her circles by 1849. And her need for a mission was still on her mind. With a note of longing, she now wrote to Martha Lamont (in reference to her new book): "Your '*life*' looks useful and satisfactory—I wish I could say the same of mine—which has been for long standing still, and looking out into the Vague."

As she had done before—it was a motif during this decade—Jane playfully daydreamed aloud about being a revolutionary. In reference to her recent appearance on behalf of the beleaguered Roman Republic, she told Miss Lamont, "I have had ideas about breakout into *insurrection*, for the sake of the excitement of the thing, and joining Garibaldi and Mazzini, or latterly the more successful Hungarians!—but have carried them no further into practice than by showing myself on the platform at a meeting for 'Roman Liberty.'"

(The *more successful Hungarians* had also established a republic, soon to meet the fate of so many rebellions of this period. In August this year, they would be defeated by the Austrians and the Russians.)

•

WHEN JANE WAS due to travel on from Rawdon to Scotland, William Edward, acting the part of a gallant tutelary spirit, accompanied her to see her off. He handled Mrs. Carlyle's arrangements at an inn at Morpeth where she spent the night before her departure, making certain the carpetbag, writing box, and pair of boxes that served as her luggage would be sent along with her. Jane's destination was Auchtertool, Fife, where she was to meet up with her Liverpool uncle and cousins.

They were staying with her uncle's son Walter Welsh, who served as minister there.

Finding herself suddenly alone in a train carriage—a rare circumstance—Jane, who had been going back and forth for days on whether to return to her hometown, made a firm decision. She *would* detour to Haddington, a side trip she termed a pilgrimage, and travel there incognito. Reluctant to go home after her mother had left Haddington for the house of her childhood, Templand near Thornhill, and even more fearful of returning after Grace Welsh died—the memories would be too painful—she had stayed away some sixteen years.

When Jane had begun her 1845 journal experiment, she had identified in letters of that time with women on the margin: a witch, a gossip, and a seduced lady. For the writing of her 1849 memoir essay, she adds a gypsy to the list. Moving in her imagination to the margins of society seemed always to free her from the inhibiting conventions of *a lady*.

Referring to the family mythology, Jane aligns herself early on in the memoir essay with her unconventional side: "I informed William Edward that my maternal Grandmother was 'descended from *a Gang* of Gipsies' . . . a genealogical fact Forster said which made *me* at last intelligible for him,—'a cross betwixt John Knox and a Gipsey how that explained all'"; John Knox representing, of course, the sterner Scottish protestant traditions. In particular she claimed a connection to a notorious pair, a gypsy king Matthew Baillie (her grandmother's great uncle) and his wife, a gypsy queen.[29] Jane appreciated William Edward's acknowledgment of her legendary dual heritage.

A private writer or artist who finds work intended for the public extremely difficult to make or to sell, because of personality as well as societal constraints, may be able to surmount such inhibitions when favorable conditions conspire to create the delicate arrangements of mind required for acts of creative assertion. Jane Carlyle, who *was* such a person, found herself in propitious circumstances. She had William Edward's warm personal encouragement, coupled with Joseph Neuberg's admiration and that recent love letter from Amely Bölte. She had received a request to produce a piece for a book. Moreover, in the spring, her creativity aroused, she had created a folding screen collage (still on display at the Carlyles' house in London) made up of "heaps of old Prints and Pictures," which her husband, with some justification, had termed "a work of art." And swirling about her was a Europe in rebellion, with invigorating talk of individual rights, including the rights of women. Affected by it all, Jane restated her wish for a useful life, gained a spurt of independence, and distanced herself from her traditional side. For the moment, she was more gypsy than John Knox.

Her memoir essay, motivated first and foremost by the importance of her visit home, was not the only account that Jane wrote of this brief trip. Before penning it, she had two trial runs. On July 26 from Haddington's George Inn, she confessed to her husband, "I wrote you a long—very long letter last night, at midnight, from this same place—But this morning instead of posting it in the postoffice I have torn it up. You may fancy what sort of a letter, 'all about feelings' (as Lady A would say) an excitable character like me would write in such circumstance."

Her natural inclination had been to tell the story of her Haddington visit in a personal letter. In her rewritten letter, she told Thomas "you can also understand how after some hours of sleep, I should have reacted against my last nights self, and thought all that *steam* best gathered back into the Vale of *Silence*." That was a phrase of his—he indeed preached the virtue of the Vale of Silence (versus practicing it, as friends so often complained). Yet he lamented the letter's destruction: "[T]he reading of it could have done me nothing but good."

His known opinions on writing about feelings, however, had influenced his wife, as when he had written of Rahel Levin Varnhagen's letters that it was wasteful "to *feel about Feeling*! One is wearied of that."[30] Only the year before Jane had told him, humorously, that she would forgo a long emotional complaint since "descriptions of feelings are only surpassed in wearisomeness by descriptions of scenery."

On July 28 Jane also sent a brief, touching account of her Haddington visit to her brother-in-law. At the moment they were on warm terms. He (whose successfully completed prose translation of Dante's *Inferno* was now out in the world) had recently helped Jane through a spell of headaches. She addressed him as "dearest John," and he promptly shared her letter with the Carlyle family in Scotsbrig where he was staying. They heard how Jane had found so much changed; how so many names of people she had personally known had been inscribed on tombstones in the churchyard. The letter made their mother Margaret Aitken Carlyle cry. She pronounced it "the *wae'est* [most sorrowful] thing she had ever heard." A high Victorian compliment to her daughter-in-law.

We should take Jane at her word that her first outpouring to her husband was more personal and subjective than the final version. These drafts (she also sent Joseph Neuberg a short note, and might possibly have copied the piece over later) allowed her in the end to write a more shaped essay, with the extra degree of perspective and objectivity that render it more accessible to a larger audience. For, although the essay was not published in her lifetime, that is how it reads. Fortunately, it was *not* left to the Vale of Silence.

•

"MUCH ADO ABOUT Nothing" is emblematic of all such journeys back to the place of one's childhood, which, while remaining recognizable, illustrate as nothing else can the passage of time: the jolting shock of the familiar having become alien, and oneself a ghost.[31]

The page she began writing on is decorated with a pair of concentric circles, perhaps symbolic to her of the overlapping of past and present. The essay's richness comes from its use of what is now called liminality. She hits on a fertile, imaginative, in-between zone for her story. It operates between the quick and the dead, the past and the present, dream and reality—what Geraldine had termed *the debatable land* of the griffin and the phoenix, "something from between the regions of truth and fiction."[32] As Jane looks out the window of the room she has just taken at the George Inn toward the house of her childhood, whose entrance is down at the end of the street through a pend (an arched, covered entrance), she writes that "it was the same street, the same house; but so silent,—dead, *petrified*! it looked, the old place, just as I had seen it at Chelsea in my dreams—only *more* dreamlike!" Her prose throughout has a rhythmic Scots storytelling lilt.

When she visits the old church, St. Mary's Abbey, where her father lay buried (her mother had been buried in Crawford, South Lanarkshire, near her birthplace), Jane gazes at her family's pew. "I looked at it in the dim twilight till I almost fancied I saw my beautiful Mother in her old corner, and myself a bright-looking girl in the other!"

Yet the potent hallucinatory image is enough to return the pragmatic Jane to reality: "it was time to 'come out of *that*.'" And she acknowledges that what she experiences as the stunning, deathly quiet of the town is partly due to the coming of the railway, which had drawn business away from Haddington's center.

Meeting various people from her past was like experiencing mirrored facets of a hanging globe, with reflections of herself turning this way and that. The responses she at first elicited caused a puzzled confusion of identity. On the train to Haddington, for instance, an old lady in widow's garb, whom Jane comes to recognize, stares at her as if she were a foreigner, speaking to her with the distinct over-pronunciation reserved for those who hardly know English. Was it even necessary to travel incognito? She later wonders if she might not have gotten away with riding through town in the style of Lady Godiva. For luggage tags, the thrifty Jane had used the backs of calling cards of her acquaintances. This leads a porter to mistakenly identify her as Mrs. Humphrey St. John Mildmay. "*No*!" she has to respond; "*I am quite another* person!"

Walking out of the George Inn, wearing a heavy black veil, she purposely takes on the role of a traveling English woman, a "stranger-in-search-of-the-Picturesque," and at a cooper's shop purchases two little cups as souvenirs. In answer to her queries about the people of the town, the cooper tells her about the sad loss of her father, Dr. John Welsh, and then the story of herself. He used to think Miss Welsh "the *tastiest* young Lady in the whole Place," though rather proud and reserved. But the cooper then informs an astonished Jane that she had gone "away into England and—died there!" More than ever, she has become her own ghost.

She later confesses who she is, and the cooper asks how many children she has. When she answers that she has none, he wonders in the blunt privileged manner of a fellow townsperson what on earth she has been doing with herself all this time, then.

The next day when Jane returns at an early hour to the churchyard, she finds the gate locked. "[S]o," she writes, "I made a dash at the wall, some seven feet high I should think, and dropt safe on the inside—a feat I should never have imagined to *try* in my actual phase, not even with a mad bull at my heels, if I had not trained myself to it at a more elastic age." She speaks proudly of her successful climb over the almost impossibly high wall, which is witnessed and later commented on by a man she had been acquainted with: "Are *you* the Lady that climbed the Church yard wall this morning? If it was *you* that did *that*—then you must be Jeanie Welsh—I thought to myself at the time it could enter no womans head but Jeanie Welsh's to get over the Wall instead of going in at the gate."

When Jane came to write "Much ado about Nothing" (thirteen pages long in the *Collected Letters*), she may have sat down at the desk in Auchtertool and, metaphorically speaking, jumped over the wall to begin. At the age of fourteen she was said to have written a five-act tragedy "as just an explosion."[33] If, finally, she had just plunged in, it would have enabled her to leap over inhibitions.

In the churchyard, Jane makes a gesture of homage. She cleans the moss off her father's gravestone inscription with "*his own* button hook with the mother-of-pearl handle." She had brought it with her for the purpose. Gazing around at the other stones, she recognizes the familiar names of so many townspeople she had known. They lay all about her.

Ceremoniously she visits one by one the meaningful sights: the street, the pend, her house, the church ruin, the bowling green, Nungate Bridge over the River Tyne, her schoolhouse (now an infants' school)—even going inside to sit a moment in her old school chair. Memory, change, the mystery of time: all wash over. Following in the footsteps of "the customary evening walk in my teens," she finds the path for the most part solitary now, yet it looks the same: "the very puddles made by the last rain I *felt* to have stepped over before."

As the essay progresses, Jane becomes more familiar to herself. The high point is a spontaneous, emotional visit to Sunny Bank, the home of family friends, the Donaldson sisters. Her godmother, Miss Jean, is upstairs in bed and ailing. But having been let inside the house by a servant, Jane approaches Miss Catherine and Miss Jess who have visibly aged, as she has also. Her heart is thumping. There's a pause and a stare before Miss Catherine cries out, "Jeanie! Jeanie! Jeanie Welsh! *my* Jeanie! *my* Jeanie!" And says they had just been talking of her. Tears all around.

Throughout her visit, she has been learning an important life lesson: "Strange that the Universe should pursue its own course without reference to my presence in Haddington!!" Their little world has been going on without her. Yet for the moment, at least, a deep need has been met. This is *home* in the way she has been searching for it. She feels similarly later on when greeting her father's old manservant, Jamie Robertson. When he heard that a lady had summoned him to call on her at the George Inn, he claimed to have known all along it was Mrs. Carlyle: "Hoots! *Who else could it be*?"

The essay moves from a statement of her customary position of dependence to a greater sense of independence. At the beginning of "Much ado" she acknowledges that because she is so unused to traveling by herself, she is grateful to William Edward for seeing to it she has a good fire and some "brandy-negus" at the Morpeth inn, which, she states, "I should not have had the audacity to order on my own basis." But at the George Inn in Haddington, she orders and makes her own negus (a hot drink of wine, water, sugar, and spices). By the end of the essay she says of her current inn bill, "I have that bill of 6/6 in my writing case; and shall keep it all my days . . . [partly] as the first Inn bill I ever in my life contracted and paid *on my own basis*" (repeating the words for emphasis).

When she reaches Edinburgh, Jane is met at the train by her cousin Jeannie Welsh and concludes, "I bid myself adieu and 'wave my lilly hand'—I was back into the Present! and it is only in connection with the Past that I can get up a sentiment for myself—The Present M*rs* Carlyle is what shall I say?" She answers with a startling phrase of Giuseppe Mazzini's: "*detestable*—upon *my* honour!" For all her involvement in their London social circles, she has known some loneliness and isolation in the city; whereas, growing up in Haddington, she had felt rooted, secure, recognized, and appreciated.

In a letter a few months later to the man (a Mr. Lea) who had witnessed her climbing the wall, Jane says that her visits home had been "altogether good" for her—she had made a second trip that summer while Thomas was traveling in the Highlands with the Ashburtons. And she emphasizes, above all, the special *affection* she had experienced there from people who had known her parents.[34]

In writing this essay, Jane had completed a circle, getting back in touch with her early self, little Miss Welsh, the girl her nurse Betty Braid had described as "a fleein', dancin', lightheartit thing that naething would hae dauntit."[35] Reconnecting allowed Jane to incorporate into the present something of that lighthearted, undaunted self.

Did anyone during her lifetime read her memoir essay? Although Thomas, years later, wrote a note indicating that he had never heard of "Much ado" before discovering it in a drawer,[36] he sent a letter July 29 to Jane at Auctertool implying he knew something of her writing plans: "you have your MS. with you to copy, if you like; a precious thing indeed!" William Edward had by that time reached Ireland, and if Jane had written to *him* mentioning the piece, he might have said something about it to Thomas. But her husband apparently did not see the essay itself.

Jane wrote Joseph Neuberg September 2 that she was going to send him "some notes of my first visit to Haddington made for *my own* edification." She claimed—having forgotten the importance of *I-ity*, or, much more likely, feeling self-conscious about it—that such work amounted to "outpourings of human egoism" and could only be sent to a trusted, sympathetic friend. Jane asked him to send the pages right back. Her phrase *outpourings of egoism* and her title "Much ado about Nothing" have of course their ironic, deflecting side. They disguise how meaningful writing the essay was to her.

Yet she who had put so many efforts into the fire carefully saved this one, and her husband and his descendants saved it too. Long in print now, it stands as a tribute to the writerly aspirations and achievements of Jane Welsh Carlyle.

EPILOGUE: A LAST WORD

IN THE NEXT SEVERAL YEARS, JANE WELSH CARLYLE WENT FORWARD WITH a new level of confidence. She attempted further writing experiments, each exhibiting talent and skill, though she showed what she wrote to very few friends. In 1852 she composed a delightful short work of fiction, "*The simple Story* of my own first Love"; and in February, 1855, a brilliant mock parliamentary report requesting funds from her husband, "BUDGET of *a Femme Incomprise*" (or unappreciated woman). She also kept a personal diary from October 1855–July 1856.

Jane did not, however, come close to turning herself into a professional author like several of her chosen friends. Geraldine Jewsbury, throughout her life, supported herself by writing works of fiction, reviews, articles, and publishers' reports. Elizabeth Paulet wrote a novel, published in 1865 by Smith, Elder: *Dharma; or, Three Phases of Love*. Amely Bölte, after she returned to her home country, earned enough from her literary work to enable her to aid those facing hardships similar to what she had suffered: she bequeathed her estate to the City of Wiesbaden "for the establishment of a foundation dedicated to improving the financial situation of the daughters of civil servants."[1]

But the point is to understand Jane Carlyle's aspirations in the context of her patriarchal times, not to consider her a novelist manqué. She devoted herself to a form of life writing, the epistolary, a literary form that we ought to value much more highly than we do. And she became one of the best letter writers in the English language—accomplishment enough.

No tidy story of steady progress can be told about Jane, nor can any neat summary be given of the rest of the Carlyles' very complicated lives. No satisfactory, definitive conclusion occurs to the Lady Ashburton story, either. While Thomas carried on his friendship with her, Jane's own connection with the lady endured, but always with an underlying suspicion. At certain moments, the two women achieved significant companionability and mutual regard. More often, particularly if Jane thought her husband was neglecting her for the aristocratic realm, she could become darkly angry, resentful, and bitter. The hurt, tension, and ambiguity that Jane experienced because of that romantic triangle would end only with the lady's death in 1857. After that Jane created—one is tempted to say *wrote*—a happier ending for herself: she made friends with Lord Ashburton's second wife Louisa and came to adore their little daughter Mary.

For the Carlyles, the 1850s and beyond would bring new experiences and new stories. Jane would make new friends, and Thomas launched his most weighty project, a multi-volumed historical biography of Frederick the Great.—But at this point let us leave Jane alive, as she will always remain in her letters.

Jane Carlyle had traveled a considerable distance between 1843 and 1849, some of the most fascinating years of her life. The accounts of her experiences during that time should eliminate once and for all any reductive summation of her as "a tragic spouse who lived a life of pain."

Two portraits from the beginning and end of this period mark the changes that Jane underwent. Although in each the features are recognizably hers, the portraits are so strikingly different that they hardly seem to be of the same woman.

An Italian artist in exile, Spiridione Gambardella, painted the first in 1843. He undertook the commission at the request of Jane's cousin Jeannie Welsh, who wished to have a copy for herself. In it Jane has a dark lace mantilla draped softly over her head and looks astonishingly girlish for an almost forty-two-year-old woman. Though Jane found a resemblance to her face in the mirror, she attempted to deny the portrait's fresh quality by claiming—in true Janecarlylean fashion—that the expression was that of "a rather *improper female* DOING a sort of St Anthony's ecstacy! and *doing* it not well." Yet the painter had seen something different: while he does give his subject a hint of mischief and sensuousness, overall his Jane appears demure, unworldly, and old-fashioned, an ideal subject for a charming Victorian cameo.

Amely Bölte, who had been creating more complicated pictures of Jane Carlyle in her letters, organized the second portrait in 1849. As she plotted her return to Germany, the governess wanted a pictorial remembrance of Jane, and arranged for her to sit for a German refugee artist and engraver, Carl Hartmann.

What he depicted records Jane's development. Though she could not have comprehended what her work would mean to future generations, as a writer she had attained a style that could speak across the centuries—a remarkable achievement, however unrewarded in her lifetime. As a woman she had grown less naïve and more worldly, having encountered in her urban circles a wide array of London's most intriguing people and issues; and having endured and survived a portion of life's tribulations. Accordingly, Carl Hartmann's portrait, in watercolors and crayon, shows an intelligent, aware, sophisticated woman. Astonishingly enough, the artist has turned her into one of her era's new women.

Jane voiced her own opinion about the 1849 portrait. She thought it a little sorrowful though not as "severe" as some, but she liked it very much, saying "an excellent little sketch he has made of me." Once Amely had moved back to her country, a copy of this portrait done in watercolors ended up on the wall above her writing desk in Dresden—where Thomas Carlyle was touched to see it on a trip he made there in 1852.[2]

For many readers, Jane Carlyle possesses an oddly modern quality. When the twentieth-century writer Diana Trilling—married to prestigious author Lionel Trilling and herself concerned about "old-fashioned frustrated female talent"—contemplated writing a book about Jane Carlyle, she aptly termed her "a strangely modern instance."[3]

In the Hartmann rendition, Jane's hairstyle has hardly changed yet now looks to be in the shape of an elegant chignon. She is seen in profile, turned a little toward us, wearing a long-sleeved jacket, her beringed hand under her chin, a slim finger just touching her cheek. She is a woman a twenty-first-century person could imagine sitting with at a sidewalk café, talking about marriage and spouses, culture and politics, as well as love, work, and friendship.

Very much a Victorian and of her era, always, Jane Welsh Carlyle during the 1840s was at the same time moving toward the future, "too much in advance of the Century" as she would later note ironically.[4] By the decade's end, Jane had already achieved that surprisingly modern aspect.

Like many still today, she was a woman in transition.

NOTE TO READERS

Quotations from the Carlyles' letters, if not otherwise identified, are from the Duke-Edinburgh edition of *The Collected Letters of Thomas and Jane Welsh Carlyle*, eds. Charles Richard Sanders, Clyde de L. Ryals, Kenneth J. Fielding, Ian Campbell, Aileen Christianson, David Sorensen, Brent Kinser, et al., 44 vols. (Durham, NC: Duke UP, 1970—). The volumes of the *Collected Letters* published so far cover the entire period of Jane Welsh Carlyle's life (later letters by Thomas Carlyle are to come). Readers who wish to explore further can find the source of quotations from the *Collected Letters* used in this book in the Carlyle Letters Online: carlyleletters.dukeupress.edu

Putting phrases from a quotation into the search box of the Carlyle Letters Online will bring up the complete letter the quotation is from, along with information such as date, name of correspondent, place of original publication (if any), the volume and page numbers of the print edition, and considerable documentation. Quotations can also be searched by date. When there might be confusion, I have provided in the endnotes the date of a quotation, the correspondent, and, if needed, the relevant footnote number from the original print edition (which can be accessed online).

Jane Welsh Carlyle's own spelling, punctuation, and capitalization have been kept, with a few exceptions. A clarification has sometimes been added in brackets; and on a few occasions, especially with longer passages that include dialogue, slight alterations have been made for readability. When that has been done, it is explained in an endnote. As is customary, italics are provided to indicate words and phrases that JWC underlined. Even when a quotation is cut short, end punctuation has been used rather than final ellipses points.

Readers might notice occasional unexplained quotations within quotations. Both Carlyles, and JWC especially, made use of coterie-speech, a style that weaves in sayings of family members, servants, friends, and acquaintances, as well as common folk expressions and literary allusions. This use of quotation allows us to hear a community of voices through the letters of Jane Welsh Carlyle.

Abbreviations in the endnotes: JWC, Jane Welsh Carlyle. TC, Thomas Carlyle. GEJ, Geraldine Endsor Jewsbury. GM, Giuseppe Mazzini. AB, Amely Bölte. WEF, William Edward Forster. *CL, Collected Letters*. And NLS, for the National Library of Scotland, which houses a vast treasure trove of materials by and related to the Carlyles.

NOTES

Introduction

1. Virginia Woolf, "Wordsworth Letters," *The Essays of Virginia Woolf*, ed. Andrew McNeillie, vol. 1 (New York: Harcourt Brace Jovanovich, 1986) 184.

2. George Eliot, "Thomas Carlyle (*Leader*, 27 October 1855)," *George Eliot: Selected Essays, Poems and Other Writings*, eds. A. S. Byatt and Nicholas Warren (London: Penguin, 1990) 344.

3. Kenneth Fielding and Ian Campbell, "New Letters of Harriet Martineau to Jane Carlyle, 1842-44," *Women's Writing* 9:3 (2002) 386.

4. Mrs. Alexander Ireland [Anne Elizabeth], *Life of Jane Welsh Carlyle* (London: Chatto & Windus, 1891) v.

5. Charlotte Perkins Gilman, "Is Feminism Really So Dreadful? Listen to Charlotte Perkins Gilman," *Delineator* 85 (August 1914) 6.

6. Elizabeth Hardwick, *Seduction & Betrayal: Women and Literature* (New York: Random House, 1974) 174.

7. The angel in the house: "Had I not killed her she would have killed me. She would have plucked the heart out of my writing." Virginia Woolf, "Professions for Women," *The Essays of Virginia Woolf*, ed. Stuart N. Clarke, vol. 6 (London: Hogarth Press, 2011) 481.

Chapter One

1. In the opening scene, words in quotation marks come from letters that JWC and TC wrote from 1 December 1843 to the end of the year, with slight alterations to ease the transition from the written word to speech. This chapter also relies on TC's long letter to JWC, 21 May 1834, describing, for the first time, their Chelsea house and neighborhood.

2. See JWC to Frances Wedgwood, 16 January 1843.

3. Harriet Martineau, *Autobiography* [1877], ed. Linda H. Peterson (Plymouth UK: Broadview 2007) 113.

4. Deirdre David, *Intellectual Women and Victorian Patriarchy: Harriet Martineau, Elizabeth Barrett Browning, George Eliot* (Ithaca NY: Cornell UP, 1987) 227.

5. Martineau, *Autobiography* 292-93.

6. Harriet Martineau, *The Collected Letters of Harriet Martineau*, vol. 2, ed. Deborah Anna Logan (London: Pickering & Chatto, 2007) 211.

7. Martineau, *Autobiography* 112.

8. Three sources are the basis for the scene concerning the destruction of TC's manuscript. (Words in quotations come from the Carlyle's letters or from Duffy's account.) The *Collected Letters*: TC to James Fraser, 7 March 1835, especially n. 1, which provides a summary of the incident including TC's 7 March 1835 journal entry, through TC to Ralph Waldo Emerson, 13 May 1835. Thomas Carlyle, *Reminiscences* [1881], eds. K. J. Fielding and Ian Campbell (Oxford: Oxford UP, 1997) 92-94. Charles Gavan Duffy, *Conversations with Carlyle* (New York: Scribner's, 1892) 169.

9. "Lily" was a nickname for Helen Taylor, who after her mother's death lived and worked with her stepfather John Stuart Mill, and dared to stand for Parliament before women got the vote.

10. "John Stuart Mill, from an unsigned review, *London and Westminster Review* (July 1837)," Jules Paul Seigel, ed., *Thomas Carlyle: The Critical Heritage* (New York: Barnes and Noble, 1971) 52.

11. Thomas Carlyle, *Reminiscences* 119.

12. "H. P." sent a temperature register for 23 December 1843 to the *Times*: "London Temperature (Letters to the Editor) H. P.," *Times* [London] 25 Dec. 1843, 3F.

13. "H. P.," *Times* 3F.

14. JWC to John Welsh, 23 December 1843, n. 3.

15. Virginia Woolf, "Geraldine and Jane," *The Essays of Virginia Woolf*, ed. Stuart N. Clarke, vol. 5 (London: Hogarth Press, 2011) 515.

16. Virginia Woolf, "The Art of Biography," *The Essays of Virginia Woolf*, ed. Stuart N. Clarke, vol. 6 (London: Hogarth Press, 2011) 187.

17. Charles Dickens, *The Letters of Charles Dickens*, eds. Madeline House, Graham Storey, and Kathleen Tillotson, vol. 3 (Oxford: Clarendon Press 1974) 614.

18. Charles Dickens, *The Letters of Charles* Dickens, eds. Kathleen Tillotson, vol. 4 (Oxford: Clarendon Press, 1977) 33.

19. Amely Bölte, *Amely Böltes Briefe aus England an Varnhagen von Ense (1844-1858)*, ed. Walther Fischer and Antje Behrens (Düsseldorf: Michael Triltsch 1955) 37. Trans. Renata Stein.

Chapter Two

1. Liz Stanley, ed., *The Diaries of Hannah Cullwick, Victorian Maidservant* (London: Virago Press, 1984) 59-60 (a very useful source of information about a housemaid's tasks).

2. Ian Campbell, "Grace Welsh and Jane Carlyle," *Carlyle Newsletter* (March 1979) 20.

3. Thomas Carlyle, *Past and Present*, ed. Chris R. Vanden Bossche (Berkeley, CA: U of California P, 2005) 203.

4. "The Profession of the Teacher," *English Woman's Journal* 1.1 (1 March 1858) 9; 1.

5. Geraldine Jewsbury's account of JWC in: Thomas Carlyle, *Reminiscences* [1881], eds. Kenneth Fielding and Ian Campbell (Oxford: Oxford UP, 1997) 62.

6. TC note on JWC to Margaret Aitken Carlyle, 27 October 1840, n. 7.

7. See JWC to Jeannie Welsh, 20 May 1843, n. 2.

8. "The Profession of the Teacher" 5-6.

9. *The Story of the Governesses' Benevolent Institution* (Southwick, Sussex: Grange Press, 1962) 14.

10. JWC to John Sterling, 16 August 1843, n. 1.

11. Amely Bölte, *Amely Böltes Briefe aus England an Varnhagen von Ense (1844-1858)*, ed. Walther Fischer and Antje Behrens (Düsseldorf: Michael Triltsch 1955) 90. Trans. Renata Stein.

12. Rosemary Ashton, *Little Germany: Exile and Asylum in Victorian England* (Oxford: Oxford UP 1986) 2; 212.

13. *The Story of the Governesses' Benevolent Institution* 30.

14. Mrs. [Sarah Stickney] Ellis, *The Wives of England: Their Relative Duties, Domestic Influence, and Social Obligations* (New York: D. Appleton, 1843) 45; 67.

15. JWC to Jean Carlyle Aitken, 11 October 1843, n. 1.

16. Jane Welsh Carlyle, "*The simple Story* of my own first Love [1852]," eds. K. J. Fielding and Ian Campbell with Aileen Christianson (Edinburgh: The Carlyle Letters, Department of English Literature, University of Edinburgh, 2001)19.

17. Harriet Martineau, *Harriet Martineau's Letters to Fanny Wedgwood*, ed. Elisabeth Sanders Arbuckle (Stanford, CA: Stanford UP, 1983) 31-32.

18. *The Story of the Governesses' Benevolent Institution* 27.

19. JWC to TC, 31 August 1843, n. 6.

20. Thomas Carlyle, *Reminiscences* [1881], ed. Kenneth Fielding and Ian Campbell (Oxford: Oxford UP, 1997) 121.

21. G. E. J. [Geraldine Endsor Jewsbury], "Social Barbarisms: Hiring a Servant," *Douglas Jerrold's Shilling Magazine* 4 (July-December 1846) 465.

22. TC note on JWC to Susan Stirling, 14 November 1843.

23. Geraldine Jewsbury, *Selections from the Letters of Geraldine Endsor Jewsbury to Jane Welsh Carlyle*, ed. Mrs. Alexander [Anne Elizabeth] Ireland (London: Longmans, Green, 1892) 228-29.

24. TC to G. L. Craik, 20 January 1847, n. 3.

Chapter Three

1. Except for generally known facts about Giuseppe Mazzini, most details and all quotations in this drama in one scene can be found in JWC's letters to Jeannie Welsh, 2 January – 9 January 1844.

2. Denis Mack Smith, *Mazzini* (New Haven: Yale UP, 1994) 38-39; 45.

3. Reginald Blunt, "Mrs. Carlyle and Her Housemaid," *Cornhill Magazine* 84 (September 1901) 467.

4. Henry Mayhew, *Mayhew's London: Being selections from "London Labour and the London Poor"* [1851], ed. Peter Quennell (London: Spring Books, 1969) 527-531.

5. JWC to Jeannie Welsh, 5 October 1844 n. 2.

6. Iris Origo, "The Revolutionary and the Prophet: Mazzini in Cheyne Row," *A Measure of Love* (New York: Pantheon, 1958) 203-04.

7. Edward FitzGerald, *The Letters of Edward FitzGerald*, eds. Alfred McKinley Terhune and Annabelle Burdick Terhune, vol. 1 (Princeton, NJ: Princeton UP, 1980) 431; 433.

8. Virginia Woolf, "Geraldine and Jane," *The Essays of Virginia Woolf*, ed. Stuart N. Clarke, vol. 5 (London, Hogarth Press, 2009) 507.

9. JWC to Jeannie Welsh, 27 January 1844 n. 6.

10. Strangely, different parts of this passage, from a 20 March 1844 letter to JWC, are found in two separate sources: Kenneth Fielding and Ian Campbell, "New Letters of Harriet Martineau to Jane Carlyle, 1842-44," *Women's Writing* 9:3 (2002) 386-87; and Harriet Martineau, *The Collected Letters of Harriet Martineau*, ed. Deborah Anna Logan, vol. 2 (London: Pickering & Chatto, 2007) 266.

11. Her section on the Carlyles: Harriet Martineau, *Autobiography* [1877], ed. Linda H. Peterson (Plymouth UK: Broadview 2007) 287-94.

12. From the 27 April 1845 entry in: "Jane Welsh Carlyle Notebook, 1845-1852," the *Collected Letters*, vol. 30, which contains non-epistolary writings of JWC.

13. Thomas Carlyle, "Characteristics," *A Carlyle Reader*, ed. G. B. Tennyson (Cambridge: Cambridge UP, 1984) 80.

14. TC to Jean Carlyle Aitken, 22 January 1844 n. 9.

15. Thomas Carlyle, "Chartism," *Critical and Miscellaneous Essays in Five Volumes*, vol. 4 (London: Chapman and Hall, 1899 / AMS reprint 1980) 197.

16. Thomas Carlyle, *Reminiscences* [1881], ed. Kenneth Fielding and Ian Campbell (Oxford: Oxford UP, 1997) 270.

17. Room descriptions and house plans are most helpfully provided in Reginald Blunt, *The Carlyles' Chelsea Home: being some account of No. 5 Cheyne Row* (London: George Bell, 1895) 65.

18. Geraldine Jewsbury, *Selections from the Letters of Geraldine Endsor Jewsbury to Jane Welsh Carlyle*, ed. Mrs. Alexander [Anne Elizabeth] Ireland (London: Longmans, Green, 1892) 78.

Chapter Four

1. Amely Bölte, *Amely Böltes Briefe aus England an Varnhagen von Ense (1844-1858)*, ed. Walther Fischer and Antje Behrens (Düsseldorf: Michael Triltsch, 1955) 57-58. Trans. Renata Stein.

2. [Philip Harwood], "Sir James Graham," *Westminster Review* 41 (June 1844) 321.

3. Jonathan Parry, "Sir James Graham," *Oxford Dictionary of National Biography*, eds. H. C. G. Matthew and Brian Harrison (Oxford: Oxford UP, 2004).

4. Harwood 336.

5. Parry, *DNB*.

6. David Vincent, "The Origins of Public Secrecy in Britain," *Transactions of the Royal Historical Society, Sixth Series, Vol. 1* (Royal Historical Society, 1991) 230.

7. JWC to TC, 31 July 1843, n. 8.

8. TC to JWC, 16 September 1844, n. 5.

9. Denis Mack Smith, *Mazzini* (New Haven: Yale UP, 1994) 41.

10. Thomas Carlyle, *Reminiscences* [1881], eds. Kenneth Fielding and Ian Campbell (Oxford: Oxford UP, 1997) 94.

11. F. B. Smith, "British Post Office Espionage, 1844," *Historical Studies* 14:54 (University of Melbourne, April 1970) 189-90.

12. Denis V. Reidy, "Panizzi, Gladstone, Garibaldi and the Neapolitan Prisoners," eBLJ [*British Library Journal*] (2005) Article 6: 2. www.bl.uk/eblj/2005articles /pdf/article6.pdf Accessed 26 September 2016.

13. F. B. Smith 192.

14. [Giuseppe Mazzini], "Mazzini and the Ethics of Politicians," *Westminster Review* 42 (September 1844) 242.

15. MS / NLS / 2883.151.

16. TC to the Editor of the *Times* [London], 18 June 1844 (published 19 June 1844) and see notes in the *Collected Letters*, vol. 18, 72-74, and the *CL* online.

17. Harriet Martineau, *Life in the Sick-Room*, ed. Maria H. Frawley (Peterborough, Ontario: Broadview, 2003) 86.

18. Kenneth Fielding and Ian Campbell, "New Letters of Harriet Martineau to Jane Carlyle, 1842-44," *Women's Writing* 9: 3 (2002) 390.

19. *New Letters and Memorials of Jane Welsh Carlyle*, ed. Alexander Carlyle, vol. 2 (London: John Lane, the Bodley Head, 1903) 112.

20. Denis Mack Smith 43.

21. F. B. Smith 198.

22. Denis Mack Smith 42.

23. Frederick Douglass, *My Bondage and My Freedom* [1855], ed. John David Smith (New York: Penguin, 2003) 278.

Chapter Five

1. Jane Welsh Carlyle, "*The simple Story* of my own first Love [1852]," eds. K. J. Fielding and Ian Campbell with Aileen Christianson (Edinburgh: Carlyle Letters, Department of English Literature, University of Edinburgh, 2001) 20.

2. Ludwig Tieck, *The Roman Matron; or, Vittoria Accorombona*, 3 vols. (London: T. C. Newby, 1845) 1: 6-7.

3. Tieck l: 145; 250.

4. Tieck 3: 199.

5. Tieck 3: 226.

6. Rev. of "Tieck's *Vittoria Accorombona*," *Fraser's Magazine* 36 (November 1847) 575; 572.

7. Amely Bölte, *Amely Böltes Briefe aus England an Varnhagen von Ense (1844-1858)*, eds. Walther Fischer and Antje Behrens (Düsseldorf: Michael Triltsch, 1955) 37-38. Trans. Renata Stein.

8. Thomas Carlyle, "Varnhagen von Ense's Memoirs (1838)," *Critical and Miscellaneous Essays in Five Volumes*, vol. 4 (New York: AMS Press, 1980) 103-04.

9. Bölte 37.

10. See Emily D. Bilski and Emily Braun, *Jewish Women and Their Salons: The Power of Conversation* (New Haven: Yale UP, 2005) 27-33.

11. See Norma Clarke, *The Rise and Fall of the Woman of Letters* (London: Pimlico, 2004).

12. George Eliot, "Margaret Fuller and Mary Wollstonecraft," *George Eliot: Selected Essays, Poems and Other Writings* (London: Penguin, 1990) 333.

13. Harriet Martineau, *Autobiography* [1877], ed. Linda H. Peterson (Plymouth UK: Broadview 2007) 99.

14. Kathryn Hughes, *The Victorian Governess* (London: Hambledon Press, 1993) 114.

15. "Hints on the Modern Governess System," *Fraser's Magazine* (November 1844) 576; 572.

16. Thomas Carlyle, *The Life of John Sterling* [1851] (New York: Scribners 1903) 144-45.

17. Tieck 2: 261-62.

18. Thomas Carlyle, "Varnhagen Memoirs" 109; 115.

19. Elizabeth Hardwick, "Jane Carlyle," *Seduction and Betrayal: Women and Literature* (New York: Random House, 1974) 174; and see Aileen Christianson, "Jane Welsh Carlyle's Private Writing Career," *A History of Scottish Women's Writing*, eds. Douglas Gifford and Dorothy MacMillan (Edinburgh: Edinburgh UP, 1997) 232-45.

20. Thomas Carlyle, "Varnhagen Memoirs" 115-16.

Chapter Six

1. Grace J. Calder, "Erasmus A. Darwin, Friend of Thomas and Jane Carlyle," *Modern Language Quarterly* 20 (1959) 39.

2. Geraldine Jewsbury, *Selections from the Letters of Geraldine Endsor Jewsbury to Jane Welsh Carlyle*, ed. Mrs. Alexander [Anne Elizabeth] Ireland (London: Longmans, Green, 1892) 348.

3. Jewsbury, *Letters* 145.

4. Jewsbury, *Letters* 158.

5. Geraldine Jewsbury, *Zoe: The History of Two Lives* [1845] (London: Virago, 1989) 218-19.

6. Amely Bölte, *Amely Böltes Briefe aus England an Varnhagen von Ense (1844-1858)*, eds., Walther Fischer and Antje Behrens (Düsseldorf: Michael Triltsch, 1955) 46. Trans. Renata Stein.

7. K. J. Fielding, "Froude's Revenge, or the Carlyles and Erasmus A. Darwin," *Essays and Studies*, ed. W. W. Robson (Atlantic Highlands, NY: Humanities Press, 1978) 84; and William James Linton, *Memories* (London: Lawrence and Bullen, 1895) chapter six, 45.

8. Bölte 46.

9. Kenneth Fielding and Ian Campbell, "New Letters of Harriet Martineau to Jane Carlyle, 1842-44," *Women's Writing*, 9:3 (2002) 387.

10. K. J. Fielding, "Froude's Revenge" 84.

11. "Sir Alexander Morison," Norman Moore, *Oxford Dictionary of National Biography*, Eds. H. C. G. Matthew and Brian Harrison (Oxford: Oxford UP, 2004).

12. Descriptions of Wandsworth: "Wandsworth / British History Online" http://www.british-history.ac.uk/report.aspx?compid=45293 (accessed 2/1/2009).

13. K. J. Fielding, "Froude's Revenge" 84.

14. Mrs Alexander [Anne Elizabeth] Ireland, *Life of Jane Welsh Carlyle* (London: Chatto & Windus, 1891) 12.

15. GEJ's account of JWC's life in: Thomas Carlyle, *Reminiscences* [1881], ed. Kenneth Fielding and Ian Campbell (Oxford: Oxford UP, 1997) 42.

16. Thomas Carlyle, *Reminiscences* 68.

17. See Kathy Chamberlain, "Illness as Speech in the Life of Jane Welsh Carlyle," *Carlyle Studies Annual* 19 (2000) 63-75.

18. Thomas Carlyle, *Reminiscences* 137.

19. Bölte 46.

20. Edward FitzGerald, *The Letters of Edward FitzGerald*, eds. Alfred McKinley Terhune and Annabelle Burdick Terhune, vol. 1 (Princeton, NJ: Princeton UP, 1980) 452.

21. Phyllis Rose, *Parallel Lives: Five Victorian Marriages* (New York: Knopf, 1983) 256.

22. See I. M. Ingram, "Margaret Carlyle: Her Illness of 1817 and Its Consequences," *Carlyle Society Papers* ns 17(2004-2005) 5-18; and David Alec Wilson, *Carlyle Till Marriage: 1795-1826* (London: Kegan Paul, Trench, Trubner, 1923) 137-41.

23. TC note on JBW to Margaret A. Carlyle, 14 November 1825.

24. Wilson 140.

25. Ingram 9.

26. Thomas Carlyle, *Reminiscences* 14.

27. Jane Carlyle, *The Collected Poems of Thomas and Jane Welsh Carlyle*, eds. Rodger L. Tarr and Fleming McClelland (Greenwood, FL: Penkevill, 1986) 115.

28. TC headnote: JWC to TC, 11 September 1844.

29. Geraldine Jewsbury, "Agnes Lee (1857)," *The Broadview Anthology of Victorian Short Stories*, ed. Dennis Denisoff (Plymouth UK: Broadview 2004) 163-85.

Chapter Seven

1. TC to John A. Carlyle, 12 October 1844, n. 1.

2. TC to John A. Carlyle, 20 September 1844, n. 4.

3. TC's note on JWC to Margaret A. Carlyle, 1 September 1834.

4. "Ellen Twisleton's Account of Life at Craigenputtoch 1828-34 [Nov.? 1855]," in the *Collected Letters*, vol. 30, 272; and the *CL* online.

5. Virginia Woolf, "On Being Ill," *The Essays of Virginia Woolf: 1925-1928*, ed. Andrew McNeillie, vol. 4 (London: Hogarth, 1994) 318-19.

6. K. J. Fielding, "Froude's Revenge, or the Carlyles and Erasmus A. Darwin,"

Essays and Studies, ed. W. W. Robson (Atlantic Highlands, NY: Humanities Press 1978) 85.

7. Geraldine Jewsbury, *Selections from the Letters of Geraldine Endsor Jewsbury to Jane Welsh Carlyle*, ed. Mrs. Alexander [Anne Elizabeth] Ireland (London: Longmans, Green, 1892) 79.

8. JWC to Helen Welsh, 1 December 1843. (Punctuation and capitalization are slightly altered).

9. Edward FitzGerald, *The Letters of Edward FitzGerald*, eds. Alfred McKinley Terhune and Annabelle Burdick Terhune, vol. 1 (Princeton, NJ: Princeton UP, 1980) 466.

10. JWC to John Welsh, 13 December 1844. In the mesmerism scene that follows, all words and word order are JWC's, but paragraphing, capitalization, and punctuation have been slightly altered to make clear her use of dialogue.

11. JWC to Jeannie Welsh, 18 December 1844.

12. Harriet Martineau's articles on mesmerism, "Letters from Tynemouth," appeared in the *Athenaeum* from 23 November to 21 December 1844, numbers 891-95. Notes to quotations from other works of hers appear below.

13. John Forster, *The Life of Dickens*, vol. 1 (London: J. M. Dent, 1927) 334; 345.

14. See Alison Winter, *Mesmerized: Powers of Mind in Victorian Britain* (Chicago: U of Chicago P, 1998).

15. Harriet Martineau, *Life in the Sick-Room*, ed. Maria H. Frawley (Peterborough, Ontario: Broadview, 2003) 138.

16. Harriet Martineau, *Autobiography* [1877], ed. Linda H. Peterson (Plymouth UK: Broadview 2007) 476.

17. Charles Buller Jr.'s letter to Lady Harriet: MS NLS ACC. 11388, the Ashburton Papers.

18. Harriet Martineau, *The Collected Letters of Harriet Martineau*, ed. Deborah Anna Logan, vol. 3 (London: Pickering & Chatto, 2007) 388.

19. "Hints on the Modern Governess System," *Fraser's Magazine* 30 (November 1844) 575.

20. Jewsbury 12.

Chapter Eight

1. "Hints on the Modern Governess System," *Fraser's Magazine* 30 (November 1844) 576.

2. David R. Sorensen, "The Letters of Harriet, Lady Ashburton, to Thomas Carlyle, Part I," *Carlyle Studies Annual* 26 (2010) 34.

3. TC to Lady Harriet Baring, 22 December 1844.

4. Sorensen 37.

5. Sorensen 38-39.

6. Amely Bölte, *Amely Böltes Briefe aus England an Varnhagen von Ense (1844-1858)*, eds. Walther Fischer and Antje Behrens (Düsseldorf: Michael Triltsch, 1955) 46. Trans. Renata Stein.

7. Sorensen 39.

8. K. J. Fielding, "Froude's Second Revenge: The Carlyles and the Wedgwoods," *Prose Studies* 4 (1981) 304.

9. Harriet Martineau, *Life in the Sick-Room*, ed. Maria H. Frawley (Peterborough, Ontario: Broadview, 2003) 94.

10. Martineau, *Sick-Room*, 91; 93.

11. Elisabeth Sanders Arbuckle, *Harriet Martineau's Letters to Fanny Wedgwood* (Stanford, CA: Stanford UP, 1983) 42-44.

12. Kenneth Fielding and Ian Campbell, "New Letters of Harriet Martineau to Jane Carlyle, 1842-44," *Women's Writing* 9:3 (2002) 386.

13. Thomas Carlyle, "On History Again" [1833], *Historical Essays*, ed. Chris R. Vanden Bossche (Berkeley: U of California P, 2002) 20.

14. *The Collected Poems of Thomas and Jane Welsh Carlyle*, eds. Rodger L. Tarr and Fleming McClelland (Greenwood, FL: Penkevill, 1986) 56-7; 175-76.

15. Anne Thackeray Ritchie, *Letters of Anne Thackeray Ritchie*, ed. Hester Ritchie (London: John Murray,1924) 208.

16. William James Linton, *Memories* (London: Lawrence and Bullen, 1895) Ch. 6, 46.

17. "The Profession of the Teacher," *English Woman's Journal* 1 (1 March 1858) 10.

18. Sorensen 40-41.

19. *The Letters and Private Papers of William Makepeace Thackeray*, ed. Gordon Ray, vol. 1 (Cambridge MA: Harvard UP, 1946) clviii-ix.

Chapter Nine

1. Edward FitzGerald, *The Letters of Edward FitzGerald*, eds. Alfred McKinley Terhune and Annabelle Burdick Terhune, vol. 1 (Princeton: Princeton UP, 1980) 472 and see n. 2.

2. FitzGerald 478.

3. David R. Sorensen, ed., "The Letters of Harriet, Lady Ashburton, to Thomas Carlyle, Part I," *Carlyle Studies Annual* 26 (2010) 40.

4. Description of Charles Lambert: Susanne Howe, *Geraldine Jewsbury: Her Life and Errors* (London: George Allen, 1935) 83-88.

5. JWC to Jeannie Welsh, 6 February 1845, n. 7.

6. Kenneth Fielding and Ian Campbell, "The Trump and Her Trumpet: New Letters from Harriet Martineau to Jane Carlyle," *Times Literary Supplement* (30 November 2001) 16.

7. Fielding and Campbell 16-17.

8. Francis Espinasse, *Literary Recollections and Sketches* (London: Hodder and Stoughton, 1893): 129 n 1.

9. JWC to Helen Welsh, 12 November 1844, n. 7 and n. 8.

10. Quotations from JWC's 13 April and 27 April entries are from vol. 30 of the *Collected Letters*: "Jane Welsh Carlyle Notebook, 1845-1852." It includes an editorial preface describing the notebook. For readability, I have sometimes altered JWC's paragraphing, punctuation, and capitalization in passages of dialogue.

11. Thomas Carlyle, *Reminiscences* [1881], eds. K. J. Fielding and Ian Campbell (Oxford: Oxford UP, 1997) 72-73; 157.

12. Charles Gavan Duffy, *Conversations with Carlyle* (New York: Scribners, 1892) 5.

13. Duffy 1-5.

Chapter Ten

1. Geraldine Jewsbury, *Letters of Geraldine Endsor Jewsbury to Jane Welsh Carlyle*, ed., Mrs. Alexander [Anne Elizabeth] Ireland (London: Longmans, Green, 1892) 165-66.

2. Jewsbury 180.

3. The lost child is described at the end of the 13 April 1845 entry in "Jane Welsh Carlyle Notebook, 1845-1852," the *Collected Letters*, vol. 30, 166-69; and the *CL* online.

4. David R. Sorensen, ed., "The Letters of Harriet, Lady Ashburton, to Thomas Carlyle, Part I," *Carlyle Studies Annual* 26 (2010) 28.

5. Bettina Lehmbeck, "Elizabeth Paulet and the Carlyles," *Carlyle Newsletter* 8 (1987) 23.

6. S. G. Checkland, *The Gladstones: A Family Biography 1764-1851* (Cambridge: Cambridge UP, 1971) 83.

7. From the description accompanying an engraving of Seaforth: J. P. Neale, "Seaforth House, Lancashire; the seat of John Gladstone, Esq. M. P.," *Views of the Seats of Noblemen and Gentlemen in England, Wales and Scotland* (London: J. P. Neale, 1824).

8. Her letter describing Seaforth House: JWC to TC, 3 August 1845.

9. TC to JWC, 19 July 1841, n. 4.

10. G[eraldine]. E[ndsor]. J[ewsbury]., "Social Barbarisms: Hiring a Servant," *Douglas Jerrold's Shilling Magazine* 4 (1846): 462-71.

11. The drama in one scene: JWC to TC, 20 August 1845. The words in quotation marks are JWC's, but for the sake of readability I have slightly changed the order, and have made a few changes in her punctuation, paragraphing, and capitalization.

12. The party conversation: JWC to TC, 16 August 1845. Paragraphing and punctuation have been slightly altered to make it clear who is speaking.

13. Joseph Slater, ed., *The Correspondence of Emerson and Carlyle* (New York: Columbia UP, 1964) 372.

14. Elizabeth Barrett [Browning] and Richard H. Horne, unsigned essay, "*A New Spirit of the Age* [1844], *Thomas Carlyle: the Critical Heritage*, ed., Jules Paul Seigel (New York: Barnes & Noble, 1971) 237-38.

15. TC to JWC, 26 September 1845, n. 4.

16. JWC to TC, 28 September 1845, n. 13.

17. Francis Jeffrey, *The Letters of Francis Jeffrey to Thomas and Jane Welsh Carlyle*, ed., William Christie (London: Pickering & Chatto, 2008) 131.

18. Jeffrey 148.

19. Jeffrey 137-38.

20. JWC to TC, 20 August 1845, n. 4.

21. Giuseppe Mazzini, E. F. Richards, and Emilie Ashurst Venturi, *Mazzini's Letters to an English Family, 1844-1854* (London: John Lane, 1920) 5-6.

Chapter Eleven

1. Charles Dickens to Madame De la Rue (27 September 1845), *The Letters of Charles Dickens*, ed., Kathleen Tillotson, vol. 4 (Oxford: Clarendon Press, 1977) 389.

2. John Forster, *The Life of Dickens*, vol. 1(London: J. M. Dent, 1927) 375.

3. Dickens 388.

4. Alan S. Downer, *The Eminent Tragedian: William Charles Macready* (Cambridge: Harvard UP, 1966) 76; 277.

5. Lord Houghton [Richard Monckton Milnes], *Monographs, Personal and Social* (New York: Holt & Williams, 1873) 223; 218.

6. JWC to Jeannie Welsh, 27 May 1843.

7. *Selections from the Letters of Geraldine Endsor Jewsbury to Jane Welsh Carlyle*, ed. Mrs. Alexander Ireland [Anne Elizabeth] (London: Longmans, Green, 1892) 189.

8. Houghton 223.

9. Ed., David R. Sorensen, "Letters of Harriet, Lady Ashburton, to Thomas Carlyle, Part I," *Carlyle Studies Annual* 26 (Philadelphia: Saint Joseph's UP, 2010) 52.

10. Jewsbury 191.

11. Jewsbury 189.

12. Amely Bölte, *Amely Böltes Briefe aus England an Varnhagen von Ense: 1844-1858* (Michael Triltsch: Düsseldorf, 1955) 38. Trans. Renata Stein.

13. Caroline Fox, *The Journals of Caroline Fox, 1835-1871*, ed., Wendy Monk (London: Elek, 1972) 164-65.

14. Jewsbury 188-89.

15. Jewsbury 199.

16. Jewsbury 196-97.

17. Janet Browne, *Charles Darwin, a Biography*, vol. 1 (New York, Knopf, 1995) 356; 379.

18. Sorensen, 35; 36-37.

19. Edward FitzGerald, *The Letters of Edward FitzGerald*, eds., Alfred McKinley Terhune and Annabelle Burdick Terhune, vol. 1 (Princeton: Princeton UP, 1980) 534.

20. See Jewsbury 194.

Chapter Twelve

1. After Peel's death, "Large numbers of working men sent in their pennies to help pay for statues in his memory": Asa Briggs, *England in the Age of Improvement* (London: Folio Society, 1999) 312. See, for instance, Sir Robert Peel's statue in George Square, Glasgow.

2. Alethea Hayter, *A Sultry Month: Scenes of London Literary Life in 1846* (London: Faber and Faber, 1965) 35.

3. Amely Bölte, *Amely Böltes Briefe aus England an Varnhagen von Ense (1844-1858)*, eds. Walther Fischer and Antje Behrens (Düsseldorf: Michael Triltsch, 1955) 40. Trans. Renata Stein.

4. Geraldine Jewsbury, *Letters of Geraldine Endsor Jewsbury to Jane Welsh Carlyle*, ed. Mrs. Alexander [Anne Elizabeth] Ireland (London: Longmans, Green, 1892) 210.

5. Hayter 47-51.

6. Jewsbury 209.

7. TC to JWC, 6 July 1846, n. 1.

8. For excerpts from GM's July 10 and July 15, 1846, letters to JWC see: JWC to TC, 6 July 1846 n. 3.

9. This quotation from GM's July 15 letter: Iris Origo, *A Measure of Love* (New York: Pantheon, 1958) 208.

10. Bölte 39.

11. GEJ's letter to AB is dated 1846 in a different hand. The date might be 20 July 1846. Varnhagen Collection, Jagiellonian University Library, Kraków: Berol. Varnhagen Sammlung 96; Dig. ORP 000478.

12. David R. Sorensen, ed., "Letters of Harriet, Lady Ashburton, to Thomas Carlyle, Part I, *Carlyle Studies Annual* 26 (Philadelphia, Saint Joseph's UP, 2010) 55.

13. Jewsbury 212.

14. TC to Leigh Hunt, 18 July 1833, and see n. 5.

15. Friedrich Engels, *The Condition of the Working Class in England*, ed. David McLellan (Oxford: Oxford UP, 2009) 54.

16. Jewsbury 214.

17. Lady Harriet's note to JWC: see TC to JWC, 20 August 1846, n. 4.

18. Bölte 40.

19. Sorensen 56.

20. Sorensen 61-62.

21. James Anthony Froude, *Thomas Carlyle: A History of His Life in London: 1834-1881*, vol. 3 (New York: Scribners, 1884) 391.

Chapter Thirteen

1. Geraldine Jewsbury, *Letters of Geraldine Endsor Jewsbury to Jane Welsh Carlyle*, ed. Mrs. Alexander [Anne Elizabeth] Ireland (London: Longmans, Green, 1892) 215.

2. Alexander Carlyle, ed., *New Letters and Memorials of Jane Welsh Carlyle*, vol. 2 (London: John Lane, Bodley Head, 1903) 113; 111.

3. TC's headnote: JWC to Susan Stirling, 26 September, 1846, n. 2.

4. Caroline Fox, *The Journals of Caroline Fox*, 1835-1871, ed. Wendy Monk (London: Elek, 1972) 172.

5. Elisabeth Sanders Arbuckle, ed., *Harriet Martineau's Letters to Fanny Wedgwood* (Stanford, CA: Stanford UP, 1983) 85.

6. Harriet Martineau, *Autobiography*, ed. Linda H. Peterson (Peterborough, Ontario: Broadview, 2007) 378-79.

7. Bell Gale Chevigny, *The Woman and the Myth: Margaret Fuller's Life and Writings* (Boston: Northeastern UP, 1994) 414.

8. Elvan Kintner, ed., *The Letters of Robert Browning and Elizabeth Barrett Barrett, 1845-1846*, vol. 1 (Cambridge: Harvard UP, 1969) 361.

9. Kintner, vol. 2, 961-63, and see n. 1.

10. Margaret Fuller, *The Letters of Margaret Fuller*, ed. Robert N. Hudspeth, vol. 4 (Ithaca, NY: Cornell UP, 1987) 244.

11. Fuller, *Letters* 245 n. 3.

12. NLS Acc. 8140.

13. Fuller, *Letters* 244.

14. Fuller, *Letters* 248.

15. Jewsbury 215.

16. Fuller, *Letters* 246

17. Fuller, *Letters* 248

18. Fuller, *Letters* 246.

19. Fuller, *Letters* 250 n. 5.

20. Fuller, *Letters* 248.

21. Thomas Carlyle, *Essay on Burns*, ed. Sophie C. Hart (New York: Holt, 1912) 63.

22. Fuller, *Letters* 249.

23. Chevigny 354.

24. Fuller, *Letters* 248-49.

25. Margaret Fuller, *"These Sad but Glorious Days": Dispatches from Europe, 1846-1850*, eds. Larry J. Reynolds and Susan Belasco Smith (New Haven: Yale UP, 1991) 10.

26. TC to Ralph Waldo Emerson, 7 May 1852, and see n. 6.

27. Fox 172.

28. Chevigny 362.

29. Chevigny 414.

30. Fuller, *Letters* 305 n. 1 (a quotation from Emelyn Story).

Chapter Fourteen

1. David R. Sorensen, ed. "Letters of Harriet, Lady Ashburton, to Thomas Carlyle, Part I," *Carlyle Studies Annual* 26 (Philadelphia: Saint Joseph's UP, 2010) 62-63.

2. "Francis Wemyss-Charteris Douglas," Norbert C. Soldon, *Oxford Dictionary of National Biography*, eds. H. C. G. Matthew and Brian Harrison (Oxford: Oxford UP, 2004.) 15 September 2016 http://www.oxforddnb.com

3. Sorensen 56.

4. Denis Mack Smith *Mazzini* (New Haven: Yale UP) 52.

5. Giuseppe Mazzini, E. F. Richards, Emilie Ashurst Venturi, *Mazzini's Letters to an English Family, 1844-1854* (London: John Lane, 1920) 31.

6. Mazzini, Richards, Venturi 36; 39-40.

7. Mazzini, Richards, Venturi 48 n.

8. Amely Bölte, *Amely Böltes Briefe aus England an Varnhagen von Ense (1844-1858)*, ed. Walther Fischer and Antje Behrens (Düsseldorf: Michael Triltsch, 1955) 45; 47. Trans. Renata Stein.

9. Bölte 43.

10. Ralph Waldo Emerson, *The Letters of Ralph Waldo Emerson*, ed. Ralph L. Rusk, vol. 3 (New York: Columbia UP, 1939) 424.

11. See Kenneth J. Fielding's introduction to vol. 22 (July 1847-March 1848) of the *Collected Letters*, especially xiii.

12. [Hallam Tennyson], *Alfred Lord Tennyson: A Memoir by His Son*, vol. 2 (New York: Macmillan, 1897) 410.

13. Edward FitzGerald, *The Letters of Edward FitzGerald*, eds. Alfred McKinley Terhune and Annabelle Burdick Terhune, vol. 1 (Princeton: Princeton UP, 1980) 553.

14. Sorensen 63-64.

15. K. J. Fielding, "Froud's Revenge, or the Carlyles and Erasmus A. Darwin," *Essays and Studies 1978*, ed. W. W. Robson (Atlantic Highlands, NY: Humanities Press 1978) 86.

16. Geraldine Jewsbury, *Letters of Geraldine Endsor Jewsbury to Jane Welsh Carlyle*, ed. Mrs. Alexander [Anne Elizabeth] Ireland (London: Longmans, Green, 1892) 228.

17. Caroline Fox, *The Journals of Caroline Fox: 1835-71*, ed. Wendy Monk (London: Elek, 1972) 171-72.

Chapter Fifteen

1. JWC to Helen Welsh, 15 July 1847, n. 2.

2. NLS 603.233.

3. The pane of glass is in a cabinet at the Temple Hotel (built 1785-90), Temple Walk, Matlock Bath.

4. Quotations from William Edward Forster in this chapter are from letters he wrote to friends and family during or close to the time of the Carlyles' August 1847 visit. They can be found in: T. Wemyss Reid, *Life of the Right Honourable William Edward Forster*, vol. 1 (London: Chapman and Hall, 1888) 204-15.

5. Wemyss Reid 205.

6. Edward FitzGerald, *The Letters of Edward FitzGerald*, eds. Alfred McKinley Terhune and Annabelle Burdick Terhune, vol. 1 (Princeton: Princeton UP, 1980) 580.

7. Wemyss Reid 205.

8. For the kitten see: JWC to Jeannie Welsh, 23 December 1848, and JWC to W. E. Forster, 19 or 25 January 1849.

Chapter Sixteen

1. Geraldine Jewsbury, *The Half Sisters*, ed. Joanne Wilkes (Oxford: Oxford UP, 1994) 160.

2. Denis Mack Smith, *Mazzini* (New Haven: Yale UP, 1994) 49-50.

3. See JWC to Jeannie Welsh, 26 February 1844, including n. 4.

4. For Henry Fleming see: TC to JWC, 15 July 1844, n. 3; and JWC to TC, 11 September 1844, n. 3.

5. Ralph Waldo Emerson, *Emerson in His Journals*, ed. Joel Porte (Cambridge MA, Harvard UP, 1982) 379-80.

6. Francis Espinasse, *Literary Recollections and Sketches* (London, Hodder and Stoughton, 1893) 164.

7. Emerson, *Journals* 380.

8. Espinasse 156-57.

9. Joseph Slater, ed., *The Correspondence of Emerson and Carlyle* (New York: Columbia UP, 1964) 43 n. 46.

10. Espinasse 163.

11. Ralph Waldo Emerson, *The Letters of Ralph Waldo Emerson*, ed. Ralph L. Rusk (New York: Columbia UP, 1939) vol 3: 443.

12. Emerson, *Letters* vol. 4: 30-31.

13. Emerson, *Letters* vol. 3: 442-43.

14. Espinasse 163.

15. Emerson, *Letters* vol. 4: 86.

16. Emerson, *Letters* vol. 3: 424.

17. Giuseppe Mazzini, E. F. Richards, Emilie Ashurst Venturi, *Mazzini's Letters to an English Family, 1844-1854* (London: John Lane, 1920) 68.

18. Giuseppe Mazzini, *Scritti*, vol. 33 (Imola: Cooperativa Tipografico-Editrice Paolo Galeati, 1903-43) 75-76.

19. David R. Sorensen, ed., "Letters of Harriet, Lady Ashburton, to Thomas Carlyle, Part I," *Carlyle Studies Annual* 26 (Philadelphia: Saint Joseph's UP, 2010) 70 and JWC to John Forster, 20 November 1847.

20. Amely Bölte, *Amely Böltes Briefe aus England an Varnhagen von Ense (1844-1858)*, eds. Walther Fischer and Antje Behrens (Düsseldorf: Michael Triltsch, 1955) 48-49. Trans. Renata Stein. All quotations from AB in this section are from these pages.

21. The torn letter: JWC to Helen Welsh, 19 November 1847 – and see n. 5.

22. Espinasse 143.

23. Fred Kaplan, "'Phallus-Worship' (1848): Unpublished Manuscripts III – A Response to the Revolution of 1848," *Carlyle Newsletter* 2 (March 1980) 22-23.

24. Jewsbury, *Half Sisters* 108.

25. Jewsbury, *Half Sisters* 396.

26. Jewsbury, *Half Sisters* 214.

27. Jewsbury, *Half Sisters* 134.

28. Jewsbury, *Half Sisters* 187; 250.

29. Jewsbury, *Half Sisters* 208.

30. Jewsbury, *Half Sisters* 219-20.

31. Jewsbury, *Half Sisters* 222.

32. Jewsbury, *Half Sisters* 391-92.

33. Jewsbury, *Half Sisters* 249.

34. Jewsbury, *Half Sisters* 247.

35. Jewsbury, *Half Sisters* 250-51.

36. Geraldine Jewsbury, *Letters of Geraldine Endsor Jewsbury to Jane Welsh Carlyle*, ed. Mrs. Alexander [Anne Elizabeth] Ireland (London: Longmans, Green, 1892) 241-44.

Chapter Seventeen

1. Denis Mack Smith, *Mazzini* (New Haven: Yale UP, 1994) 56 and passim.

2. See JWC to Jeannie Welsh the following year, 29 January 1849: "I never go out in the evening, indeed there have been no evening invitations for *me* yet,—excepting one to Lady Lyell's."

3. Amely Bölte, *Amely Böltes Briefe aus England an Varnhagen von Ense (1844-1858)*, eds. Walther Fischer and Antje Behrens (Düsseldorf: Michael Triltsch 1955) 60. Trans. Renata Stein.

4. JWC to Jeannie Welsh, 12 February 1848, n. 1.

5. Ralph Waldo Emerson, *The Letters of Ralph Waldo Emerson*, vol. 4, ed. Ralph L. Rusk, (New York, Columbia UP, 1939) 30-31; 43.

6. Francis Espinasse, *Literary Recollections and Sketches* (London: Hodder and Stoughton, 1893) 169.

7. Emerson 43.

8. Emerson 34.

9. Emerson 43.

10. Most information and all quotations in this description of the Chartist demonstration are from the blow-by-blow account given in *The Illustrated London News* (15 April 1848). See www.chartists.net/insurrection/monster-meeting-on-Kennington-Common-April-1848/ accessed 4 September 2016.

11. Mike Rapport, *1848: Year of Revolution* (New York: Basic Books, 2008) 329.

12. Quotations in this section not otherwise attributed are from WEF's diary account of his May 1848 Paris journey, as excerpted in: T. Wemyss Reid, *Life of the Right Honourable William Edward Foster* (London: Chapman and Hall, 1888) 228-45.

13. Bonnie S. Anderson, *Joyous Greetings: The First International Women's Movement, 1830-1860* (New York: Oxford UP, 2000) 157-8. See Chapter 7: "Volcano Time."

14. Caroline Fox, *The Journals of Caroline Fox: 1835-1871*, ed. Wendy Monk (London: Elek, 1972) 191.

15. Emerson 73-74.

16. Emerson 76.

17. Rapport 190.

18. Emerson 72.

19. Mary Gabriel, *Love and Capital: Karl and Jenny Marx and the Birth of a Revolution* (Little Brown: New York, 2011) 148.

20. Rapport 208.

21. TC to Jean Carlyle Aitken, 19 July 1848, n. 5.

22. *Emma Darwin: A Century of Family Letters*, ed. H. Litchfield, vol. 2 (London: D. Appleton, 1915) 95.

23. Francis Espinasse, *Literary Recollections and Sketches* (London: Hodder and Stoughton, 1893) 267.

24. Frederick Niecks, *Frederick Chopin, as a Man and Musician* [1902], vol. 2 (New York: Cooper Square, 1973) 285.

25. TC to Lady Ashburton, 17 October 1848.

26. Ian Campbell, "Grace Welsh and Jane Carlyle" *Carlyle Newsletter* 1 (March 1979) 19; and JWC to Eliza Stodart, 8 March 1923.

27. In 1855 Lady Ashburton gave JWC for Christmas the gift of a black silk dress, which deeply insulted her and caused much distress. Iris Origo who wrote about the incident as an example of JWC's "touchiness" later explained that she had been ignorant of the fact that in mid Victorian society "a silk dress was the recognized present for a housekeeper and a friend of the family would have felt bewildered at receiving it. . . . [Having been given such a gift] was a sign of social inferiority." Origo learned this from the writer Rebecca West whose great aunt had known of the episode and called it "a most extraordinary thing for Lady Ashburton to have done." *Images and Shadows: Part of a Life* (London: John Murray, 1970) 179.

28. See TC to Alexander J. Scott, 5 August 1848 and 18 September 1848.

29. Bölte 64.

30. David R. Sorensen, ed., "Letters of Harriet, Lady Ashburton, to Thomas Carlyle, Part I," *Carlyle Studies Annual* 26 (Philadelphia: Saint Joseph's UP, 2010) 87.

31. JWC to John Welsh, 7 January 1851.

32. TC's note on JWC to Susan Stirling, 29 December, 1846.

Chapter Eighteen

1. Alan and Mary McQueen Simpson, eds., *I Too Am Here: Selections from the Letters of Jane Welsh Carlyle* (Cambridge: Cambridge UP, 1977) 197.

2. Bell Gale Chevigny, *The Woman and the Myth: Margaret Fuller's Life and Writings* (Boston: Northeastern UP, 1994) 461.

3. Chevigny 464.

4. Chevigny 467.

5. Chevigny 469.

6. Chevigny 479-80.

7. Denis Mack Smith, *Mazzini* (New Haven: Yale UP, 1994) 225.

8. See TC's note on JWC to Susan Stirling, 29 December 1846.

9. See GEJ's account of JWC in Thomas Carlyle, *Reminiscences* [1881], eds. K. J. Fielding and Ian Campbell (Oxford: Oxford UP) 65.

10. Hilary Macaskill, *Charles Dickens at Home* (London: Frances Lincoln, 2011) 53-61.

11. JWC to Jeannie Welsh, 17 May 1849, n. 2 and n. 4.

12. Janet Flanders, *Inside the Victorian Home: A Portrait of Domestic Life in Victorian England* (New York: W. W. Norton, 2003) 253-91; 481.

13. Words and emphases are JWC's, but I have changed punctuation, capitalization, and paragraphing—and added the initials—for readability.

14. From TC's *Journal*: TC to Margaret A. Carlyle, 22 March 1836, n. 11.

15. JWC to Jeannie Welsh, 17 May 1849, n. 4; Jenny Uglow, *Elizabeth Gaskell: A Habit of Stories* (New York: Farrar Straus Giroux, 1993) 225.

16. The report of the phrenologist Cornelius Donovan is appended to JWC to TC, 12 August 1849.

17. Amely Bölte, *Amely Böltes Briefe aus England an Varnhagen von Ense (1844-1858)*, eds. Walther Fischer and Antje Behrens (Düsseldorf: Michael Triltsch, 1955) 93. Trans. Renata Stein. And see TC to JWC, 25 September 1852.

18. Bölte 70.

19. Bölte 71.

20. Bölte 67.

21. Bölte 91.

22. Elizabeth Barrett [Browning] and Richard H. Horne, unsigned essay, "A New Spirit of the Age" [1844], *Thomas Carlyle: The Critical Heritage*, ed. Jules Paul Seigel (NewYork: Barnes and Noble, 1971) 237-38.

23. See two essays by Lowell T. Frye: "' Vocables, Still Vocables': Linguistic and Religious Despair in Thomas Carlyle's *Latter-Day Pamphlets*," *Literature and Belief: Thomas Carlyle*, eds. Paul E. Kerry and Jesse S. Crisler (Provo UT: Brigham Young University, 2005) 197-216. And "Thomas Carlyle's *Latter-Day Pamphlets* and the Condition of England in 1850," *Thomas Carlyle & the Totalitarian Temptation / Studies in the Literary Imagination* 45.1 (Atlanta: Georgia State University, Spring 2012) 113-38.

24. Bettina Lehmbeck, "Elizabeth Paulet and the Carlyles," *Carlyle Newsletter* 8 (1987) 25.

25. GEJ's famous letter to JWC: Geraldine Jewsbury, *Selections from the Letters of Geraldine Endsor Jewsbury to Jane Welsh Carlyle*, ed. Mrs. Alexander [Anne Elizabeth] Ireland (London: Longmans, Green, 1892) 345-52.

26. Mary Wollstonecraft, *A Vindication of the Rights of Woman*, ed. Carol H. Poston (New York: W. W. Norton, 1988) 8.

27. Bölte 65.

28. "The Property of Married Women," *Westminster Review* (July & October 1856) 331-360; 336; 338.

29. See TC to JBW, 28 November 1825 n. 9: a daughter of John Knox had married a John Welsh, but TC's nephew Alexander Carlyle said that JWC was instead a descendent of John Welsh's older brother, David Welsh of Colliston. Matthew Baillie's wife was "Margaret Euston"—apparently Mary Yowston or Yorkston. JWC may have believed all she said concerning her ancestry, but the point was also her delight in claiming such a contradictory heritage.

30. Thomas Carlyle, "Varnhagen von Ense's Memoirs (1838)," *Critical and Miscellaneous Essays in Five Volumes*, vol. 4 (New York: AMS Press, 1980) 109.

31. "Much ado about Nothing" (MAAN) is published in full, with documentation, in the *Collected Letters*, vol. 24, 159-71; it is also available in the *CL* online.

32. Jewsbury, *Letters* 98.

33. See GEJ's account of JWC in: Thomas Carlyle, *Reminiscences* 47.

34. Simpsons 197.

35. Lawrence and Elisabeth Hanson, *Necessary Evil: The Life of Jane Welsh Carlyle* (London: Constable, 1952): 4.

36. TC note, 3 August 1866.

Epilogue: A Last Word

1. The information was taken from an online entry by the Women's Museum in Wiesbaden in honor of Amely Bölte's 200th birthday. Trans. Renata Stein.

2. TC to JWC, 25 September 1852. It is very likely that this was a copy of the Carl Hartmann portrait since Amely had commissioned it so that she could have a copy to take with her to Germany.

3. Diana Trilling, *The Beginning of the Journey: The Marriage of Diana and Lionel Trilling* (New York: Harcourt, Brace, 1993) 349.

4. Jane Welsh Carlyle, "*The simple Story* of my own first Love" [1852], eds. K. J. Fielding and Ian Campbell with Aileen Christianson (Edinburgh: Carlyle Letters, Department of English Literature, University of Edinburgh, 2001) 20.

ACKNOWLEDGMENTS

MY GREATEST DEBT is to the editors, past and present, of the Duke-Edinburgh edition of the *Collected Letters of Thomas and Jane Welsh Carlyle*. This ongoing project has already produced forty-four printed volumes, as well as the invaluable Carlyle Letters Online. To read through the *Collected Letters* is to watch, close up, as daily life in Victorian Britain—and so much more—unscrolls before your eyes. My profound thanks to current editors Ian Campbell, Aileen Christianson, Jane Roberts, Liz Sutherland, David Sorensen, and Brent Kinser, as well as to Sheila McIntosh and the late Kenneth J. Fielding, and also to David Southern, managing editor of the Carlyle Letters Office at Duke University Press. Additional thanks to the editors in the Carlyle Letters Office, Department of English Literature at the University of Edinburgh, for their collegiality and hospitality. This book could not have been written without the meticulous scholarship and organizational skills of all these talented, hard working individuals. A fascinating story remains to be told of the history of this superb project, some sixty years (so far!) in the making.

Words cannot express what I owe the learned and delightful members of the Women Writing Women's Lives seminar, affiliated with the City University of New York's Graduate Center. I cannot imagine a better "transitional group" within which to negotiate the tortuous, many-years-long path from private writer to published author. I am especially grateful to historians Dorothy O. Helly and the late Claire Morris Stern (and their "Victorians Table," around which so much work got done), and Diane Jacobs. They discussed every chapter with me. I also owe thanks for very specific help with this book to WWWL members Evelyn Barish, Bell Gale Chevigny, Kate Culkin, Johanna Garfield, Gail A. Hornstein, Polly Howells, Patricia Laurence, Dona Munker, Victoria C. Olsen, Sydney Ladensohn Stern, and Donez Xiques.

I owe a great deal to the network of international Thomas Carlyleans, known for being considerably more congenial and progressive than the man they write about, and their memorable conferences, scholarly articles, books, and anthologies; and to other "transitional groups": the stimulating New York University biography seminar; the English Department at the Borough of Manhattan Community College / CUNY, especially Robert Lapides, editor of *Hudson River*, Dickens scholar, and impresario of faculty forums; the CUNY Victorians seminar; the OWN journal writing group and its founder, Eva Kollisch; and the West Village insight meditation sangha. I would also like to thank Clare Cain, Tara C. Craig of the Rare Book and Manuscript Library / Columbia University, Elizabeth Ely, Emily Fairey, Lowell T. Frye, Sally Harrower of the National Library of Scotland, Catherine Heyrendt, Kathy Hintz, Robert Lepley, James P. O'Brien, Edith Penty, Linda Skippings, curator of the Carlyle House in Chelsea, Renata Stein, and Arnold Wishnia. For assistance with illustrations, tremendous thanks to Winnie Lee.

My agent Georges Borchardt has been a prince of patience and kindliness. I'm deeply grateful to Peter Mayer, publisher of The Overlook Press and Duckworth, and to editor Tracy Carns, and their excellent staff.

I thank my friend Elizabeth Strout for reading and commenting on my manuscript. For their support during the years I worked on this book, I wish to thank the Chamberlain-Zweig-Jen-Lepley-Thornton-Lynner extended family, most of all my dear husband, Michael Zweig.

INDEX

Adam Bede (Eliot), 235
Addiscombe Farm, 172, 207, 219, 290; Jane at, 172, 174, 207–9, 215, 275, 291, 292, 315, 328; Seaforth House compared to, 176, 177
"Agnes Lee" (Jewsbury), 121–22
Albert, Prince, 45, 258
alcoholism, 40, 164–65, 340; Helen Mitchell's, 40, 86, 236–37, 340
Alcott, Amos Bronson, 107, 252
Alcott House, 107
Angel in the House, The (Patmore), 16, 197
animal magnetism. *See* mesmerism
Arkwright, Richard, 278
Arnold, Matthew, 54, 170
Arrowsmith, Jane, 129, 132
Ashburton, Baron, first (Alexander Baring, father-in-law of Lady Harriet Baring), 77, 116, 174, 196, 199
Ashburton, Baron, second. *See* Baring, William Bingham
Ashurst, Eliza, 264–65
Ashurst family, 264–65, 266, 272, 296, 339. *See also* Ashurst, Eliza
Athenaeum, 128–29, 132, 133, 134
Austen, Jane, 14, 91, 174, 184, 276
Austrian Empire, 79, 81, 83–84
autograph collecting, 74, 95, 328–29

Bacon, Theresa. *See* Revis, Theresa (mother)
Bagley, William, 287–88
Baillie, Matthew, 355, 383n29
Bamford, Samuel, 227
Baring, Lady Harriet (Lady Ashburton), 77, 363; appearance of, 13, 139–40, 206; childhood of, 205; impressive intellect of, 204, 209, 221; marriage of, 77, 123, 140, 228, 256; in Nice in 1844, 138, 139, 140–43, 155–56; place of, in upper-class society, 139, 176
—and Jane, 172–74, 197, 200–201, 206–10, 290–92, 311; class difference between, 139, 262, 381–82n27; correspondence with, 148, 155–56, 228–30, 292–93, 307; and country-house visits, 172–74, 199–201, 207–9, 215, 256–62, 275, 291, 292, 306, 315, 328; first meeting of, 173, 197; Jane's ambivalence about, 173–74, 199–202, 207, 261–62; Jane's distrust of, 116, 174–75, 208, 215, 258; sometime friendship with, 204–5, 206–7, 209–10, 231
—relationship of, with Thomas, 13, 139–40, 160, 198, 206–7, 221; and country-house visits, 116, 172–74, 199–201, 215, 232, 256, 260, 261–62; intimate letters between, 140, 173, 187, 205–6, 221, 223, 225, 232–34, 259, 269, 292; Jane's anxieties about, 40, 77, 140, 146,

172–75, 196–98, 215–26, 238, 255, 258, 289, 311; platonic nature of, 13, 269, 331; tensions within, 232, 242, 261–62, 269

Baring, William Bingham, 140, 208, 258, 294; as husband of Lady Harriet, 77, 123, 140, 228, 256; as MP, 200, 258; as second Baron Ashburton after 1848, 327, 332, 363

Barrett, Elizabeth. *See* Browning, Elizabeth Barrett

Bath House, 197–98

Bay House, 199–201, 229, 232, 233, 258, 260–61, 306; Jane at, 199–201, 256–62

Beeton, Mrs. Isabella, 238

birthdays, Jane's, 171, 212, 218–19, 275, 308, 312

Blanc, Louis, 315, 318, 321–22, 347–48,

bluestockings, 96, 139, 266

Boadicea, 186–87

Bölte, Amely (Amalie), 30, 44–45, 46, 347–48, 362; ambitions of, 45, 73, 171; and European events of 1847–49, 285, 296, 297–98; illness of, 137–39, 140–43, 149, 150; and mesmerism, 126, 127, 130, 132, 134–35; religious skepticism of, 50–51, 57, 75, 139; and Thomas, 86–87, 140–42, 143, 204, 219, 230–31, 248, 266–67, 297–98, 346–47; as translator, 87, 101; views of, on women's place in society, 266, 298, 346, 353; as writer, 52–53, 95, 362

—as governess, 44–45, 73–75, 84–86; for the Bullers, 51–52, 57, 69–70, 84, 123, 124–25, 134–35, 137–38, 143, 149–50

—and Jane, 36, 142, 218, 275, 297–98, 330, 345–48, 350–51; admiration and love for, 92–93, 275, 297, 364; annoyance caused to, 45–46, 47, 72–73, 171, 208; in Cheyne Row visits, 45–46, 48–50, 70–73, 116, 142, 171; correspondence between, 30–31, 33–34, 36, 57, 200–201, 208, 218, 275; and Jane's "employment bureau," 44, 45, 51–53, 104

—and other friends of the Carlyles: and Geraldine Jewsbury, 53, 73, 220; and Karl August Varnhagen von Ense, 93, 94–95, 142, 208, 219, 266, 297–98, 311, 330, 346; and Lady Harriet Baring, 138, 139, 140–43, 155–56; and Richard Plattnauer, 107, 108, 116, 120, 139, 143–44

Bonaparte, Napoleon, 93–94, 315, 338

Book of Household Management (Beeton), 238

Boudicca. *See* Boadicea

Braid, Betty, 239, 360

Brindley, James, 278

British Factory Act (Ten Hour Bill), 263

Brontë, Charlotte, 46, 135, 351. See also *Jane Eyre*

Brontë, Emily, 311

Brontë sisters, 14, 92, 311. *See also* Brontë, Charlotte; Brontë, Emily

Brown, Anne, 244, 260, 263, 274, 283, 293, 328, 333, 335

Browning, Elizabeth Barrett, 54, 214, 230, 294, 354; and Margaret Fuller, 245, 252; on Thomas's writing, 182, 348

Browning, Robert, 60, 214, 230, 245

Buller, Arthur, 69, 70, 138

Buller, Charles, Jr., 70, 74, 294; in Barings' social circle, 200, 208, 258, 290, 327; early death of, 333; and Jane, 126, 133; as MP, 57, 70, 208, 258

Buller, Charles, Sr., 70; death of, 333. *See also* Bullers, the (Charles and Isabella)

Buller, Isabella, 70, 76, 116, 133; and Amely Bölte, 73, 84, 85, 126, 134–35, 137, 150; as friend of Jane, 115–16, 173, 197, 274, 334; illness and death of, 334; and Lady Harriet Baring, 150–51, 173, 197; and mesmerism, 126, 127, 134–35; Thomas's opinion of, 116, 141; as would-be novelist, 152. *See also* Bullers, the (Charles and Isabella)
Bullers, the (Charles and Isabella), 70; and Amely Bölte, 51-52, 69–70; and Theresa Revis, 51–52, 69, 70, 84, 150–51, 152, 334
Burdett-Coutts, Baroness Angela Georgina, 187–88
"Buried Life, The" (Arnold), 54, 170
Burns, Robert, 33, 124, 248
Byron, Ada (Lady Lovelace), 119, 342
Byron, Lady (Anne Isabella Byron), 65
Byron, Lord (George Gordon), 65, 90, 119, 276

Canning, George, 295
Carlyle, Alexander (Thomas's brother), 12, 42, 268
Carlyle, Alexander (Thomas's nephew), 216
Carlyle, Dr. John (brother of Thomas), 42, 274; and Jane, 53–54, 138, 191, 193, 287, 290, 312, 356; as translator of Dante's *Inferno*, 127, 193, 274, 356
—and Thomas, 90, 277, 297, 298; Thomas's letters to, 84, 120, 125–26, 147, 230, 232, 240, 241, 246, 277
Carlyle, James (Thomas's father), 42, 69, 119, 286
Carlyle, Jane Welsh: appearance of, 12, 18–19, 47, 59, 61, 88, 106, 177, 218, 234, 246; birthdays of, 171, 212, 218–19, 275, 308, 312; bouts of depression suffered by, 161, 170–71, 189, 207, 213, 238; childhood of, 11, 112, 96, 119, 150, 222, 235, 328, 355, 357–58; distinctiveness of, as letter writer, 21, 92, 145, 326–27; "employment bureau" operated by, 53, 54, 86, 174, 333, 336; family of, 11, 12, 30, 41, 241, 253, 355 (*see also* Welsh, Dr. John; Welsh, Grace; Welsh family in Liverpool); and irony, 84, 98, 211, 217, 361; life of, in Cheyne Row house: *see under* Cheyne Row house; notable sense of humor possessed by, 11, 98, 102, 181, 211, 213, 220 ; and Thomas: *see* Carlyles' marriage; and Thomas's brother (Dr. John Carlyle), 53–54, 138, 191, 193, 287, 290, 312, 356; and Thomas's mother (Margaret Aitkin Carlyle), 208, 291, 356
—country-house visits of, 13; at the Barings' estates, 172–74, 199–201, 207–9, 215, 256–62, 275, 291, 292, 315, 328; at Seaforth House, 175–86, 187, 189, 190, 215–21, 260
—health of, 48, 54, 113, 125, 127–28, 241, 242–43, 255, 260–61, 275, 295; headaches, 48, 54, 161, 172, 192–93, 229, 281, 295, 356; insomnia, 72, 147, 199, 207, 281; opium taken for, 212, 241, 243, 272, 312
—non-epistolary writings by: "BUDGET *of a Femme incomprise*." 362; "Jane Welsh Carlyle Notebook, 1845–52," 161–69, 183, 188, 213; "Journal, October 1855–July 1856," 362; "Lines to Lord Byron: From his daughter, Ada," 119; memoir essay by ("Much ado about Nothing"), 349, 357–61; occasional ambitions for, 99–100, 153, 161–69, 183, 188–89, 213; "*The simple Story* of my own

first Love," 86, 252, 362, 364
—views of: on mesmerism, 130–31, 132–34, 136; on poverty, inequality, and class differences, 32–33, 164–66; on propriety, 106, 136, 161–62, 228, 264, 288–89, 335; on religion, 50–51, 165–66, 178, 184; on women's place in society, 29–30, 97, 98, 154–55, 162, 184–86, 187–90, 243, 352, 353–54
Carlyle, Margaret Aitkin (Thomas's mother), 69–70, 118–19, 120, 286; and Jane, 208, 291, 356; letters from Thomas to, 68, 309, 341; religious beliefs of, 69, 195, 267
Carlyle, Thomas: appearance of, 19, 24, 149, 154, 204, 240, 267, 294; childhood of, 11, 119; and 1847–49 political upheavals, 70, 167, 227, 310, 317, 323–24, 329; family of, 11, 30, 41, 42, 270, 278, 196, 278 (*see also* Carlyle, Dr. John; Carlyle, James; Carlyle, Margaret Aitkin; Scotsbrig farm); growing conservatism of, 65–66, 249–50, 271, 348–49; insomnia of, 72, 147, 199; and Jane: *see* Carlyles' marriage; life of, in Cheyne Row house: *see under* Cheyne Row house; at Seaforth House, 187, 221–23
—views of: on Ireland and the Irish, 166–68, 242, 268–69, 329, 348; on music, 60, 325, 347; on poverty and unemployment, 164–65, 213, 295, 324, 329, 348; on religion, 23, 118, 165–66, 248, 267–68, 270–71, 281, 348; on romantic love, 77, 230–31, 301; on slavery, 65–66, 67, 83, 249–50; on universal education, 70; on women's place in society, 29–30, 70, 298, 347
—as a writer, 68, 92, 97–98, 349; growing reputation of, 12, 28, 66, 182–83, 213, 230, 348; Jane's admiration for, 28, 199, 271; in letter to *Times*, 76, 81, 84; on Oliver Cromwell: *See under* Cromwell, Oliver. See also *Chartism*; *French Revolution, The*; *Life of John Sterling, The*; *Past and Present*; *Reminiscences*; *Sartor Resartus*
Carlyles' marriage, 153, 230–31, 273; age difference in, 21–22; companionship in, 277, 296, 301; and disagreements, 29–30, 67, 90, 167, 168, 300; equality and inequality in, 29–30, 43, 135, 148, 210, 223–24; friends' observations of, 14, 66, 146, 214, 296, 297–98; "gaslighting" in, 221–22; growing tensions in, 212, 216–34, 239, 255–58, 286–90, 330–31, 362–63; Jane's comments on, 231, 273; lack of romantic love in, 230–31, 301; and music, 124, 325; near-daily correspondence between, when separated, 49, 220, 223, 227, 231, 329; physical aspects of, 146–48; shared laughter in, 12, 20, 24, 102, 148, 248, 282, 296; stereotypical beliefs about, 14, 146; tender feelings in, 148, 231, 275; and trip together to Derbyshire and Yorkshire, 275–83
Cavaignac, Godefroy, 321–23
Cavaignac, Louis Eugène, 321–23
Chalmers, Dr. Thomas, 270–71
Chambers, Robert, 182
Chapman, Edward, 103, 157, 230. *See also* Chapman and Hall
Chapman and Hall, 103, 104–5, 162, 299, 307
Characteristics of Women (Jameson), 65
Charteris, Frank, 258–59
Charteris, Lady Anne, 258–59
Chartism (Thomas Carlyle), 70, 167, 227

Chartist movement, 75–76, 82, 310, 314–17, 320, 328; Thomas's essay on, 70, 167, 227
Chelsea, 17, 18, 22, 36, 66. *See also* Cheyne Row house
Cheyne Row house (No. 5 [later No. 24] Cheyne Row, Chelsea), 18, 59, 72, 231, 333; fireplaces in, 20, 39, 71, 128, 140, 293; lighting in, 21, 124, 193; preservation of, as historic site, 12, 69; provisions for, from Thomas's family in Scotland, 41, 42; and street noise, 22, 60.
—Jane's life in, 18–25, 39, 58, 72, 255, 283, 333; housemaids employed by, 86, 239–44, 341, 344 (*see also* Brown, Anne; Mitchell, Helen); housework done by, 25, 40, 42–43, 97, 188, 239 (*see also* sewing)
—Thomas's life in, 22, 23, 72, 193; and Cromwell book project, 19–21, 22, 23, 24, 63, 153, 203
Chimes, The (Dickens), 129
cholera, 48, 334
Chopin, Frédéric, 13, 317, 324–26, 336
Christie, Dr. John, 126, 216, 271
Christmas, 31–32, 145, 201. See also *Christmas Carol, A*
Christmas Carol, A (Dickens), 31–32, 36, 129; as inspiration to Jane, 31–32, 34, 91, 130
Clough, Arthur Hugh, 317, 350
Club des Femmes, 318
Coleridge, Samuel Taylor, 248
Coleridge, Sara, 248
Communist Manifesto (Marx and Engels), 309
consumption, 166, 278, 321, 326, 334
Corn Laws, 21, 200, 213–14
Craigenputtoch farm, 12, 43; as Carlyles' home in first married years, 12, 22, 41, 120, 146, 147, 185, 292; income from, 123; legal status of, 43, 353
Cromwell, Oliver, 20, 64, 65, 181, 294
—Thomas's writing project on, 21, 63, 65, 86, 92, 123, 126, 153, 154, 162, 175, 216; frustration of, 19–20, 22, 23, 24, 33, 59, 63, 67–68, 153, 185, 203, 204; in print, see *Letters and Speeches of Oliver Cromwell;* recovery from, 187, 190, 194–95
Cullwick, Hannah, 37
Cushman, Charlotte, 136, 203, 265, 294, 304, 351, 354

Dante, 33, 61, 290; *Inferno* by, 127, 193, 274, 356
Darwin, Charles, 13, 54, 67, 206
Darwin, Erasmus Alvey, 13, 102, 108, 125–26, 206, 288; as close friend of the Carlyles, 81, 102–3, 109, 111, 113, 117, 128, 144, 160, 271; generosity of, 102, 113; and Mazzini, 60, 81
David Copperfield (Dickens), 342
de Staël, Germaine, 99, 103, 298
de Vere, Aubrey, 329–30
Dial, The, 246
Dickens, Charles, 35–36, 41, 129, 144, 188, 295, 342–44; in Carlyles' social circle, 13, 31–32, 34–36, 191–92, 294; charitable work of, 45, 60, 299; and Jane, 35–36, 129, 164; and Mazzini, 60, 83, 263; writings by, 41, 46, 129, 272, 342 (see also *Christmas Carol, A*; *Dombey and Sons*)
Dickinson, Emily, 101
Dilberoglue, Stavros, 227, 230
divorce, 223–24
Dombey and Son (Dickens), 222, 243, 272
Donaldson sisters, 359
Donovan, Cornelius, 345
d'Orsay, Alfred, Count, 74, 163–64

Douglas Jerrold's Shilling Magazine, 204, 208
Douglass, Frederick, 83
Drago, Maria (mother of Giuseppe Mazzini), 61–62, 76
Duffy, Charles Gavan, 166–68, 187, 229, 242, 269

Ecclefechan, Scotland, 11, 62, 69, 190, 286
Edgeworth, Maria, 91
Edinburgh Review, 164, 185
"Egyptian, the." *See* Lambert, Charles
electricity, 129
Eliot, George (Marian Evans Lewes), 12, 96, 235, 246, 253, 288–89, 294
Ellis, Sarah Stickney, 47, 228, 245, 353
Emerson, Lidian, 268, 295, 296, 313
Emerson, Ralph Waldo, 13, 37, 285–86, 292–96; on the Carlyles' marriage, 296; on 1848 events in Europe, 313, 314, 317, 319; and Jane, 252, 293, 295; and Margaret Fuller, 244, 247, 249, 251–52
—and Thomas, 182, 242, 260, 293–94, 295–96, 314, 325; correspondence with, 52, 153, 182, 242, 250, 260, 267–68; opinions on, 182, 268, 271, 294, 296, 323, 324
"employment bureau," 53, 54, 86, 174, 333, 336
Engels, Friedrich, 226, 309
Espinasse, Francis, 300–301
Evans, Marian. *See* Eliot, George
Examiner, the, 199, 314, 323–24, 325, 333

female education, 45, 60, 150, 251; in *The Half Sisters*, 301, 302, 305
FitzGerald, Edward, 13, 36, 63–65, 154; and Thomas, 63–65, 117, 127, 153–54, 207, 230, 268, 280
Flanders, Janet, 343
Fleming, Henry, 230, 290–91, 327, 334
fog, 21, 31, 200, 297
Forster, John, 323, 325; in Carlyles' social circle, 35, 129, 191–92, 294; Jane's correspondence with, 161–62, 243, 288, 297, 299, 300, 306–7, 311; as writer and editor, 191, 299, 300
Forster, William Edward, 278–82, 294, 349–50; and Ireland, 279, 360; and Jane, 279, 282, 283, 295, 318–19, 349–50, 355, 360–61; and Thomas, 279, 280, 281–82, 360–61; on trip to France, 317–21
Fox, Caroline, 204, 243, 251, 272–73
France, 263, 313–14, 315, 317–24, 329, 338
Fraser, Vivian Blair, 287–88, 289
Fraser, William, 287, 289
Fraser's Magazine, 89, 135, 137
Fraser v. Bagley, 287–89
French Revolution, The (Thomas Carlyle), 12, 25, 28, 216, 314, 348
Froude, James Anthony, 234
Fuller, Margaret, 13, 36, 60, 244–52; advanced views of, 244, 247, 253, 305; death of, 251; in Italy, 252, 337–38, 339; Jane and, 244, 246–47, 251–52, 335; Thomas and, 246, 247–50, 251. See also *Women in the Nineteenth Century*

Gambardella, Spiridione, 363
Garibaldi, Giuseppe, 286, 338–39, 354
Gaskell, Elizabeth, 13, 228, 342, 344, 354
gas lighting, 342
"gaslighting," 221–23
"George Sandism," 77, 214, 301, 307
Gilman, Charlotte Perkins, 14–15
Gladstone, John, 175
Godwin, William, 352

Goldsmid, Sir Isaac, 346
governesses, 44–45, 46–47, 50, 70, 135, 137. *See also* Bölte, Amely
Graham, Lady Fanny, 73, 75, 84
Graham, Sir James, 73, 74–76, 168; and postal scandal, 79–80, 82, 83, 85, 157, 183
Greene, Henrietta, 162
Guizot, François, 315

Haddington, Scotland, 30, 112, 235, 258, 273, 355–61
Hahn-Hahn, Countess Ida von, 214, 230
Half Sisters, The (Jewsbury), 274, 285, 298–308; Jane's involvement with, 91, 227, 298–300, 306–8
Hallam, Arthur Henry, 154
Hardwick, Elizabeth, 15
Hartmann, Carl, 364, 384n2
headaches, 125; Jane's, 48, 54, 161, 172, 192–93, 229, 281, 295, 356
Helps, Arthur, 159, 160, 228
Helps, Bessy, 159, 160, 226
Holland, Baron, 290
Hunt, Leigh, 224
Hunt, Thornton, 344–45
hypnotism. *See* mesmerism

"I-ity," 82, 135–36, 197, 331, 361
illiteracy, 70
Industrial Revolution, 32, 278
Inside the Victorian Home (Flanders), 343
insomnia: Jane's, 72, 147, 199, 207, 281; Thomas's, 72, 147, 199
invalidism, 54–55, 102, 131, 135, 295
Ireland, 181, 242, 279, 350; potato blight and, 195, 200, 242, 309–10; Thomas and, 229, 242, 268–69, 280, 327, 329, 345, 348. *See also* Irish
Irish, 166–68, 181, 316; Jane and, 67, 166–68, 187. *See also* Ireland
Irving, Edward, 11, 96, 273
Italian Free School, 60, 263
Italy, 59, 76, 77–78; awakening in, 286, 296, 309, 312, 337–39; Brownings' elopement to, 230, 245; Margaret Fuller in, 252, 337–38, 339. *See also* Mazzini, Giuseppe

Jameson, Anna Brownell, 65, 214, 224, 294, 354; and Jane, 276, 282–83; and Thomas, 65, 248
Jane Eyre (Charlotte Brontë), 46, 135, 226, 272
Jean of Haregills, 118
Jeffrey, Francis, 147, 164, 184–85, 188, 344
Jerrold, Douglas, 263, 266, 342. See also *Douglas Jerrold's Shilling Magazine*
Jewsbury, Frank, 104, 158, 159, 226, 227, 228
Jewsbury, Geraldine, 47, 53, 55, 56, 126–27, 274, 285, 295; advanced views held by, 47, 103, 157, 214, 285, 304, 305–6, 308, 352–53, 354; and bouts of depression, 170, 176; as fiction writer, 13, 121–22, 213, 274, 304, 362 (see also *Half Sisters, The; Zoe*); journalistic writings by, 203–4, 208, 362; romances and infatuations of, 38–39, 156–59, 160, 179–80, 181, 203, 230, 265, 305; at Seaforth House, 178–81, 182, 215, 218, 260; views of, on servants, 56, 177, 204, 260
—as best friend of Jane, 47, 170–71, 174, 204, 226–27, 228, 297, 308, 352; advice to Jane by, 135, 171, 175, 272, 308; and Geraldine's books, 91, 103, 104–5, 157, 175, 227, 298–300, 306–8; missing correspondence between, 144, 170, 203, 246

—and other friends of Jane, 317, 318, 321; Amely Böldt, 53, 73, 220; Elizabeth Paulet, 104, 175, 299, 300; Giuseppe Mazzini, 60, 61, 157, 159; Lady Harriet Baring, 197, 204–5; Margaret Fuller, 246–47, 352
Jewsbury, Tom, 228

Knox, John, 12, 355, 356, 383n29

Labour Rate Act, 242
Lamartine, Alphonse de, 315, 320
Lamb, Charles, 283
Lambert, Charles, 156, 158, 186, 317; and Geraldine Jewsbury, 156, 158, 160, 179, 180, 304
Lamont, Martha MacDonald, 29, 181, 248, 353, 354
Latter-Day Pamphlets (Thomas Carlyle), 349
Levin, Rahel. *See* Varnhagen, Rahel Levin
Letters and Speeches of Oliver Cromwell (Thomas Carlyle), 199; second edition of, 213, 214. *See also* Cromwell, Oliver: Thomas's writing project on
Lewes, Agnes Jervis, 344–45
Lewes, George Henry, 246, 289, 344–45
Lewes, Marian Evans. *See* Eliot, George
Life in the Sick-Room (Martineau), 131, 145
Life of John Sterling, The (Thomas Carlyle), 97–98, 349
lighting, 21, 124, 193
"Lily." *See* Taylor, Helen
Lind, Jenny, 274
Linton, William James, 263
Livingstone, David, 291
Logic (Mill), 105
London and Westminster Review, 93, 158
Louisa (Bölte), 346
Louis Napoleon, 315, 323, 338, 339
Louis Philippe, king of France, 202, 313–14, 315, 321
Lovelace, Lady (Ada Byron), 119, 342
Lucas, Frederick, 166–68
Lyser, Madame, 125–26

Macaulay, Thomas Babington, 83
Macleary, Kenneth, 88
Maclise, Daniel, 129
Macready, Catherine, 34–35, 60, 114, 125, 192, 211, 213
Macready, William Charles, 34, 51–52, 192, 202, 210–11, 294, 334
Macready family, 34, 51–52, 202, 210–11, 274, 324, 333, 334. *See also* Macready, Catherine; Macready, William Charles
Marioni, Ubaldo, 352
marmalade, 328
Married Women's Property Act, 354
Marston, John Westland, 246
Martineau, Harriet, 13, 60, 74, 82, 102, 109, 295, 305, 354; as invalid, 23, 54; in Lake District, 66, 134, 158; and Margaret Fuller, 244, 245; on mesmerism, 128–34, 136, 202; and Thomas, 50–51, 65–66, 133, 202, 248; as a writer, 24, 40, 96, 128, 129–30, 131, 134
—and Jane, 65–66, 133, 230; correspondence with, 13–14, 23, 65–66, 133, 144–45, 202; fading of friendship with, 133, 202
Martineau, James, 181–82
Marx, Karl, 46, 309
Mary Barton (Gaskell), 228, 342
Mathew, Father Theobald, 33
Matlock Bath, Derbyshire, 276–78, 279
Maurice, F. D., 194
Maxwell, James Clerk, 129
Mayhew, Henry, 60–61

Mazzini, Giuseppe, 13, 58, 74, 249, 263–66, 290, 320, 339; and Geraldine Jewsbury, 60, 61, 157, 159; and his mother (Maria Drago), 61–62, 76; school founded by, 60, 246, 263; and Thomas, 78, 81, 325
—close friendship of, with Jane, 13, 58–59, 61–63, 78–79, 92, 116, 174, 203, 266, 312; cooling of, 216–17, 255–56, 265, 339; correspondence with, 216–17, 222, 296
—dedication of, to Italian independence, 59–60, 77–78, 188, 203, 217, 249, 309, 313; in Italy in 1848–49, 309, 317, 337, 338, 339; and Young Italy, 59, 286, 296
—support for, in London social circles, 60, 76, 77, 83, 264–65; fundraising by, 60, 263, 264, 272, 312; and post office scandal, 76, 78–81, 83–84, 85
menopause, 212, 312
mesmerism, 13, 126–33, 134–36, 202
Mill, John Stuart, 60, 158, 366n9; and Carlyles, 13, 25–28, 77; and Harriet Taylor, 13, 26–28, 148; writings by, 28, 105
Milner-Gibson, Mrs. Arethusa, 264
Milnes, Richard Monckton (later Lord Houghton), 258, 279, 281, 294, 317
Mitchell, Helen, 20, 39, 82, 236–38, 244; alcoholism of, 40, 86, 236–37, 335–36, 340–41; duties of, 22, 39, 49, 58, 59, 71, 114, 128, 133, 195, 239; and Jane, 40–41, 42, 71, 236–37, 242, 253, 256, 340–41; leaving and return of, 236–38, 239, 253, 335–36, 340–41; and Thomas, 87, 237
Mitchell, John (brother of Helen Mitchell), 236, 237, 253
Moffat, Robert, 291
Montagu, Anna Dorothea, 188
More, Hannah, 187–88
Morison, Sir Alexander, 110, 111, 112, 113, 114, 115
morphine. *See* opium
Moxon, Edward, 155
"Much ado about Nothing" (memoir essay), 349, 357–61
Mudie, Bessy, 43, 55, 56, 104
Mudie, Juliet, 43, 55, 56, 104
Mudie, Robert, 43, 44

Neuberg, Joseph, 350, 355, 357, 361
Neuberg, Rosetta, 350
Neumann, Baron Philipp von, 79
Newton, Elizabeth Nodes, 184
Newton, Reverend Robert, 184
New York Daily Tribune, 249, 337–38, 339
Nightingale, Florence, 16, 54
Norton, Caroline, 199, 324

"Occasional Discourse on the Negro Question" (Thomas Carlyle), 349
O'Connor, Feargus, 316
O'Hagan, John, 166–68
opium, 129, 243, 341; Jane and, 212, 241, 243, 272, 312
Ossoli, Giovanni Angelo, 251

Papers on Literature and Art (Fuller), 251
Parkes, Bessie Rayner, 353
Past and Present (Thomas Carlyle), 38, 49–50, 68, 144
Patmore, Coventry, 16, 197
Paulet, Elizabeth Newton "Betsey," 182, 184, 299, 352; as friend of Jane, 178, 188, 203, 204–5, 215, 220, 260, 297, 328, 350; at Seaforth House, 178, 182, 215, 218, 294–95; on trip to France, 317, 318, 319–20; and William Edward Forster, 319–20, 350; as a writer, 175, 362. *See also* Paulet family

Paulet, Mark Étienne, 175, 177, 202, 317, 350; at Seaforth House, 175, 177, 179, 180, 294–95. *See also* Paulet family
Paulet family, 177–79, 182–83. *See also* Paulet, Elizabeth; Paulet, Mark Étienne; Seaforth House
Peak District, Derbyshire, 276, 279–80, 350
Peel, Sir Robert, 73, 74, 200, 213–14, 376n1
Pendennis (Thackeray), 152
penny post, 82
People's International League, 263–64
Pepoli, Elizabeth Fergus, 62, 230
Perry, Sir Erskine, 354
Persuasion (Austen), 91
phrenology, 110, 345
Pigot, John Edward, 166–68
Pius IX, 286, 337
Plattnauer, Richard, 34, 105, 120–21, 275; and Amely Bölte, 139, 143–44; and Jane, 34, 105–12, 113–18, 120, 121, 122, 139, 156, 160, 174, 202, 203, 272; mental illness of, 105–12, 113–18, 119, 120–21, 132, 156, 202–3; and Thomas, 117, 119, 120–21
potato blight, 195, 200, 242, 309–10
poverty, 32–33, 45, 46, 60, 164–65, 295; in Ireland, 348; for women, 55–56
Pride and Prejudice (Austen), 174, 276
property laws, 43, 223, 353–54
prostitution, 55–56, 166, 294, 303
Punch, 80, 83, 347

Quakers, 111, 246, 281. *See also* Forster, William Edward; Fox, Caroline
Queen's College, 45

Rachel (actress Rachel Félix), 252, 318
railways, 207–8, 211, 257, 277, 357
reform banquets (France), 263
Reminiscences (Thomas Carlyle), 54, 78, 119, 163
Revis, Theresa (mother), 70, 138, 143
Revis, Theresa "Tizzy," 51, 106, 143, 150–52, 334; Amely Bölte and, 57, 72, 84, 138, 149; behavioral problems of, 125, 137–38, 149, 151, 334; in Buller household, 51, 57, 70, 86, 116, 150–51; literary characters based on, 149, 151–52; parentage of, 69, 70
Richardson, Samuel, 114
Ritchie, Annie Thackeray, 149
Robertson, Jamie, 359
Robertson, John, 158–59, 160, 305; and Geraldine Jewsbury, 158–59, 160, 179, 181; and Jane, 34, 43, 165–66, 181, 230, 321–22
Rogers, Samuel, 342, 343–44
Roman Matron, The; or, Vittoria Accorombona (Tieck), 87–90, 99, 101, 103, 155, 303
Rubáiyát of Omar Khayyám (FitzGerald), 13, 64
Russell, Lord John, 213, 242, 279
Russell, Mary, 201, 238, 241, 244, 312

Saint-Simonianism, 156
Sand, George, 157, 252, 296, 324; writings of, 77, 103, 265, 298, 301
Sandwich, Lady (Mary Anne Julia Louisa Harriet Lowry-Corry), 205, 259, 331–32
Sartor Resartus (Thomas Carlyle), 12, 40, 105, 163; inspirational effect of, 12, 66, 271, 348
Scotsbrig farm, 196, 200; Thomas's visits to, 187, 190, 196, 225, 267, 283, 291, 356

Scott, Sir Walter, 74
Seaforth House, 175–76, 187, 294–95; atmosphere of, 176–79, 183; Geraldine Jewsbury at, 178–81, 182, 215, 218, 260; Jane at, 175–86, 187, 189, 190, 215–21, 260; Thomas at, 187, 221–23
sewing, 19, 25, 43, 272; by Jane, 18–19, 25, 117, 161, 264, 272, 293
Shelley, Mary, 274, 276
Shirley (Charlotte Brontë), 91–92, 351
skepticism, religious, 50, 61, 73, 75, 268, 270
Smith, Barbara Leigh, 353
Speke Hall, 220
"spiritual magnetism," 136
Sprague, Elizabeth, 341
Spring, Marcus, 245
Spring, Rebecca, 245, 249–50
Sterling, Anthony, 159–60, 230, 315, 326, 340, 345
Sterling, Charlotte, 159–60, 207, 226, 340
Sterling, Edward, 160
Sterling, John, 97–98, 123, 135, 279; and Jane, 87, 90, 135; and Thomas, 97–98, 123, 349
Stirling, Jane Wilhelmina, 324–25, 326
Swanwick, Anna, 34, 159

Tarnow, Fanny, 52
Taylor, Harriet, 13, 26, 27–28, 148, 288
Taylor, Helen ("Lily"), 27, 366n9
Taylor, John, 27
Templand, Thornhill, 71, 355
Ten Hour Bill (British Factory Act), 263
Tennyson, Alfred, 191, 268; in Carlyles' social circle, 13, 36, 207, 294; Jane and, 154–55, 163, 192, 193–94; writing by, 154, 248
Thackeray, William Makepeace, 36, 46, 64, 149, 152, 272, 295; in Carlyles' social circle; 13, 35, 74, 268, 342, 347. See also *Vanity Fair*
Thames, the, 18, 61, 66, 72
Thomson, James, 260
Tieck, Ludwig, 88, 99. See also *Roman Matron, The; or, Vittoria Accorombona*
Times [London], 31, 79–81, 160, 261 310, 324; Thomas's letter to, 76, 81, 84
"To a Swallow Building under Our Eaves" (poem, Thomas Carlyle), 147
Toulman, Camilla, 228
Trilling, Diana, 364
Trilling, Lionel, 364
tuberculosis. *See* consumption
Turner, J. M. W., 246
typhus, 43, 48, 112, 138, 215, 334

Vanity Fair (Thackeray), 149, 151–52, 272
Varnhagen, Rahel Levin, 95, 98–100, 356
Varnhagen von Ense, Karl August, 49, 93–95, 99, 298, 346; and Amely Bölte, 93, 94–95, 142, 208, 219, 266, 297–98, 311, 330, 346; and Jane, 74, 98; and Thomas, 49, 93–94, 98, 267
Victoria, Queen, 45, 98, 202, 258, 276
Vindication of the Rights of Women (Wollstonecraft), 96, 285, 352
visuality (term), 21
Vittoria Accorombona. See *Roman Matron, The; or, Vittoria Accorombona*
von Arnim, Elizabeth (Bettina), 298
von Reichenbach, Count Oskar, 120
von Willisen, General Wilhelm, 49–50

Wandsworth Lunatic Asylum, 108, 109–11, 113, 116, 159
Wedgwood, Fanny, 50, 76, 102, 145, 325

Wedgwood family, 60, 76, 102, 325. *See also* Wedgwood, Fanny
Welsh, Dr. John (Jane's father), 11, 20, 30, 112–13, 321, 357; early death of, 50, 119, 358; inheritance from, 12, 43; and Jane's childhood, 112-13, 321; Jane's mourning for, 54, 113, 119, 359
Welsh, Grace (Jane's mother), 11, 30, 37, 54–55, 124, 144; and Jane's childhood, 11, 112, 150, 328; Jane's mourning for, 22, 54–55, 71, 145, 243, 355, 357
Welsh, Helen, 41, 74, 144, 230, 239, 241, 244, 275; correspondence of, with Jane, 41, 124, 154–55, 209–10, 231, 233, 255
Welsh, Jane Baillie. *See* Carlyle, Jane Welsh
Welsh, Jeannie "Babbie," 41, 310–11, 328, 363; correspondence of, with Jane, 41, 126, 144, 201, 310–11, 312, 313, 328, 330, 339, 342–44
Welsh, John (Jane's uncle in Liverpool), 31–32, 41; Jane and, 41, 128, 130–31, 132–33, 183–84. *See also* Welsh family in Liverpool
Welsh, Margaret, 259–60
Welsh, Walter, 355
Welsh family in Liverpool, 41, 114, 120, 224, 264, 311, 354–55; Jane's visits to, 84, 85, 86, 100, 175. *See also* Welsh, Helen; Welsh, Jeannie; Welsh, John
Whistler, James McNeill, 69
Whittington Club, 266
Wives of England, The (Ellis), 47, 245
Wollstonecraft, Mary, 89, 100, 245, 317, 352. See also *Vindication of the Rights of Women*
Woman in the Nineteenth Century (Fuller), 244, 245, 253
Woolf, Virginia, 11, 16, 32, 65, 125, 365n7
Wordsworth, William, 97, 317
workhouses, 45, 55, 341
Wuthering Heights (Emily Brontë), 272, 311
Wynn, Charlotte, 346
Wynyard, Mrs. Montagu, 129–30, 131, 132, 133, 136, 145

Young Italy, 59, 76, 286, 296

Zoe (Jewsbury), 103–5, 156–58, 175, 299–300, 307; Jane's involvement with, 103, 104–5, 157, 175, 299–300